Psychic Journey

THRU THE MISTS

Jo Hammers the Mystic

Paranormal Crossroads & Publishing

Psychic Journey Thru the Mists © 2015 by Jo Hammers

All rights reserved. No part of this book may be reproduced or transmitted in any form or by any means without written permission of the author. For information, address Paranormal Crossroads & Publishing, Po Box 5056, Bella Vista, AR 72714.

ISBN 978-0-9911540-2-9

www.paranormalcrossroads.com

This work is fiction. All of the characters, organizations, and events portrayed in this novel are either products of the author's imagination or are used fictitiously.

The publisher does not have any control over and does not assume responsibility for author or third-party Web sites or their contents.

The scanning, uploading, and distribution of this book via the Internet, or via any other means without permission of the publisher is illegal and punishable by law. Please purchase only authorized electronic editions and do not participate in or encourage electronic piracy of copyrighted materials. Your support of the author's rights is appreciated.

Image copyright Jo Hammers, 2015.

Table of Contents

Introduction – What is a mystic?	7
1. January – The Book of Understanding	9
2. February – The Book of Portals	51
3. March – The Book of Visitations	95
4. April - The Book of Resurrections	157
5. May – The Book of 'Out of Body' experiences	215
6. June – The Book of Twists & Turns	269
7. July – The Book of Light & Dark Powers	320
8. August – The Book of Healing	370
9. September – The Book of Divine Powers	417
10. October – The Book of the Dead	465
11. November – The Book of Prosperity	514
12. December – The Book of 'Passing It On'	558

DEDICATION

This book is dedicated to Tom C. Lyle, author of a book titled 'The Magic Power of Pragma Psychics'. For ten years, his book became my 'Holy Bible'. I, a light being named Barjoraven, was confused and lost on Earth, due to a damaged silver cord communication line. Tom's book became my road map to higher understanding and healing for my communication cord. Thank You Tom! . . . Barjoraven in the Heavens/Jo Hammers the Mystic on Earth.

INTRODUCTION

WHAT IS A MYSTIC

A mystic is an orb soul that is traveling in a male or female human body vehicle on Earth for one human lifetime. A mystic knows where he has entered Earth life from, as well as his purpose for being on Earth. Mystics are masters and forerunners of chosen prophets, new dispensations, and advancements in thought. John the Baptist was the forerunner of a master orb known as Christ. Masters walk amongst you today, traveling earth in human bodies. They hold the secret keys to unlocking the future. Each master traveling Earth has a specific mission.

I, Jo Hammers the Mystic, am a trumpeter of words. My trumpet's sound calls man to rise in his thinking, to be caught away, to rapture. There are other trumpeters besides me that are scattered all around Earth. We are trumpeting angels. We are light being orb souls traveling in human flesh. This page of written words is the sound of my individual trumpet. "Hear ye your trumpet sound!"

CHAPTER ONE
JANUARY

THE BOOK OF UNDERSTANDING

January 1

THOUGHT FOR THE DAY – Have you ever considered that you are a spirit being traveling in a human body, like a man climbs in and drives an automobile?

YOU ARE MORE THAN YOUR HUMAN BODY VEHICLE

The human body has intelligence, a mind that looks out thru a pair of human eyes and makes decisions about survival in it's Earth surroundings. The human body and its intelligence, or natural mind, is like the electronic intelligence built in to an automobile. Without the electronic intelligence, a human body is a car that has its key removed and its engine shut off. Without the human mind intelligence, a human body is a vehicle that will not run or move about.

Just as an automobile has to have a driver to activate it, the human body also has to have a driver. The driver of the human body is a Spirit Being, not the human mind. The Spirit Being travels in the human form. The Spirit Being is a supernatural, spiritual driver of the human form vehicle. It can drive the human form body/vehicle, or it can climb out and travel the Heavens at will, obtaining needed information, or just visiting with friends and associates there. We climb out of our cars at the end of our Earth work days, not giving it a second thought. We enter our houses and eat and visit with family and friends. Humans are the vehicles. Spirit Beings are the drivers. In death, we lay our human forms down. It is our Spirit Being that lives forever.

I, Jo Hammers the Mystic, am a Light Being that is traveling in a human form for a lifetime on earth. I am a trumpeter of words. Christ was a Light Being. He traveled in a human form for a lifetime/mission on earth. You are either a light being, or a dark being that is traveling in a human form for a lifetime on earth.

January 2

THOUGHT FOR THE DAY – Have you ever climbed out of your human form when it sleeps? If you fly, levitate, or walk above the ground looking down in what you call dreams, you have exited your human vehicle.

KNOWING YOUR PURPOSE

As a human being, you have been born on Earth with the purpose of mastering free-will choice. Each human is endowed with certain talents. What his talents are is the key to knowing what his purpose on Earth is. A human is to use his special creative talents in a fashion that will further the advancement of Earth plane society. His purpose is not the degrading of Earth society. When he makes good free-will choices, his Spirit Being within him awakes. Some call it discovering his spiritual side.

A free-will choice pendulum swings back and forth. We are on it. It swings from light to dark, with a dividing point between the two. Those seeking perfection, spirituality, and enlightenment will make free will choices that are on the light side. Those not seeking perfection, spirituality, and cutting edge higher knowledge will make choices that are on the dark side. Shades of gray, wobbling and trying to keep a grip on things (the pendulum) can fall off the pendulum in either direction. They are the unstable ones.

The mastering of free-will choice is a lesson that humans must ace. The failing of a human to master free-will choice results in hell on Earth coming to call. Those failing to master free-will choice are the humans who fall off the pendulum onto the dark side, wrecking their human vehicles, and becoming broken down shades of gray. Shades of gray are those humans who are sometimes good as gold and sometimes vicious in their dealings with others. They are the ones who climb out of their addictions for awhile, and then go back to them. They are the criminals who give up their vices for awhile, but then return to their chosen illegal activities. They are the unstable ones.

Are you seeking to be a master of higher thinking, or a dark gutter rat with no desires for anything better in life?

January 3

THOUGHT FOR THE DAY – Holding on to old ways of thinking and archaic literature prevents an individual from embracing that which is on the cutting edge of advanced thought.

WHY DO I FEEL SO DISCONNECTED IN LIFE?

Traveling in human vehicle forms are Spirit Beings. You and I are Spirit Beings. In our Spirit Being state, free from our human bodies, we have a silver cord that connects us to our source of all knowledge and wisdom. Some people call that source God. The cord is similar to a land phone line, or a cell phone signal. The cord carries the voices of communication

The Silver Cord has form. It looks like a long skinny, strip of silver/gray cloud. You can see thru it, like looking thru a frosted window on Earth. In shape, it looks like a floating rope or cord. If you view a loose strand of a cob web billowing and blowing away in a heavy breeze, you have seen a thing that is similar to the look of a silver cord. The Silver Cord billows and moves as thought being moved about by a breeze. The cord appears to be gray or silvery because it is a beam of white light that glistens and looks silvery when other light sources shine on it, illuminating it.

Although referred to as a cord, the Silver Cord is like a cell phone signal, except that it can be seen. It does not bind a Spirit Being like a chain would a dog on Earth. Although it is there, it can be walked thru like it is a mist. On Earth humans can walk thru cell phone signals or radio signals and never know it. The only difference being is that the Silver Cord signal can be seen in the Astral/Heavens. The Silver Cord is a Spirit Being's connection to all that is in the way of supernatural knowledge and wisdom.

Silver Cords can be injured or snapped when a Spirit Being chooses to enter the River of Life to enter a human form and live a lifetime on Earth. Injured cords allow some communication to get thru during a human form existence. An occasional visitation or communication with a spirit guide/angel might occur. A snapped cord cuts off all communication. The Spirit Being basically goes to sleep, leaving the driving of the human vehicle up to the human mind/intelligence. Having no spiritual connection, the snapped cord individuals often become atheists.

Those having fully intact cords are the psychics, mediums, and other deeply spiritual leaders such as the Buddha or Christ.

January 4

THOUGHT FOR THE DAY – Your purpose in life is to use your talents to support yourself, add to the advancement of Earth life society, and point those about you to paths of enlightenment.

USING YOUR TALENTS

Once you come to the realization that you are a Spirit Being, possibly on a learning mission on Earth, you will realize that your talents are different from those around you. Each Earth life mission requires certain talents to complete it. To ace learning assignments on Earth, an individual must use his talents in a fashion that will further the advancement of Earth plane society. It is not an individual's purpose to use his talents to degrade the quality of Earth life.

I feel very blessed when my sister (a really good cook), shares with me tidbits from her baking. She makes a Buttermilk Chocolate Cake that melts in your mouth. Her special talent is cooking and baking. I, in turn, share with her my writings, my special gift or talent. If she gave up cooking, she would be degrading/denying society her specialness. If I give up writing, I would be degrading/denying society the talent given me. Another friend of mine is a truck driver. He lives and breathes the subject. He is a master in transporting items needed by Earth's peoples. One such item is toilet paper. If he, and other talented drivers like him, went on strike there would be no toilet paper in my or anyone else's bathroom. Society would take a step backwards and use leaves, corn cobs, or fingers for wiping. Are you using your special talents to better society, or short changing it?

Take one tiny step today toward putting yourself out there and blessing Earth life with your talents. If you are a violinist, go outside with your instrument and stand on your steps. Play an evening song as the sun goes down. Bless those about you with your special gift. If you are a baker, share your pies with a neighbor. The neighbor, more often and not, will eventually share back with you something they have created using their talents. My grandsons once surprised and shoveled an elderly lady's snow covered drive. A week or so later, she made and delivered to them a plate of homemade cinnamon rolls.

What goes around comes around. You will get out of Earth life what you contribute to it.

January 5

THOUGHT FOR THE DAY – Twelve, champion horses

stand prancing in a row. Eleven are black and one is white. Dare to use your power of free-will choice to stand out from the crowd.

UNANSWERED QUESTIONS

Have you ever considered that you, a Spirit Being traveling in human form, have a home, family, friends, and an identity that are non-Earth related? Earth life is like going overseas in the military. The soldiers in your group are your brothers, but not your real/biological ones. An army barracks is your home, but not your real home. Your ID tags give you a number as a name. At home you have a name given you by your biological parents.

Our real home is in the Astral or Heaven. Home is a working society, not a place where we lay around on clouds and eat grapes fed to us by mystical angels. There, we have an occupation, home, family, friends, and an identity/name. Have you ever asked yourself what your name in the Astral or Heaven is?

My name in the heavens is Barjoraven. My Earth mother named me Barbara Jo, thinking she heard my name spoken to her. Her connection to supernatural intelligence was a little fuzzy at the time. However, she got it almost right. In the heavens, I am the Spirit Being known as Barjoraven.

When entering Earth life, we sometimes have our silver cords injured or snapped. When this happens, our memories of home/the Astral/Heaven are sometimes forgotten. Thus, we assume we are the human vehicle that we travel in, and the name our Earth parents have given us. As our cords start to heal or grow back, we sometimes get hints of who we are in the Heavens. Sometimes it comes in dreams. Other times, you will hear a voice calling your name in the night, a name your parents didn't give you.

Have you heard someone calling you a strange name in your dreams in the night? Your name in the heavens is not the one you go by on Earth.

January 6

THOUGHT FOR THE DAY – You are two in one. You live two lives at once, one on earth and one in the heavens when your human form sleeps.

DREAM COMMUNICATIONS

Dreams are one tool that Spirit Guides use to communicate with us. Our angelic guardians/guides project to us dream scenarios, coded information dreams concerning the twists, turns, and forks in our life paths. The dream scenarios are sort of an 'in-between worlds' game of charades. The dreams give the clues. You and I are the guesser/decoder/interpreter of them.

My best friend, in her late twenties had a dream. In it, her grandmother came to her and played a pin-ball machine with her. In her grandmother's day, pinball was the in game of the time. Instead of putting in coins to activate the machine, she put in three pink balls and two blue ones. The meaning of the dream message was not understood for a few years. MY friend, who was not supposed to be able to conceive, had two boys (the blue balls). My friend's cousin, also a granddaughter of the grandmother and childless, had three girls afterward. The grandmother calls on my friend on a regular basis in her dreams. She has chosen to be my friend's Spirit Guide.

Who speaks to you in your dreams? Which of your deceased friends and loved ones has chosen to guide you? Have you decoded their messages?

January 7

THOUGHT FOR THE DAY – When you look about yourself on Earth, is there something missing? Could you be homesick for your other life?

BEING HUMAN AS WELL AS DIVINE

In dream scenarios, you may have someone address you by your heavenly name. On awakening, you may find it amusing that you were called by a wrong name in what you consider to be a crazy dream. You live two lives and have two identities. On Earth, you are the driver of a human vehicle. In the heavens, you are a Spirit Being who has a name, position, and life there. You are two in one. Christ was two in one. He was human as well as divine! He was a Spirit Being traveling for a lifetime in a human form. He has returned to his home and identity in the heavens. He is a Master Being. You and I are human, as well as divine. We are human on Earth and Master Beings in the higher heavens who have occupations, homes, identities, families, friends, etc.

Jesus was a Master Being in the heavens, and was divine. He came down to Earth, entered human flesh, and worked as a carpenter's helper till he started his lifework as a Prophet/Preacher/philosopher. He was human. He was two in one, both human and divine.

The Buddha was both human and divine, as was Christ,

Mother Theresa, etc.

January 8

THOUGHT FOR THE DAY – If Earth life frustrates you, it could be because you are used to a more advanced form of living in the Astral and Heavens. Earth life is like going on a campout.

ASTRAL HEALERS WHO TRAVEL IN HUMAN FORMS

Spirit Beings like you and I have communication systems called Silver Cords. The rope like, misty, see thru, cloud-like form is a line that connects us to Divine Intelligence. There is war in the Heavens. One of Dark Being Forces favorite methods of warfare is to attempt to sever the Silver Cords of Light Beings, if they can. When war wounds occur, the damaging and severing of Silver Cords, a light being's memory of his divine Astral identity sometimes become static plagued and fuzzy. Those beings who have fully snapped cords are totally cut off from their memories of who they were in the heavens. Spirit Guides use whatever tools are necessary to re-establish/heal communications. Without supernatural heavenly healing of cords, Light Beings will wander the Earth thinking they are merely human and wondering why they feel so disconnected. These are the beings that just can't seem to get their acts together.

Dreams are a healing tool used by guides. Bliss dreams heal Silver Cords. If you dream an especially happy blissful dream, your Spirit Guide is a healer, and is sending healing to you. Christ healed. Sprit Guides heal. I am a writer of words on paper that heals. I am a healer. A minister's sermon heals. He is a healer.

All Light Beings, traveling in human forms on Earth, are healers. We are just commissioned to use our healing gift in different forms.

January 9

THOUGHT FOR THE DAY - You may have deceased loved ones who are trying to contact you by sending dream scenarios. When you brush your dreams away as crazy, you are actually throwing away a letter from Heaven.

INTERPRETING DREAM MESSAGES

A man says, "I had a wild dream last night. It must have been something I ate that caused it." Food does not cause dreaming. Your Spirit Guide and Spirit Beings such as deceased loved ones are the projectors of dreams. No dream is crazy. Dreams are communications.

Man creates his own pocket translator for interpreting dreams. He assigns meanings to people, places, colors, events, numbers, etc. according to how he has experienced them in his day to day experiences. His assigned meanings become his codes for translating.

No two humans will have the same codes. Take the color red, for instance. I have always hated the color. To me, for some reason, it brings a feeling of disgust. My mother loved red. To her, it represented warmth and joy. Should the two of us receive twin coded dreams where everything was red, our interpretations or translations would be different. I would see my dream as telling me that something disgusting was going to happen in my world. My mother, however, would see an outpouring of warmth and joy coming her way.

To decode or interpret your dreams, you must assign an associated meaning to each thing happening in it. Only you know what each item, color, person means in your world. Only you can decode your dream communications from your Spirit Guide. Dreams are sent in code from the afterlife/astral/heaven to keep darkness from knowing Heaven's secrets.

January 10

THOUGHT FOR THE DAY – Closed minded men fear and brand what they do not understand as dark and of the occult/devil in origin. Open minded men live on the cutting edge of higher understanding/advanced thought.

WHAT ABOUT FRIGHTENING DREAMS?

All dreams must be decoded, no matter what their content. Once decoded, you may find that your frightening dreams are actually warnings sent from a deceased relative, friend, or Spirit Guide. Their efforts to make you fearful, due to a dream, may cause you to sit up and take notice of what is happening in your human world. You could have Spirit Beings of darkness, walking all about you in human forms, out to get you in one way or another. Perhaps your Spirit Guide, or deceased relative, is trying to tell you that you have reasons to be afraid.

Just like crazy dreams, you have to take what you feel and assign a meaning to what frightened you in your dream. My traveling mate on Earth is deathly afraid of wasps. To him, should he dream of them, the wasps would represent painful disaster coming to him. To you, getting stung by a wasp could represent a person in human life sticking it to you. To a diabetic, the same wasp stinging him might mean to check the sterile quality of his insulin needles. Each man must decode his own dreams by assigning meanings to what he interacts with in his daily Earth life.

January 11

THOUGHT FOR THE DAY – You have a name in the heavens that is not your Earth one. You may be Jack in Earth life, but Master Jericho in the Heavens.

LIVING TWO LIVES

Once you realize that you are a Spirit Being traveling in a human form that has its own mind, you realize that you are two in one. The human mind with its eyes looks outward into the physical world and makes judgments about it, as well as chooses what it needs to do to survive. The Spirit Being mind with what is called a third eye/spiritual eye, looks inward and upward retrieving supernatural guidance. Intuition comes to the human mind from the Spirit Being traveling in his human form. The human mind is like an automobile's electronics that tells the human engine to run and survive in everyday Earth life.

We live two lives. We are a Spirit Being that is able to climb in and out of a human form, like it is an automobile. As Spirit Beings, we can park our human vehicles, get out, and return to the heavens, our other home. Just like a man waking up in the morning, getting up, and going to work; we can return from the heavens to our parked in bed human vehicles, wake them up, and resume our human lives.

You are a divine being on an Earth mission, traveling in a human form vehicle.

January 12

THOUGHT FOR THE DAY – Your human body is like an automobile. You are the driver. You are not the car. It is transportation for you, a spirit being.

LIVES BEYOND THE HUMAN FORMS WE DRIVE

When Silver Cords are snapped in the entry to earth process, Spirit Beings entering human forms go into a sleep stage. Their spiritual connection is shut down. Their human form car, and its intelligence, has no interest in spiritual matters. Some of these humans, with sleeping Sprit Beings, become agnostics and atheists. They hear and read about Divine Source, but God/Divine Source is like a relative that lives at a far distance that you have never seen or heard from. You know and hope they are well and alive, but there is no communication, and therefore no real knowledge of them. They could be dead or non- existent in the atheist's human thinking.

Dissatisfied humans, with feelings of being disconnected, go on spiritual quests to find their distant God. They seek to see if he is real, and not a fairytale like Santa Claus or the Easter Bunny. They quest in various ways. One will try the kneeling at an altar approach. Another will start to read and study old writings. Another will study the lives of the great masters such as Buddha, Christ, etc. Others will sit still and go within in, meditating.

Any beginning path to seek divine Source is acceptable.

However, some paths will get you there quicker. Those who lay aside religious roots and go within seeking for truth are those who will resurrect, rapture, enter heavenly states of enlightenment, and come to know the masters of Heaven.

Automobiles are parked in garages at night. The driver exits the car and goes about his business doing other things. Human vehicle forms are parked in beds at night. The driver, a spirit being, exits and goes about his business. In the evenings, humans entertain. In a Spirit Being's evening, he does the same. He interacts with his friends, family, and acquaintances in the astral. We are Spirit Beings. We have lives beyond the human forms we drive. We are children of the stars.

January 13

THOUGHT FOR THE DAY - Did you know that Spirit Guides wear costumes and facial masks, like a man would wear on Earth going to a costume ball?

SPIRIT GUIDES

The First Heaven/Astral shore is where Spirit Guides work. There, they keep an eye on their charges on Earth, as well as on other planets. Spirit Guides are in charge of sending messages to guide their charge's paths. Spirit Guides are communications specialists/masters.

THE ASTRAL SHORE/FIRST HEAVEN HAS THREE PURPOSES

1. It is a disembarking shore for those traveling there thru portals, similar to a train station.

2. It is the place where all light being and shades of gray souls are judged for their deeds, missions, life lessons, etc.

3. Spirit Guides are stationed there, and are in charge of communications between Heaven and Earth (and other planets).

The higher heavens are the dwelling places/homes of the masters. A Spirit Guide can be a master who goes to work every day on the Astral Shore.

Visions are also orchestrated by Spirit Guides. They come down to you via a portal. Spirit Guides can also travel down portals to visit you, if he feels it is necessary. Even though your guide is a Spirit Being, he can put on a form/costume/mask that you can understand. He particularly makes visits to those who have snapped/severed Silver Cords. Spirit Guides can appear in costumes and masks as angels, masters, medicine men, shamans, etc. etc. Some humans expect to see angels with wings, others with no wings.

In the higher heavens, Spirit Beings/Guides are master orbs of pure light. They put on costumes to appear to Earth men, as well as beings of other planets. Costumes are worn by beings in the first and second heavens. Spirit Beings wear costumes and masks to communicate with life forms on different planets, who understand nothing more than the forms of the beings that walk their planet. The WHITE BUFFALO WOMAN of the Native American Indians is a Spirit Guide (Orb of Light) wearing a costume to communicate in a way the Native Americans understand.

January 14

THOUGHT FOR THE DAY – Heaven's lighted portal is within you!

.SOME SWEET DAY I WILL SING UP THERE

'Some sweet day' never comes for day dreaming humans who are looking out into the natural universe for answers. The some sweet day is found by going inward, seeking the spiritual, and then realizing that you are a spirit being traveling in a human form. Heaven is within you. It is accessed in moments of enlightenment, as well as when you learn to pop from your human form when it is sleeping. Dream Portals are accessible 24 hours a day. Meditation portals are for those who go inward seeking higher truths, perfection, enlightenment, etc. In meditation, a spirit being can leave his human body and enter knowledge portals.

Like automobiles on Earth, the human body vehicle can be left in the driveway bed while its owner does other things. Just like getting out of an automobile and entering your Earth home's front door, you and I are capable of exiting our human body vehicles and entering the portal door of our Eternal home for a little rest and visits with friends and family there.

SOME SWEET DAY I WILL SING UP THERE comes when the human body sleeps. It is a rapture that takes place inward. Master Spirit Beings can pop or exit their human body vehicles, leaving them in idle, while they take flight to the Astral when they wish. They are the seers, mediums, psychics, etc. They have mastered the going away and the coming again, just like Christ. They are fellow masters with him. They are the perfected ones. They have sought enlightenment and found it.

January 15

THOUGHT FOR THE DAY - A closed mind is a gate that holds you captive in primitive thinking.

LIVING TWO LIVES AT ONCE

Once you realize that you are a Spirit Being traveling in a human form that has its own mind, you realize that you are two in one. The human mind with its eyes looks outward into the physical world and makes judgments about it, as well as chooses what it needs to survive. The Spirit Being mind, with what is called a third eye/spiritual eye, looks inward and upward, traveling and retrieving supernatural knowledge and guidance. Intuition comes to the human mind from the Spirit Being who is driving him like he is an automobile. The human mind is like an automobile's electronics that tells the engine to run.

So, we are two in one. We live two lives at once. Not only are we human, we are a Spirit Being that is able to climb in and out of our human form.

As a Spirit Being, you and I can travel the heavens, visiting with all sorts of beings and crossovers that dwell there. At the sound of an Earth alarm clock, or a knock at our earth door, we can return to our human forms and live Earth lives.

You are a divine being traveling on Earth in a human form, driving it like it is an automobile.

January 16

THOUGHT FOR THE DAY – Humanity walks about in spiritual blindness on Earth because their Silver Cords/connections to the Heavens and afterlife are damaged, or severed. When a phone line is down on Earth, communication becomes static ridden, or totally non-existent. The same applies to the Silver Cord.

SILVER CORDS

In our Spirit Being state, free from our human bodies, we have a silver cord that connects us to our source of all knowledge and wisdom. The cord is similar to a land phone line or a cell phone signal. Shape wise, the Silver Cord looks like a long skinny, strip of billowy cloud. You can see thru it, like looking thru a frosted window on Earth. If you have ever seen a loose strand of a cob web that is floating off on a breeze, you have seen something that is similar looking to the Silver Cord.

The Silver Cord does not bind a Spirit Being, like a dog on Earth might be secured on the end of a chain. The Silver Cord is a Spirit Being's supernatural connection to all that is, all the infinite knowledge and wisdom of Divine Source/God.

Humanity has been asleep spiritually on Earth, because there is war in the Heavens. Darkness/fallen angels have sought to cause havoc in the lives of Light Beings/Spirit Beings who have traveled the River of Life to be born in human forms on Earth. It is considered a great victory by fallen angels/darkness, if they can sever or injure the Silver Cords of Light Beings that are entering Earth life. With no functioning Silver Cord communication systems, Spirit Beings in human forms sleep.

A world of humanity walks about with no spiritual understanding, or desire to seek it. The atheists are Spirit Beings with severed Silver Cords. They do not know from whence they have came, or where they are capable of going.

January 17

THOUGHT FOR THE DAY – Seeking Enlightenment is a healing path for damaged and severed Silver Cord beings.

WHY SHOULD SPIRIT BEINGS IN HUMAN FORMS SEEK ENLIGHTENMENT?

There is war in the heavens. Earth is one battlefield, as are other planets. Forces of Darkness have chosen to attack Light Spirit Beings as they travel the River of Life to be born in human forms on Earth. In military wars, there are some warriors that go unscathed in battles. Others are injured slightly, or seriously. In the war in the heavens, Silver Cords are damaged or severed.

There are three types of Light Beings/Spirit Beings that exist on Earth.

1. Those that are fully connected, Silver Cord intact Light Beings

2. Those that have their Silver Cords damaged by the enemy

3. Those that have their Silver Cords fully severed by dark forces.

The injured and severed cord beings, traveling in human flesh, have to seek enlightenment in order to heal their spiritual connections to Divine Source. Seeking enlightenment, higher truths, heals or restores their communication system. Spirit Beings, with fully severed Silver Cords, have to blindly believe there are a Heaven and a Divine Source that exist after Earth death of their human form. We have all had faith preached to us. It is the belief in the unknown/unseen. Belief heals.

January 18

THOUGHT FOR THE DAY - Are you rubbing shoulder with Dark Beings on a daily basis? Perverted Demons of Darkness walk all about you in human forms. Some of them are possibly family members.

HOW TO KNOW DARK BEINGS

I recently read about two folk artists, who live in different areas of the United States. One was obviously a Dark Spirit Being, the other one a Light Spirit Being.

Artist one worked in the medium of scrap wood, patriotic color paints. He took scrap wood and created hanging pieces of modern art that resembled American flags. When asked why he did it, when he was such a busy man pursuing other mediums he was interested in, he said, "I just want to share my passion for flags. I have loved them since I was a little boy. My passion is worthless, if I don't share it with others. I want someone to see the beauty I see in flags."

Artist two was in to metal sculpting. He welded and turned scrap pieces of metal into not so polite, provocative likenesses of local politicians, public figures, and ex girlfriends. He displayed his works in his front yard along his road frontage that led into town. When asked why he produced what he did, he half cursed and stated, "I do it to piss them off."

So, we have two artists. With one, it is passion that motivates/drives him. Passion and sharing are love. The second artist is driven by an inner dark need to piss people off, which is a form of abuse. So which is a Light Being and which a Dark one? Dark Spirit Beings have one goal; to abuse and destroy others who are trying to do good things in their communities, etc.

To recognize dark beings, pay attention to the words spewing from their mouths, what is created by them, what they wear, their daily deeds, and their reasoning for what they do. A man with sexually explicit naked women tattooed on his body says he has no respect for women, or children. Disrespect is a characteristic of a dark being.

January 19

THOUGHT FOR THE DAY – Heaven and Hell exist side by side on Earth. Angels and demons dwell in human flesh.

WHERE IS HELL?

Heaven and Hell exist side by side on Earth. Dark beings/demons/devils travel in human forms the same as Light Beings do. Human forms are the pits that darkness/Hell resides in. The gates of Hell open when a devil/demon/dark being in human flesh chooses to open up and play havoc with, or inflict, destruction on another.

Hell comes to call when a light being decides to accept a marriage proposal from a dark being in human flesh. A marriage bed can be hell. Hell comes to call when a light being's human form is abducted, raped, and murdered by a dark being. Hell comes to call when a dark being parent beats a child to death or deprives them food, or other basic necessities. Hell comes to call when a vicious gossip spreads evil untruths about you that cause you to be abandoned by family and friends. Demons, devils, dark souls are what they are. They cannot be changed. They don't want to be changed. Fallen angels/dark beings have already been kicked out of heaven. There is no salvation or redemption for them.

Fallen Angels/ beings of darkness will choose vulnerable light beings in society to attack, the ones with damaged or severed Silver Cords.

January 20

THOUGHT FOR THE DAY – Marrying darkness is a choice. Walking away from a dark marriage is another.

Have You Made Your Marriage Bed In Hell?

In religious circles, there is the belief that if a person marries, that marriage is forever because God expects it. Women and men stay married to dark beings on Earth because of this belief. They are denied their right to turn from darkness and walk in a different direction, a light one.

Men and women search for that perfect soul mate on Earth. The truth is that perfect soul mates only exist in the upper heavens. Perfection doesn't exist on Earth. Traveling companions on the Earth plane is what can be expected. Sometimes humans, with damaged or severed Silver Cords, make bad choices in partners/traveling companions, or are tricked in to believing that a dark being pursuing them is their soul mate. The term 'soul mate' is used by humans much too loosely.

God does not join his Light Beings in marriage to Dark beings. If you have made a bad, dark choice of a traveling companion on Earth, choose differently. God expects us to walk towards his light, not hang on to the arm of a dark being till you have wasted your human existence. You are on Earth for a reason. Being chained to darkness is not the reason.

As light beings, we are not to join ourselves with darkness in any fashion. Kicking dark angels out of our personal heavens is admitting we have made bad choices. Afterward, we are to run like crazy from them, our past choices, never looking back.

January 21

THOUGHT FOR THE DAY – Would you let your children hang out with a perverted dark being that you knew would possibly harm them? Of course, you wouldn't. Why do you willingly rub shoulders with the adult perverted beings in your daily existence?

DARK UNIONS

Just as we develop relationships with the angels in our lives, we also forge, unknowingly, relationships with devils and demons of darkness that walk about us in human forms. Just as there are angels, there are fallen angels. When we come to the realization that we have free will choice, we are faced with the decisions of whether to forge or not forge relationships with those moving in and out of our worlds.

The most common union of dark with light is marriage. The result of the union is domestic violence inflicted on the light being. There are other dark unions on Earth that possibly does not catch the attention of the press or law enforcement. In the business world, a light being joins forces with a business associate who clearly display under the table, questionable, business practices. A light being man meets a prostitute and befriends her. Befriending a daughter of the night attracts dark pimps and other criminal types to his door. Associating with child abusers, murderers, rapists, thieves, con artists, liars, etc. will bring you experiences to call that will not be pleasant. There is war in the Heavens. Darkness wants to destroy Light. If darkness can convince you to join them in some minor way, they have their foot in your door, to piddle about and subtly destroy the light of your world.

Do not marry, befriend, or consider joining forces with darkness in any fashion. If you have entered a union with darkness, you have the free will choice to exit the union and join forces with those of the light instead. Hanging out with darkness will turn you into a shade of gray, and eventually totally put out the light that you are.

If you have made your marriage bed in Hell, rise up, run, and never look back. There is no way to make a marriage bed of horror into one of roses. It is what it is, a dark union. The same goes for the other types of dark unions you may have entered into.

There is war in the heavens. Light is at war with darkness. It is not Divine Source's will that his warriors of Light cross enemy lines and embrace those of dark forces. Fallen Angels/Dark Forces were kicked out of Heaven. Why would God/Divine Source take them back in, or send his angels of light to be abused doormats for the warriors of darkness.

Heaven and Hell exist side by side on Earth. Devils and Light Beings exist side by side in human forms. Every day of human life we rub shoulders with both good and evil. We are at war, and must choose our unions wisely! God/Divine Source is our Military Commander. Don't be a traitor to Him, the light.

January 22

THOUGHT FOR THE DAY – Attitude is everything. It can make or break you in the business world and in personal relationships. Biting your tongue is the mastering of attitude.

SKUNK TYPES

I have a home that some friends live in, due to my not needing it at the moment. Three times, during the last five days, they have called stating that a pair of skunks has taken up residence beneath the house. They complain that the stench of the night spraying is driving them crazy. So, each morning I have driven many miles to check and smell the house, at their request. Each time, I have smelled nothing. However, to appease them I have put out skunk traps.

Earth life is sometimes plagued with friends and acquaintances that are skunks. They can stink to high heaven to us, but those about us don't smell them for what they are. So, it is sometimes necessary to trap or catch the skunks in our lives. For instance, a woman hires a detective to follow her skunk of a husband that she feels is running around on her. The detective trap works. I have a friend with a different type of skunk in his life, a thieving one. Someone was stealing change and bills from a hall table where he unloaded his pockets every evening after work. So, he set a trap. He started leaving one crumpled dollar bill on the hall table. Then, he invited all his friends and relatives, one at a time, to visit. When the bill disappeared, he knew exactly who the thieving skunk was in his life. His skunk trap worked. Skunk types, dark beings, invade our worlds.

There are some rabid, seriously stinking skunks (sociopaths) who are intent on doing secret physical harm to light beings. For instance, they will spit, pee, poop, put chemicals in, or drug an unsuspecting Light Beings' food or drinks. What a lot of humans think is stomach flu, is actually dark being skunks assaulting them. Other types of skunks will break out windows, porch lights, and mirrors. Others will rip or tear up curtains or clothing, not to mention those who will stuff your toilet stool with rolls of paper. Then, there are the children who will draw on your freshly painted walls with markers, tease the dog, curse at you, continually bully others, kill small animals, go on school rampages, etc. Darkness is out to physically harm you and what belongs to you. He sees your things as an extension of you, like having a third arm.

Both light and dark Spirit Beings enter Earth life thru the birth process. Little dark being skunks grow up to be adult dark being skunk sociopaths. Darkness is what it is, whether it exists in adults, children, or babies. There is war in the Heavens. Earth is one battlefield. All warriors, light and dark, enter Earth life thru the birth process of human forms. Just as there are very young privates in military ranks, there are older, seasoned commanders. In darkness there are very young private types, as well as older seasoned demons of darkness.

January 23

THOUGHT FOR THE DAY – looking outward into the universe is not where you will find supernatural experiences. Going within is the path to all there is.

TIME TRAVEL and THE FOUNTAIN OF YOUTH

Humans look outward desiring supernatural visitations and events. They look outward thru human eyes in search of the Fountain of Youth, as well as for machines to Time Travel in. Also, they look outward for angel visitations, and ghostly encounters with deceased loved ones. Looking outward, most often than not, is not where you will find the supernatural experiences that they or you desire.

We are spirit beings traveling for a lifetime in a human body. The body is like an automobile. It can run with us in the seat, or idle without us in the driver's seat. We can leave our car, or our human vehicles, running in idle while we run into our houses to get something we have forgotten. As Spirit Beings, we are not our human bodies. We are the drivers of them. Leaving our human forms in idle, sleeping, or meditative states, we can exit them and run into our heavenly homes to get what we need.

Time Travel is a mode of transportation available to us as Spirit Beings. When a human dreams of going back in time and being part of different history episodes, he is traveling backwards. He is Time Traveling. The same goes for when he travels into the future in his dreams and visions. It is Time traveling. Time travel does exist, but it is for those beings who go inward and then upward to the Astral where those travel stations/machine types are available.

The much sought after Fountain of Youth is also found by going inward and upward. The Fountain of Youth is for the Spirit Being, not the human car they travel in. Light Beings are able to heal all of their injuries and imperfections by visiting the Fountain of Youth on the Astral Shore/First Heaven. It is sort of like a human form returning home after a long, arduous day on the Earth Plane. He takes a much needed soaker in a hot tub to revive him-self. In the Heavens, a Spirit Being has a home. In it, he has a hot tub, but it is the Fountain of Youth. It is a place the soul renews itself. When a soul is renewed, it never dies. The soul is young and filled with vitality forever.

The Fountain of Youth is not for humans. It is for Spirit Beings that travel inside human forms.

January 24

THOUGHT FOR THE DAY – You can vacation in the same old spot every year, or you can choose to adventure into the unknown.

TRAVEL TO OTHER PLANETS

With every truth learned, there is another to master.

When we discover that we can exit our bodies at night and return to the Astral /Heaven's Shore, we have to face the fact that there is more to the Heavens than the astral shore or beach. The inner heavens are vast, and we have the power to travel them.

Vacations are nice, but no one wants to hang out on a beach forever. Sooner or later, a being gets tired of collecting shells, eating ocean fish, and getting sunburns from lying on the beach and basking too long in the sun. Life is progressive. You can choose to vacation and travel to the same old spot every year, or choose to venture in to the unknown.

Spirit Beings on Earth pop from their human forms and return to the Astral Shore, when their human forms lay sleeping. They travel by portals. Dreams are one of those portals. Spirit Beings on other planets also travel to the Astral Shore, via their inner portals. We are not the only ones out there. On the Astral Shore, Spirit Beings that are home from other planets mill about and mingle with those from Earth.

John, of the book of Revelations, was caught up to the Astral Shore/Heaven. He saw beasts with seven heads, etc. He could not explain what he saw there. Men with human minds are still trying to interpret the book of Revelations. As I have mentioned in previous writings, dream scenarios can only be interpreted by the one who receives them. They are in code. So, John left behind his experience of being caught away and what he saw. He did not leave behind his interpretation, due to his limited knowledge and thinking of that day. He had a vision, but failed to interpret it for the benefit of those coming after him.

Just like John's creature with multiple heads, beings arriving on the Astral Shore from other planets do not necessarily look like us. They could be beast like creatures with a strange head, or seven heads. Beings could have four arms, instead of the two we have. They could have tails, or no tails. I am sure the first man to spot a giraffe on Earth was in awe of his long neck. If you are first to portal walk to another planet, I am sure that you are going to be in awe of beasts and beings there. John the Revelator was a portal walker. He saw many things that he could not interpret.

Once arriving on the Astral Shore from Earth, we can choose to enter a portal that goes to other planets. If we are brave enough, we can explore them and then return to the heavens and take our own portal back to Earth.

January 25

THOUGHT FOR THE DAY – The resurrection of the dead is taking place all around you on a daily basis.

RESURRECTION OF THE DEAD SOUL

When a spirit being is disconnected from his Divine source, due to injury or the severing of his Silver Cord communications system, he is blind or dead to whom he really is. The atheist, with a severed cord, is dead spiritually. He has no communications with the heavens and sees himself as just a human being who will live, die, and cease to be. He believes he is a product of animal evolution and the failure of his parents to use birth control. The blind spiritual being knows there is something out there, as he puts it, but feels whatever it is, it doesn't have any interest in communicating with him. He sees his God/Divine

Source as an uncaring God that has left him to fend for himself. Only Spirit Beings with fully intact communication systems, Silver Cords, understand they are powerful light beings who can reap from the heavens the knowledge they need for surviving whatever situation on Earth they find themselves in.

Searching for enlightenment is the path for those with damaged Silver Cords. Only a few blind/damaged cord individuals are able to think themselves out of their blindness. Elevating ones thoughts is the first step on that path. The next step is going inward, and then upward. The path to enlightenment is healing for them. The path of believing in faith that there is something beyond us is the healing path for severed cords. The human mind must believe in faith, in order to awaken/reattach his dead/severed/sleeping Spirit Being.

Both the damaged and severed cord types experience resurrection and being caught up to God when their Silver Cord communications systems are healed, or reconnected. The fully intact Silver Cord beings know their source and experience the going away and coming again/returning to their Earth bodies on a regular basis. Those left behind are the humans who look outward with human eyes for a resurrection. They let their inner spirit being sleep. A sleeping being does not rise.

January 26

THOUGHT FOR THE DAY – Spirit Guides can appear in forms that you are comfortable with. To one it could be an angel with wings. To another it could be an angel without wings. Spirit Guides are guardians.

SPIRIT GUIDES

The First Heaven/Astral Shore is where spirit guides work, keep an eye on their charges on Earth, and send messages to guide their paths. Communications between Earth and Heaven are sent and received there. The higher heavens are for those who have mastered their Earth lives and are moving on to other things. That does not mean that the masters of the upper heavens can't return to the Astral Shore, if they choose to guide other spirit beings still in school or on missions on Earth. A Spirit Guide can be a master, a friend or associate in the heavens, or an Earth family member that has proceeded in death.

The astral shore is a disembarking place for souls that are returning to, or traveling to the heavens.

There are dark as well as light spirit beings milling about there. Earth is heaven and hell existing side by side. The Astral shore is the returning place for light and shades of gray angels, and the judgment place for the shades of gray. Dark souls may be deported, sent back to their hell on Earth. Thus, Spirit Guides have to be careful in the messages they send to their charges from the Astral. Dark spirit beings would love to interrupt communications while they wait their turn at the judgment seat. Shades of Gray know they have turned from the light and their current presence on the Astral Shore might be their last.

Crazy Dreams are coded messages sent to you by your Spirit Guide. Being in code, Dark Beings cannot intercept and sabotage communications between heaven and Earth. The same goes for visions. Your Spirit Guide is your guardian.

Your Spirit Guide is capable of taking on a form that you are comfortable with seeing. In the higher heavens, spirit beings, including spirit guides, are orbs of pure light. Forms are put on like costumes and used in the first and second heavens. The First Heaven is a place of judgment. The Second Heaven is a garden, and the welcoming home place for light beings that have aced their turn at judgment. Costumes are worn in the second heaven, because returning Spirit Beings are still used to being known as who they were on Earth.

January 27

THOUGHT FOR THE DAY - Angels are actually orbs of light. They can, if they desire, put on human form or other costumes that men will understand.

DO ANGELS HAVE WINGS?

You and I just travel in the human bodies we have chosen for transportation on Earth. Just as we step in and drive an automobile, spirit beings step in and drive/travel in human bodies. Angels are spirit beings from the realms beyond Earth. Just like those of us who have chosen to travel in human forms, Angels can choose what form they wish to appear in (travel in) to perform whatever their tasks or interests are.

Angels may choose to enter, use, and travel in human forms like you and I, or they can wear costume bodies if they are just making a short appearance. Angels may choose to appear winged or un-winged when they are wearing costumes. They can also choose to appear in the costume forms of guardian animal or tribal shamans.

Angels are spirit beings with appointed missions. They are not limited to man's idea of what they should look like. Have you ever met a human that was so sweet in all their ways that they were unbelievable? Perhaps you were entertaining an angel unaware, one who was traveling in a human form and on a mission for one lifetime on earth. Has a dog ever run between you and danger? Perhaps you have entertained an angel in costume. Angels are spirit beings. Out of form or costumes, they are orbs of light. Out of human form, you and I are orbs of light. We are not the human form costumes we travel in. Angels are not the human form costumes they occasionally travel in. To truly know an angel, you would have to know him in his orb light state.

Take photos at family reunions and see if any orbs appear in your camera shots. You might be surprised at the fact that you have had supernatural visitors. Pay attention to who the orb appears over. Some orb angels are guardians, or protectors. They will appear in photos over those they are commissioned to follow about on Earth.

January 28

THOUGHT FOR THE DAY – You have to grow up to be an understanding human, before you can grow up spiritually to be understanding of the mysterious creatures and beings of astral life.

CRUDE LAUGHING OR UNDERSTANDING

My father was raised Methodist, and his grandfather was a minister back in the late 1800s. Methodists were very stiff and starchy. Most Methodist families rode to church in a buckboard or a buggy. Teen boys, back then, rode horses (the equivalent of first cars) to church. My father was proud of his horse. Back then, girls didn't consider you suitor material, unless you had a horse.

One summer, a new Baptist minister moved into the farming community, and he had a very beautiful teen daughter. My father developed a crush on her. So, on a couple of Sunday mornings, he ditched his own Methodist church services, and rode across a back field to attend the Baptist one.

The Baptist minister and family did not ride in a buggy or buckboard to church. They each rode a horse, including the stunningly beautiful daughter. After a couple of Sundays, my father worked up the courage to ask the girl if he could escort her home on horseback after Sunday service. She agreed. So, after Sunday morning services my father and the girl rode their horses side by side in front, while the minister father and his wife rode horses behind them. The minister's wife, and the girl, rode their horse side saddle.

It was spring and during Sunday morning services, a storm had blew thru, causing the creek (they had to cross to get home) to rise. Trying to be a gentleman, my father let the girl go first. Afterward, he planned to follow and then the minister father and wife behind them. Teens don't always make good decisions. When she entered the deepest part of the rushing creek, those on the creek bank realized that the water was deeper than the belly of her horse. The father was instantly off of his horse and wading out into the creek to assist her. My father was in teen shock and didn't know what to do. He remained on his horse.

Suddenly, the beautiful Baptist girl's horse got excited and lost its balance in the water. The horse stumbled to one side losing its footing in the water. Then, the perfectly long dressed, gloved girl with perfect hair fell off into the rushing creek. The horse struggled to regain his footing, as the girl flailed about in the rushing water.

My father, seeing that the Baptist minister was going to the aid of the girl, made a scramble to assist the horse. After my father had assisted the spooked horse to shore and had quieted it, he turned to look at the girl. Seeing what a soaked wet mess she was, he laughed. She was not amused.

My father, back at that time, could not understand why the girl refused to let him accompany her home anymore. I think it came down to understanding that he had chosen to rescue the horse and not her.

In the Astral, there are many exotic, beautiful, royal supernatural spirit beings. If you are granted permission to accompany one of them on a journey into their world, show respect (be gentlemanly). However, should something happen to that being that you don't understand, it is best to not be crude in your understanding and laugh at their calamity. You just might not be granted future portal travel with them.

January 29

THOUGHT FOR THE DAY- The underdog cannot sleep peacefully till the upper dog quits using and gnawing on his weaknesses.

WHEN WILL THE LION LAY DOWN WITH THE

LAMB?

Let me remind you that there is war in the heavens. The heavens are found within. Hell is also an inner place, a sad state of a pit that man chooses to lower him-self into, such as drug addiction, alcoholism, prostitution, welfare living, etc.

Some men give totally over to the call of darkness and choose to become demons/devils in human flesh. Then, battles between demons of dark states are at war with the light beings that have chosen heavenly lamb states of being. Hitler chose to embrace darkness, and then became a monster devil lion.

I embrace two thoughts as to when Peace will come to Earth.

1. When man quits eating them physically, the animal kingdom will feel safe enough to lay down with the lion, who becomes a non meat eater, a vegetarian.

2. A lamb lays down in peace when his or her abusive enemy is imprisoned, put to death, or dies. Peace comes to one lamb at a time.

Lions are many and walk about us in human forms. They are devils who are intent on devouring us. A lion is the church gossip. She lives to tear apart decent beings with her vicious tongue. A lion is the parent or family member who sees nothing good that you have ever done. They put you down, and eat your emotional state till you feel you are going to lose it. You can be a lion and kill a person without them physically dying.

Peace will come individually to lambs on Earth, when lions lay their gossiping, belittling, abusing, teasing, etc.

down, or are forced to lay their darkness down thru imprisonment and death. Peace may come when a rapist is captured and caged in a prison. Peace may come when an abusive family member dies. Peace may come when your abusive boss gets fired. A lamb laughs and lays down when a rapist is sent to prison. A worker breaks out in smiles when he gets to watch his lion of a boss clean out his desk. A lamb smiles, while looking down into the casket of an abusive family member.

January 30

THOUGHT FOR TODAY - There is a higher path for you to travel. The writings on this page are your trumpet sound to rise and be caught away to the heavens within you. Hear ye your trumpet sound.

THE CALL TO DIVINITY

There is a higher path to travel. It winds in and out of Earth life, as well as the inner and upward heavens, and thru portals on the Astral Shore to other planets. Free will choice is a divine power. Used wisely, it brings out the God in all of us, our Divine side. Used poorly, it puts our divinity to sleep, a spiritual dark comatose state.

Beings on Earth start to walk paths to enlightenment at different ages, in different religions, and in world wise locations. The Buddha was bored with his royal position and left it behind. He sat beneath a tree like a homeless, jobless street person while he sought all that there is. He was a master of perfecting ones inward self and the traveling of the inner and upward heavens. Christ started his mastership as the son of a carpenter and then an independent rogue preacher for his day. Independent thinking was one of his powers, as were healing and the power to call back Spirit Beings from the Heavens to return to their human forms. We just lost (she returned to the Astral Shore) a famous Psychic of the United States. She started her magnificent journey in Kansas City, Missouri. She was a carrier of messages and a writer of books.

What are your powers? You are a divine Spirit Being traveling in a human form for a life time on Earth.

I, Jo Hammers the Mystic, (known in the heavens as Barjoraven) am a trumpeter of words. I point souls with damaged Silver Cord connections to the CATCHING AWAY, which is within. My power on Earth is the written page, a path to enlightenment and a portal to the heavens. My mission is to make a road map for Spirit Beings coming after me. Someone has to write the manuals for becoming and make road maps.

All around the Earth, in every town, city, and religion, Divine Beings/Spirit Beings walk about in human forms. Every being starts their search for enlightenment somewhere. It does not matter where. Because you have started your journey, you have attracted me and my writings into your life. It is your turn to be caught away to God/Divine Source. I am your trumpet sound.

January 31

THOUGHT FOR THE DAY - Why wait for others to follow in your footsteps? Leave your foot prints for others to follow. Then go on about your calling to rapture in thought and Spirit.

WE ARE THE GOING AWAY AND COMING AGAIN

Once we realize that we are able to pop/exit from our human forms and then return to them, we realize that we are the promised 'GOING AWAY AND COMING AGAIN". It is not physical bodies that will rise. It is the Spirit Beings in them that will rapture.

Christ said he would go away, but come again. He did. He laid his human, physical body form down in death. His Spirit Being went home to the Father. After his body was laid to rest in a tomb, he returned from the Father and revived his human form. The Spirit Being Christ was a Master Portal Walker, a master of the going away and coming again. You and I are portal walkers, those who go away and come again, while our human forms lay sleeping.

Don't be fooled in thinking that your particular religious persuasion will be the only religious group that will be found in the Heavens. Spirit Beings travel in human forms in all religious persuasions all around the globe. It does not matter what religious persuasion path you start your journey on. It is the mastering of individual inner paths, wherever they lead, that counts. All men are born somewhere around planet Earth. All men start their spiritual journeys somewhere around the globe. The starting point is not what is important. The finishing point is. When a Spirit Being, traveling in a human form, has mastered his personal path and the going away and the coming again, he has mastered life and death.

Resurrection comes to those who seek to know more than what their religious persuasion roots have offered them on Earth. 'Resurrection' is the popping from human forms in thought, or in journeys of the Spirit to the Astral/Heavens. The 'Coming Again' is when the Spirit Being returns to his human body and wakens his physical form.

I, Jo Hammers the Mystic, am a Spirit Being, traveling in a human form. So are you! Be caught away to all that you can be! Travel the Universe in thought and spirit being form. You are divinity traveling in human flesh. The resurrected ones are the new inhabitants of the New Heaven and New Earth that is coming down, a new dispensation beyond the New Testament Age.

CHAPTER TWO
FEBRUARY

THE BOOK OF PORTALS

February 1

THOUGHT FOR THE DAY – Portals are like elevators. Spirit Beings travel up and down in them from Earth (and other planets) to the Astral Shore, or First Heaven.

WHAT ARE PORTALS?

Portals are like the inside of soda straws, but larger. Spirit Beings can travel up and down in them like they are elevators. They are also like the eye in the center of a tornado or hurricane, passageways that Spirit Beings can use to travel to and from the Astral Shore, or First Heaven. Some portals are to Earth. Some are to other planets. Spirit Beings from Earth are not the only intelligent life forms traveling the universe via portals. Spirit Beings from other planets also travel via portals to the Astral/First Heaven.

Spirit Beings traveling down portals and in and out of human forms are called Light Beings. Those traveling down thru portals from the Astral to the hells on Earth are called Dark Beings, or Fallen Angels. From the other planets you have a variety of beings with Characteristics of their own. Some are called Holy Beasts, others Guardians of the Universe, etc. All are called Portal Walkers. Also, on the Astral Shore, you will find Rainbow beings and Invisible beings, not to mention all sorts of beasts that humans have never even considered, beasts with multiple heads, eyes, or mouths. The Astral Shore, before judgment, looks a wee bit like a side show carnival. Royalty from other planets may be walking along the shore wearing crowns and robes. On Earth, we prefer cats and dogs for pets. On other planets, they may prefer creatures that you and I are totally unfamiliar with, and be walking them on leashes on the shore.

Portals empty out on the Astral Shore. The shore is like the waiting room of a train station or an airport. It is filled with strangers of different body types. Some may have four arms where you and I have two, or have three eyes instead of two. Some beings may have wings and others bodies that can be seen thru. John the revelator, in the New Testament Book of Revelations, saw beings and beasts with multiple heads that he didn't understand, when he traveled to Heaven in a vision portal. Only he could interpret what he saw. He did the best he could with the knowledge of his day. John was a Portal Walker, but did not understand his ability to do so. He referred to it as being caught up to Heaven.

In the Christian's New Testament, it speaks of a New Jerusalem coming down and its many gates. Gates are the entrances and exits to portals. Is it possible that the Kingdom of God/New Jerusalem/Kingdom of the Divine is coming down to open its gates to more than one planet?

Keep an open mind, an open gate, to all that is coming down to you. Some of it has landed on this written page for you to read.

February 2

THOUGHT FOR THE DAY – When you awaken inside spiritually, you find yourself starting over.

STARTING OVER AFTER AWAKENING

When you awaken as a Spirit Being, after going on a quest to find God/Divine Source/etc., you find yourself starting over. Your life is suddenly governed by higher thoughts, desires, and ways of being. You have awakened to the fact that you are more than the human form you travel Earth life in. Your goals change, and you start to look at yourself from a higher perspective. Your path as a Spirit Being on Earth becomes more important than the path your human form has been traveling.

One of the first human things you will lay down is the belief that a soul mate exists for you in the human world. You discover that soul mates are perfect, and human form life is not perfect. Earth is a learning experience. The attractions of the human body (a necessity to keep it reproducing) are not love, but fleeting moments. The human form, the reproducing form, can be attracted to another human who is really a dark, mean spirited person on the inside. A man can wake up in bed with a gorgeous human form next to him, but inside that form is a dark, mean spirited being. The same goes for a woman waking up next to the handsomest man ever, but a devil within. Light and dark cannot be soul mates. The war between light and darkness eventually surfaces in such a relationship. Then, those in the union go for each other's throat. What was once a union that was thought to be between soul mates turns out to be a marriage bed in Hell on Earth!

Soul mate unions are awarded in the Third Heaven, the home of the perfected ones. On Earth, we have free will choice and may choose a traveling companion. In the land of the perfected ones, Divine Source does the matching. The most that we can expect on Earth is to have a compatible traveling companion. Remember, you are a Spirit Being traveling in a human form. You are not the form. Choose to travel Earth life with a Light Being who shares your goals and understands that unions are made in the heavens, not on Earth. A portal walker should choose another portal walker as a traveling companion.

A soul mate is the other half of you. He/she is a perfected master, an orb of light who dwells in the Third Heaven. Soul mates are awarded, or matched by God/Divine Source. He is the perfect matchmaker.

February 3

THOUGHT FOR THE DAY – Being a permanent, comfortable, couch potato will let you miss out what is next in life for you.

CHANGE COMES WITH A PRICE

Some stepping stones in Earth life are slippery and hard to stand on, but they are the next step to reaching whatever is next on your Earth path. We would all like to have perfect lives where nothing goes wrong. However, the Spirit Being within that we are will not awaken, unless we have our 'on our knees' life jolting moments. Comfort is a sleeping state for the Spirit Being that lives within.

A comfort zone is not a good place to be. Failing to move forward in life beyond roadblocks on your path will leave you without an education, suited occupations, future children, living in larger homes, having greater wealth, making higher class friends, eating in better restaurants, embracing new and enlightened religions, etc. etc. etc. The comfort zone will keep you living in what will soon be the past. Being a comfortable couch potato will let you miss out on what is next in life.

Change comes with a price. That price is to be willing to leave the familiar, the comfortable, and step out to embrace the fork in your road and its surprises, no matter what bumps in your road it offers.

February 4

THOUGHT FOR THE DAY - To discover that you are not your human form can be a frightening experience. You do not want people to think that you are crazy.

TURNING POINTS/WAKE UP CALLS

Turning points are just bumps or forks on our life paths that cause us to look and travel in a different direction. Also, they aren't always pleasant. Sometimes, they are the most frightening experiences of our lives. They are events we can't go around, under, over, or thru. Some discover they are Sprit Beings traveling in human forms during these moments. They have to awaken, as Spirit Beings, in order to find a way thru their sudden disastrous events of tumultuous, frightening change.

When things are going well, a human being doesn't think about changing courses, or approaching, embracing, and awakening his spiritual side. So, life presents a bump in the road, a splash of ice cold water in the face. Disaster slaps the human face with a wakeup call. These calls come in many forms. For instance:

1. Your brilliant child suddenly has failing grades

2. Someone hits your car and totals it

3. Your cake in the oven falls,

4. Your skin breaks out with a ring worm or seed warts

5. Your hair turns prematurely gray in your early twenties

6. You fall and knock a front tooth out

7. Your practically new water heater goes out

8. Your friends at church, or school, shun you, and you don't know why

9. You get fired for something someone else did

10. You move in with relatives because you are unable to pay your rent

11. Your mortgage holder hits you with a balloon payment

12. You find a snake or a mouse that has managed to get into your house,

13. A child dies

14. Your doctor tells you, a baker and doughnut loving fool, that you are diabetic

15. Etc. etc.

Turning points (or little bumps in life's road) are wake up calls. As little as some are, they can put you on your knees in tears. Portals to Divine Source and the heavens open up when Spirit Beings are forced to wake up.

February 5

THOUGHT FOR THE DAY - The real winners in Earth life are those who stay focused on the path in front of them, not the path of the past. The future is happening. The past is not.

WHO IS RAINING ON YOUR PARADE

My mother made yeast rolls on special occasions. She had a knack for making them rise to great heights. After punching down her dough once, she made her perfect mound of yeast dough into rolls and placed them in a baking pan to rise. She always timed it so that they went into the oven at a precise time to come out of the oven hot for the meal.

One Easter, my eight year old brother was fascinated by the kids Easter song that went, "Here comes Peter Cottontail . . . hopping down the bunny trail." He would end the song with "Hop-hop-hop!" My mother had her rolls sitting on the kitchen table, in preparation to pop them in the oven. The phone rang and she was momentarily distracted. My brother wandered into the kitchen, spotted the rolls, and pretended two of his fingers were bunny feet hopping. Right down the center of my mother's perfect rolls he went. Two finger holes were made in each roll right down the center of the pan, flattening them. He didn't realize it, but he had just rained on my mother's parade. She had accomplished something really spectacular, perfectly risen rolls. My brother came along and stole from her the joy that comes with accomplishment.

In life, we have blissful moments of accomplishment that are destroyed by phony hopping rabbits. Perhaps we have just received a promotion, a bonus, etc. Instead of getting to enjoy our accomplishment, someone says something nasty to us, or tries to diminish our moment. We have our promotion, our bonus, our hot rolls moments that should be times of joy. Instead, along comes a hopping fake rabbit to flatten our spirits and joy. My mother had her accomplished rolls moment flattened.

We cannot help the hopping rabbit individuals that are all about us. What we can do is realize that no matter what disaster comes our way, it doesn't mean that we can't make another pan of perfect rolls. Life is about new beginnings. In my mother's new beginning, she placed her rolls on top of the refrigerator till it was time to pop them in the oven. In each of our new beginnings, we must take steps to guard ourselves from those who want to rain on our parades. Putting up our umbrellas of knowing how special our accomplishments are, we must let the harsh, spiteful, jealous words of others just run off into the gutters of life. Our accomplishments won't always be important to others.

My mother didn't yell, spank, or discipline her hopping rabbit in response to her flattened rolls. Warring with others about what they say or do to us accomplishes nothing.

Perfected ones focus on making their next pan of perfect rolls.

Portal Walkers are accomplished astral travelers who are always seeking a new spiritual horizon and portal to master. They don't have time to waste on the hopping rabbits about them who want to hop and rain on their parade, destroying the joy of having accomplished perfect rolls.

February 6

THOUGHT FOR THE DAY – Portal gates are to be kept open, not locked.

PORTAL GATES

We are spirit beings traveling in human forms. To enter portals to the heavens, we must climb from/exit our human forms. Then we travel upward toward a round light, which is beyond the upward exit of the portal. It is the light of the Astral Shore. The actual portal is like traveling thru a misty, foggy tunnel. On the Earth end of some portals are invisible gates. The structures are built/erected by frightened humans whose Spirit beings within are asleep. They are afraid of the unknown, what they have no understanding of.

Dream Catchers, of the Native American Indians, are gates. They hang them to keep bad dreams out. They have no understanding that frightening dreams could be messages from their Great White Spirit/Spirit Guide. They fear Kachina, supposedly evil ones. What they fear could actually be their Spirit Guides, wearing costumes and masks. Not all messages sent to humans on Earth are flowery pretty ones. Warnings of disaster and danger come down as frightening dreams.

Humans can put up all sorts of gates to block their individual portals. They hang and sprinkle potions, incenses, crosses, etc. They actually put up roadblocks to their own spiritual advancement. If you want an open portal to higher understanding, visitations, and astral travel, throw out your dream catchers, crosses, potions, etc. Protection is not what you need. What you need is to study and learn how to interpret your dreams, as well as understand portals and your Spirit Being within that travels them.

February 7

THOUGHT FOR THE DAY – Humans who seek visitations from deceased loved ones, using the gift of another, has a Spirit Being of their own within that is asleep, or has a silver cord that is severed.

VISITATION PORTALS

When loved one die, we mourn that which is familiar to us. We long for the face of our mother, the hands of our father, and the hugs of a child. We grieve for that which we once saw and felt. We fail to think about, or grieve for, the loss of the Spirit Being that traveled in the human form of our mother, father, child, etc.

Missing the familiar, human aspects of our deceased loved ones; men approach psychics, mediums, mystics, witches, seers, etc. in an effort to speak once more with them. Most want their deceased loved ones to appear as their human forms once looked, forgetting that their deceased loved ones' human forms are abandoned; ashes to ashes and dirt to dirt. Some forms have been worm eaten, cremated, or scattered to the four corners of the Earth. Visitations come from the Spirit Being that lives in, or travels in, a human form.

Should a Spirit Being desire, he can use a visitation portal to appear to former human family members on Earth. Because of long lines waiting to use these visitation portals, the use of them is limited to about thirty seconds of Earth time. During that time frame, a Spirit Being can choose to send down a message just in words, or he can travel down the portal for a 30 second visitation to stand before whoever they wish to visit and speak with.

Just as angels (orbs of light) can choose to appear on Earth with or without wings costumes, the Spirit Beings of deceased relatives can also choose to appear in a costume. It can be a replica of their Earth human body, or altogether different. The Spirit Being has no real interest in the human form he has just abandoned. Worn out, discarded in death human forms are like old, dented wrecked cars on Earth that have been sent to a salvage yard to be crushed and disposed of.

Should you request a visitation from your deceased mother, father, or a dead child; don't expect them to appear exactly as they once were. Your father may be wearing tropical shirts and carrying a fishing rod, when in Earth life he was a book worm who wore very conservative gray clothing. The mother you remember wearing an apron on Earth, may wear nurse's whites and a cap in their visitation to you. The child, who once lavished you with six year old hugs, may appear as a grown man who extends his hand to shake with you. Spirit Beings only traveled in human forms on Earth. In the Astral and upper heavens they are approximately thirty years old and have lives there. I am a mystic trumpeter and a writer on Earth. In the heavens I am Master Barjoraven, a keeper of paths and portals.

All deceased loved ones, Spirit Beings without human forms, are about thirty Earth years in age in the Astral/Heavens. When asking for a visitation, ask to see them as they truly are. It is a request that is respectful. Your dead six year old child could be a thirty year old angel, or spirit guide, who extends his hand to shake with you on his visitation.

February 8

THOUGHT FOR THE DAY – Spirit Guides can wear costumes to appear in when visiting humans on Earth. The White Buffalo Woman of the Native American Indians is an example.

SPIRIT GUIDES

The First Heaven/Astral shore is where Spirit Guides work. From there, they keep an eye on their charges on Earth, as well as on other planets. Spirit Guides are in charge of sending messages to guide their charge's paths. Spirit Guides are communications specialists/masters. Portals are their means of sending messages down to, or descending and making visits to the Spirit Being traveling in a human form that they guard.

The Astral Shore/First Heaven has three purposes:

1. It is a disembarking platform/shore for those traveling via portals, similar to a train station or a bus station.

2. It is the place where all light being and shades of gray souls are judged for their deeds, missions, and life lessons on Earth and other planets.

3. Spirit Guides are stationed and work on the Astral Shore.

The Higher Heavens are the dwelling places/homes of the masters. A Spirit Guide can be a master who commutes and goes to work every day on the Astral Shore.

Visions and dreams are orchestrated/created by Spirit Guides. Dreams are sent down to you via a portal. Spirit Guides can travel down portals and appear to you in what is called visions, if he feels it is necessary. Even though your guide is a Spirit Being/Orb of Light, he can put on a form/costume/mask when he is making a visit, in order for you to understand the reason for his vision visitation. Spirit Guides can appear in costumes and masks of angels, masters, medicine men, shamans, etc. etc. Some humans expect angels to have wings, others with no wings. He is a master and can appear both with and without wings. His true form is that of an orb of light.

The White Buffalo Woman of the Native American Indians is a good example of a Spirit Guide appearing in a costume that a particular planet's inhabitants understand.

February 9

THOUGHT FOR THE DAY – Your biological parents gave you a name on Earth. Who are you addressed as in the heavens?

WHAT NAME ARE YOU CALLED OVER THERE?

Have you ever considered that you, a Spirit Being traveling in human form, have a home, family, friends, and an identity that are non Earth related? Earth life is like going overseas in the military to Heaven's Spirit Beings. Soldiers in the military are your brothers, but not your real/biological ones. An army barracks is your military home, but not your real home. Your ID tags give you a number as a name. At home you have a name given you by your biological parents. We basically have a home away from home, as well as an identity and social life that go with it.

Our real home in the Astral is not a place where we lay around on clouds and eat grapes fed to us by mystical, winged angels. The Astral/Heaven is a working society, just like Earth is. There we have a home, family, friends, an occupation, and an identity/name. Have you ever asked yourself what your name at home in the heavens is?

My name in the heavens is Barjoraven. My Earth mother named me Barbara Jo, thinking she heard my name spoken to her. Her connection to supernatural intelligence was a little fuzzy at the time. However, she got it almost right. In the heavens, I am Barjoraven. Have you heard someone calling your name in your dreams? Was the name one that your Earth biological parents didn't name you?

February 10

THOUGHT FOR THE DAY – Atheists have severed Silver Cords.

ASTRAL AMNESIA

Spirit Beings have communication lines called Silver

Cords. The misty, see thru, cloud like, rope of a form is a line that connects us to Divine Intelligence. When entering Earth life, sometimes our Silver Cord is injured or severed by attacking Dark Beings. The Astral Shore at times is a minor battleground between light and dark beings, because the judgment seat is there. Both dark and light beings mill about there waiting for their call to judgment. During the milling stage, dark beings see it as their last chance to assault, war against, Light Beings who happen to catch their attention.

One of Dark Beings favorite methods of assault is to try to sever Silver Cords communication lines. Sometimes, all they can manage to do is bruise or injure the cords. When injured Silver Cords happen; a light being's memory of their Astral identity may become static plagued, fuzzy, or temporarily forgotten till their cords heal (Temporary Amnesia). The fully severed cord being is totally cut off from memories of his astral identity (Amnesia). Assaults on cords take place on the Astral Shore, as well as on Earth.

When injuring or severing of silver cords occur, Spirit Guides use whatever tools are necessary to re-establish communications. This would be termed healing in the thinking of Earth men. It is a powerful reconnection/healing that is only available to Light Beings that are traveling in human forms.

Without healing and reconnection, Light Beings could wander Earth for an entire life time experience with a sense of being disconnected, or being out of control. Those beings are as sweet and good in Earth life as they can be. However, they just can't seem to get their acts together. Reconnection comes in dream states. Blissful dreams heal Silver Cords.

February 11

THOUGHT FOR THE DAY – To read and understand higher thoughts is to portal walk words.

WRITTEN PAGE PORTALS

It is important that we leave behind a record of our spiritual triumphs, and the many twists and turns on our paths that led us to our final mastering of life's moments on earth. As awakened Spirit Beings, we are responsible for point the way for those coming behind us. We must leave behind trail markers for those who have just entered Earth life, or those just reaching Earth maturity and are about to embark on their spiritual journeys. Without maps and markers, there is nothing but wilderness of mind, the briars and overgrowth of Dark Age thinking. We must pioneer paths for those behind us.

I am a writer. So, I am leaving behind what I know about enlightenment and Astral life on the written page. Hopefully, a couple hundred years after I am gone from Earth life, someone will read my written pages and be inspired to awaken and pursue a path up distant mountains of advanced thought to even greater plateaus of enlightenment. I am willing to be someone else's stepping stone.

Women who make friendship quilts are interesting. They are very accepting of each other and the unique block each brings to a sewing bee to share and stitch into a quilt. No two blocks are ever the same in color or design. However, each block tells a simple story of who made it. One quilter will put her name and date on her block, while another will put her baby's name. Someone else might put their divorce date. One will make an all blue block, while another makes one of rainbow colors. They each have a unique spark in them that they share thru their invested block. New Age thinkers are just as unique and diversified in their colorful thoughts and writings. No two writer blocks/blogs will be the same.

Quilt blocks, just like books, can be read (portal walked). They each have a special story to tell.

February 12

THOUGHT FOR THE DAY – Some beings from other planets are frightening looking. We are possibly frightening looking to them. We tend to fear what we don't understand and are not familiar with.

PORTALS TO OTHER PLANETS

There are portals to other planets. Spirit Beings do not need slow man-made spaceships to travel there. Just as we go within and travel to the Astral Shore, beings from other planets can do the same. Thus, on the Astral Shore we can use their portals to visit their planets, just as they can use ours to visit Earth.

On the Astral Shore, you will encounter travelers from other planets who are more than happy to share information about travel there. In turn, we share with them information about Earth and its points of interest to travel to. One of my favorite places on Earth is Lake Tahoe in winter. The view of snow on the mountains is breath taking. I have pointed a few travelers from other planets there, and explained to them what costumes they should wear to fit in. Travelers from other planets arrive on the Shore in Spirit

Being forms, usually wearing look a-like costumes of the forms they travel in on their planets. They also bring their Spirit Being pets, who wear look– a-like costumes of their planet's animal forms. This accounts for the strange beasts and beings seen when Earth Spirit Beings visit the Astral thru dreams or visions. A disciple of Christ was caught away in a vision and encountered beasts with seven heads, etc.

Just as we can choose to walk about the Astral Shore in a look-a-like form of our Earth human bodies, the beings and animals from other planets can do the same.

Man fears what he does not understand. When he dreams or has visions, he fears the beasts and other beings that he is not familiar with. If he would have an open mind, he would have the opportunity to intermingle with beings and animals from other planets. Also, he could use their portals to travel to other planets. Man, using his human form mind, limits himself with his fears and thinking.

February 13

THOUGHT FOR THE DAY – When man relaxes and his human vehicle sleeps, his spirit being within often climbs out and travels forward and backwards in time. His human mind thinks that he is dreaming.

TIME TRAVEL

Just as you and I are spirit beings traveling for a lifetime in human vehicles, time travel is a mode of transportation for the soul. Time Travel is a dream portal vehicle that we can take, just as the human body is a vehicle we can take to travel in on the Earth Plane. The Heavens and the Astral are advanced in intelligence and inventions. Modes of light speed transportation exist that human minds are not capable of comprehending.

Time travel in the Astral is a skill that the youngest of Spirit Beings (the equivalent of an Earth two year old child has mastered. Time travel is like first steps are to a human earth baby. I am sure that Earth human efforts to time travel via machines amuses Master Beings of the Heavens.

Our Spirit Beings can pop from our human forms and enter a Time Travel portal. From there, they can travel backwards and relive past experiences or travel backwards to observe past history. Time Travel is available to you, but it is in your spirit being state that it is available. When man relaxes and his human vehicle sleeps, (like an automobile having its engine shut off) his spirit being often climbs out and travels forward and backwards in what man calls dreams.

Time Travel is a specialty feature in Dream Portals, like air conditioning or windshield wipers are on a car.

February 14

THOUGHT FOR THE DAY – Enlightenment is the path to perfection and the Fountain of Youth.

THE FOUNTAIN OF YOUTH

Just as humans have sought without to find a means to time travel, they have also longed to find the Fountain of Youth, thinking it to be a magic garden and pool somewhere on Earth. They are oblivious to the fact that it too is a place within that the Spirit Being pops from its human form and travels to. The Fountain of Youth is called the Eternal Fount. The Eternal Fount is the source of all life. Some call the Fount God, Divine Source, Jehovah, Supreme Father, etc. etc. The Eternal Fount is not a pool of magic water that one swims in. It is knowledge. A Spirit Being that has mastered perfect knowledge never dies or grows old. All masters of perfection in the heavens live forever as thirty year olds.

A woman trying to hide her wrinkles with a magic cream is an example of a human mind trying to stop aging, dip in a magic de-aging fountain of youth. A man might have his bald head implanted with supposedly magic hair cells. Someone else might have plastic surgery to get rid of aging flaws, while others will try body building or extreme diets. No one tries going within to where the Fountain of Youth actually exists.

I am Jo Hammers the Mystic. I am a spirit being traveling for this lifetime in a human body vehicle. My Earth body/car has its share of wrinkles, dents, and fender repairs. At the same time, it is not me. I am the Spirit being driving it. I am eternal, and will live forever, whether in this human form, orb form in the heavens, or in another human body form, should I choose to do another incarnation. I will be looking for you on the Astral Planes. Perhaps, as popping Spirit Beings, we will time travel together and then renew our minds in the Fountain of Youth.

February 15

THOUGHT FOR THE DAY – Life begins in the seed/

sperm of the man, not the woman. Men have killed more new life forms than women have ever thought about doing. How? They spill their seed/sperm on the ground.

DO CHILDREN ASTRAL TRAVEL?

Do children Astral Travel? Much younger than you think! You have to take into consideration that a Spirit Beings starts his Earth journey by swimming the River of Life in a sperm form, known as man's seed. Swimming is the entry to Earth life experience. Astral travelling is the popping from, or exiting from, Earth life experience.

Human babies and children, who die young, are Spirit Beings that are traveling in human forms. They pop from their youthful human forms to return to the Home of the Soul, having pre-planned short life missions on Earth. The Spirit Beings of the babies and children astral travel to do so. Remember, it is not the human form that lives on. It is the Spirit Being in the form. Human forms, baby or adult, are like costumes or dresses that can be put on, or taken off and discarded as worn out and no longer wearable.

As children grow, they begin to dream. In dream states, they can travel the Astral by being little poppers who go away (go home to the Astral) and come again (return to their human forms to experience their day to day Earth life.

February 16

THOUGHT FOR THE DAY – Men with closed minds fear what they don't understand. In fear, they limit themselves from entertaining supernatural, mystical beings from the Astral, as well as other planets.

CHILDREN'S GUARDIANS & SPIRIT GUIDES

Some children in the toddler stage see beings standing in their closets, or at the foot of their beds. Guardians/Keepers/Spirit Guides make personal, visible visitations to children, although toddlers don't always know who it is that is watching over them. Their human minds have not fully developed yet and the Spirit Being within them has not awakened yet. The sleeping Spirit Being sees inward and upward. The human body with its eyes looks outward into the Earth plane. So, guardians put on costumes and interact in visitations with the human mind and eyes. The Spirit Being does not awaken until the toddler grows to a certain stage, knowing right from wrong, and begins their life's spiritual journey.

My grandson was continually seeing a man named Gene in his closet till he was about five. He had to have asked the man/guardian his name in order to know it. We had no one named Gene amongst our family or friends. It is possible that the guardian introduced himself to my grandson as a Genie, and my grandson understood him to say Gene. Thus, my toddler grandson, not knowing what a genie was, called him Gene. In the Astral, there are all sorts of magical mystical beings. Men with closed minds fear what they don't understand, or will blow it off as not possible.

My first remembered moment of astral traveling was when I was about the age of 8. In a dream state, I traveled to the First heaven, the Astral Shore. Standing there, a great ladder descended from a cloud like place above me. I looked up and Christ was standing at the top, in a Second Heaven, with his arms outstretched to me, I was raised in a strict holiness, Christian persuasion. A visit from Christ was appropriate for me at the time. We visit, and are visited by, those we are familiar with. Others might be caught away to the Astral in a dream state compatible with their masters and religious persuasions. It does not matter what religious persuasion you, I, or your neighbor was born in to. What matters is that we find our path and ace our life missions. Astral traveling is not limited to one religious persuasion.

Light Beings enter Earth life all around the world into every religious community, via the River of Life. The same beings exit Earth life by popping from/climbing out of their human forms. They astral travel/ portal walk home to the heavens. A Light Being is a Light Being no matter where he is stationed around the globe, as well as what religious persuasion he is born into. There is no one true religion on earth.

February 17

THOUGHT FOR THE DAY – Spirit Beings, from other planets, return to the heavens via death portals; just as Spirit Beings from Earth do.

JUDGEMENT PORTALS

All Spirit Beings return to the heavens via death portals when their human form vehicles die. These portals open onto the Astral Shore, which is a place of bright lights and somewhat of a carnival atmosphere, due to so many beings arriving from different cultures. Also, beings from other planets return thru death portals emptying out on the Astral Shore.

Returning to the home of the soul, our missions or lessons on Earth are critiqued at a place called the judgment seat. It is sort of like getting an employee review on Earth. If you have done well, you move up the ladder in whatever business you are employed by. Spirit Beings have one goal, to reach Master Status. Masters are over seers who are CEO types who travel to Earth and oversee large groups of beings. Christ is a master and responsible for the Christians. The Buddha is a master and responsible for leading his followers. You are responsible for sharing your knowledge of the inner heavens with at least one other person before exiting Earth life. You are a map maker. Your supernatural, pioneer, mystical accomplishments are marked paths for those coming after you to follow.

At your judgment seat review, you will be asked if you have left behind a map for at least one severed Silver Cord Spirit being to follow and find their way home thru the death portal. We are responsible for the spiritually blind Light Beings we travel Earth with.

February 18

THOUGHT FOR THE DAY – Channels retrieve information from the heavens for others. Pentecostals channel a being they call the Holy Ghost. They let him speak thru them.

CHANNELS & MEDIUMS

Channels and Mediums let beings from the heavens speak thru them. Angels, masters, teachers, deceased relatives, and friends can send down messages and use channels' mouths to speak with beings on Earth. Channels and

Mediums retrieve messages for those who cannot make portal communication connections for themselves. Mediums mostly relay messages from deceased loved ones or friends. Channels can relay lengthy sermons or orations from masters, etc.

Channels and Mediums are individuals on Earth who decide to go inward and let their Spirit Being (that is traveling in them), take control. The Pentecostal religion refers to it as the Holy Spirit or Holy Ghost taking control. The open channel lets his voice, as well as his body, be used. Shouting and speaking in tongues is the result of a human being going inward and giving himself over to his Holy Ghost/Spirit Guide to use to relay messages to Earth. Pentecostals are channels. They let those of the other world/afterlife speak thru them. The Holy Ghost is in the afterlife. Holy Ghost is a nick name for him. He has an actual name in the heavens. I will go into that in a future blog.

Man likes to brand anything he does not understand as occult. In doing so, he denies himself supernatural communications from angels, etc. that he so desires. Man limits himself!

February 19

THOUGHT FOR THE DAY - Someone speaking a foreign language to you from the heavens is useless, unless there is a translator.

PENTECOSTAL SPEAKING IN TONGUES

On the Astral Shore/First Heaven, just crossed over (severed cord) beings are milling about in costume forms like their human ones that lay dead on earth. Arriving on the Astral Plane from all over Earth, they speak many languages. Desperate to send back messages to their friends and families left behind, they will try to speak thru channels/mediums/seers/etc. They have not been to judgment yet and had their Silver Cords reattached and their memories restored. They are still holding tightly to who they were on Earth.

Members of the Pentecostal faith go inward and upward in search of deeper experiences. Those experiences include what they call the Gifts of the Spirit (speaking in tongues, interpretation of tongues, prophesy, word of knowledge, etc.). These gifts are the basic gifts of all awakened Spirit Beings. We go inward, listen to our Holy Spirit Guide, retrieve messages, and then return to Earth life, deliver posts, and share our experiences. Occasionally, we carry, interpret, and relay messages in languages we do not understand. The interpretation of tongues is a Channel position of being a translator between worlds. The Pentecostals speak a message in a foreign tongue, and then some translate/interpret.

The Pentecostal's Holy Ghost is a Light Being in the heavens. He can be seen thru like looking thru a piece of glass. He is transparent. That is the reason he has been nick named the Holy Ghost. He can be seen thru like we could look thru a misty ghost. The Holy Ghost is a personal friend of Christ in the heavens, and he works as a Spirit Guide on the Astral Shore. Pentecostals are one of his mouthpieces on Earth. Seers, mystics, channels, mediums, etc. are also.

The Holy Ghost is not the only Spirit Guide in the heavens. There are special Spirit Being guides who are available to guide those of other world religions.

When the Holy Ghost Guide is passing on messages of importance to the Pentecostals, he is allowing those on the Astral Shore of different Earth languages to send down messages to Earth and speak thru those who channel. A Pentecostal, who is speaking in tongues on Earth, is allowing himself to be a channel of English or a foreign language message. A master Pentecostal channel can also interpret or translate the language messages. The Holy Bible says that the person speaking in tongues should also pray that he be able to interpret. Messages without interpretation are wasted communications from the heavens.

February 20

THOUGHT FOR THE DAY – If we close a door to enlightenment, we become one of those who are left behind (standing on the outside looking in).

ARE TAROT CARDS A PORTAL?

A reader asked me if Tarot Readers were occult dark beings. I had to laugh to myself. Humans try to brand anything they don't understand as belonging to the occult. Man fears and labels what he doesn't understand.

If a human has encountered something or someone of a spiritual nature that he doesn't understand, it would be better for him just to shelf the person and the idea for the present, till his understanding clears. Cutting the 'not understood' off and labeling it occult only roadblocks a person's inward climb to spiritual understanding. It is like closing a door. If we close a door to enlightenment, we become dull of mind.

There are many portals to enlightenment/First Heaven/Astral Shore. The Tarot is a portal there, just like dreams are. Tarot cards have to be interpreted, just like dreams have to be. Whoever created the Tarot; did so after discovering a portal. There are many other portals that have not, as yet, been discovered by humans. They will be just as mystical as the Tarot, and with items that have to be interpreted. With the Tarot, it is scenes on cards. With Dreams, it is movie like scenarios.

February 21

THOUGHT FOR THE DAY – There are many portals around the globe. The Tarot is just one. Its reader is a channel.

INTERPRETING TAROT MESSAGES

The following are two cuts from another blog of mine on dream interpretation. Tarot interpretation is similar.

(Every individual on Earth will associate different feelings and meanings for colors, people, events, time, etc. in their lives. Their accumulated association meanings are their pocket translators. Thus, when they dream, what is shown them is according to their take on things.)

The Tarot Cards must be interpreted according to what the client's associated word meanings are. Interpreting the Tarot Cards according to what is in a book doesn't work. Someone else's meaning associations for the pictures on the cards would be like using or trying to guess someone else's code. Every human has his own code to interpret his dreams. The true Tarot reader will understand that it is his client that must interpret. He is just the in-between world shuffler, the medium for a message to come thru.

(Consider the color red. I have always hated the color. To me, for some reason, it brings a feeling of disgust. My mother loved red. To her, it represented warmth and joy. Should the two of us receive twin coded dreams where everything was painted red, our interpretations would be different. I would see my dream as telling me that something disgusting was going to happen in my world. My mother, however, would see an outpouring of warmth and joy coming her way. To decode your crazy dream, you must assign a meaning to each thing happening in it. Only you know what each item, color, person means in your take on things. That is how you decode your dreams/ your communications from your Spirit Guide and others. The reason for codes is to keep darkness from knowing Heaven's secrets.)

Interpreting the Tarot is the same. Dreams are a portal between worlds. The Tarot is a portal between worlds. Both are available to individual seekers. However, a Tarot Reader is a channel and can only read or relay what the message cards are. His set of interpretation codes will be different from the person sitting in front of him. The Tarot Reader and his client are like my mother and I, and our different associations with the color red.

A Tarot Reader is a seeker of the unknown, just like you. He has discovered a portal between worlds and has taken a different path, one you are possibly unfamiliar with. You have taken a different path in Earth life than your biological family members. All paths exploring, and seeking communication and understanding of the Heavens are acceptable.

PORTALS: Dreams are the number one portal used by humans. Tarot is another. Native Americans have Dream Catcher portals. Masters of Enlightenment's portals are thru meditation and literature. The written page is a portal. Peaceful music is a portal. Artists' hands on a brush can be portals. The sound of musical instruments can be a portal. Dream Catchers are portals. Your secret closet could be a portal!

February 22

THOUGHT FOR THE DAY – Prayer portals open, if requests are made after going inward and upward to the third eye in the middle of your inner forehead. The third eye is where the silver cord is connected. The third eye is the open or closed gate to between world communications.

A PRAYER PORTAL

I had a Pentecostal lady minister friend who was referred to as Sister Norma. When she was a teen, she was attending a store front mission church, and felt that she was called to preach. Lady preachers were not accepted back at that time. Men tried to keep women in their place at home and in church. So, she was bucking the system insisting that she felt called.

It was common practice back then for everyone to gather around the front and pray for the evening service. These were not short flowery prayers. They were on your knees, tears running, verbal beseeching of God to come down, be present, and bless the service.

Sister Norma took her place on the women's side up front to pray. In tears she prayed for Christ to show her if she were truly called. The men had been on her case, as they say now-a-days. As she prayed, with tears running down her face, she heard a voice behind her speaking from across the room on the men's side. The voice was calling her name.

"Norma Jean . . . ," the male voice called.

Sister Norma raised her head and turned it toward the voice. In shock, she saw Christ standing with his hands outstretched to her. In haste, she turned around on her knees and was too weak in the knees to rise. She lifted one hand to him and started to crawl across the floor toward him.

Again, Christ spoke, "Norma Jean . . . will you follow me?"

"Yes, Lord!" she answered thru tears as she continued to crawl towards him.

Again, Christ spoke, "Norma Jean . . . will you feed my sheep?"

"Yes, Lord!" she again replied thru tears, continuing to hold out one extended hand towards him.

"Feed my sheep!" He replied reaching forth and touching her. Then poof, he was gone.

On knees, in tears, and inward searching, she had opened a portal to heaven and her Master Christ came down and graced her with a visitation, as well as a calling to preach his gospel. Sister Norma opened an inward prayer portal.

February 23

THOUGHT FOR THE DAY – "Here on this seat my body may shrivel up, my skin, my bones, my flesh may dissolve, but my body will not move from this seat until I have attained Enlightenment . . . Gautama Buddha

THE BUDDHA'S PORTAL TO ENLIGHTENMENT

Siddhartha Gautama, the Buddha-to-be, had been dwelling on the banks of a river with five ascetic followers, practicing austerities for six years.

Ascetics – the practice of restraint with respect to actions of body, speech, and mind. It is the refraining from sensual pleasures and the accumulation of material wealth. The austere lifestyle is seen as an aid to the pursuit of physical and metaphysical health.

Austerity – severe disciplines and the self denial of luxuries.

The Buddha, realizing that austerities/severe living could not lead to realization/obtaining, he abandoned them. His five ascetic companions, disgusted at his seeming failure, deserted him. He then journeyed towards a village where he was offered rice milk by a Brahmin girl. After her, he accepted a grass mat from a grass-cutter. Then, the Bodhisattva seated himself beneath a papal tree facing east. There, he resolved not to rise again until enlightenment was attained.

Sister Norma, in my previous writing, and the Buddha had a lot in common. Both wanted something that could not be attained by human means. She wanted confirmation from her God that she was called. The Buddha wanted enlightenment from his. Both received, even though they were from different religious persuasions. The Buddha sat on a grass mat facing east and went within. Sister Norma knelt in the front of her church and went within. Both had portals that opened. Supernatural visitations from supernatural beings then entered their space.

All men have inner portals. Only those who take the time to go within will awaken and have their master portal doors opened. Not all Spirit Beings traveling the Earth Plane are masters. To many, Earth is a learning experience. The Buddha and Sister Norma attained, which made them masters.

Due to being extremely busy, I hire my lawn mowed. My grass cutter is a short little man about the age of 30 who speaks with a lisp. What would happen, if he would suddenly weave his grass clippings into a mat, sit down beneath my Formosa Tree, and then vow not to rise till he attained enlightenment? The answer is that his Spirit being would awaken. He would then go within and climb upward till he reached that which he sought.

February 24

THOUGHT FOR THE DAY – States of limbo, such as being the mistress of a married man, are hells on Earth.

HELL'S PORTALS

Fallen angels were kicked out of the heavens on to Earth. Thus, they set up their kingdom of darkness on Earth. The fallen angels are the devils/demons of Hell, and they created hells on Earth.

Keep in mind that a Spirit Being is the driver of a human vehicle body, but is not the human form. The human form's eyes look out ward, like the headlights on a car. The Spirit Being's eyes look inward and upward for guidance for driving, or choosing paths. If a human is not seeking an inward experience or spiritual experience, his Spirit Being sleeps within and the human form with its mind can be enticed by what he sees around him. What he sees can be many forms of Hell on Earth.

One day, a human form's intelligence uses its free-will choice in error and finds him-self in hellish conditions that just sort of sneaked upon him. With the Spirit Being asleep, it is like leaving a car parked in neutral. It can roll down a hill, off of the road, and down into a hell of a deep ditch. Hitting life's ditch, and finding himself in a not so pleasant place, he turns within and prays for help. It is at that point that his Spirit Being awakens.

The hellish ditch the driver finds himself in could be a bad marriage, a financial disaster, the death of a child, getting fired, serious health issues, etc. etc. Up to the point of impact in the ditch, he has basically been asleep spiritually. Then in a sudden moment of crash, fear, and panic, he finds himself needing help from angels or a God that he has no relationship with. He doesn't have a clue as to how to tow himself out of his hell in the ditch.

Hell comes to call on men in many forms on Earth. Perhaps, in the crashing moment, he instantly loses friends, family, social outlets, jobs, fiancés, homes, wives, husbands, cars, health, etc. Perhaps he suddenly needs a tow truck driver, a life coach to get him hauled up and out of his dark, muddy ditch hell. Perhaps, he needs a healer or a grief counselor. Awakening in a disaster, men find themselves instantly walking down a totally new path. The dark path of grief, over the loss of a child, is a hard new path to walk.

To move forward in life, and climb up out of hells on Earth, a man has to make up his mind he is tired of living in the gutter hells of life. A man stands with one foot on the grassy side of a narrow, trickling stream that he is familiar with. However, his future lies on the other side of the stream. In an attempt to move forward, he lifts one foot and puts it down on the opposite bank. He is for the moment stranded in time and space between the old familiar and his future. He can choose to remain in his past hell and step backwards, or he can step forward into what lies ahead. Living in a state of limbo with a foot in the hells of the past and one in the future is not a pleasant limbo place to be.

There are many states of limbo. A lifetime of grief is a state of limbo. Holding on to hope that a cheating spouse, who has left you, is going to return to you is a state of limbo. Holding on to the hope of getting your old job back is a state of limbo. Holding on to friendships that have soured is a state of limbo. Holding on to a lover who no longer wants you is a state of Limbo. Being the mistress of a cheating husband is a state of limbo. Working year in and year out at a job you hate is a state of limbo. Being comfortable where you are is a state of limbo. States of limbo are hells.

February 25

THOUGHT FOR THE DAY - Someone encouraging you to overeat is an enticement for you to enter the subtle hell portal of obesity.

HELL'S PORTALS ARE SUBTLE

Hell's portals are different from Astral/Heaven portals. They have dark beings standing at the entrances handing out invitations. The dark beings are fallen angels that were kicked out of the inward and upward heavens. Earth is where they were kicked out to.

The fallen dark beings have no portals to return to the Astral or Heaven's Shore. They have already been to judgment and stripped of their portals. So, their only way to invade the Astral/First Heaven is to entice/recruit new members on Earth to darkness, those who haven't returned home to the Astral and faced judgment yet. Light Beings, who are failing their Earth missions, are good candidates. The failing candidates can return home to the Astral and invade (play havoc or wage war against) Light Beings till their turn comes to face their judgment. Hell's keepers, or fallen angels, know that is their only way to get even with those who had kicked them out.

Hell's portals on Earth are subtle and don't look like tunnels. For instance, a simple hand that is enticing you with one pill or a powder dose of an illegal narcotic is an invitation to walk thru a door/portal to hell. A dark, evil, abusive man offering marriage to a woman, who feels she has no hope of ever finding a mate, is an invitation to her to enter a marriage gate/portal to hell. A dark child enticing another to shop lift or bully others is opening a subtle door to hell. A church gossip, encouraging you to pass on a bit of nasty gossip, is darkness enticing you to enter a subtle portal. Someone encouraging you to overeat is enticing you to enter the hell of obesity.

Once you have entered darkness' subtle portals, and are hooked on drugs, alcohol, over eating, stealing, lying, etc., you are captive of the fallen angels, the demons of darkness. It is almost impossible to climb up and out of Hell's burning pits/portals on Earth.

February 26

THOUGHT FOR THE DAY – Your yesterday choices are your life today. Choose wisely today and live your wise choices in your tomorrow. Choose welfare living today, live in its gutter tomorrow.

WELFARE PORTALS TO HELL

Women complain that they can't escape their welfare states, or that it is someone else's fault that they and their children are where they are in life. Not so! To begin with, a woman chooses the man she wants to be with, as well as to have children by him. She could have chosen to remain single, have no children, and get an education. Her current welfare state is the result of her choices. If you have chosen a dud for a mate, it was your choice.

When the dud/bread winner man, the welfare woman has chosen, dumps her, she is faced with having to make choices again. She can spend a day filling out applications for employment, or filling out a welfare application. The first step to escaping a welfare state is to return to the point where you started/made your first choices and choose wisely the second time around. Without welfare as an option, our dumped woman would have, undoubtedly, chose to fill out employment applications.

We are our choices in life. Some women (and men) just don't want to work and better themselves, unless life forces them to do so. They want an easy way out. Wanting a free living is a characteristic of a dark Spirit Being. Using and coning systems, friends, family, food banks, and other social services are darkness. There is free will choice on Earth. Both dark and light beings have that freedom of choice. Children of the light are intent on working and making good lives for their children. A dark being will be intent on not working and raising his/her children in the gutters of life.

Welfare parents choose to live year after year in the gutters of life. The same parents have probably made other bottom basement choices. They may have chosen not to go to church, when doing so would let their children associate with those of higher classes. Choosing to stay home on Sunday and barbecue for all the local low life and drug dealers will not provide children with role models. Welfare parents choose to send their children to ghetto schools, when they could choose to home school them in order to give them a safe, quality education. After all, 'stay at home' welfare parents have the time to go to church and invest their time in their children's education. Even lower than welfare choosing parents are those who choose to take their food stamps and sell them to fund their alcoholism and drug addictions. There are gutters in life, and then below it are pits of Hell. Some parents willfully choose to raise and abuse their children in gutter life and pits of Hell.

There are basics in life that we have to have to survive. We need water to drink, food, clothing, a place to bathe, and a place to sleep. When worlds come crashing down, humans find themselves in the position of having to make new choices to fill those needs. There are always two options. One will be a wise choice, one will not.

Where you are in life right now is the result of your yesterday choices and no one else's. If you don't like where you are, turn and make new choices so your tomorrows will be what you want them to be.

February 27

THOUGHT FOR THE DAY – Both Light Beings and Traitor Beings return to the Astral Shore via the portal of death at the ending of their human forms' lives.

ASTRAL STALKERS

On Earth, when walking alone, smart individuals do not as a rule walk into dark tunnels, underpasses, or alleys alone. We have street smarts and are aware that there are sadistic, criminal elements on Earth that frequent those places. The Dark Beings stalk lone beings there, with the intention of robbing, assaulting, kidnapping, or possibly murdering the unaware. Portals to the afterlife are also stalked by predators. The predators are the dark beings that have crossed over and have not faced judgment yet on the Astral Shore.

Spirit Beings of Light, as well as forces of Darkness mill about on the Astral Shore and the exiting point of the death portal. The Astral Shore is a disembarking place for those heading for the judgment seat. Fallen angels cannot travel there. However, those light beings that they have enticed on Earth can. So, Light beings that have embraced darkness on Earth become the long arm of the fallen angels/

demons of darkness on Earth. The Astral shore is the chosen long arm battlefield of darkness. Traitor light beings (those who were enticed on Earth into darkness) stalk and do war with light beings who are returning home after a lifetime on Earth in a human form. The death portal can be a frightening, dangerous place.

(Remember from my previous writings, the Spirit Being lives in a human form, but is not that form. Therefore, a Spirit Being does not suffer from human form illnesses. Epilepsy is a human form illness, and has nothing to do with the driver of the human form, the Spirit Being).

A while back, I met a man (in his late twenties) whose human form suffered from epilepsy. He would fall in the floor and violently seizure. The young man told me about an experience he has when he seizures and looses consciousness from his epilepsy.

Quote "When I seizure and pass out, I am suddenly on the end of a long chain that is secured to a collar on my neck like I am a dog. A monkey is on the controlling end like I am a dog he is walking. The laughing, dark, sadistic monkey starts twirling me in a circle like I am a kite on the end of a string. He twirls me so fast that my body leaves the ground and I am in a dizzying spin that has me totally terrified. The monkey laughs at me, and seems to get intense pleasure from my terror. Every time I have an epileptic seizure, it is the same. I pop from my body and am once more chained like a dog and at the mercy of the monkey. It is always the same, and has been for years."

The above is a prime example of an Astral Portal Stalker. The monkey is a dark force being who has chosen to wear the costume and facial mask of a monkey. The young man's

Spirit Being was popping from his human form when it had a seizure. Out of his human form, he found himself in a place he didn't understand, and at the mercy of a terrifying dark being wearing the costume of a monkey.

Just as a human stalker on Earth gets obsessed with stalking one particular human, the dark being in the monkey costume, in the young man's personal portal, was obsessed with assaulting him.

Be aware of your surroundings when you enter and exit your portal to between worlds, just as you would when entering a dark alley or passageway on Earth as a human.

February 28

THOUGHT FOR THE DAY – Is there a portal open in your world? The strange sounds you hear, are they the sounds of beings coming and going?

A NEW BORN BABY DIES – A PORTAL OPENS

My father, born in 1909, used to tell an interesting story about the corpse of a new born baby that had been laid out on the closed top of a treadle sewing machine till time for burial. The event took place on a farm near Stout land, Missouri around 1920 or so. My father was possibly six or seven at the time.

My father came from a large family with two sets of twins in it. One set of twins did not survive infancy and had been buried. A second set of twins came along and one of them died shortly after birth. This story is about the one that died in the second set.

My father related that the corpse of the new born baby had been washed by family members, dressed, wrapped in a baby quilt, and laid out on the top of his mother's treadle sewing machine till arrangements for burial could be made. Night time was falling. Back then, all graves were hand dug. The grave would have to be dug the next morning. A minister was to come and preside over the burial, but he would not arrive till late the next day. He hadn't even been sent for yet. So, the baby was laid out for the night in wake fashion till final arrangements could be finished. Family members from near farms had gathered in to sit up with the dead, as they called it. The decision was made that one person would sit up with the baby corpse at a time, taking turns thru the night. All took their appointed turns, but by morning, no one was left to sit with the corpse. Frightened, due to a supernatural occurrence, all had vacated one at a time on their shift.

When darkness had fallen on the night the corpse of the baby was laid out, the sewing machine treadle foot started to move as though someone was sitting at the machine with their foot moving it. The machine was closed and there was no one sitting at it. There was no chair. The sewing machine, even though it was closed, began to hum with the sound of the machine sewing machine needle going up and down. My father, who was too little to be afraid, said the sewing machine sewed all night long on its own. He had sat down in the floor and watched the treadle foot move. Everyone, during the night, was afraid to move the dead body of the baby, open the machine, or get near the supernatural occurrence. The next morning, family members quickly dug a quick grave and the baby was buried at daylight. Frightened, they did not wait on a minister.

A baby died, a visitation portal opened, and a sewing machine sewed. A guardian had come down to escort the soul of the baby over. Apparently, the guardian was fascinated with the sewing machine and decided to sew all night.

February 29 – Leap Year

THOUGHT FOR THE DAY – Men speak of certain individuals having a good and a bad side. Could it be that both a Dark Sociopath and a Light Being dwell in the same human form?

LEAPING IN AND SHARING HUMAN FORMS

Once every four years, we get an extra day in February. The month has an extra day, a leaper of sorts. In the Astral, every now and then, an extra being leaps or somehow falls into a human form. You might say it is a leap year of a sort. Schizophrenia is one result of this unexpected, not often happening event. Schizophrenia is leap year in portal incarnations.

We have discussed in previous writings how both dark and light beings travel in human forms. Also, I have written about how dark souls mill about on the Astral Shore with Light beings, as they both wait their turn at the judgment seat. There is war in the heavens and it is between the dark beings on the shore and the light ones there. The dark Spirit Beings do all they can to play havoc with and do harm to those arriving home and those entering portals for new life missions on the Earth Plane. Sometimes, two or more dark beings will assault a light being who is about to enter his appointed portal to travel down to Earth and enter a new conception, via traveling in a sperm. If the fight between light and dark gets rough, an accidental fall might occur and two or more dark beings might fall into the portal with the one light being they are assaulting. Thus, we have a new born who grows to adulthood and is diagnosed with Schizophrenia. This accounts for the multiple personalities in the human individual. Some are light and gentle of nature, while others are cruel, vulgar, dark sociopaths. The battle and assault continues within the human body, the dark wanting to dominate.

The legal system puts the human body form of a sociopath murderer to death. Spirit Beings, dark or light, that reside in or drive human vehicles cannot be put to death. A dark, killer, sociopath spirit being lives on in a popper stage and returns to the Astral Shore for judgment. If he manages to find a light being about to take a portal back to earth for another lifetime, he will do his best to overcome the light being and steal the new conception form that he is about to enter. If he can't overcome the light being, he may try to hang on to the light being and fall into the new conception. Thus, a new conception on Earth has both a dark and a light being traveling in its human form. This may not be a psychiatrist's opinion, but it is the way it is in the Astral. I am not an Earth doctor. I am a mystic, a Spirit Being traveling for this lifetime in a human form. I speak of what I see and know of life beyond this one.

Travel safely . . . Portal Walker. May our paths/portals cross in the near future, as we journey. At that time, may we get to know each other for the unique beings that we are. I am Jo Hammers the Mystic on Earth, and Master Barjoraven in the heavens.

CHAPTER THREE
MARCH

THE BOOK OF VISITATIONS

March 1

THOUGHT FOR THE DAY - If you have seen a being in your dreams that had blue skin or maybe three or five eyes, you have had an encounter with an alien from another planet.

PLANETARY TRAVELERS

Just as we are spirit beings traveling in human forms, there are beings on other planets that also travel in forms. Just as we can pop from our human forms and fly thru a portal toward the light of the Astral Shore. Spirit Beings on other planets can do the same. From the Astral Shore, we can take portals and visit other planets. Beings from other planets can enter our portals and visit us. Thus, we have visions or visitations of sometimes strange looking creatures and beings. You and I, here on Earth, are not the only ones out there!

On planet Earth, we have a variety of odd looking animals, birds, insects, etc. We also have humans of various colors of skin and size. The other planets have the same. Blue or purple is not uncommon on other planets. Animals that can fly are common. Flight isn't restricted to birds and insects.

When a Spirit Being on Earth awakens from his sleep in a human form, he can climb out of his human body like exiting an automobile. Then he can fly, walk, run, etc. up his personal portal toward the light, or exit point onto the Astral Shore. Spirit Beings on other planets can do the same. Freshly out of forms, beings from all planets may choose to wear costume forms for their Astral Shore traveling experience. The costume forms are look-a-like twins of human and other planet bodies that they have exited. Remember, Spirit Beings are actually orbs of light, balls of energy. Costume forms worn by visitors from other planets may have four arms, three eyes, two heads, wings etc. etc. They may see us as odd, and we might see them as odd.

We are Portal Walker Space Travelers. Visions of strange beings and creatures that humans have written about in holy books are actually chance encounters with 'Portal Walker' travelers from other planets. They come down to us on Earth thru portals, just as we go up our portals and then down theirs to visit them.

March 2

THOUGHT FOR THE DAY- When your tire flattens, it is a sign.

THE BROKEN WHEEL GUARDIAN

I had a friend named Henry Turner. He is deceased now and has been for thirty or so years. His parents decided to immigrate to the United States when Henry was two. Having loaded a hand cart with what few possessions they could take with them, they headed out on a fifteen mile journey to the shore where their passage on a ship had been secured. About five miles from the shore, a mishap happened. The wooden wheel on the cart they were pulling fell off. In order to fix it, they had to stop and unload it.

Everything seemed to go wrong for the frantic couple, who barely had time to get to the boat. The fixing if the wheel took twice as much time as it should have. Finally, after much exasperation, they got the wheel back on, reloaded their things, and pulled as fast as they could toward their destination. When they got there, they were horrified to see that their ship had already left the dock and was heading out to sea. They had missed it. Then, they had to wait for almost a month for passage on another ship. They thought, at the time, that fate had dealt them a really bad hand. However, it was more like fate was a guardian angel who chose to disable their cart wheel to protect them. The ship they were to take was the Titanic. They would have been in the hole with all the lower class passengers who drowned.

Henry Turner, two years old, came to the United States with his immigrant parents. As a young adult, he became a door to door salesman of Bibles. Later in life, he became a Pentecostal minister. His oddity was that he lived his whole life in a converted yellow school bus camper on a tiny plot of land outside Kansas City. He never married, nor had children. In my opinion, Henry was a Light Being, a called one with a future destiny to fulfill. His guardian angel did what he had to do to protect him; he broke a wooden cart wheel.

Henry met my parents during the depression in Springfield, Missouri where he was traveling and selling Bibles. The friendship lasted a lifetime. Times were hard back then, and shoes were bought for the children who were going to school. I was not in school yet and my parents were putting cardboard foot cutouts inside mine to make them last a little longer. Henry popped by one September morning, and gave my mother money to go buy me a pair of shoes. Why did he buy me shoes? I think he knew that one day I would grow up, remember, and tell his story. Paths do not cross without reason. His story lives on thru me.

If you have a flat tire today, consider that it might be your guardian angel protecting you from a major horrendous experience on your path ahead. Be thankful for the flat!

March 3

THOUGHT FOR THE DAY - As the arrow flies, so flies the days of your youth. Make every arrow flying day a treasured one that hits the mark.

CHASED BY A BLUE ORB

Does anyone have an ex earth life traveling companion besides me? Well, we all have those quirky little stories we tell on them. I have an ex traveling companion named Don. He was pleasant enough, except when he drank. Then, he didn't care what bar fight he got into, or how much bigger the other fellow was than him. (The fighting and drinking was what made him my ex.) Anyway, he was a force to deal with, except when it came to a back bedroom in an old house we bought outside of Anderson, Missouri. He was deathly afraid to go into its back room.

Don said that while I was gone to work one evening, he went into that back bedroom to retrieve something. A blue ball of light appeared out of nowhere and floated along the wall of the room and then chased him out of the room. He said that he was sure that whatever the thing was, it had come for him. From that night on, he insisted that the back bedroom door always be kept close. Also, he found excuses to be away from home on the nights I worked. I laugh about it now. My scrapper ex traveling companion feared and cowered before what he could not explain.

People fear what they do not understand. My ex did not understand that orbs of light are supernatural beings, such as angels. Angels can appear in costumed human forms with wings or no wings. However, their true self is that of an orb of light.

So, did an angel come to brawl and win a fight with my ex scrapper? If so, the angel won. Don wouldn't set a foot in that back room. He feared the orb killing, or abducting him. - A Shared Story

March 4

THOUGHT FOR THE DAY - One person has a vision of an angel with wings, another sees one without wings. Both are costume forms that angels wear. Angels in the higher heavens are orbs of light.

WINGS OR NO WINGS

The First Heaven, or Astral Shore, has a mixture of beings milling about there. Some are travelers from other planets. Some are Light Being workers such as Spirit Guides. Others are angels who are preparing to descend down portals to appear in visitations to Earth humans. Also on the Astral Shore are student Spirit Beings that are waiting judgment, or final grades for lifetimes spent on Earth as well as other planets for learning experiences.

Those failing educational lessons on Planet Earth, as well as other planets, are not perfected ones. Thus there are shades of gray beings. Failing to buckle down and ace life learning lessons is a sign of a new Spirit Being choosing to be a dark force instead of one of the light. Human school drop outs become less than they could be, choosing a gutter type lifestyle. So, you have the straight 'A' spirit beings returning to the astral shore to stand at the Throne of Judgment, as well as the F ones. 'A' students are light beings; 'F' students are not. Human students, graduating from high school with high scores, move on to be the educated masters of Earth life. Human drop outs become the less educated and lower segments of society.

Dark Forces/Dark Spirit Beings, as well as Light Forces/Light Beings move about on the Astral Shore waiting to be called to the throne of judgment. These beings may choose to wear the form, or costume, of their former human or alien body, till their friends and families left behind on Earth and other planets cross over. It is a temporary identity and recognition thing.

Angels can also put on costume forms, if they choose, in order to communicate in a recognizable form to Earth humans. Man on Earth has been taught, as a whole, that angels have wings. In all actuality, they are orbs of light. In the higher heavens, they need no forms or costumes to move about in. Costume forms with wings are recognizable things Earth humans understand. They want Spirit Beings to have wings like birds to fly with. They have no understanding of vibration, energy, thought, soul, or astral travel.

God chose to appear and speak in the form of a burning bush to Moses. Angels can take whatever form they wish. If a being on Earth expects wings, angels can take that form. An advanced thought human might want them to appear without wings. Angels can appear that way also. Angels can appear in forms not human as well, just as God appeared as a talking burning bush. Dogs have been known to pull children and babies out of burning buildings. Forms are like costumes that Angels can use at will.

In the first and second heavens, Spirit Beings crossing over can choose to travel in, or stand before judgment wearing costumes. The Astral, or first Heaven, is like a giant masquerade ball. Those traveling to it, or crossing over to it, can wear form costumes like the human body they have just exited. Christ still appears in his Earth form in the first two heavens, as well as in visitations/visions to his followers on Earth. In the higher heavens, Christ is a master. Like the angels, he is an orb of light/a light being.

Abstract or odd portraits of angels are painted by Spirit Beings on Earth who have their Silver Cords injured. (I did a blog in January on what Silver Cords are). With an injured communications cord, or bad reception, an artist's perception of what an angel looks like may be an abstraction. Artists paint what they see. Angels with wings, no wings, orbs of light, or abstractions are all correct when painted.

March 5

THOUGHT FOR THE DAY – Truths are keys that are scattered thru all the religions of the world. To know spiritual truth is to study all. Closed minds put up fences declaring their religion to be the one and only.

Pizza Slice religions

Let me start by saying that I believe there are enlightenment seekers in all religions of the world. You cannot put a fence around your little corner of the religious world and demand that all see you as the one and only. God/Divine Source/Mother Father God is the Supreme Being of the whole world, not just you and yours. Closed minds put up fences.

Earth is like a round pizza cut into slices/sections. Each piece represents one of Earth's religions. All slices are pieces of pizza. All slices are paths to Divine Source/God/Etc. The paths are just located differently in the pan. Where all the points of the pizza slices meet is Heaven and our creative source, or God.

Some slices of pizza are a little toaster brown than others. Some have more cheese or pepperoni pieces. Some have exotic toppings. Whatever the differences are, they are still pizza. No one slice or religion has the market leading to where the points meet, Divine Source. It is my opinion that we must study all religions in order to find all the keys to enlightenment and perfection. Truths are keys, and they are scattered thru all the religions of the world. If you want to know it all, you have got to read and consider all.

I, Jo Hammers the Mystic, am a Spirit Being, traveling in a human form for a lifetime on Earth. I happen to have been commissioned to dwell and sound my trumpet in the slice of pizza that is known as the Bible belt of the United States. There are others like me on missions in the other slices of the world and its religions. Divine Source/Mother-Father God is the god/goddess of all.

March 6

THOUGHT FOR THE DAY - Your path, Heavenly or Hellish, is chosen and walked by you! Your spiritual path to enlightenment is chosen and walked on by you! You are your choices! You live your choices.

MY MOTHER'S DEATH BED VISITATION

One fall afternoon, my mother made her way down the hallway to my bedroom where I was reading and asked, "Did you come into my room and hit me?"

It was a shock to be asked that. I assured my 84 year old mother that I had not hit her and that I would get up and look thru the house for an intruder, which I did. No one was in the house with us. The doors were locked.

My mother then proceeded to tell me that she had seen a blonde headed woman standing at the foot of her bed. The blonde woman, she had thought was me, had slapped her foot hard. In my younger days, I liked experimenting with hair color and had been blonde a few times. So, in my thinking, my mother had probably been dreaming and assumed her visitor was me.

Looking back now, 14 years later, I realize that the blonde headed woman was my mother's sister, my aunt named Golden. As an infant, Golden had white golden blonde curls. That is why my grandparents named her Golden at birth. Sometimes, those crossed over will come to accompany us over at the point of death of our human forms.

In the upper heavens, we are Orbs of Light. On the Astral Shore and in the First Heaven, we can choose to wear a costume form of our human body that we have just exited on earth or other planets. It is like putting a paper dress on a paper doll. It is a costume for an orb of light to appear in. Otherwise, he is invisible or seen only as light. Orbs put on costume forms for visitations to the Earth and other planet Realms, simply because humans and other planetary beings relate to them.

A Spirit Being, who has a severed silver cord, might climb from his human form at death and not know to travel up his portal and toward the light of home. (I have written about Silver Cords in January. They are communication lines. Sometimes they get injured or severed by dark forces, when spirit beings enter earth life. There is war in the heavens.) The Severed Cord being only understands life as what he has known it in human form. Orbs Beings can put on human form costumes to return to earth in, for visitations or to escort others over. The costumes are not human bodies. Dead Human bodies do not live again. They rot in their graves, are cremated, eaten by wild animals, or consumed by fish if buried at sea.

So, my mother's visitation continued like this: In the middle of the afternoon, my mother always took a nap. She had done so since I was a child. When she napped for the next week, she suddenly felt someone slapping her foot. She would open her eyes. Standing at the foot of where she was napping was a beautiful, blonde headed woman who always told her to get up. My mother was experiencing a dream or in-between world's state.

Each afternoon, my mother would immediately arouse after the encounter and would get up and proceed down the hallway to where I retreated when she napped. Each time, I could see in her facial expression that she was a annoyed with me.

"Why did you slap me?" My mother asked each time in an annoyed voice.

"I didn't slap you, mom. I have been sitting here reading!" I replied each time. Then I would ask each day, "Who slapped you? Describe the person to me."

"She had blonde curls and stood at the foot of my bed. She slapped my foot telling me to get up. I was really sleeping sound. It had to be you. Have you been bleaching your hair again?"

"Mom, look at me. I don't have blonde hair at the moment; and I would never slap you for any reason!" I replied. Then I would help my 84 year old mother back to her afternoon sleeping spot.

For about a week, the same event happened every afternoon. My mother napped, was slapped on the foot by a blonde curly haired woman, and told to get up. By the end of a week, I was starting to get a annoyed that my mother was accusing me of slapping her every day. However, I loved my mother and bit my tongue.

Once more it was afternoon and my mother had gone to lie down and take a nap. Within fifteen minutes or so, my mother again came down the hall and confronted me.

"Did you come into my room and slap my foot?"

"No, Mom, I didn't!" I once more assured her, also knowing that all the doors to the house were securely locked by me.

This time she replied differently and had lost the annoyance in her voice. "I think I might be seeing an angel. Today, she said something new to me after slapping my foot!"

"What did she say?" I quickly asked, happy that she had gotten off my case.

"She slapped my foot and told me to get up like she always has. This time, she told me she had brought someone with her that she wanted me to meet. Then she said it was almost time for me to go."

"Who did she bring to meet you?" I quickly asked.

"I woke up. I don't know!" She replied, as she turned and wandered back down the hall to her room.

That was the moment I realized that my mother's blonde headed woman was her guardian, and possibly her deceased sister. Her supernatural visitor was trying to get my mother's Spirit Being to wake up and climb out of her human form to return to the home of the soul. My mother passed on just weeks later.

On the final visitation, the curly, golden haired, female being brought three male beings to my mother's bedside. On her death bed, the blonde headed woman brought with her Mark, Luke, and John from the Bible. My mother was holding a conversation with the four when her spirit exited her body, and her human form was laid down in death. I was privileged to hear her side of the conversation with them. Apparently, they were old friends.

On her death bed, just before she crossed over, my mother sang the words to an old hymn that went something like this: I WILL WORK – I WILL PRAY- IN THE VINEYARD – IN THE VINEYARD – OF THE LORD.

It is my personal opinion that my mother (a Spirit Being) lived a life in a human form in the days of Christ. In my thinking she was possibly a vineyard worker who became a follower.

March 7

THOUGHT FOR THE DAY - You cannot lose what is not yours to have in the first place. Stolen spouses are ill gotten gain. Theft of any sort is a characteristic of a dark one/devil/fallen angel/etc.

VISITS WITH DECEASED LOVED ONES & DEMONS

Humans, who have no spiritual connection, find the death of a loved one devastating. Some think their loved one is gone for good, or lies in a grave of dirt somewhere waiting for a call to rapture. Others feel their loved one has crossed over, but are unsure of where to. When they have no supernatural visitations or communications from them after death, they think their family member is possibly in Hell. Others hope that their loved one is alive and well in a Heaven they hope exists.

All Spirit Beings pop from their human forms when their

body vehicle goes 'kaput'. Until a new cross over receives judgment on the Astral shore/first Heaven, they wander about in spirit form costumes that resemble their exited human ones on Earth. It is during this transition time that they can, in costume form, appear in an understandable form to those friends and family left behind on earth.

Those left behind on earth, or other planets, experience the Hell of losing someone they love. Those earth beings that know their loved one is a spirit being that has gone on, experience a comfort of knowing that they too will one day pop from their human forms and join them. Those not having the same comfort suffer loss.

If you are immediately visited by a deceased loved one in your dreams, be comforted. Your loved one is on the Astral Shore/First Heaven, waiting for his/her turn at the Throne of Judgment yet. At the same time, that loved one could be a dark or light being.

You are a fool if you ask for a visitation from a being that was dark on Earth. After judgment, a dark being returns to Earth to join the throngs of other dark beings in hell. Heaven and Hell exist side by side on Earth. To ask for a visit from a dark one is to ask devils/demons/dark ones to enter your life and talk to you.

March 8

THOUGHT FOR THE DAY - We create our own Heavens and Hells on Earth. Free will choice is the tool we create them with.

ASKING FOR A VISITATION FROM A DEAD CHILD

Ghosts don't always appear in the form they were seen as in Earth life. When human forms die, they are autopsied, embalmed, cremated, painted pretty, buried beneath the ground to rot. etc. Only the Spirit Being traveling in a human form rises, or climbs out of the human body at death. Spirit Beings, who enter Earth life, are Orb beings from the Upper Heavens who are working on the equivalent of master degrees. Mastering Earth life is one course they take. So, your four year old child dies. The Spirit Being climbing out of him/her is not a four year old. The being is an adult orb.

A grieving parent on Earth may ask for a visitation from their deceased child, wanting to know they are okay. The child's human body is no more. It has either been cremated, or lies rotting in a grave somewhere. What the grieving parents might get, in the way of a visitation, is an orb of light. The adult orb can put on a form costume, should he choose to be so. However, Spirit Beings are souls or orbs. Dreams are the commonest way for an orb to visit those left behind in Earth life. A visitation is a gift, but it doesn't necessarily mean that the Orb Being will choose to appear in a costume form of his former child body. In the heavens, the orb is an adult. He may choose to appear in adult form to his grieving Earth parents. The parents may mistake him for an angel, or other supernatural being they are unfamiliar with. However, it is the soul/spirit being orb of their child. Orbs can also appear without costume forms, thus being seen as an orb of light or energy.

If you should encounter a ghost wandering about on Earth, he is a Spirit Being who has climbed out of his human form and has found himself lost between worlds. He may choose to create a costume body to roam about in, or he can choose to be seen as an orb or shadow. If a ghost spirit being chooses to create a costume form, like that of your dead child, to appear to you in, it is his gift to you. Perhaps he feels sorry for you in your grief. Keep in mind that both light and dark Spirit Beings climb out of human forms when they die. The ghost appearing to you could be a being from the dark side.

I had a cousin that everyone dreaded coming for a visit. One year, at about age ten, he beat to death a whole batch of new kittens with a hammer when no one was looking. He grew up to be an abusive adult who lived to pick fights with other men. He abused children and the women in his life, not to mention his under table dealings in the business world. My cousin died young because he picked a fight with a dark being traveling in a human form that was stronger than him. The other sociopath killed him. My cousin was a dark Spirit Being, who traveled in a human form. Just as light beings rise/climb out of their human forms when they die, his dark spirit could do the same. Light Beings resurrect and go upwards to the light. Dark Beings/devils climb out of their human forms also. However their resurrection goes downward, a descending. A dark being's heaven is called Hell.

Laws sentence sociopaths to death. However, it is only their human form bodies that die from lethal injections or electrocution. The dark, sociopath Spirit Being climbs out of his electric chair fried human form and looks for another to possess. Dark Spirit Beings are fallen angels. Hitler of yesterday was a sociopath. Today, he may be hiding, living again, causing havoc in a new human form.

March 9

THOUGHT FOR THE DAY – A Spirit Being on Earth, who has a severed silver cord communications line, has no memories of the Astral/Home of the Soul/Heaven. When his human form dies, he becomes a ghost with nothing better to do than haunt the Earth locations he is familiar with.

Earth Bound Spirits/Ghosts

Not every Spirit Being travels to the light of home when they pop from their human forms. One who has their Silver Cord severed has no memories of where home is. They are disconnected. Thus, when they pop from their human bodies, they cling to their former lives, places, and people in it. (I have discussed injured and severed Silver Cords in previous writings in January and February.)

Ghosts (as humans refer to them) are Spirit Beings without Silver Cord connections. They do not know to look upward and travel up their portal to the light. Instead, they roam the familiar. They haunt the homes they once lived in, their previous jobs, or places of familiarity. They haunt their family members, in an effort to get them to hear them. Sometimes, they haunt strangers, who they hope will hear or see them.

I encountered one Earth bound spirit when I was a senior in high school. The being was not a family member. It was a brief chance encounter with a stranger, a female ghost.

It was in the spring of 1964 that I saw my first ghost/severed cord being. I had just recently met a guy named Sam, and we had been dating for about three weeks. He had picked me up for a date in his red convertible, and we were just cruising, you might say. On the west side of my home town is a road they call the bypass, part of route 66 back then. The highway had two lanes running North and South. My date and I had just turned on the bypass and were heading south. There was a short stretch of vacant fields that lay on either side of the road between Kearney Street and a train overpass. It was on that short stretch of road that I saw her.

An elderly woman, possibly in her seventies, suddenly appeared on the shoulder of the other side of the road. She was wearing a plaid house dress, house shoes, and a sweater. Too my horror, she darted across the road in front of us. I screamed bloody murder and then watched as she barely made it to the other side of the road, with us just missing her. It was like a frozen moment in time. I could look out the car's windshield and into her eyes. Her eyes were dark with a lost look in them. This may seem strange to you, but she spoke to me with her eyes. My date's car just moved on down the highway. I quickly spun around in my seat and swiveled my neck to get a further at her. My date, Sam, still had his 'pedal to the metal; as they say. In front of my human eyes she disappeared. "Poof' she was gone.

My new boyfriend was annoyed with me and asked why I had screamed. I was shocked to realize that he had not seen her. So, I explained the ghost I had just seen. Needless to say, I lost my new boyfriend. He saw me as a wacko nut case.

There was a county nursing home near the area where I saw the woman. It is my opinion that she died in the nursing home and was trying to find her way home to where she lived prior to being put there. I can still see what she was wearing - the color of her hair, her eyes, and her pink sweater. I have been down that short stretch of road hundreds of times since, but have not encountered her again.

March 10

THOUGHT FOR THE DAY – Some ghosts are souls that have severed silver cord communication lines. When they pop from their human forms, they do not know to return home to the Astral Shore.

GHOSTS

Ghosts are Spirit Beings that have climbed out of their dead human forms, but are lost as to where they are to go from there. They have Silver Cords that have been severed. Having no communications link to the afterlife, they don't realize that one exists. So, they roam Earth life trying to figure out what is going on and why those about them can't see or hear them.

Silver Cords are a cloud like, misty, see thru, cord that connects Spirit Beings with Divine Source in the heavens. It is like a telephone line. It has form, but it is like a force field that you can walk thru and not disturb its existence. The cord, if seen on Earth, is similar to a body aura. In the heavens it has a gray/silver rope like appearance.

The Silver Cord carries intelligence and spiritual communications from the upper heavens to Spirit Beings wherever they may be, on Earth or other planets. Beings with severed Silver Cords think they are merely human. Many of them become atheists as adults, because they have no personal spiritual communications with their Divine Source.

Severed Cord Beings become ghosts after their human forms cease to be.

Ghost can be nice, or a little mean spirited, just as human beings in Earth life sometimes are. Their nature depends on their choices on Earth as well as their passing or failing of Earth life lessons. Some Spirit Beings on Earth are strictly there for learning/educational experiences. The mastering of free-will choice is one of those lessons, as well as the passing up or overcoming of obesity, alcoholism, drugs, gossip, etc. When returning to the Astral for judgment, beings on learning ventures will be judged for their attempts at mastering those subjects. Just like in Earth human schools, some returning home Spirit Beings will get good grades, some will get poor grades, and the class goof offs and hooky players will fail.

There are three types of severed cord, Spirit Being Ghosts who have been on earth for educational adventures.

1. Congenial ghosts are those who got good grades in Earth School and mastered free will choice. An encounter with one of them will be a pleasant one. The only reason they are a ghost is the fact that their silver cord has somehow been severed and they have astral amnesia.

2. Ghosts who had poor grades in Earth School may be a little nice, as well as be a bit mean spirited. He is a recycler who will live several lives on earth till he gets it right. His second time at Earth life will probably go better for him, because he will not be plagued with a severed silver cord. These ghosts might be nice one day, and leave you the scent of a rose in your house. The next day, they may let you pick a rose and get thorn stuck.

3. Failure Ghosts are those who got nothing right in

Earth life school. Also, they willfully chose to goof off and not attain/pursue anything worthwhile in Earth life. They will be the haunts who appear to you with worms or bugs spewing from their mouths. They will be totally dark, mean spirited ghosts. If they did not have a severed cord, they would go straight to judgment and be kicked out of the Astral/Heaven for their choice to not attain and fulfill their missions on Earth.

When lost souls/spirit beings wander into the land of ghosts, they become ghosts. The change is sort of like an Irishman coming to the United States and assuming our lifestyle. The Land of Ghosts exists between Earth and Heaven. It is part of a parallel universe.

March 11

THOUGHT FOR THE DAY – You are only as good as what you invest in educating and perfecting yourself.

HAWAIIAN LEAPERS

The Hawaiians believe that their soul journeys to a special spot called Leina when their human forms die. (Leina is a place where their souls leap from island life to the nether world.) They also believe they have two portals to leap into for their journey. One is Waipio Valley on the Big Island. The other is Kaena Point on Oahu. The Big Island Waipio portal is believed to be an entryway into the place of the gods.

When you are on the Astral Shore, it is interesting to watch how different peoples exit the portals from Earth locations, as well as other planets. Hawaiians leap out of their two. I guess you could call them 'Leaping Spirit Beings' when they are out of their earth bodies. Their nether world is the Astral Shore. The Buddhist first heaven is the Astral Shore. Your heaven is the Astral Shore. My home is just above the Astral Shore. All beings arrive there thru their different portals. It does not matter what religion, country, or planet a soul arrives there from.

Have you ever had a souvenir hula dancing girl doll that you stick on your dash? I had one a few years back. She was lost, when I braked to miss having an auto accident. She leaped off my dash and rolled under my auto's seat. I thought back at the time that her exit from my dash was probably similar to our exit from our human bodies at death. Her jump from my dash was quick, as well as her rolling into her portal beneath my seat. She leaped, rolled, and disappeared.

After the braking incident, I couldn't find her. I searched beneath the seat for days, almost to the point of being obsessed with it.

Spirit Beings in the in-between world (a realm of ghosts that exists between Earth and the Astral) are able to move some things about in our world, in an effort to snag our attention. Pictures can fall off of walls, book pages flutter, microwaves run, radios turn on, light switches flip, etc. It is possible a Hawaiian earth bound ghost caused my hula girl to leap, roll, and disappear.

Take time today to consider the things in your world that have been moved about, that you cannot explain. Once, I found my electric coffee percolator in the refrigerator. To this day, I do not know how it got there.

March 12

THOUGHT FOR THE DAY - Just as light beings travel in human form on earth, dark beings do also. In the ghost world, there are dark and light beings as well.

ARTISTS WHO PAINT GHOSTS

Artists and non-artists will attempt to try to paint on canvas what they have seen in the way of a ghost. It is hard for them to describe in words what they have seen, so they try to put it on paper. Some shared characteristics they paint is haunting lost eyes, missing lower feet, and views of them floating, not walking. If visited by a dark being ghost, they will see mangled bloody bodies that might have maggots crawling from them. They might have also been chased by their ghost with knives or other fierce weapons, or possibly been bitten with teeth.

Ghosts wander about the earth on a ghost plane that exists just slightly higher and unaligned with earth. When humans encounter a ghost, the out of alignment of worlds is the reason that ghosts are seen without their lower feet and seem to be floating.

Writers and singers are artists, just in a different fashion. If a writer writes (or a singer sings) entirely about blood and gore, horrendous murders of men and animals, dark deeds, etc., they are dark beings using pen and song to assault you. If the writer is a light being, he will write your religious books, history books, futuristic prediction books, rags to riches books, training manuals, assembly instructions, etc. Light being singers will sing of love or positive thoughts. A dark singer will sing of black deeds. A dark musician will play music that hurts the ears, as well as so loud it offends anyone in hearing distance. A stereo can be a weapon of darkness, if used to annoy neighbors.

If you should encounter a ghost, judge his projections by whether they are positive or negative (light or dark). If you meet an artist, writer, or musician, judge their creative works by the same. If you meet a politician, judge him by the above. Judge your friends by standards of light and dark.

March 13

THOUGHT FOR THE DAY – Not all souls cross over to the afterlife, after they climb out of their deceased human forms. Some enter the in-between world, the land of Ghosts.

GHOST FOOTSTEPS

It was in the 1980's when I had an encounter with the deceased spirit of a child. I was young at the time and had three children to support, two of which were elementary age. One child was in Kindergarten, one was in First Grade. An older child was in the Seventh. I had just moved in to a worn out ten wide trailer in a white trash trailer park in the south. It was all I could afford, and I was doing what was necessary to make ends meet and survive back at that time. At the time, I was working the night shift so my children never missed my being home, even though I was sleeping sometimes.

It was during the time I worked nights that my two youngest children got in the habit of not fully closing the refrigerator door. I had been onto them about it on a regular basis for two or three weeks. I tried to explain to my children that we could not afford to have our food spoil. It seemed to go in one ear with them and out the other. All parents occasionally have little things that their children do that drives them crazy, and the children never seem to understand or quit doing it.

My children walked with other children in the trailer park to school at that time. We were just a block and a half from the elementary school. After they left for school, I always went to bed to sleep. Working the night shift, days were sleeping hours. One morning, I was about to doze off in my bedroom, in the back of the trailer, when I heard my trailer door open and a child's footsteps in the kitchen. Then, I heard the refrigerator door open. In disgust, thinking one of my two younger children had returned home and was raiding the refrigerator; I rose and headed to the kitchen. Too my surprise, there was no one there and the refrigerator door was closed. I went to the front door and found it locked, as well as dead bolted on the inside. No one could have gotten in. Thinking I was letting my imagination run wild, I returned to bed and went to sleep.

For three mornings straight, I had the same experience. On the second morning, I called the school and inquired if my two youngest children were there. They were. On the third morning, I was a little spooked as I lay down to sleep. About thirty minutes later, I once more heard the front door of the trailer open, footsteps, and then the sound of the refrigerator door opening. Rising, I found no one in the trailer, the door locked and dead bolted as usual. However, this time the fridge door was open. I didn't know what to think.

After my next night shift, the morning was a Saturday. So, I stayed up to watch cartoons with my children. Later in the morning, I stepped outside with a cup of coffee in hand, and visited with a neighbor who walked down from a couple trailers up to get acquainted and chat. She made a strange inquiry, asking me how I was making it in the trailer. I wasn't sure what she was referring to, thinking possibly she was going to give me pointers as to how to get repairs out of my landlord. I proceeded to tell her that everything was going fine for me, except that someone was entering my trailer and messing with my refrigerator. I then told her that I was sure that it was one of my children, but that I hadn't caught them yet.

As the words spilled out of my mouth, I saw my neighbor's face get flush, and she seemed suddenly edgy. I asked her what was wrong. Sputtering, she told me that a child had been murdered in my trailer a few years back. The child was starved on a daily basis by a stepfather when the mother was at work. The hungry child had sneaked home one morning from school, thinking the stepfather was gone. He entered the trailer and went straight to the refrigerator for food. The step father was not gone, but was in a drunken stupor in the back room. He rose and beat the child to death for daring to open the refrigerator door.

It was at that point, that I realized I had the ghost of a child haunting my white trash, trailer park mobile home. Needless to say, I never again scolded my children for opening the refrigerator door and leaving it open. After hearing the tragic story from the neighbor, no more footsteps were heard. – A shared story

March 14

THOUGHT FOR THE DAY – The Pentecostals have a specific Spirit Guide, referred to as the Holy Ghost. He is an orb of light energy, and chooses not to wear a body costume. His particular mission is comfort.

THE PENTECOSTAL GHOST

On the Astral Shore/First Heaven, spirit beings there mill about in costume body forms like their human one that they have just exited on Earth. Some of the beings are light and some are shades of gray (beings that have failed their education experience or mission on Earth.) The same beings may continue to speak in the languages that they were familiar with on Earth.

So, we have spirit beings that have just exited human forms on earth. Some are sad to leave behind those they traveled earth life with (family, friends, associates). In desperation, these beings may try to send back messages to those left behind on Earth. Their only hope of sending a message back is to speak to, or thru, an earth channel, medium, seer, etc.

Pentecostals go inward and upward in search of deeper experiences. Those experiences include the speaking in tongues, interpretation of tongues, prophesy, word of knowledge, etc. Those supernatural gifts are the basic gifts of all mystics. The Pentecostals have chosen to be channels for one gift in particular. They let those of the heavens speak thru them in languages, unknown tongues. They refer to it as a Holy Ghost speaking thru them. More advanced Pentecostals have mastered the interpretation of tongues. The messages coming down are from those in the beyond, sent via the Pentecostal's Spirit Guide postman, the Holy Ghost.

The Pentecostal's Holy Ghost is not the only Holy Being that is acting as a Spirit Guide and relaying messages to earth's mystics and then to its inhabitants. There are Spirit Guides/Holy Ghosts available to guide men of all earth light religions. Holy Ghosts are master orbs of light and energy. They live in the higher heavens, and have no need for body costumes.

The Holy Spirit/Holy Ghost/Spirit Guide/Holy Ones comfort those in need. Also, they pass down messages to mystics, who pass them on to Earth men. Those on the Astral Shore have just arrived from Earth and other planets. Their languages will be many. A Spirit Guide/Holy Ghost may send language messages down thru Pentecostal channels. Naturally, the channel speaks, but does not know the language he is speaking. He is just speaking in tongues. A perfected Pentecostal channel will be able to interpret the tongues/unknown language.

Channels that speak in tongues on Earth, but have not mastered the gift of Interpretation of Tongues, are wasting their Holy Spirit/Holy Ghost/Spirit Guide's time. They are allowing them-self to channel unrecognizable words.

March 15

THOUGHT FOR THE DAY – As a Spirit being, you have the powers of creative thought and free-will choice. Heaven and hell in earth life are created by you. If you choose to lash others with your tongue, you create hell for others and become the dark force ruler in it.

SHOCKED BY A VISITATION

Ghosts don't always appear in the human form they were known as in Earth life. When human forms die, they are autopsied, embalmed, cremated, painted pretty and then buried beneath the ground to rot. Only the Spirit Being traveling in a human form rises/ resurrects/climbs out of the human body at death. Spirit Beings, who enter Earth life in new conceptions, are orb beings from the Upper Heavens, who are working on the equivalent of master degrees. Earth life and freewill choice is one course they take. So, the adult orb of the heavens starts his learning journey traveling in a human infant vehicle.

To our horror, your one year old child dies. The Spirit Being climbing out of him/her is not a one year old toddler. He is an adult orb, a light being. If you ask for a visitation from your one year old, what you will get is one from an adult light being. He may choose to appear in a costume form of an angel, or whatever he chooses. Adults dress themselves. I am sure he would be appalled to appear to you in a diaper costume of a baby.

Ghosts are severed communication cord, Spirit Being Orbs in costume who don't know to return to the heavens via the light. Their Silver Cord communication's line was severed when they entered earth life. If they were fully connected, they would automatically head for the light of their personal portal and home beyond it. Ghosts have the equivalent of amnesia. They are lost beings who hang around earth in a lost state, wondering why humans can't see or hear them.

A grieving parent on Earth may ask for a visitation from their deceased child. The child's human body is no more.

It has either been cremated, or lies rotting in a grave somewhere. What they might get in the way of a visitation is a ghost Spirit Being who has put on a form costume, such as that of a toddler. A visitation could also be from an adult orb of the heavens. It is up to the Master Orb whether he wears a human form costume or not. Strangers in dreams and visions could actually be Orbs that once traveled in the human form of a deceased loved one of yours. If you have asked for a visitation from a deceased child, be open to him/her appearing to you in an adult form or orb of light.

On the Astral Shore, Spirit Beings can choose costume bodies to walk about in till they appear at the Throne of Judgment. You must remember that they are Spirit Beings when they leave the human form. As adult spirit beings on the Astral Shore, they can choose to wear costumes of who they once were on Earth, exotic ones of their choosing, or no costume at all. When they wear no costumes at all, they appear as orbs or shadows. Many people take photos and orbs appear. Others have orbs of light that float about in their homes like balloons, or reflect in mirrors and door glass.

Something else to keep in mind is that dark spirit beings also climb out of human forms and may choose to appear to you. If it is a light being appearing to you in costume form, there will be joy, bliss, and the being will be radiant or clean. A dark being appearing in costume form might be seen as a dirty, dark child, with a mouth filled with worms or other creepy crawlers. Sociopath children on earth have Dark Spirit Beings traveling in them. They will appear to you as the darkness they embraced. You will see the ghost children killing small animals, wielding knives, and wearing dirty, ragged costume forms. If they appear in adult forms, you will see them as adult rapists, murderers, thieves, etc. in your dreams. Remember, it is only the child human form that is young. The Spirit Being in the child (light or dark) is an adult.

I had a cousin that everyone dreaded coming for a visit. One year, when he was about ten, he beat to death a whole batch of new kittens with a hammer when no one was looking. He lifted anything he could get his hands on from neighbors. When he grew up, he became an abusive adult who lived to pick fights with other men. At home, he abused his children and the women in his life. In the business world, he conned anyone he could. This cousin died young, because he picked a fight with a dark being traveling in another human form that was stronger than him. (Only human bodies die!). My demented cousin was an adult, dark Spirit Being who traveled in a human form. That form was once a baby, a toddler, a child, teen, adult etc. He was a sociopath child, as well as an adult.

Laws put sociopaths to death. However, it is only their human form bodies that die. The dark, sociopath, Spirit climbs out of the electric chair fried human form and moves on to cause havoc in the form of an invisible demon or in the costume of a dark ghost. Dark Spirit Beings are fallen angels. Hitler was a sociopath. Him and his mistress may have committed suicide, killed their human forms. However, they did not die as spirit beings. Today, they may be hiding, or living again in other human forms.

March 16

THOUGHT FOR THE DAY – The wise men of Bethlehem were Astrology gurus, the New Age thinkers of their day who dared to follow a star.

ASTROLOGERS 'CAME AND WENT AWAY'

The wise men of Bethlehem were Astrology gurus, forward thinkers who dared to follow a star. They were seers/psychics/mystics/master spirit being types traveling in human forms. They had fully connected silver cord communication lines, and received communication from the heavens via dreams. They dared to be the forward thinkers of their day. They were Astrologers who 'Came and Went Away" at the birth of the Master Spirit Being Jesus.

(In the time of King Herod . . . wise men from the East came to Jerusalem, asking, "Where is the child who has been born king of the Jews? For we observed his star . . . When King Herod heard this, he was frightened . . . Then Herod secretly called for the wise men and learned from them the exact time when the star had appeared. Then he sent them to Bethlehem . . . ahead of them went the star . . . until it stopped over the place where the child was.) from the Christian's Bible.

Today, we have wise men that are following a new star, and it leads to a New Dispensation of Time (the stepping over from the New Testament Age into the New Age of Enlightenment. Are you aware there are master beings being born into earth life that will spearhead the New Age? Like the wise men and Christ, they will be masters of the 'going away and coming again' to their human forms. They will travel between heaven and earth at will, as well as to other planets. The Master Wise Men of the future will not ride camels. They will be time travelers.

I, Jo Hammers the Mystic, am a Spirit Being, traveling in a human form for a life time on earth. Like the Wise Men, I know my dreams relay messages to me from my guide in the heavens. The star I follow is leading me, a wise man, into the New Dispensation of Time and to its many masters. The old is passing away. Be wise enough to see it!

March 17

THOUGHT FOR THE DAY – Young Spirit Beings of an impish nature might choose elf or other children form costumes to wear while playing around in portals.

ARE THERE REALLY LITTLE PEOPLE

I always thought Leprechauns were just a myth, till I had an experience with them. Once, I inadvertently opened a portal that was not mine, but belonged to someone who had lived in my house before me. I was in my early twenties at the time, and hadn't discovered there was anything supernatural that went on outside the four walls of my fenced in religion, yet. Spiritually blind best described me at that time. I had not discovered New Age Thinking, or the possibility of Astral traveling at will yet, due to having a damaged Silver Cord that had not been healed, or repaired.

At the time of my little people visitation, I was lying flat of my back and staring at my bedroom ceiling, waiting for night sleep to overtake me. I was concentrating on one certain spot on a seam in the ceiling drywall, when suddenly it opened up, like it had been ripped or unzipped. The edges of the unzipped/ripped open ceiling dipped down and touched both sides of my full size bed. The opening was about ten feet long, and ran the same direction as my body (head to toe).

As the edges of the ceiling touched my bed, eight or so little men fell down out of the ceiling and started jumping up and down all around me on my bed, trying to frighten me. They looked like jumping dolls, due to their height only being about two feet. They were all male, wore knee britches, green vests, black shoes, and black hats. There was no denying they were Irish Leprechauns/little people.

Instead of conversing with them, and learning more about their world and what they were like, I made the decision to tell them to leave me alone and go away. However, I was not afraid of them, or their impish, childlike efforts to frighten me.

Boldly staring at them, I demanded, "Go back to where you came from!"

Immediately, the little men returned to the space above the ceiling, floating upward head first. Then the ceiling closed, re-plastered itself, and became as it was before the visitation.

The house where I experienced the visitation was in Springfield, Missouri on Clifton Street, off of Nichols. The house has long been torn down, but I am sure the portal probably still exists. The owner before me didn't close it, and I didn't either. I knew nothing about opening or closing portal doors at that time.

Visitations of a supernatural nature come thru portals from the Astral Shore. The Astral Shore is like a giant airport or bus station waiting room. Beings exit portals there from Earth, as well as other planets. Till judgment, arriving beings walk around in body and face form costumes they are familiar with. You will find two types of beings milling about there, portal travelers and those returning to the home of the soul due to the death of their human body. Spirit Guides and angels also put on and wear costume forms on the Astral Shore that their charges will understand, when they visit them in dreams or visions. Dreams and visions are sent down from the Astral Shore.

The portal in the house I lived in years ago was owned by an Irish man. I am sure he expected visitations in his portal to be from those he understood or fantasized about. Moving from his house, he apparently forgot to close his portal. Thus, I was visited by his Leprechaun costumed little people.

March 18

THOUGHT FOR THE DAY – Shaman Oarsmen are time travelers. In a one evening journey, they can travel around the world obtaining what information they need from the future.

ROWING WITH MYSTICAL OARSMEN

Have you ever rowed a shaman's canoe? It is a journey of the spirit into the in-between worlds. A group of psychic travelers sit on the floor, as though they were in a canoe. They begin to row physically, but see where they are headed with their inward spirit eyes. These shaman oarsmen are seasoned travelers of the mystical night sky.

One night, I joined an oarsman group who were passing over. I was sitting and rowing alone in the floor of my bedroom, when a group passed over head. They slid their mystical shaman's canoe alongside mine, stopped, and let me on board. Their canoe enlarged mystically to accommodate me. I sat down and started rowing with them. My physical body was still rowing on Earth in one location in my bedroom. Their physical bodies were still rowing on Earth in their locations. In the night sky, we rowed southwest. We rowed with groaning words of the soul matching the rhythm of the rowing.

In this night adventure, I suddenly saw a great tornado in the night sky at our level, at least a hundred feet off the Earth's surface. It was intent on destroying me. I screamed. The other oarsmen just continued to row. Then, the tornado disappeared and I saw my boss firing me. The vision/visitation took place maybe a hundred feet off the ground, in a mystical canoe, and in the company of psychic oarsmen who were strangers to me. I guess you might say we were all on a vision quest.

Returning to my bedroom from the mystical, shaman's canoe journey, I popped back into my human state, and laid down my mystical invisible oars. Tired to the bone, I rose and went to bed.

The next day at work, I got fired. After that a series of devastating events took place forcing me to pack my bags and move to a huge city to find work. The tornado represented forced change coming that was out of my control. Had I not gotten fired, I would not have moved. The move led me to the psychic world and those who could heal my damaged Silver Cord.

(I discussed Silver Cords in January. When entering Earth life, sometimes Silver Cords, or communications lines, can be injured or severed. When severed, Spirit Beings have no supernatural communications or memories of their life in the Upper Heavens. The cordless being usually becomes an atheist on Earth. An injured or bruised Silver Cord results in a Spirit Being having fuzzy or static plagued communications with his source in the heavens. I was a damaged cord Spirit Being at that time.)

With my Silver Cord healed, I became alive spiritually. With my spiritual communications' line healed, I became aware of my true identity. I am Master Barjoraven of the Heavens. On Earth, I am Jo Hammers the Mystic.

I, Jo Hammers the Mystic, am an oarsman who once rowed a shaman's canoe to a place of future predictions/ knowledge. In the night sky, with strangers for fellow oarsmen, I traveled into the future and saw my future for the next day. Time travel backward and forward is available to those rowing shaman's canoes.

March 19

THOUGHT FOR THE DAY – Just because a child dies, it does not mean the spirit being within the child human form will automatically go to heaven and become an angel. Dark Spirit Beings enter human bodies to travel earth, the same as Light Beings.

DEMONS CAN ATTACH THEMSELVES TO OBJECTS

On Earth, both light and dark beings travel in human, vehicle forms. At the death of the human form, Spirit Beings climb out and either journey toward the light and future incarnations, or are earth bound and look for humans or objects to enter or attach them-selves to.

For instance, when children died young a hundred years or so ago, it was a popular practice to take locks of the deceased child's hair and put it on a doll, making an angel of death doll. If the child body form before death was inhabited by a dark Spirit Being, the unsuspecting maker of the Angel of Death doll created an invitation for a Dark Being Demon to attach itself to the object/doll. In doing so, the demon gains an avenue in which it can cause havoc for anyone picking up the doll to play with, or admire it. Dybbuc/Jewish demons can attach themselves to personal objects belonging to their former human host, such as hair, playthings, clothing, shoes, watches, jewelry, eye glasses, etc.

Back in the 1960s I was invited to dinner by a mother and her two grown sons who were in their twenties. The three were slightly mentally challenged, but able to function in society. They were able to work and make themselves a living. Back then, the three would have been referred to as 'slow of thinking'. On the occasion of my invitation, the older boy asked me if I would like to see something very special to his family. "Of course," I replied, being a good guest.

The guy went to a glassed in cabinet and pulled out what looked like a bird nest. When he returned, I saw that it was a bowl like structure made of what looked like chicken feathers. He held it down for me to look in. I assumed I would be viewing a couple of dried up Robin eggs, or something similar. Too my surprise, there was a lock of human blond curls lying in the nest like structure. "Tell me about it!" was all I could manage to say, not knowing what in the world it was supposed to be. I was young in human years at that time, and was unfamiliar with Dybbuc and their object gates/portals between earth life and Hell.

The guy proceeded to tell me that they had a baby sister who died when she was about a year old. He further informed me that the feather bowl was created by unknown forces inside her pillow case, when she lay dying. Her head had made the impression and the chicken feathers had somehow formed into the nest. He then told me that they had cut the baby's blonde hair, before she was buried, and placed her locks in the feather nest. The nest of human hair was an object that a Dybbuc demon could attach itself to.

Objects of the dark deceased can be portal gates. When opened, they allow the dark demons that had exited the human form to return to cause havoc in the lives of anyone coming in contact with the object. Portal Gate objects can be watches, hand mirrors, small boxes, dolls, toys, tea cups, etc. If you are aware that a deceased member of your family was a dark sociopath being, who abused, raped, murdered, etc. do not keep any of his possessions. Burn them. If you do keep them, each object is an invitation for him to return to you, haunt you, and assault you in the fashion he did to his victims.

Taxidermy animals can be objects a demon might attach him-self to. The taxidermy animal then becomes a portal gate. Mess with a taxidermy head, eyes, or mouth and you might open Hell's gate, unsuspectingly. Doing so is an invitation for demons to call on you!

March 20

THOUGHT FOR THE DAY – You can know a dark being by what spews from his human mouth. Cursing and gossip are two forms of oral attacks by darkness.

The Cursing Dark Being

Back in the early 1970s, I met a very religious, older couple who had just emigrated from New Zealand. The woman in her 50s seemed very devout in her faith. The controlling 60ish man was an odd character who claimed to be a non-denominational minister. In the 1960s and 1970s there was a lot of moving about due to the hippie age being in. This couple was embracing that lifestyle. In my opinion, back at that time, the New Zealand couple was a little too old to be doing the hippie thing. However, I kept my thoughts concerning them to myself.

After getting to know the woman, she confided in me that she and her husband were actually newlyweds, having only been married a year or so. She then told me a story about her new husband that she was having mixed emotions about. The validity of his Christian experience was in doubt by her. She went on to tell me that a few months prior, her husband had surgery. Being a devoted wife, she had sat night and day with him at the hospital. After surgery, in the intensive care unit, he had lost his mental faculties for almost a month. She said that he did not know her, and that he was just totally off the wall with his behavior to the point of having to be restrained. She then added that the dark man in the ICU hospital bed was not the meek religious man she had married. Naturally, I asked her what she meant.

She then went on to state that her husband cursed and used filthy, offensive, demeaning language to her, the nurses, and anyone coming into the room to care for him. She related that she had never heard such vulgarity in all her 50 plus years of life. For days, he called the nurses the worst of demeaning names, and didn't speak a sentence that didn't have sexual innuendos or vulgarities in it. She didn't know what to think at that time, or in the presence. He had returned to being the religious man she knew before surgery. She said that back at the time of the vulgarities, she was totally embarrassed for him, as well as for herself being married to him. She ended her story by saying that he had verbally spouted all dark views that she had spent her whole religious life opposing.

As we have discussed in previous chapters, both Light and Dark Spirit Beings travel in human forms on Earth. Dark Beings like to disguise themselves in Earth life as prominent, up and up, good people in order to entice those about them into their hells. To recognize a dark being in a human form, you must listen to what spews from his mouth, as well as make note of his deeds, body language, etc. The human form, known as her husband, was driven by a dark being, like a human driving an automobile. In true evil fashion, the demon in a human form had managed to keep his dark side hidden, in order to attract his light being wife into his marriage hell snare.

Demons want to control light beings. A demon, who manages to pass himself off as a minister, rabbi, priest, etc. is an example of a demon choosing an occupation where he can control light beings.

March 21

THOUGHT FOR THE DAY – Ghosts don't always appear to humans in the image of the body they once traveled Earth life in, especially those of children. Ghosts are adult orbs of either light, or darkness. They can choose to costume their orb body in the likeness of former human bodies, if they choose. Some choose not to.

SHOCKED BY A CHILD'S GHOST APPEARANCE

Ghosts don't always appear in the costume human form they traveled as/in on Earth life. When human forms die, they are autopsied, embalmed, cremated, painted pretty and buried beneath the ground to rot. Only the Spirit Being traveling in a human form rises, or climbs out of the human body at death to live on in another form. Spirit Beings, who enter Earth life, are orbs of light beings from the Upper Heavens. To pursue education or missions on earth, they enter or put on human bodies. So, your four year old child dies. The Spirit Being climbing out of him/her is not a four year old. He is an adult orb/light being from the upper heavens.

Ghosts are Spirit Being Orbs from the upper heavens, who had their silver cord communication lines severed when entering earth life. If they were fully connected, they would automatically head for their portal and the light of the heavens beyond when their human bodies died. Having no connections, they get lost in the in-between world, which is a parallel existence about a foot off the surface of the earth. Ghosts who appear to be floating are actually walking on the surface of the in-between world that is just above ours.

A grieving parent on Earth may ask for a visitation from their deceased child, to let them know he/she is okay. The child's human body is no more. It has either been cremated, or lies rotting in a grave. What the parents might get in the way of a visitation is a ghost Spirit Being who has chosen to wear a costume form of his former human body. A visitation from a deceased child could be in orb form. It is up to the Ghost or Spirit Being whether he puts on and appears in a body costume or not. Adult strangers in dreams and visions could actually be Spirit Beings that once traveled in the human child/toddler/baby form of a deceased loved one of yours.

On the Astral Shore, Spirit Beings can choose costume bodies to walk about in, till they appear at the Throne of Judgment. You must remember that they are ageless, timeless, adult Spirit Beings. As eternal adult spirit beings, they can choose to, or not to, wear costumes of who they once were on Earth, exotic costumes from other planets, or no costume at all. When they wear no costumes at all, they appear as orbs of light or orb shadows. Orb shadows are dark beings.

If you encounter a ghost wandering about on Earth, he is a Spirit Being who has climbed out of his form (baby, child, or adult) and has found himself lost between worlds, due to his communications/silver cord being severed, or cut. He may choose, in the world of ghosts, to create a costume body to roam about in, or he can move about as an orb or a shadow. If he chooses to create a costume form like that of your dead child to appear to you in, it is his gift to you. Perhaps he feels sorry for you in your grief. If it was a dark orb traveling in your child's human form, the costume he may put on for you will be one with worms or maggots crawling out of it. There are sociopath or dark children.

I had a young cousin that everyone dreaded coming for a

visit. One year, at about age ten, he beat to death a whole batch of new kittens with a hammer when no one was looking. He grew up to be an abusive adult who lived to pick fights with other men. He abused children and the women in his life. He conned the business world with under table dealings. My cousin's human form died young, because he picked a fight with a dark being traveling in another human form that was stronger than him. The other sociopath killed his human form. My cousin was a dark Spirit Being who traveled in a human form. That form was once a baby, a toddler, a child, teen, adult etc.

Laws put sociopaths to death. However, it is only their human form bodies that die. The dark, sociopath spirit being climbs out of his electric chair fried human form and moves on to cause havoc in the ghost world. He will incarnate in a new conception, if at all possible. Dark Spirit Beings are fallen light orbs/angels. Hitler was a sociopath, a dark spirit being traveling in human flesh. Today, he may be hiding, or living again in another human form.

March 22

THOUGHT FOR THE DAY - Do not fear your crossing over! Death is but a winding path upward that we take to reach our Astral/Heaven home.

INCARNATIONS

As Spirit Beings, traveling in human forms, we sooner or later exit our human body vehicles and return to the inner/upper heavens, which is our Home. On Earth, when you get off work, you exit your place of employment, and return to your house till it is time to go to work again. That is the way it is with reincarnation. Earth life is one work place/school for spirit beings.

In a previous blog, I discussed how dark, sociopath souls (like Hitler) exit their bodies (just like Light Beings) when their human forms die. Dark souls return to the realms of hell (their heaven) and then look for new earth human form, or other planet form, to enter and travel again. The electric chair only fries the human form that dark sociopath souls enter and travel in on Earth. Lifetime lockup/containment would be a harsher punishment for them. Only Divine Source, or a perfected warrior of the heavens, can actually destroy a dark soul. There is war in the heavens between light and dark forces.

In the Hindu religion, Rama is the 7th avatar, or incarnation of Vishnu. Krishna is the 8th avatar, or incarnation, of Vishnu. Etc.etc. When Spirit Beings return to Earth for a first, second, third, fourth ,fifth, sixth, seventh, or eighth lifetime, etc., they have new human forms they enter into earth life in. Rama was a warrior. Krishna was a child who was obsessed with playing the flute. Both were the same spirit being living in human flesh, just in different time periods and different bodies.

Have you ever run into a male stranger, whose witty remarks reminded you so much of your deceased grandmother? Do you have a female child born into your family circle who displays all the emotional makeup and quirks of a male family member who died ten years prior? The Spirit Being that once traveled in the human form of your deceased loved one may be back for another incarnation. He could be traveling, or living a life, in a male or female form. The quirky Spirit Being is who he has always been.

There are other planets with civilizations besides earth. They have portals to the inner and upward heavens the same as we have. Spirit Beings on those planets do incarnations, the same as ones do on Earth. Your loved one, whose human earth form has died, may choose a life on another planet for his next life incarnation. One from another planet may choose to do an incarnation on earth. Those obsessed with astrology have probably lived former lives on other planets. Children obsessed with a certain planet have probably lived a life there.

March 23

THOUGHT FOR THE DAY - Who says Spirit Guides/guardians/angels/ dead loved ones have only pleasant words to relay to us? Suppose you have a soul mate in the upper heavens that is unhappy with your earth activities?

SOUL MATES DO NOT EXIST ON EARTH

This may shock you, but soul mates on Earth do not exist. Soul Mates are perfect Spirit Beings who have mastered all their earth and other planet lessons and are prepared to live a life of perfection in the upper heavens. Humans are not perfect. Perfected states only exist in the upper heavens. So, that perfect other side of you does not exist on Earth.

Furthermore, soul mates are not chosen in the upper heavens, they are paired by Divine Source. So, if you are looking for your soul mate in human form, forget it. Face it, a couple meets and is physically attracted and then thinks the other person has to be their soul mate. Then the new wears off and the attraction fades. Disappointment sets in and the search begins all over again. Human forms are animals and their attractions are a built in program to keep the species reproducing. They have some intelligence, but it is the Spirit Being within them that is on a mission on Earth, or pursuing higher education. Perfection doesn't happen till a Spirit Being completes his last Earth educational assignment and then returns to the Throne of Judgment for his grades. So, the perfect side of you does not exist till after your throne graduating experience. You are not the perfect side of another, till both of you complete your last earth or other planet educational course and return to the throne to receive your master degree.

The most a being on earth or other planets can expect is to have a traveling companion that is compatible with his life mission and understands where he is at in his educational studies. Free-will choice is one of Earth's life lessons. A spirit being traveling in a human form may choose a traveling companion on earth life. When doing so, it must be a companion who understands that soul mates exist only in the upper heavens. Non-compatibility causes lots of problems. Just because a woman is gorgeous, or a man is extremely handsome, doesn't mean they are compatible. Compatibility means two beings interested in the same spiritual paths, morals, ideals, etc. Compatibility is not sex, physical attraction, charming voices, alluring eyes, touch, etc. The difference between the two is light and dark.

A Soul Mate is an orb being that has passed his master courses on earth and other planets. That orb being will have returned to the upper heavens. Perfection only exists in the upper heavens.

The first heaven is the Astral Shore and it is a place where both dark and light beings appear before a throne for judgment. It is an imperfect place because of those of light and dark milling about there. The Second Heaven is the first heaven of perfection. Darkness cannot enter there, nor the imperfect who have not mastered their life lessons. Reincarnation, or recycling of gray souls to earth for further education, takes place on the Astral Shore.

Masters from the higher heavens entering Earth life are a different group of beings than those on earth for educational studies. They are perfected orbs who choose to live a life on Earth to do the will of Divine Source. They are spiritual map makers, leaders, and keepers of the four corners of the earth. They are God's Divine presence on Earth, you might say. Their soul mates await them in the upper heavens.

March 24

THOUGHT FOR THE DAY - If a Jinn or Genie likes you, he may encourage your cat to have 12 kittens instead of 3. He sees it as a prosperity promise to you.

JINN OR GENIES

On the Astral shore, you will find spirit beings from all religions of earth who have returned to the heavens for judgment of jobs done and reassignment. During dream states, we can pop from our human forms, travel up our personal portals and visit the Astral Shore/First Heaven. There, we can mingle with the unusual supernatural beings from all religious persuasions that have exited Earth life and returned there.

Milling about on the Astral Shore, you will encounter

Masters of the Hindu faith, who are recycling. Also, you will find Jinn, or Genies, on the Astral Shore, as well as magical beings from other planets that are recycling to the Astral and then entering different planet's life forms in the pursuit of assigned missions there. Ghosts and Angels are not the only supernatural beings in parallel worlds, hells, and heavens, not to mention unique supernatural beings from other planets existing invisibly beside you that you are totally unaware of. They cannot be seen with human eyes. Only the spirit eyes of spirit beings can see them.

In Eastern cultures, Jinn/Genies are supernatural spirit beings that live side by side with humans. Some take human forms. Others do not, preferring spirit form. Some Jinn/Genies are merely observers, while others have agendas to trick or be nasty to humans. Although Jinn are not Hindu in origin, they have been adopted into their beliefs. Adoption comes from Earth humans having visits or encounters from such. Jinns/Genies actually originate in Islamic and Buddhist cultures.

Just as there are light beings and dark beings on Earth traveling in human forms, Jinn/Genies can also be light or dark.

When you stand next to a person at a casino slot machine who puts one coin in and wins hundreds of dollars, you could be standing next to a Jinn or Genie who is living or traveling in a human form. A dark Jinn or Genie may assault you by making your billfold, change jar disappear, or you to be a loser as a gambler. Thieves can be dark Jinn or Genies in human form disguise. They make your prosperity disappear.

If a Jinn or Genie likes you, he may encourage your cat to

have 12 kittens instead of 2 or 3. He sees it as a prosperity gift of promise to you. You may see it otherwise, especially when you are sitting on a corner with a box of twelve kittens, trying to give them away. What is happening in your world? You could be being blessed, or cursed by a Jinn/Genie.

March 25

THOUGHT FOR TODAY - Dealing with Earth life and all its problems, without a spiritual connection, brings out the animal in man. He approaches his problems like a dog scratching at fleas till his skin is hairless and raw. Yet, the flea lives.

SUICIDE GHOSTS

I was reading a Buddhist article about a suicide ghost. It was described as a skinny necked ghost with a pencil size mouth, who haunted live humans because it couldn't get any type of food into its mouth. For food, or energy, the suicide ghost chooses to suck the life out of live humans who are in the process of committing suicide. A suicide feeding ghost gets his food by scouting for opportunities to help foolish people commit suicide. The hungry ghost was once a human on Earth who committed suicide by hanging/strangulation, thus limiting what can go down his throat as a ghost. He haunts and feeds on what he understands, the energy of others committing the suicide act.

Face it . . . , humans do crazy things for crazy reasons, especially if they have no spiritual connection to keep them on a level headed track. Because they have no spiritual connection, their inner spirit being is asleep. The inner being has his communication silver cord disconnected, or severed. Pursuing life and all its problems, using only a human animal's mind, can cause all sorts of self abusive situations, like a dog scratching fleas till his skin is hairless and raw. On my father's side of the family, we have had three males (in the last fifty or so years) commit suicide.

My favorite Uncle was despondent over his wife leaving him. He was older, disabled, and on a very small pension. He feared he could not make it, financially, in his later years without her. A suicide ghost may have whispered to his human mind, "Why don't you just kill yourself, instead of just thinking about it." My uncle put a sawed off shotgun to his mouth and pulled the trigger. The Suicide suggesting voice got what he wanted, my uncle's life energy.

A cousin of mine lost an eye in an automobile accident. As a result, most of his life he had trouble finding work. His one great accomplishment, in his mind, was meeting and marrying a very beautiful woman. She made everything alright in his thinking. Then one day, she met someone else and told him that she was leaving. It is possible my cousin heard the voice of a Suicide Ghost telling him, "Without her, you are nothing. Do you want to live all alone the rest of your life in your ugly one eyed body?" My cousin killed himself with a rifle. The Suicide Ghost voice sucked his life energy out of him. In reality, my cousin was a very handsome man in his forties, who happened to have a glass eye due to an accident. He wasn't ugly at all.

The third suicide in my family was a drowning. I was elementary age at the time. A brother of my father showed up one morning at our house carrying nothing but a transistor radio. He had been making the rounds of all his siblings, stopping for short visits that same morning. After leaving our house in Springfield, Missouri, he hitchhiked to St. Louis Missouri where he jumped from a bridge into the river below. He left his billfold and the radio on the bridge railing. Who says he wasn't hearing a suicide voice ghost over the transistor radio telling him to say his last goodbyes, before jumping to his death. A dark suicide ghost sucked his life energy out of him.

Occasionally, man hears suicide and other voices in his head. However, he has a power bestowed upon him by Divine Source. It is free-will choice. Man has the right to obey the voices he hears in his head, or to say no. Mastering free-will choice is what life school is all about. There has to be valley moments in order to choose well and overcome.

Suicide is failing life lessons. However, it does not mean that a suicide person will not be given another chance to repeat the life lesson in another incarnation. On earth, lots of kids have to repeat a grade of education.

March 26

THOUGHT FOR THE DAY – In Eastern religions there is a ghost called a 'KITCHEN STOVE HUNGRY GHOST'. This ghost, supposedly, loves to hang out in the kitchens of lazy women who rarely use their cooking stove. Beware homemaker, if you are one who eats fast food and carryout all the time. You may be leaving open a portal for a ghost to take up residence in the oven of your prized, stainless steel, never used, kitchen range.

THE KITCHEN COOK STOVE GHOST

Jo Hammers

While studying writings about ghosts of the Far East, I came across a type of ghost that I was amused with. It is one of over 30 ghosts the Hindu and Buddhists call hungry ghosts. Hungry ghosts supposedly have pencil size mouth openings that they can't get normal size food in to. So, they feed off of the energy of those who are alive, like breathing/sucking in laughing gas.

The hungry ghost that amused me was one they called the 'KITCHEN STOVE HUNGRY GHOST'. This ghost, supposedly, loves to hang out in the kitchens of lazy women who rarely use their cooking stoves. The hungry ghost, that amused me, was one they called the 'KITCHEN STOVE HUNGRY GHOST'. This ghost, supposedly, loves to hang out in the kitchens of lazy women who rarely use their cooking stove. The reason being, they want to hide in the cold, dark, ovens. I am in agreement. A black oven would be a good hiding spot, if I were a Kitchen Ghost.

When I was eighteen and first out on my own, all food was cooked from scratch. I recall one cold day creating from scratch one of the most beautiful tuna and noodle casseroles. The bread crumbs were crumbled perfectly on top, and the oven had been set to preheat. Taking the casserole dish in one hand, I opened my apartment's kitchen cook stove door to pop it in. When the white porcelain door let down, one mad mouse jumped out in my face, causing me to drop my perfect casserole and scream bloody murder. If there was a kitchen stove ghost dwelling in my oven that day, in the form of a mouse, he was one hot footed mad one. My screaming and kicking further agitated the mouse that had landed on my foot. I started to jump up and down in hysteria. In fright of me, the mouse proceeded to run between my legs, causing me to further jump up

147

and down, in the spilt ingredients of my casserole. Was I the ghost scaring the mouse, or was the mouse the kitchen ghost scaring me?

I apologize little, hungry, hot footed, mouse ghost for being your tormentor that day in my kitchen. It was unintentional.

March 27

THOUGHT FOR THE DAY - The Holy Ghost of the New Testament appearing in the form of a dove is an example of a Spirit being putting on a costume.

THE INVISIBLES WHO HAVE THREE EYES

There exists an invisible world beyond earth that can be traveled to by portals from the Astral Shore. Only those seeking higher paths and mastering their earth educations have access to those portals. The Invisibles are advanced civilizations. Their beings travel planet to planet in thought and to the upper heavens via personal portals.

We have discussed in previous writings how orbs of light can put on the costume form of a human in order to travel down portals and make appearances to humans on Earth who are seekers. The invisibles from other planets can do the same. The invisibles can travel to the Astral Shore, put on a costume form, and then travel portals downward to earth, in pursuit of travel or opportunities to study Earth and its colorful life forms. Beings and creatures in the invisible are invisible. They are like earth's air. They can walk by you and you will feel their presence as a chilly breeze. They are there, but you cannot see them, unless they choose to put on a human costume form. The invisibles have three eyes, but you cannot see them.

Invisibles are not ghosts. Ghosts are severed cord Spirit Beings that have popped from human forms, but are oblivious to where to go from there. They don't know that the bright light they see is a portal gate to the Astral or home. Ghosts are lost souls.

March 28

THOUGHT FOR THE DAY – Strategy is better than guessing. Approach your spiritual life with strategy, instead of fantasy. Plan and execute your walk with your master.

KNEE ANGELS THAT CRY HOLY

In my thinking, congregations of churches, temples, etc. are there for the social aspect of church life and not for a supernatural experience. You can judge the difference between the social religious person and the one there for an experience by the bowing of their knees. There are pew sitters and then there are altar bowers. (A pew can be an altar if bowed at.)

For instance, a minister gets up in a traditional protestant church and gives an altar call. Then he calls for workers to come forth and bow at the altar to pray for church or member's needs. In big congregations, you might see four or five walk down front and kneel to pray for the needs presented. Some bow their head in their pews. One or two might kneel at their pew. The rest will sit with their eyes closed and occasionally open one to peek to see if the prayer time is over.

It does not matter what religion a human seeks God (Divine Source) in. What does matters is their dedication and desire for a deeper spiritual experience. Willingness to practice 'knee-ology' is the opening of a gate to supernatural religious experiences. The same experiences will not be made available to those with eyes closed in the pews, because the invitation was to come and kneel before the Almighty. Failure to come and failure to bend on knee are defiant acts of rebellion against having to prostrate oneself before God. Either you respect your god, or you don't! Those who fail to answer their call to kneel are showing disrespect and will not be rewarded with spiritual experiences for it.

So, a church congregation has a handful of individuals that gather in the front of the church and prostrate themselves before the altar. They are KNEE ANGELS, or THRONE ANGELS traveling earth life in human forms. The invitation in all religions to prostrate oneself can either be seen as a chance to touch and be touched by the divine, or a chance to sit back in disrespect and turn ones back on his invitation.

A throne angel, traveling in a human form, will sing words such as, "I bow on my knees and cry Holy . . . Holy . . . Holy . . . to the Creator of my soul."

The peeping pew sitter will bow his head and mutter to him-self, "Is the preacher/rabbi/priest ever going to shut up and let us go home?"

The one bowing at the pew will say a few pleasant, flowery prayers and then cry, "I have got to get up God . . . my knees are killing me."

I, Jo Hammers the Mystic, am a Spirit Being, traveling in

a human form for a lifetime on Earth. So are you! I am a trumpeter, a Keeper and Sounder of Words. I am a trumpet angel. What kind of Spirit Being/light being/angel are you? If you are Christian, are you a Throne Angel or a Fallen Angel who sits on his pew and peeps?

March 29

Thought for the day – Guardians of the Four Corners of the Earth are commissioned to guard earth, air, water, and fire. Kill or maim one of them, the balance of nature will go out of kilter in the area of earth where they are commissioned to protect. Wiccans are guardian spirit beings traveling in human forms.

WICCANS GUARD EARTH'S FOUR CORNERS

As I have said many times in my writings, man fears what he does not understand. Witches are guardian light beings, not Satanist dark beings. Wiccan followers are commissioned helpers of the Master Guardians of the four corners of the earth. Kill or maim one of the helpers and the balance of nature will go out of kilter in the area of earth where they are commissioned to protect. (Fierce tornadoes, floods, hurricanes, ice storms, dust storms etc.) Some religions seek to maim, incarcerate, or burn at the stake the guardians' helpers. The pious abusers are dark beings traveling in human forms. They cause natural disaster curses to fall on their area of the globe. Light Beings are born into all religions around the world, and are positioned there for reasons.

As we have discussed in previous writings, Spirit Beings in the higher heavens are orbs of light and energy. They can descend and enter Earth life traveling in invisible spirit or human forms. These Higher Beings can enter earth life for various reasons such as being world religious figures, guardians of animal life, or of elements, etc. If you are fortunate enough to have an encounter with a guardian or one of his Wiccan followers, be respectful, if you don't want your parade rained on literally.

One morning, about 1974 I think, I looked out my window in Cassville, Missouri and was in shock to see that the creek behind our house had risen. My yard was filled with muddy creek water that was running at least three feet deep. A flood was happening! When I managed to wade out of the rising water, which rose quickly to above my waist, I looked downstream and saw my dog on top of its doghouse floating away in the rapidly moving water. One of the four guardians of the four corners of Earth was unhappy with someone in my neighborhood that morning. Have you ever questioned the why of natural disasters in your life?

My dog came home three days later, following the creek bank. There is no telling how long of a journey downstream he took, or what guardian of animal life looked out for him.

SUGGESTED READING – Wiccan literature on the subject of the four elements. You cannot glean the truth about anyone, or any religious persuasion by going to their enemy, who will demean and want to see them literally burned at the stake. Wiccans are not Satanists. They are keepers of the earth and its elements. They are light beings. Satanists are dark beings.

March 30

THOUGHT FOR THE DAY - The belief in a goddess or god starts with an ordinary, everyday individual having a supernatural visitation of some sort. Needing a god to believe in, he enthrones, or designates his supernatural visitor as being a god or goddess.

GODDESSES

The Hawaiians have a ghost/goddess story about a female, earth bound, Spirit Being that resides in the craters of the Mauna Loa Volcano. Some natives believe she is the goddess of the volcano. Others are convinced that she is the earth bound ghost of a woman who died in one of the Volcano's eruptions. It is rumored that she appears just before a volcanic eruption, in an effort to warn residents of the area about impending doom and death if they remain. It is said that she always dresses in lava fire red and has a ghost dog with her. Some native inhabitant's of the area leave her food and drink sacrifices, believing that she is a goddess.

The belief in a goddess or god starts with an ordinary, everyday individual having a supernatural visitation of some sort. The visitation is real, whether from an Earth Bound Spirit, Angel, Alien, Astral Traveler, or a Master. It is what the individual does with their supernatural visitor's appearance that enthrones/designates them as being a god or goddess. Humans, in the area of an occurrence, hear about the supernatural visitation and adopt the supernatural visitor as their goddess or god, becoming followers. They have had no supernatural experiences or visitations of their own to relate to. The followers are the Severed Silver Cord Beings who have their communication line to the heavens cut off. Thus, following in faith is all they have to hold on to. Someone else's god or goddess becomes theirs. (I have discussed severed Silver Cords in previous writings.)

Mary, the mother of Christ, has been made into a goddess by Catholic followers. They also make saints out of individuals. The Hawaiian earth bound, red dressed, volcano woman has been made into a goddess by native Hawaiians. The man Christ has been enthroned and designated as a son god. Men's writings (THE HOLY BIBLE) have made and designated him so. Mormons have created a world religion around their Joseph Smith and his visitation. Gods and goddesses are created. Somewhere in the ancient of days, someone had a visitation from an astral visitor and it was a very loving one. Thus, we have the goddess of love.

Man's need for something spiritual/supernatural to hang onto enthrones and designates space and astral light visitors as gods and goddesses.

The writings of Matthew, Mark, Luke, & John in the Holy Bible made, created, designated, and enthroned Christ into being a son of god. Christ was a Spirit Being traveling in a human form for a lifetime, just like you and I. He had a fully intact Silver Cord communications line. With his communications line fully functional, he was psychic (for lack of a better term) and could retrieve information and powers from the heavens to heal, raise the dead, etc. He is a Master Spirit Being who dwells in the inner and upward heavens. There are other master beings besides him.

March 31

THOUGHT FOR THE DAY - You are a Portal Walker, one who is learning to travel between Heaven and Earth at will. When you have completed your supernatural education, you become a Master, a god of the heavens. You are divinity in the making.

THE MOST IMPORTANT SPIRIT BEING ON EARTH

The most important Spirit Being is you! Why? You can't do anything about those about you, other than give advice and offer assistance. Due to the gift of free will choice, each Spirit Being, in partnership with the human mind, is responsible for his own accomplishments and well being. You alone must stand before the Throne of Judgment when earth life is over and give account for either passing or failing in your life mission.

Earth is a graduate school for Light Beings, other than the masters who are on earth on missions. The Keepers of the Four Corners of Earth are Master Light Beings. You are a spirit being traveling Earth in a human form. You are either here for education, or on a mission. If you are a student, all the triumphs and lows in your life are lessons.

Your student purpose on earth is to become an enlightened, perfected, resurrected one. Christ was an enlightened, perfected, resurrected one. He rose from his dead body and returned to it after death. Buddha sat beneath a tree and pursued enlightenment till he attained. He was an enlightened one, a perfected one, a resurrected one. If you have chosen to follow a spiritual path, you are on your way to becoming a spiritually enlightened, perfected, and resurrected one. Resurrection comes with learning. You can't become a chef, without first opening a cook book. You can't become an enlightened, perfected, and resurrected one without first mastering your earth life studies.

You are the most important Spirit Being on Earth. It is your duty to show respect for yourself, seek enlightenment, perfect yourself, and become a mature Master of the inner and upper heavens, as well as the universe. You are a Portal Walker, one who is learning to travel between Heaven and Earth at will. When you have completed your supernatural education, you become a Master, a god of the heavens. You are divinity in the making.

I, Jo Hammers the Mystic, am a Spirit Being, traveling for this lifetime in a human form. In the upper heavens I am known as Master Barjoraven. I am a trumpeter, a keeper and sounder of words. To publish words is to sound a trumpet calling men to rise in their thinking. I am the trumpet sound calling you to rapture!

CHAPTER FOUR
APRIL

THE BOOK OF RESURRECTION

April 1

THOUGHT FOR THE DAY - We are entering a New Dispensation of Time that is beyond the New Testament Age, just as the New Testament Age was a dispensation beyond the Old Testament age. It will be an age of the 'Resurrected Ones', those who are able to step out of their human forms at will and then return and enter them again. They will be the masters of the going away and coming again.

COMMUNICATIONS WITH OUR KEEPERS

My neighbor John was telling me an interesting story about his dog understanding the English language. He had been in his garage working, when he realized he needed gas for some project. However, he couldn't find his gas can. He went inside to ask the lady of the house if she knew where it was. His little dog followed him inside. John then proceeded to tell the lady of the house that he needed the gas can. His dog immediately left the house. A minute or so later, the dog came back carrying the gas can, by its handle, in its mouth. The dog had not been trained to retrieve it, or any other object.

My point for the morning is this . . . if a dog (that doesn't speak human words) can understand (master the English language) and retrieve a gas can just by listening to a conversation; it is absolutely possible for us to master communications with our Spirit Guides/Guardians/keepers in the heavens.

It is time this morning for us to resurrect from being just human. We are intelligent, divine, spirit beings traveling in human forms. We are capable of assisting, interacting with, and communicating with our John types (guardians & keepers) in the heavens.

I am sure that my friend John gave his dog a treat for his intelligence and act of helpfulness. Our Spirit Guides/Keepers/Guardians will treat us for our efforts. What do you want from the heavens? One wants to speak with a deceased loved one. Someone else wants enlightenment. I want an angel to oversee my writings, so that they will be read two or three hundred years down the road and help someone who is struggling to discover who they really are. Not every dog wants the same flavored dog biscuit.

I, Jo Hammers the Mystic, am a Spirit Being, traveling in a human form for a lifetime on Earth. So are you! Seek to speak and know that which you think is beyond your capabilities.

April 2

THOUGHT FOR THE DAY – We may be called on to be the resurrecting hand that shakes another to an awakened state of spiritually.

WILL SOMEONE PLEASE WAKE UP WILBUR

Several years ago, I attended a small mission church in the downtown area of a large city. The small mission had a charity outreach program with extended hands to the poorest of the city, transients and street people. The Pentecostal church mission was run by a lady minister who was not afraid of anything. The downtown area just didn't seem to bother her. She slept and lived in the back of the mission, using her wages as a night nurse to pay the rent.

Twenty five people were considered to be a big congregation in her services. Non-street people were afraid to venture to the downtown location after dark. I guess what I saw in the lady minister that intrigued me to attend her services was religious determination. She knew what she was called to do, and she let nothing get in the way of what she felt she was called to do. She paid no attention to the danger that lurked on the streets and sat on her pews. Her name was Sister Norma and she was a force to deal with.

One man in her congregation was named Wilbur. He was an extremely obese man who probably weighed close to 4oo pounds. Rather than let him sit on her wobbly, fragile, antiquated, slat back pews, she provided him with an overstuffed huge recliner at the end of the front row.

Wilbur had one bad habit. He would stay awake for the song service and then doze off when the lady minister would begin to speak/preach. Then he would break out in very loud, wake the dead, snorts and snoring. The congregation was always amused, and would get distracted by his snorts and sounds. Numerous snickers would break out as she spoke.

Sister Norma, the lady minister, would lay down her bible, which she always held in one hand when speaking, and then demand, "Will someone please wake Wilbur up!"

A member of the congregation, mostly transients and street people, would rise and go shake Wilbur till he was awake. Wilbur would then stretch his 400 lbs., blink his eyes, grin, and look about to see if he had annoyed anyone. Then he would enthusiastically 'amen' Sister Norma till he dozed off again.

Just as Wilbur needed someone to awaken him, it sometimes takes the sound of the voice of another to awaken spiritually sleeping spirit beings. You may be called on to be the resurrecting hand that shakes others from their sleeping spiritual state.

April 3

THOUGHT FOR THE DAY - Masters of Enlightenment are required to leave behind road maps for seekers coming after them. The written page is a road map.

PASS IT ON

When I was growing up, we had one single mother in our neighborhood. The men looked down on her, because she worked out in the public, taking a man's place in a factory as the men put it. In their thinking, she didn't have a husband to keep her home barefoot, pregnant, and in her place. What was worse, she dared to see herself as a weekend, 'hands on' builder and owner of houses. The men were outraged that she didn't have a man telling her where to hammer her next nail, and the fact that she didn't ask them for advice.

The neighborhood's single mother was a woman who had dared to flee from a bad marriage, work, raise her child alone, save her money, own property, and become a landlord that men had to pay their rent to. Her name was Doris and she was a self made, or self resurrected woman.

When you start over penniless and against all odds, focus only on journeying upward to the top, beyond the limits that man would set for you. Like Doris, you are capable of becoming a self-made/ resurrected man or woman. (Women - don't let any man tell you that your place is at home abused, serving him, barefoot, and pregnant. Your place in life is on a mountain top, with men paying you rent. The same goes for men in abusive situations.

In your spiritual life, the story of Doris has applications. When you first begin your spiritual journey, you don't always know for sure where your new path is going to lead you. However, it has to be better than where you were. Desire and work for more.

Women ministers were looked down on in the early 1900s, as were divorcees and homosexuals. A divorced minister back then might as well have hung up his shingle. Divorce was considered taboo. So, those considered sinful outcasts had to stand tall, work hard, and step over many obstacles to become. The enlightenment seeker, straying from traditional religions, may find himself out in no man's land, only with Divine Source as his companion. Doris had her child, a hammer, and a dream.

The New Age Thinker (mystic, seer, psychic, etc.) is a

seeker. Men may scoff at them for their wacko ways of looking at things. However, the seeker will rise in spiritual awareness and become a master of his physical world, higher thought, and his inward and upward path into the heavens. The neighbor scoffer will be the one be left behind, due to his closed mind. When you rise in higher thought (spirituality) you become a resurrected one, a master. Those scoffers, who once put you down, will be paying you rent, because you have overcome and become a Doris type. The scoffer becomes he that is left behind in Dark Age thinking.

You have the capability of being a Master Spirit Being. Just as there are high school students on Earth who have chosen to go on to college, and then master degree programs, there are Spirit Beings like you that are perfectly capable of acing basic supernatural lessons (the equivalent of high school) and then move on to seek enlightenment, perfection, and master degrees.

Masters of Enlightenment are required to pass on to their followers, life path road maps. These road maps can be sermons, speeches, books, etc. This blog that I am writing is what I am passing on to those coming after me. I am responsible for sharing with at least one other light being what I know about life on earth, astral life, and the higher heavens. Masters are like pioneers. They go first, and their followers come after.

April 4

THOUGHT FOR THE DAY - The human body is like an automobile. You can get in it, or get out of it for a spell.

In dream and meditative states, Spirit Beings/Souls often climb out of their human forms and move about in the heavens.

ARE YOU A RESURRECTED ONE?

We are Spirit Beings traveling in human flesh vehicles. When we step/pop/climb from these vehicles, due to sleep dreaming, comatose state, or death of the human body . . . we resurrect or return to our source. We climb out of our human bodies and go home. We rise to live again. If we are astral travelers that have experienced the climbing from human forms many times, we have experienced multiple resurrections. Also, we have experienced multiple 'coming again' experiences as we have returned and climbed back into our human forms.

Astral Travelers, masters of resurrection, know that they are souls that never die. They realize that they, like Christ and other Masters, are the 'Resurrection and Life'. They are masters of the 'Going Away' and the 'Coming Again'. They travel back and forth between Heaven and Earth. Man has always believed in angels, but never gave any thought to the fact they were masters of the coming to earth and going away.

The human body is like an automobile. You can get in it, or get out of it for a spell. In dream and meditative states, Spirit Beings/Souls often climb out of their human forms and move about in the heavens. When it is time to return to everyday Earth living, the Spirit Being can climb back in his human flesh vehicle and continue to drive, or travel Earth life in it.

Is there a difference between souls and spirit beings within? In the higher heavens, souls are orbs of light and energy. They do not have forms that resemble human or other planets' life forms. Souls are born thru the river of life into human forms. When they choose to return home to the Astral/First Heaven, they may choose to wear a body costume that resembles the human it has just exited. Costume bodies are like paper doll dresses. A soul in costume is a spirit being. When you, a soul, dreams or astral travels, you wear a body costume like the one you leave sleeping in the bed. Those you encounter on the Astral Shore will also be traveling in costumes, instead of an orb of light.

Angels are a good example of costumed travelers. In the higher heavens they are orbs of pure light. When appearing to humans on earth, they put on costumes with (or without) wings to speak to man in a manner that he understands. Men have been conditioned to believe that angels must appear to them wearing white, halos on their heads, and have wings. Thus, orb angels of the higher heavens may choose to put on body costumes to appear to men of conditioned thinking.

April 5

THOUGHT FOR THE DAY – Young orbs/spirit beings of the heavens experience a lot of the same phenomena that human children do. Motion sickness puking is one.

ELEVATOR UP . . . . .

There are some people who just can't ride in the back seat of a car. They get deathly nauseated. I suppose it is some form of motion sickness. My father was one of those. If he wasn't driving and had the steering wheel to hold onto, he got nauseated and complained of his world spinning.

There are other people who can't ride an elevator, or sail on a boat without experiencing the same symptoms.

Have you ever ridden in a car with a preschooler who can't ride any distance without throwing up? Sometimes, they manage to wait till you get the car stopped, sometimes not! The same little spontaneous 'PUKERS' can't handle riding in boats or elevators. Motion brings out the 'puking' quirk in their physical makeup.

Standing in a slow moving, stopping and starting elevator, you happen to glance down at a stranger's child who is standing next to you in an elevator's tight box quarters. The child looks up at you with big eyes. Just as quickly, he turns and looks up at his mother. Then, he returns his big eyed, sick stare back to you. It then dawns on you what is about to happen. You try to take a quick step backwards. However, you are on the back row and there is no place to back up to. Then it happens! Rather than throw up all over his mother's shoes, he lets your new shoes have it.

There are young Spirit Beings (like the elevator child) that have been sent down portals (astral elevators) to earth for schooling. When they make their first trip down a portal, many are antsy like the elevator puking child. Master Beings sometimes accompany these young Spirit Beings as they descend to enter a human form. Just like human children, some are big eyed and are about to lose their cool.

Should you find yourself traveling up or down in a portal with a group of strangers, don't stand near the little spirit being with big eyes! The young spirit beings of the heavens have not perfected themselves yet. Astral, motion sickness puke is something you don't want to deal with. Trust me!

April 6

THOUGHT FOR THE DAY - People think that sociopaths are just killers and rapists. Not so, there are life time dark being users/rapists of social systems, church charities, food stamps, etc. Heaven is not a welfare state. It does not cater to sociopaths.

SOCIETY'S SOCIAL SYSTEM USERS

You have to believe in and experience personal resurrections, before you can experience resurrections of the Spirit Being that lives within.

I have a sister-in-law named Patsy. She was not raised in a family that attended church. So, when she discovered God and started attending church in her thirties, it was a big thing. She resurrected from a non attending church state to one of perfect attendance, plus she read the Holy Bible thru something like seven times. This is a type of personal resurrection.

Other women (or men) might start their climb out of less than desirable states in other ways. A homeless woman could take a live in position caring for someone, thus providing shelter for herself. She could go on to get a nursing degree, and move on further up in society from there. Personal resurrections start at ground zero. People think that sociopaths are just killers and rapists. Life time dark being users/rapists of systems are also sociopaths. If the shoe fits, wear it! Remaining a homeless person, a rapist of systems, or a non-religious person makes an individual automatically one who will be left behind in the catching away to all that there is. Heaven is not a welfare state. It does not cater to user sociopaths.

A welfare mom goes back to school in order to make a better life for herself and her children. Her choice pays off. She gets a good job, and then moves her family out of ghetto life. You can't become more than what you currently are, if you do not take steps to make it happen. Resurrection is taking one step and then another toward becoming.

Free will choice is given to each human on earth. You can choose to learn, rise, and become a positive addition to society, or you can choose to be a user of society. Welfare recipients are users. They have no intentions of rising for anything other than to get out of their chair and walk to the mailbox to get free money and food stamps. A person who embraces a lifetime of welfare or disability living is not a person of resurrection.

Might I further add . . . Heaven is not a welfare state! Those trying to con others out of free finances and food on earth are considered to be dark beings there. At the judgment throne they are recycled to earth (kicked out of heaven). They become part of the legion of darkness. They are not given second chances and cannot return to the heavens, because they have been given demon/devil/dark being status and have been kicked out.

Those of the resurrection are those who are taking baby steps and advanced steps toward being all they can be in earth life as well as in spiritual life. Those left behind will be the sociopath users and abusers of social systems (church charities, food stamps, welfare, disability, etc.) and those who free load on those about them. Those who are not taking baby steps to get out of the gutters of life are dark beings, or demons.

April 7

THOUGHT FOR TODAY – Read your life path signs like they are pages of a cookbook. The more attention you pay them, the quicker you will perfect yourself and master your Earth lessons.

GREASE THAT ROOSTER

Have you ever cooked or baked something in your kitchen that tasted just awful, or was so greasy it gave you indigestion? At that moment in time, you absolutely knew that you followed the recipe. However, you made the casserole or pie that, when throw out to the dogs, they wouldn't eat. I have been there and done it.

When I was just out of high school and had a place of my own, I decided I was going to bake a chicken. Everything was made from scratch back in those days. You didn't run to Wally World for one of their already baked lemon or traditional birds in a plastic carrier. As a new cook, I got out my cookbook and read the directions.

First on the list was to get out the roasting pan. Next, I was to grease the rooster well. As directed, I lathered my bird up good with shortening, plopped him into the dry pan, and popped him into the oven. After the bird had been in the oven for an hour, I re-read the recipe instructions and discovered it said to grease the roaster, not the rooster. It was supposed to have been the pan that was lathered up with shortening. Needless to say, I served up some pretty greasy chicken.

Beginning again in life is like my chicken story. You may not follow your first road path signs exactly right, but at least you are out there cooking. Each individual must take baby steps in life, letting him-self decide what life's directions/recipes mean to him. Becoming the professional chef of your future is a learning and resurrection experience. You may have a misstep now and then in the learning process. However, as you rise in knowledge, you become a perfected one who can come and go in his kitchen of life at will, no longer greasing roosters. Individuals not taking steps toward rising and mastering earth lessons are the couch potatoes, the losers/ dark ones of life.

Seeking higher thoughts, perfection, enlightenment, etc. will have its greased chicken moments. The humor of your trial and error cooking life mistakes will make you laugh later when you look down from resurrected heights. So, when you find that you have goofed up in some way, while cooking your future, don't get depressed or mad at yourself. Just laugh at your honest mistakes, and then put on your glasses and follow your spiritual path markers a little clearer in the future.

SMILE UPDATE – Today, I buy my birds already baked at Wally World. I use my kitchen cooking time to write instead. We must make choices in life. I choose to spend my time cooking and baking words to share with you. What are you cooking or baking in your earth life experience that you could share with me?

April 8

THOUGHT FOR THE DAY – Resurrection and fulfilling ones' true calling is a free will choice thing.

WALKING DEAD MEN

The Walking Dead move about you on a daily basis. They do not lay down in graves or wooden boxes. Human bodies are their caskets. For instance, a man works at a job that he hates. He is a human that is experiencing walking shut down. He has chosen not to let the light of resurrection shine on him. He ignores his call to rise and be more than what he is. He is a walking dead man.

My father said he was called to be a minister. However, he never answered his call and worked in a railroad tie yard his whole life, as a crane operator. He had night dreams that kept reminding him that he was called. Today, I understand that it was his Spirit Guide trying to get him back on the right tract or path. Instead of pursuing and being what he was called to be, he was one of the walking, emotional dead. My oldest brother, who is dead now, also said he was called to be a minister. Like my father, he never pursued his calling. He too was a walking dead man. My father and brother were not alive on the inside, because they were not fulfilling their missions on Earth. If you are called to be a carpenter, but work as a cook in a nursing home, you are one of the walking dead. There are many callings.

There are other humans who walk about as dead men. A woman, abused by her husband is a member of the walking dead. A man can be equally demeaned and emotionally abused/killed by a wife. He is one of the walking dead. Children can be put down by parents till they are dead on the inside. Being a withdrawn child is being dead. Working at a job you hate is being dead!

As mourners for the walking dead, we would like to look down into their walking grave forms and yell, "Hey you, down there in the death of despair, rise to live again and be who you are supposed to be! Climb out and run like crazy from your dark situation." Resurrection and fulfilling ones' true calling is free will choice. Either a man chooses choose to climb out of his walking hell, or he remains in his chosen state. A woman can stay in an emotionally abusive grave, or she can choose to grab her coat, hat, and purse, and walk away to rise again into the newness of life. If you are stuck sitting on a church pew because your father is the minister, you are the walking dead. To choose your own church, mosque, temple, circle, etc. to attend is a step toward inner coming forth from the grave.

Children have the right to grow up and abandon dark, abusive parents. If an adult does not visit an earth parent, there is usually a reason.

April 9

THOUGHT FOR THE DAY - Children climb up ladders and then slippery-slide down. Adults climb life ladders to enlightenment. Instead of slipping backwards/downward, they should spread their wings and fly to even greater heights.

DOWNWARD RESURRECTIONS

There are dark forces and light forces existing side by side on Earth. Our planet has Spirit Beings, inhabitants of Heaven and Hell, walking about rubbing shoulders with each other on a daily basis.

Hell's inhabitants are Spirit Beings that have crossed over to the Throne of Judgment and then been kicked out of the Astral for having embraced darkness. They join the fallen angels, who are the rulers of Hell and its many pits.

Light Beings who enter earth life and then embrace its

lifestyles of Darkness, become willful demons or devils. They then take on many personalities as they intermingle with light beings, trying to cause havoc, or assault those of the light. A pimp, who entices young girls to do his bidding, is a being who has chosen to be a Dark Being. The bully at school has chosen to be a dark being. The drug runner is a dark being who has chosen to ruin the lives of others. The sociopath who rapes and murders is a being that has chosen dark deeds.

In the Christian's Bible, it says by their fruit you will know them. In other words, you will be able to recognize dark beings and fallen angel dark beings by their actions, words, and deeds, as you rub shoulders with them on a daily basis. Giving someone the finger is a dark action. Cursing is dark words, as is the telling and writing of blood and gore stories. Singing songs that have curse words or sexual innuendos is a sign that the songster is a dark being. Slicing tires, spitting in someone's food, or shoplifting are dark deeds perpetrated by dark beings. Some shoplifting dark beings travel in human children bodies. In spite of the fact we would like to believe that all children are innocent, not all children are light beings.

Beware of those you rub shoulders with on a daily basis. If they have chosen dark ways, they are sons and daughters of Hell in the making. Light beings go inward and upwards, resurrecting upwards. Dark beings resurrect/descend downward. Hell is the name of dark beings' heaven.

April 10

THOUGHT FOR THE DAY – Anyone who remains on

social system welfare rolls longer than three months is a dark being. Light beings try to improve themselves and the world about them. Dark beings continuously try to rape the world about them.

A DARK RAPPER CONFESSES

I have a female acquaintance who has chosen to be a rapper. It is her choice. Others, interested in the music field as a vocation, might choose rock, opera, or country. As long as the music's words are not cursing/dirty, the pursuit of a career in such music is fine.

My female rapper acquaintance was raised by devout Baptist grandparents. I suggested to her that she should not embrace anything in the music world that her grandparents would not be proud of. They are light beings, steadfast, hardworking, decent people who hold to high religious principles. This woman's reply revealed her con artist, subtle dark side.

"I choose to rap dirty! My grandparents would not be proud of my choice of dirty words, so I don't rap in front of them. Rapping dirty is my preference, part of my signature in the music world. I just keep my secret world of dirty rapping hidden from my grandparents and aunt. What they don't know won't hurt them."

Dark forces know they are dark. They use their power of free will choice to spew cursing and dirty words, think dirty thoughts, and verbally abuse the ears of the unsuspecting. At the same time, they will hide their dark deeds, if necessary, from anyone they need to use. My acquaintance needs her grandparents for financial support. She takes money from them for one thing, and uses it for another. She does others the same way, raping their finances and time. Her children are a noose around her neck, preventing her from pursuing the dark career she wants to embrace. So, she needs an unsuspecting aunt to baby sit her children while she takes off on jaunts to another city to rap and embrace the dirty side of life. She is a dark being who uses and abuses the light beings in her life to get what she wants. By their fruits, ye shall know them.

The dirty rapper could turn from her ways. However, she still has a record of having turned from the light she was raised in. In her turning away, she has become a shade of gray, one who must repeat life lessons in order to prove themselves. Lazy dark beings who rape welfare systems, food banks, disability programs, family finances, etc. rarely turn and change. They like the freebees of life that they do not have to work for. Anyone who remains on social systems longer than three months is a willful dark being.

Light beings try to improve themselves and the world about them. Dark beings continuously try to rape the world about them.

April 11

THOUGHT FOR THE DAY - There is a difference between willful choice of dark ways and not fully fulfilling your earth mission or lessons

HEAVEN IS NOT A WELFARE STATE

Heaven is not a welfare state, nor inhabited by shades of gray. Either you are pure and have aced your earth missions and educational lessons, or you don't progress beyond the Throne of Judgment and enter the 2nd Heaven and above.

Shades of gray are sent back to earth for a second round of earth lessons. If they fail their second chance, they are permanently kicked out of heaven and become one of the legions of darkness (demons and devils). There is no further redemption for them.

The Astral/First Heaven is home of the Throne of Judgment. Both light beings and shades of gray arrive there after Earth life to present their personal accountings of what they accomplished in earth life. Light Beings proceed to travel upwards, beyond the throne, to the home of the soul (the Second Heaven and Upper Heavens). The shades of gray failures are either kicked out of Heaven, or are given second chances to get it right by living a second life on earth. Salvation by another will get a shade of gray to the First Heaven/Astral Shore/Throne of Judgment. It will not get them past the throne into the upper heavens.

There is a difference between sinning and not fully fulfilling your earth mission or lessons. Christ the Rescuer Master can help you turn from your sinning and get you as far as the First Heaven, the Astral Shore. However, your choice to not fulfill your earth mission or lessons is between you and those who sit on the Judgment Throne. Everyone reports in, including Christ. Everyone must stand on their own two feet and reap consequences for failed (or ignored) missions or studies. No one can hide behind the skirt/robe of another like a toddler.

Christ can rescue you, and get you to the First Heaven/Astral Shore. From there, you are on your own. All light beings must stand naked before God/Divine Source and account for their missions on Earth, as well as other planets, in-between worlds, ghost worlds, etc. Demons and devils traveling in human forms do not go to heaven. Their heaven is hell.

April 12

THOUGHT FOR THE DAY - The punishment for failing earth life missions or lessons is to be sent back to earth life for another go round, experiencing the same mission and lessons again.

JUDGE MEN BY THEIR DEEDS

An elderly neighbor asked me to take her to the Dollar Gen shopping, because she was out of a few things. I was agreeable and accompanied her. The woman put one thing in her cart and then proceeded thru the store putting small items, such as a bottle of aspirin in her high pocket, down the front of her blouse. I was surprised to discover that she was a thief. Darkness is darkness, no matter what the age of the human body! As light beings, we must be careful who we embrace and associate with.

I recall a story that a dark being dispatcher told me back in the 1960s about his assault on a firehouse of unsuspecting firemen. It was Christmas time. The firemen, who had to work Christmas Eve and Christmas Day, were taking festive dishes of holiday food in to the firehouse to share. The dark ex-dispatcher told me about putting a whole pack of chocolate laxatives in a pan of fudge he had made and took to the feast. As he told me the story, I could tell that he was reliving the pleasure he had gotten out of watching his fire buddies have the trots for the holiday weekend. He was a dark force, who had assaulted his co-workers in a subtle, unsuspecting way. Your employees, fellow students, or associate workers might be dark beings who are secretly assaulting you in such a manner. Pay attention!

Shades of Gray Light beings on Earth, who have embraced dark friends and ways of life, will resurrect/return to the Astral Shore to face judgment. Depending on their shade of darkness, they could get kicked permanently out of the heavens. The only second chances given are to light shades of gray. Their punishment/sentence is to be sent back to earth life for another go round. It is like a student being given a repeat test. Not all students/gray light beings are awarded that second repeat chance.

APRIL 13

THOUGHT FOR THE DAY– When we get drama sidetracked in Earth life, we lose our focus on climbing our own personal ladder to enlightenment/resurrection.

KICKING MYSELF

Have you ever gotten mad at yourself for not being perfect? As Spirit Beings, traveling in human forms, we would like our lessons and missions on Earth to be nice and easy to ace. We would prefer to have no bumps in the road, or birds flying over us that relieve themselves on our heads. In a perfect life situation, we would have no sickness or emotional pains. So, we beat ourselves up when we can't seem to get our acts together and get it right, or when we are wiping off bird crap.

I am currently mad at myself for getting mixed up in someone else's drama. This morning, I am suffering the fallout from being in the middle of two friends who are at war with each other. The pair are relishing in the chosen mud that they are throwing at each other in the form of words. Mouths can be nasty pig pen mud pits. If you wallow in the pig pen (nasty verbal assaults) with swine, you are going to come out mud covered. Then you have to ask yourself how you managed to get side tracked and in the pig pen drama to begin with, and off your own path. When you find yourself in someone else' mud hole, the important thing is to crawl out of the mud, shower, return to your own path, and leave the drama behind.

My two friends, a father and a daughter, are at each other's throats. The father is in his fifties and the daughter in her thirties. Both are mature adults. However, they are mouthing each other like spoiled brats. Down deep, I am sure they both have their reasons. However, they take the little things that they have done to each other and blow them all out of proportion. For awhile, they chose to share a house living situation. The father suddenly moved out. She accused him of owing her rent money. He says she sucked his finances dry and watched him walk away penniless. Since I am friends with both, I am caught in the middle. They both ring my phone and unload their grievances in my ear. Listening, more than once, to their exaggerated ramblings is wallowing in the mud with them.

So, I am mad at myself this morning for letting myself be in the middle of someone else's drama. Their pig pen isn't mine! Would you sleep on someone else's dirty sheets, eat off dirty dishes, or bathe in a tub of water after them? Of course not! Then why do we allow ourselves to wallow in other's pig pen dramas? When we get drama sidetracked, we are not focusing on climbing our own personal ladders to enlightenment.

I have psycho analyzed my participation in my friends'

drama. Now, it is time to ask myself if my two friends are light or dark beings? Did I bother to check them out before associating with them? There is a trend amongst professional women to hire a detective and check out a man before getting seriously involved. Wouldn't it also make sense to check out those whom we would take into our inner circle of close friends?

Darkness/Devils walk about on Earth in human forms, rubbing shoulders with us on a daily basis. The dark ones would love to draw you in as a spectator and then a participant in their dark wars. When you are a spectator, you are not focused on your own path. When you become a participant with darkness, you willfully become a shade of gray. So, I am mad at myself for letting myself become friends with these two dark individuals to begin with. I have discovered their dark sides, by judging their use of their tongues as vengeful, dirty swords. It is long overdue on my part to walk away from them, which is a bleaching of my tarnished shade of gray.

This is a personal resurrection moment for me, as I write this. When we choose to walk away, abandon drama, and start again, we are having a personal resurrection.

There are many hellish pits and human devils in Earth life. My two swine natured friends/ex-friends are wallowing in a pit of hell that they have created. I do not have to crawl into the mud pit and wallow with them. You do not have to crawl into a mud hole and wallow with the swine in your world!

April 14

THOUGHT FOR THE DAY – It is better to be a slow turtle in a fast paced race with hares, than to be a laughing hyena standing on the sidelines scoffing and going nowhere.

YOUR PERSONAL TRUMPET CALL

The followers of Christ think they are going to fly off into the sky somewhere in a rapture seen by human eyes. They believe their dead loved ones, buried in graves, are going to jump up out of their coffins, resurrect, and join them in the flight. I hate to disappoint them, but the rapture and the resurrection of the dead isn't going to happen that way. Spirit Beings do not die. They pop from their human forms at the point of human death. Only rotting human flesh is buried in the dirt.

Resurrections of the dead happen every day in hospitals, on highways, in the gutters of life, in war, etc. When a human form dies of natural causes, or is murdered, its Soul/Spirit Being immediately pops/climbs out of it and heads for the light of home. A soul's resurrection takes place at the point of death, not hundreds of years down the road when a trumpet sounds.

What about the trumpet sound? Isn't it supposed to happen just before the resurrection of the dead?

The trumpet sound is the voice of Master Light Beings. I am a trumpet sound. My words on paper call to you. There are others like me calling you to rapture in thought and the climbing out, or rising, from your dead spiritual state, as well as leaving your human form to Astral travel. The trumpet sound is words, whether spoken, written, or sung. I am your trumpet sound! I am calling you to rise to higher states of living, thought, and to leave your human body to 'go away' like Christ, and then 'come again' to your human form.

We are spirit beings that travel in human forms like they are automobiles. We can climb out of the vehicles to return home to the heavens/astral at will. Once we discover that we are not the human body vehicles we drive, we can exit them and go home to the heavens for a little rest and recuperation, just like human drivers get out of their cars and enter their houses to sleep at night. When we are rested, we can return to the human forms we drive, get in and tackle earth life again. We, who enter dream and meditative states and then climb from our human forms to Astral and Time travel, are the resurrected ones.

I, Jo Hammers the Mystic, am a Spirit Being, traveling for a lifetime in a human form. So are you! Awaken, rise, and be the god/goddess that you are. Christ was a master of life and death. You can also be a master of the going away and coming again. I am your trumpet sound!

April 15

THOUGHT FOR THE DAY – Friends in the heavens watch out for each other. When one friend is assigned a mission on Earth, the other stays behind and often becomes the other's spirit guide. The same thing happens between soul mates.

FRIENDS IN THE HEAVENS

In the heavens, spirit beings have friends and family just like humans do on earth. Because the upper heavens are the home of masters, angels, and perfected ones, friendships there are perfect bonds. Friends there often act as Spirit Guides for each other, when one is assigned a mission on earth to be lived in a human form.

When a spirit being from the upper heavens descend to earth on a mission, he can request help from his spirit guide/heaven friend when necessary. Naturally, that perfect friend in the heavens is going to do his best to assist and grant his pal's requests. The miracle performing being on earth, when his human form dies, is then dubbed a Saint. In the Catholic faith, parishioners can pray to the miracle working saint for help.

All the gods and masters of the upper heavens descend to earth and travel for life times in human forms. Before entering earth life, they ask a friend to act as their spirit guide. A silver cord connects the one descending with the one who guides. The cord is a communication's line between heaven and earth. The saint friend on earth has an open channel of communication with his spirit guide friend in the heavens. So, a saint definitely has the ear, or attention of his master friend in the heavens who is guiding him. He can also perform what man calls miracles when needed. He receives information from his friend in the heavens as how to accomplish the miracles needed.

At the death of a human form, the Saint friend on earth climbs out of his human form, steps into a portal of light, and returns home to the heavens. He resurrects from his human form. If you have befriended a saint (a master) on earth, you have his ear. There is the chance he will assist and help you, once he has returned to the home of the soul, because you befriended him. A saint is a perfect friend of his master spirit guide friend. You can befriend a saint. If you do, he/she will come to your assistance in the way of healing, or other needs. Not everyone is a friend of the heaven's masters. However, everyone should be.

I, Jo Hammers the Mystic, am a Spirit Being, traveling in a human form for a lifetime on Earth. On Earth, my human birth parents named me Jo Hammers. In the heavens, my name is Master Barjoraven. Christ is my friend, as are many other masters of the heavens. In the upper heavens, there are masters besides Christ who have traveled for lifetimes in human forms in all the religions of earth and other planets.

April 16

THOUGHT FOR THE DAY – In the upper heavens, there are masters besides Christ who have traveled for lifetimes in human forms in all the religions of earth and other planets. Each master has his/her followers.

AREN'T THE DEAD IN CHRIST SUPPOSED TO RISE FIRST?

In the time of disaster, the worst victims of a tornado, etc. are seen first in an emergency room. Spirit Beings enter earth life with a silver cord communications line connected to them. Sometimes these cords are damaged or severed. Those with severed cords lose all spiritual connections to their Divine Source and their memories of the Astral, upper heavens, family, friends, and their positions in the afterlife. They are dead to whom they once were, and believe themselves to be simply human. They suffer from Astral Amnesia.

The dead in Christ are severed cord beings who choose to

follow a master on earth by faith of the human mind. Their spirit being within is cut off, asleep spiritually. Christ's mission is to save/rescue those severed cord beings that follow him in faith. They cannot save themselves. Thus, the dead in Christ will rise first. He will save or rescue the severed cord being followers first, because they are unable to find their way home to the heavens otherwise. After them, he will save the damaged cords beings that have followed him. The damaged cord beings know there is a heaven, but need a little bit of help getting there. Their communications are fuzzy. Christ is a rescuer, a saver of Light Beings, not devils.

We are now living in the time of the awakening/resurrection. Spirit Beings are stepping from human forms and traveling to the heavens at will, and then returning again to them.

What about the great sinners like Hitler, rapists, and mass murderers? Do they have sleeping spirits within who will awaken?

Christ's mission is to save/rescue severed silver cord light beings. Hitler, rapists, and mass killers are dark spirit beings, the offspring of fallen angels and inhabitants of hell. When they leave their human forms, they resurrect downwards to Hell's pit, not inward and upward to the light.

There are masters on earth traveling in human forms, as well as on every planet of the universe. Christ is one Master, a rescuer or saver of severed silver cord light beings. He is also now a Spirit Guide for current day followers. There are many other Masters like Christ, with special fields they work in. I am a Master trumpeter of words.

April 17

THOUGHT FOR THE DAY - A couch is a bad choice to physically sit on when choosing to go inward and astral travel. You do not wish to share your energy or travel experience with anyone (possibly a dark soul) who might sit down next to you. If you take a dark soul with you to the light, you might find yourself facing the Throne of Judgment for compromising the security of the Heavens.

MASTERING GOING INWARD AND UPWARD

You can go inward and upward to the light of the Astral Shore three ways. One is at the death of your human body. The second is in dreams. The third is in meditative states. Rising after the death of the human body and in dreams are automatic. The third, meditative states, is learning to become a master of the 'going away and coming again' while the human form is awake.

If you decide to take an inward journey, while your body is awake, you must start by calming your human form.

Closing the eyes is the beginning. Next start at your toes and work upward stretching and relaxing all parts of your body. When you reach the head, wrinkle your forehead and then relax. Take a couple of slow deep breaths and then yawn a couple of times to free tension from your head. Now, you are ready to take an inward journey.

As you sit in a perfectly relaxed position, look with your inner eye, not your two human ones. Inwardly, see with a third eye in the center of the forehead, knowing that eye belongs to the spirit being within which is the real you. You will become aware that you are another being that dwells within your human flesh. As you concentrate on your inward Spirit Being, you will experience a popping, and then discover that you are no longer a human sitting in a chair. You are a Spirit Being that is free to levitate and fly out thru windows and upward thru ceilings.

When you reach a certain spot in flight, where you can see the Light of Home/Heaven/Astral Shore, you may be shocked to see that the entry light looks like a bright round, white star, with two rows of silver white beams radiating from its edge. (The beams of light emitting from the edge of the light portal turn two ways at once, like machinery parts. I cannot explain how the edge of the light turns clockwise and counter clockwise at the same time. It just does. It has to do with time travel forward and backwards. The Light of Home is also a time travel machine.)

Facing the star Portal of Light; walk, fly, run, float, leap, or step thru it. The experience will be like stepping thru a round elevator door. Once thru the portal door, you will find yourself on the Astral Shore or somewhere forward or backwards in time. Mastering of the portal and its three possibilities for travel will come with time. The three possibilities are travel to the Astral Shore/First Heaven, time travel backwards, or time travel forward.

When your visit to the light and beyond is over, you will automatically pop back into your human form, because your earth mission is not complete. You will also pop back, if someone enters your room, some loud noise occurs such as a car backfiring, or a knock at your human house door sounds. The rushing back into your human form may leave you exhausted. If you have been light years away in the upper heavens, you have a right to be tired from the split second return trip!

April 18

THOUGHT FOR THE DAY - If you suddenly find yourself in a group where there is a new leader who is embracing Dark Age thinking, it is best to move on. Dark Clergy will slowly poison your thoughts and the thinking of those about you.

SPIRITUAL FOOD POISONING

Have you ever been to a family dinner or restaurant, where you were served food that was so salty or vile, that you had to grab for a glass of water to wash it down? Sermons, lectures, temple lessons, and speeches are served up spiritual food for the soul. Have you ever had disgusting words served you in a church, temple, mosque, etc. that were too off the wall, prejudiced, or spicy to take in? Did you have to rise and leave your church host's table to find water elsewhere?

Spiritual food poisoning moments cause us to seek water, refreshing of the spirit elsewhere. When you outgrow children's literature, you must choose when to move on to the teen and then adult reading sections. There comes a time in human life that we outgrow our meeting places, temples, churches, mosques, etc. In order not to stunt our growth with bad food/sermons being served us, we move on to find water or the refreshing elsewhere.

Seek the promised 'Latter Rain', the end time refreshing. The latter Rain is the antidote for spiritual food poisoning. There is healing for the soul in the latter rain. The latter rain falls, man's spirit rises and abandons what he once was. A spirit being that has drank in (been bathed) in the latter rain becomes new. His damaged silver cord/spiritual connection to the heavens heals.

April 19

THOUGHT FOR THE DAY - One of darkness' greatest battle strategies is to try to capture a clergy position. There is war in the heavens, and Earth is but one battleground. Dark and light clergy battle for pulpits and the souls of men.

BIBLE TOTING DEVIL

I know a woman, whose husband claimed to be a minister, an evangelist. She was young when she married him, and a firm believer that marriage was forever in God's eyes. It was easy for the dark being minister to prey on her naiveté and convince her that he was god's gift to her. She was a Christian and wanted God's will in her life.

After marriage, he refused to work to support them. He spent all her savings, and put her to work supporting him. Every night he raped her, not giving her any choice as to whether they had relations or not. During their ten year marriage, he possibly preached 5 sermons a year. After a few years (as she matured) the young woman's blinders came off and she saw her husband for what he was. He was a rapist, one who lived off of the finances of others, and a minister impersonator who could not preach his way out of a wet paper sack. Maturing, she recognized him for the dark being he was and walked away.

Light Beings have the right to walk away from darkness, if they awaken and find themselves living with devils in the dark shadows of life. God does not join light and darkness. Furthermore, soul mates (perfect ones) only exist in the heavens. When one, of a pair of soul mates, accepts a mission on earth; the other stays in the heavens and becomes his spirit guide.

April 20

THOUGHT FOR THE DAY - Children are not taken away by social services and adopted out without reason. Usually, they have dark parents that have abused them in some manner. Not all parents are light beings.

BEAT TO DEATH WITH A HAMMER

About 2001, I lived across from a couple who had a mentally challenged daughter who was married to a man who had mental problems in other ways. The daughter had lost a couple of children to the welfare system, before marrying the guy who had mental illness problems. The two children that had been taken away from her had been neglected, not fed, and raised in knee deep filth. After marrying the man with mental problems, she continued to pop out babies. Social services kept stepping in and taking them. We will call him Ed and her Mary.

The first of the two babies by Ed was named Violet. Violet was taken within a week by social services, because of Mary's extreme history of child neglect. Mary immediately got pregnant again. In their mental craziness, they decided to run off in a beat up old pickup to Texas, so they could keep baby number four (number two by Ed). In their thinking, a Texas birth certificate was all they needed to keep baby four. Anyway, it was on a return trip with the newborn fourth baby to visit her parents that their mental illness peaked and a dark tragedy happened. A murder took place.

The father of Mary was in a wheel chair. On the day Ed and Mary arrived home from Texas, there was a male friend visiting Mary's disabled father. For some reason, Ed and Mary had placed baby number four in the lap of Mary's disabled father and went about their business. Supposedly, Mary lay down in a back room to take a nap. The father was out back somewhere.

Suddenly, Ed (the mentally ill husband) picked up a claw hammer out back and slipped in the back door of his father-in-law's house. He then beat Mary's father to death as he sat helpless in his wheelchair. He also attacked and beat the other older man with the hammer. The visitor spent weeks in critical care, but survived. The visitor was holding the infant at the time of the claw hammer attack, and was also limited to what he could do, because he was protecting the newborn infant from the blows. When the police arrived, they immediately removed the infant and placed it with social services.

I have often wondered what Mary's four children will feel, when they one day search and find that their mother was a mental case breeder of neglected and unplanned babies. Even worse, how will they feel when they discovered that their father is prison for killing their grandfather with repeated blows from a claw hammer? Children are not taken away by social services and adopted out without reason.

Little do those four little girls realize, the welfare system stepping in, taking them, and adopting them out was the first step to a better future/resurrection for them! Sometimes, we are given the opportunity to help others in their climb out of poverty, abuse, and neglect situations. Social workers are angels, although they get a bad rap sometimes. The social worker that placed the infant girl, who had survived a blood bath on the lap of a man being beaten to death, into a good home gave her a step up in life. The police man, who took her from the arms of the bloody half dead man, gave her a step up in life. The couple who was willing to adopt her, the child of two mentally deranged parents, was angels.

Before the baby Violet was taken away, I got to see and hold her a couple of times. A few months after her removal from Mary's care, and purely by accident, I ran into a couple at McDees who were telling me how happy they were to be adopting an infant girl they were toting in a carrier. The couple was seated at the table next to mine. When the very respectable woman took the baby out of her carrier, I recognized her. It was baby Violet.

I was so pleased to see that the baby girl was clean, dressed well, and adored by her prospective, new parents. The red headed adoptive mother was kind and gentle with her. The young father prayed over their burgers and fries before they ate them. I did not tell the strangers that I knew the baby, nor did I inform my white trash, mentally challenged, deranged neighbor that took a bath maybe once a month, that I had been privileged to see her. I kept my mouth shut and left Violet to enjoy her resurrection at the hands of her new light being parents who would let her grow up in respectability become all that she could be.

Heaven and Hell exist side by side on Earth. Sometimes a light being baby ends up in hellish conditions with dark being parents. Personal resurrections, for those who can't help themselves, sometimes start at the hand of another.

Adoption and a chance to grow and succeed in life is a good thing. That chance in life is a resurrection orchestrated by others.

April 21

THOUGHT FOR THE DAY - Failing students and those failing assigned missions on earth and other planets sometimes try to hide on the Astral Shore in its mists, to keep from having to appear before the Throne of judgment. The Throne of Judgment has angels who hunt down non-appearance beings. The angels are the equivalent of earth bounty hunters.

ASTRAL BOUNTY HUNTERS

The Astral Shore is where spirit beings first step out of portals from earth. It is like a huge train station or airport terminal, except there are not buildings with walls like on earth. It is more like a huge beach with a moving, fog like mist covering it. Spirit beings mill about on the misty shore, and create scenarios to hang out in, till it is their turn to appear at Judgment. The Astral Shore is the First Heaven. The Upper Heavens is home to angels, keepers, masters, spirit guides, perfected beings, etc. The Astral Shore/First Heaven is a place of arriving and leaving.

Returning home to the Astral Shore from planet Earth are light beings that have been on missions and educational assignments. Some of the student beings have aced their assignments. Some higher beings have completed their missions successfully and have returned home. The student and the higher being will make a brief appearance before the Throne of Judgment, and then move on beyond the throne and enter the upper heavens, like crossing a border.

Students who fail education assignments are recycled back to earth for repeat life lessons. Those beings failing life missions appear before the Throne of Judgment to explain their failing actions. If the higher being has failed due to embracing darkness, he will be kicked out of heaven permanently, as were the original fallen angels. So, the Astral Shore is a disembarking place for light beings and student beings who have returned home triumphant, or in disgrace.

Failing students and failure mission beings sometimes try to hide on the Astral Shore, in its mists, to keep from having to appear before the Throne of judgment. There are beings at the Throne of Judgment who are the equivalent of earth bounty hunters. Some Astral Bounty Hunter Beings pursue 'playing hooky from the throne' students. Other Astral Bounty Hunters track down the hiding 'failure light beings' in the fog mists of the Astral Shore, and in the in-between world of ghosts (those refusing to go to the light).

Keep in mind, spirit beings from other planets disembark on the Astral Shore also. Astral Bounty Hunters deal strictly with beings who have failed to make their court date at the Throne of Judgment, no matter what planet they are from. Instead of carrying guns and clubs, Astral Hunters carry a see thru, crystal, light stick that is the equivalent of a stun gun. Not only can it stun a runner into submission, it can also be used to send the runner, in a levitating manner, at dizzying speeds back to the Throne of Judgment.

So, what does this have to do with resurrection, our subject this month? It has to do with the fact that the catching away/rapture/resurrection only gets light beings back home to the Astral Shore, or First Heaven. Only the acing of lessons and life missions will get light beings beyond the Throne of Judgment and into the Second and Upper Heavens where perfection is the standard. Hooky players and shades of gray failures only return to the first Heaven or Astral Shore.

Beings from other planets travel by portals to the Astral Shore. If you visit the Astral Shore, you will undoubtedly see body form costumes that you are not used to, such as ones having four arms, two heads, or three eyes or more. Earth is not the only planet inhabited by spirit beings traveling in life forms.

April 22

THOUGHT FOR THE DAY - Earth life, at times, can feel like wallowing in a muddy pig pen. Those we are dealing with on a daily basis are some pretty nasty swine.

ASTRAL LAUNDRY TIME for MUDDY PIGS

Resurrection is like doing laundry. You are a light being, basically white, but have your moments of gray that needs a little bleaching/laundered. Earth life can present many unclean situations for you to fall into. At times, earth life can feel like we are living in a muddy pig pen, and those we are dealing with some pretty nasty swine. Dealing with nasty swine beings, we sometimes get stained.

An acquaintance of mine is a hard working woman, who holds down two jobs. She is a good mother and is always talking about the good things she is doing with her grandchildren. At the same time, she has a son, age 30, who repeatedly hangs out with the wrong crowd and is addicted to drugs. It seems that no matter how much she tries to help him (money, programs, encouragement); he willfully chooses to rejoin his dark friends in their drug infested pig pen life, after his mother manages to get him cleaned up. One female addict, in particular, lives to entice him back into his old lifestyle. A dark human attraction can be a lifetime rope around some men's necks, and the cause of gray stains on their light being garments.

Recently, my friend's drug addicted son woke up naked in the middle of a field, in the middle of nowhere. His clothing, shoes, phone, money, everything was gone. I, personally, would have considered that to be a serious wake up call. Half frozen, he managed to make it to the highway and then home. His mother signed him into a rehab program for the ump-teen time. He rewarded her by returning to drugs, as soon as he was out of rehab and he called a female addict to come pick him up.

My friend's son has freewill choice. What she doesn't understand is that it has to be his choice to clean his life up. He must willfully walk away from his dark, drug lifestyle and launder his own life's clothing. It doesn't matter how many times the mother takes her water hose to him, in an effort to clean him up, he is going to disregard her efforts and return to the drug scene. His personal resurrection won't happen permanently till he makes the decision he no longer wants to wallow in drug life mud.

My friend currently has her son in a new rehab program. The individuals running the program will diligently clean him up once more. However, it will be his choice to stay clean and pursue life as a light being, or run for the mud hole of drugs again, as soon as his mother lets her guard down.

Resurrection from a life of drug addiction can happen, but only if an addict chooses to use his power of free will choice to do so.

Some people have pig pen personalities. They don't choose good places to hang out in, nor do they choose good things, friends, jobs, spouses, or what they put into their human bodies. Pig Pen/ Gutter Living situations are chosen ways of life. Only on their death beds will they try to change. That is not because they want to. It is because they fear judgment and the afterlife.

I, personally, know that there is not death bed salvation for dark souls or light beings who have chosen to embrace darkness and its addictions. The standard of the Heavens is perfection. We, as spirit beings, enter earth life on education assignments, as well as missions. A death bed individual, two heart beats from crossing over, cannot complete whatever his life mission was. A student cannot repeat, in his crossing over moment, an ignored lifetime of uncompleted lessons.

"I am sorry!" does not cut it, when you stand before the Throne of Judgment for your deeds, and they are weighed in the balance against the standard of perfection. A being that has skipped doing his earth lessons, or performing his mission, has had his back turned to the standard.

Death bed repentant individuals willfully choose to do nothing about their dark deeds till they are suddenly two breaths from crossing over to the afterlife. They have willfully embraced darkness their whole lives, and have done nothing to clean themselves up, or walk away from their choices. If they were not on their death beds, they would run back to wallow in their many pig pen pits.

Men willfully choose back door, illegal, sociopath, drug and alcohol addicted dark lifestyles. They don't want to do the work of perfecting themselves and acing earth life. At the point of death, they want an easy fix, a way into heaven by a back door. Salvation by another is a quick easy fix in their thinking. Little do they know that saving by another will only get them to the Astral Shore or First Heaven!

The First Heaven is a disembarking place where all spirit beings report to a Throne of Judgment to give account for their life missions and educational assignments. The death bed repentant will be asked to present an account of his accomplishments, just like everyone else. He has made it to Heaven, but that does not mean he will remain there. Only the perfected are allowed beyond the Throne of Judgment to enter the upper heavens where the perfected ones, angels, keepers, masters, etc. dwell.

The Christian's prodigal son tale is a death bed repentance story type of one who had squandered his life. One must keep in mind that the Bible was written by humans. Human emotions do not want any of their human relatives or friends left behind, much less to burn in hell. So, they try to find back doors to get them into heaven, to pacify their own grief. The prodigal son story was written by one of them. Darkness is darkness. Devils are devils. Life squanderers are willful squanderers. Holy books are only as light as the one who writes them. One who promotes easy access for dark ones is a shade of gray themselves.

All light beings, traveling in human forms, must account

for their life's missions and do their own dirty laundry. They are responsible for their own perfection, or lack of it. Just like the mother above saved her son for the moment by putting him in rehab, Christ rescues and sees that lost spirit beings make it as far as the Astral Shore/First Heaven. Once they are there, they are on their own and have to do their own explaining at the throne. He has taken them to heaven with him.

Astral students, who willfully choose to ignore life lessons, are recycled to earth for a second learning experience. It is like repeating the third or fourth grade. If the student chooses the second time around to ignore his lesson assignments, he will be deemed dark and kicked out of the First Heaven, just as fallen angels once were. The same goes for those not fulfilling their life missions. The fairy tale prodigal son did not fulfill his life mission. Failure is not rewarded in the heavens.

April 23

THOUGHT FOR THE DAY – The Wise Men of the New Age Dispensation of Enlightenment, will not ride camels, as they did at the time of the birth of Jesus. They will be portal walkers and time travelers.

THE MANGER WISE MEN/ASTROLOGERS

The wise men of Bethlehem were Astrology gurus, forward thinkers who dared to follow a star. They were seers/psychics/mystics/master spirit beings, traveling in human forms. They had fully connected silver cord communication lines, and received communication from the heavens via dreams. They were Astrologers who 'Came and Went

Away" at the birth of the Master Spirit Being Jesus.

In the time of King Herod . . . wise men from the East came to Jerusalem, asking, "Where is the child who has been born king of the Jews? For we observed his star (portal) . . . Then he (Herod) sent them to Bethlehem . . . ahead of them went the star (time travel portal) . . . until it stopped over the place where the child was.

Today, we have wise men that are following a new time travel star. It leads to a New Dispensation of Time (the stepping over from the New Testament Age into the New Age of Enlightenment). Are you aware there are master beings being born into earth life right now that will usher in a New Age? Like the wise men and Christ, they will be masters of the 'going away and coming again' to their human forms. They will travel between heaven and earth at will, as well as to other planets. The Master Wise Men of the future will not ride camels. They will be time travelers.

April 24

THOUGHT FOR THE DAY – Human blood has no powers, except to be the life force of a human form, like gasoline is to an auto. Christ was not his human form's blood. He was a Spirit being that traveled in a human form vehicle named Jesus, like it was an automobile.

SAVED BY HUMAN BLOOD – OR A SPIRIT BEING?

(What about the blood of Christ? Aren't you supposed to be able to be washed clean of sin in it?)

The Master Being Christ entered earth life being born into a human form the same as you and I. His human body was fallible and succumbed to being murdered, or crucified, by human hands. At the death of his human form, his flesh entered the rotting/decaying stage as soon as the Master Spirit Being Christ stepped from it, discarding it. The life force blood died and started decaying right along with the organs and other parts of his human form. It was the Master Spirit Being traveling in the human form that rose and went away to the heavens.

Human blood has no powers, except to be the life force of a human form. I am not the human form I travel earth life in, neither are you! Our human forms are modes of transportation. We enjoy the ride in them, but we are not our human body cars. We are spirit beings, either dark or light.

Sin is a simple term covering all sorts of dark deeds, words, and thoughts. The word error is a better term. Sins/errors are the result of spirit beings using free will choice to embrace dark/evil ways. Christ was a light being. Satan who tempted him was a fallen angel, a spirit being who had embraced darkness. Lucifer/Satan was kicked out of Heaven for having embraced darkness. There is a standard of holiness/light in the heavens and all abide by it.

When human forms start to die, the spirit beings that travel in them are suddenly aware that they are going to have to face judgment for their lifetime of free will choice of deeds, words, and thoughts of darkness. Dark beings always look for an easy fix. Trying to get another, like Christ, to take the rap for them is a strategy of dark beings to find an easy way out. Death bed repentance is a ploy of dark beings.

The Master Christ is a rescuer, a saver. However, it is not

dark spirit beings that have willfully chosen darkness that is his mission to save. His mission is to save, or rescue, light spirit beings traveling in human flesh that have their communication lines damaged or severed. Those lost light beings are his mission. Christ told the dark spirit being Lucifer to get behind him.

When entering earth life, spirit beings have silver cord communication lines attached to them. The cords attach light beings to their Divine Source. There is a war in the heavens between light and dark forces. One of fallen angel's favorite war tactics is to try to sever communication lines. Some light beings' lines are damaged and others completely severed. Christ is a rescuer of fallen light being soldiers. He rescues those injured light beings that cannot save themselves.

Christ is a Master Light Being. He was sent down to live a lifetime in human flesh, and to save or rescue severed and damaged silver cord light beings. Those he came to save were light beings to begin with. He was a paramedic type. He did not come to earth to save Lucifer or dark force beings like him.

Heaven and Hell exist side by side on earth, which is a battlefield. Light beings and Dark Beings traveling in human forms rub shoulders, or war with each other, on a daily basis. There are casualties in war. Christ was like a paramedic or an ambulance driver sent down from the heavens to rescue the fallen. Christ was sent down to be a savior, but not of those of darkness.

The thief on the cross asked to be remembered in the afterlife. The Master Christ told him that they would that day be in paradise. Paradise is the Astral Shore or First

Heaven. Christ's salvation or rescuing was extended to him to get him as far as the astral shore or First Heaven. After that, he was on his own. Keep in mind that dark beings don't go to heaven after death. They go downward to their heaven which is hell. The thief had to be a lost light being that was in survival mode.

I, Jo Hammers the Mystic, am a spirit being, traveling in a human form for a lifetime on earth. So are you! We are not our human forms or the blood that courses in our human veins. We are Spirit Beings (orbs of light), when not traveling in human vehicles. Light beings do not have blood. Light is our life force. A car runs on gasoline. A human body runs on blood. A light spirit being runs on light energy. A dark spirit being runs on the energy of pain he inflicts.

April 25

THOUGHT FOR THE DAY – Masters are educated specialists in different occupational fields of the Heavens. Christ and Buddha were masters. However, they are not the only masters! Light Beings who have perfected themselves on earth are masters as well. Light Beings who have perfected themselves on other planets are also masters.

MASTERS OF THE HEAVENS

In human understanding, masters have two meanings. One type of master is the owner of human slaves, such as a plantation owner who has individuals forced to work for him that are not paid. A pimp is a modern type of slave owner in the U.S. He enslaves and owns young girls that are forced to work for him. The second type of master is one who graduates college and then goes on to get a master's degree in a specialized field.

In the Astral or Heavens, there are masters. Those masters are perfected or educated ones, who have advanced in specialized occupational fields of the heavens. They are not slave owners. The slave ownership of other beings is a characteristic of darkness. Pimps are not light beings. Masters of the heavens will have followers, not slaves. The followers are free to come and go at will.

One specialized transportation field, of Masters of the heavens, is the ability to travel in Spirit Being form between heaven and earth, and other planets. That master skill is a necessity for a rescuer, or a saver. There are light beings that get stranded on earth as well as on other planets, due to having damaged or severed silver cord communication lines. Rescue/saver masters are like special op, military commando beings that are willing to go in to the worst situations in order to bring an injured or severed cord light being home to the heavens.

Christ was a Master. He was not an owner of slaves, nor was he a pimp type master. He was a rescuer, or a saver of light beings. His followers during his lifetime on earth were beings who had damaged or severed silver cord communication lines. The damaged cord being knew that a savior was said to come to rescue them. The severed cord beings had no spiritual communication lines and just followed Jesus in faith, believing that he was who he said he was. Christ did not come to save darkness; he came to save lost and spiritually blind light beings.

A pimp is a demon of darkness. A rapist is a demon of darkness. A sociopath killer is a demon of darkness. The three would not be on Christ's list of light beings to save.

If your communication line is damaged, it is easy to be lost, not knowing your purpose or place in earth life. Occasionally, you have a fuzzy dream, but that is the limit of your spiritual encounters. You are a lost soul, who is trying to reconnect and find your way home. A Christ type master being, travelling in a human form, may come to your rescue and save you with enlightened words. The Master Christ was an orator. I am a writer.

If you are a severed communication line light being, you are spiritually blind, due to having all astral/heaven communications cut off from you. It takes a master being to convince you that heaven exists, as well as convincing you to believe in them and the afterlife by faith. The Master Christ, in his day, preached believing by faith.

In Christ's day, human minds were not as advanced in technology or higher perspectives of seeing things, as they are now. They labeled the things and people of their world according to their cultures and what they were told was correct or error. Man as a whole, did not think for himself. He believed in various supernatural gods someone else had an experience with. Also, he and the receiver of the supernatural visitation really did not know what title of the heavens to correctly label them. They labeled supernatural visitors as either: angels, gods, or devils. They had no understanding that all types of Spirit Beings of the heavens could travel in human forms.

Christ is a Master Light Being in the Heavens. There are many like him. They are specialists in various occupation fields. On earth they would be the equivalent of engineers. Christ's special expertise/field is rescuing/saving light beings that have their silver cords damaged or severed when entering earth life. He helps them find their way back home to the heavens. He is a savior of lost men, but not in the fashion that Christians have portrayed him. His mission is not to save dark beings. Dark beings traveling in human forms are devils/demons/fallen angels/etc.. Hitler was a dark being devil that traveled in human form. Drug dealers, pimps, alcoholics, addicts, murderers, rapists, con artists, church gossips, etc. are also dark beings.

The Master Christ isn't commissioned to save dark beings such as: devils, demons, fallen angels, etc. They have already been to the Throne of Judgment and been kicked out. They were once light beings, but are no more. The Master Christ is commissioned to save/rescue light beings that have lost their way, due to damaged or severed silver cord communication lines.

The trumpet is sounding! The long awaited rapture, or catching away, is happening now (as you read this) in an inward and upward experience, not a fairy tale flight off into the natural sky seen by human eyes. It takes the eyes of the Spirit within to see it. Christ was a spirit being who traveled in a human form. Your ticket to your rapture flight or catching away is within. You are not your human form!

April 26

THOUGHT FOR THE DAY - Choosing to remain in an abusive marriage is lying down in a dead grave. Depression is a dead state. Seeing no need for a spiritual path is a dead state.

LOW IN OUR GRAVES WE LAY

When individuals on earth are oblivious to the fact that they are spirit beings, they sometimes use the human mind to choose and create personal graves. They become the walking dead. Graves do not necessarily have to be designated plots of earth where tomb stones loom. The human body itself can be an earthen grave.

Depression is a dead state. Human minds, that can no longer handle situations that are going on in their day to day existence, lower themselves into mental graves that are cold and dark. They see no reason for living, so they become one of the living dead that lay in self dug, mental graves. The graves are an escape from their unwanted human life, which is all they think there is.

Seeing no need for a spiritual path is another dead state. The Spirit Being inside a human form sleeps, when the human mind ignores its need to embrace a religious persuasion. Millions of humans walk about in dead states, who have never stepped foot inside a church, temple, mosque, etc. They have chosen a grave for themselves, that of being an atheist.

Choosing to remain in an abusive marriage is lying down in a dead grave. People give a lot of excuses for staying in dead marriages year after year such as: I can't make it on my own financially. My kids aren't grown yet. He will kill me if I leave. I am not about to let his mistress have half of what I have helped work for. My church says I must remain, it is god's will. Man has free will choice to sit up in his grave, rise, climb out, and walk away.

So, low in our graves we lay waiting and hoping for an outside source to sound a trumpet and call us forth to a better life.

Where is your emotional state on the resurrection scale? Are you lying in your grave, sitting up in it, or rising from it? Self resurrection is a personal choice. When you have a head cold, no one can blow your nose for you. When you are in a grave state, no one can climb out of it for you!

April 27

Thought for the day - All gods or light beings traveling in human flesh have individual personalities and different missions. All have one thing in common. They must live by the standards of Heaven, not the sub standard rules of human thinking. Heaven's standards are strict, perfect, and embrace holiness.

EASTER SERVICE or STRIP CLUB?

Easter has come and gone. You were possibly inspired on the holy day to arise in spirit and live a more spiritual life in the coming year. You have risen from last year's dark grave existence, because you have chosen to use your power of 'free will choice' to walk a higher path.

In your new beginning, what are you going to stand for? I, personally, intend to take a stand for holiness, as part of my mission. You may choose to further religious education. Others will change jobs, throw out liquor bottles, stop smoking, go on diets, open and read holy books, etc. All resurrected gods in human flesh must choose how to pursue their new beginnings. Souls are free to use the power of free will choice to choose and embrace a new path. There are many holy paths, religious persuasions.

Why have I chosen to take a stand for holiness? I attended Easter morning services in northern Arkansas with my family who lives there. Had the Master Christ been in attendance, he would probably have gotten up and whipped one of the singers off stage, as he did the money changers out of the temple. The singer, who wore a much too short dress, sat on a high stool where she pulled one leg up and rested it on the top rung of the stool, in a strip club pose for the entire Easter musical production. I could have sworn that I was in a strip club, instead of in church for one of the holiest of services. If my friend, Christ, was in attendance, and sitting with me on one of the front rows, I am sure he got his eye full! She showed her legs to within an inch of her panty line, and her underwear crotch to those sitting in direct view. It was an open attack by darkness on light beings and all that is Christian holy. In Christ's day, she would have been labeled a whore, and stoned for.

There is war in the heavens. Earth is but one battlefield. The seductive, inappropriately dressed singer was a warrior of darkness. Also, I have my concerns about the pastor. He made no effort to remove her from the church's stage.

I, Jo Hammers the Mystic, am a light being traveling for a lifetime in a human form. I am a trumpeter of words, calling men to rise and claim their positions as light beings. I now have chosen to take on an extra mission, to be a trumpeter calling human men and women to stand up for holiness.

April 28

THOUGHT FOR THE DAY - The pouring sands of time,

in the hour glass of the New Testament Age, is ceasing. The sands in the hour glass have dwindled to a few grains. A New Dispensation of time is now beginning. Have you resurrected in spirit to see its great sign, the catching away within?

STANDARDS OF 'HOLY'

It does not matter what religious persuasion you choose, there should be a standard of holy (what is, and what is not acceptable when approaching your chosen religion's deity). Cultures are different, and the standards for religions will vary in some ways. The important thing is that the follower is true to his religion's standards. You, as a spirit being, will be held accountable for your adherence to your chosen religion's standards.

Many try to defy standards and see just how far they can go (stretching their religion's standards) without being kicked out by their chosen church, temple, circle, mosque, etc. Those who stretch and defy standards, right up to the cutting edge point of breaking them, are those who secretly desire the dark side. Those individuals can be demons infiltrating a religion, or light beings who have turned to shades of dark gray in their abandonment of light being ways, or standards. Dark Spirit Beings, traveling in human forms, have a goal in churches, temples, mosques, etc. They are out to destroy, defy, and dirty 'All that is Holy'.

EXAMPLE . . . There is a branch of Pentecostals who believe that women cannot wear any item of clothing pertaining to a man, such as a pair of pants or jeans because of its zipper. It is their standard. The women are supposed to wear skirts or dresses. Some of the women's choice of skirts is the walking up to the edge of their standards to see how close they can get to sinning without doing it. Denim skirts, with the zipper up the front, is a good example of Holiness Pentecostal women defying their dress standard code. The blue denim zippered skirts have the opening and the zipper in the front, just like men have for a reason in their jeans. The zippers are as close as those women can get to sinning, without doing it. They are walking a fine dividing line between darkness and light.

I do not feel there is anything wrong with women wearing jeans. However, it is wrong for Pentecostal women to do so, because it is their religious standard. Each religious persuasion will have its standards, and those will be influenced by the culture of the area and their religious leaders' interpretations of their holy scriptures.

If you embrace a religion and its standard of holiness, you are responsible to God/Divine Source/Etc. for keeping it. It falls under the headings of faithfulness and integrity.

April 29

THOUGHT FOR THE DAY - Christ had a forerunner, John the Baptist. There have been several forerunners, like him, for the New Age Dispensation. They have left their human bodies, traveled to the light, and then were told to return to their dead bodies that it was not their time yet.

FORERUNNERS OF A NEW DISPENSATION OF TIME

Well, Easter is over and all the hype and holiday excitement has hopped away like rabbits. Your tomb house is empty. Visiting angel and non-angel guests have flown away. Wilted lilies are in the trash can, along with the colored eggs and leftovers from the dining table. What now?

"What now?" is probably what the disciples asked after Christ arose from the dead and then ascended. In the New Testament Age, they chose to establish a church throughout the world. We are now entering a new dispensation of time. New Masters are walking the earth, and the New Testament Age is ending as you read this. Men are being called to rapture; a catching away between the Old (New Testament Age) and the New Age Dispensation coming in or down.

Christ had a forerunner, John the Baptist. There have been several forerunners for the new age dispensation. They have left their human bodies, traveled to the light, and then were told to return to their dead bodies that it was not their time yet.

The rapture or catching away, longed for by Christians, is a travel experience that starts inside the human form, not out in the sky that human eyes scan. Beings must learn to travel between heaven and earth at will, like a baby learning to walk. A baby doesn't just take off walking in just one direction. If he does, he is going to walk smack into the wall or coffee table, over and over and over. A baby must learn to walk in all directions, and backwards eventually. After you master the going away and coming again to your earth body, you must learn to travel backward and forwards in time, and to other planets. You have only just begun.

Being 'caught away', or traveling to the Astral Shore/First Heaven is a minor experience, like a child being able to walk alone for the first time into a convenience store to buy a soda or candy bar. There is so much more available to those who master the 'going away and coming again'. For instance, the red planet of Mars is inhabited by (invisible to human eyes) red fog like orb beings. Traveling to other planets, Masters are able to interact with other unusual beings and creatures. Masters also will time travel backwards and forward.

April 30

THOUGHT FOR THE DAY - Some people attend church, mosque, temple, etc. strictly for its social programs. They are the spiritually asleep couch potatoes sitting on the pews of the world's religions.

THE COUCH POTATO'S TRUMPET SOUND

Have you heard someone say, concerning some extreme, obnoxious noise, "It was so loud, that it could have raised the dead!"?

When it comes to spiritual couch potatoes, it takes a major, catastrophic, loud call for them to rise from their sleeping positions on pews. They are used to ignoring all that is going on about them. They can sleep thru a hundred voice choir, a fire and brimstone yelling evangelist, and every type of altar call given. They even go so far as to snore.

In Springfield, Missouri a few years ago, a gas line to a house water heater blew up. The disaster leveled the house, destroyed neighbor properties for a block, and knocked out house windows for many blocks around. It was so loud and powerful, that the house I was sleeping in, at least ten to twelve blocks away, shook on its foundation. I thought the city had been bombed. I sprang from my bed and ran in a panic for my front door, as did a male guest sleeping in another room. We then joined frightened neighbors out in the middle of the street trying to make sense of what had just happened. Huge green clouds of smoke and debris were floating over head.

Anyway, one of my neighbors at that time was a couch potato. He was the last one to exit his house.

In true characteristic form for a couch potato, he rubbed his eyes and asked, "Did I miss something?"

At the time, I just shook my head in disbelief. His house had rocked on its foundation, the same as mine, not to mention the bombing noise that could have been heard by a deaf man.

What kind of supernatural noise will it take to wake a spiritually dead couch potato?

Some people attend church, mosque, temple, etc. strictly for its social programs; others to be seen in their Sabbath best. Some had ministers or rabbi for fathers, so they can't disrespect them and not show up. Others go because they have nothing else to do on Sunday, the golf course being closed for the season. I think the term 'pew couch potato' describes them. They are the spiritually asleep of the world's religions. They are oblivious to the possibility that the rapture, resurrection, or catching away to higher thought and inward realms is taking place as they snore.

There are Master Beings (Trumpeters), traveling the earth in human forms. They are sounding the trumpet call to come up higher, or resurrect. I am a Master Trumpeter, a sounder of words calling men to rise in their thinking. Those who hear me discover how to master the 'going away and coming again'. They learn how to lay their human forms down, and rise as spirit beings to explore the heavens and then return to their human forms. I am your trumpet sound. Are you a spiritually dead couch potato? Will you be left behind?

CHAPTER FIVE
MAY

THE BOOK OF "OUT OF BODY" EXPERINCES

May 1

THOUGHT FOR THE DAY - Like a child learning to use a cell or land line phone, you may have to learn to dial astral 911 as a first 'Earth to Heaven' connection learning experience. Go inward and picture your emergency, astral 911 operator/helper in the center of your forehead, where your third eye communications line is connected. Then yell "help," which is the same as dialing 911 on an earth land line phone.

TALKING TO THE DEAD

When you call a number on your cell phone it is just a matter of seconds till you are wirelessly connected to your wife or kids at home, who are also on cells. The calls travel the air waves using a code of number signals/vibrations. Those who have crossed over to their eternal home are just as easily accessible. The same air vibrations/signals exist.

Today, we can sit in front of a computer screen and talk

face to face with our family and friends at a distance. Computer screens between heaven and earth have existed since Adam and Eve's day. Dreams are the ancient cell phone viewing connection.

When dream calls come, there is no jumping from your bed to grab your pants, comb your hair, put on your makeup, or pop your denture plate in. When, 'DREAM SCREEN CALLS' come down to you, is at the discretion of those who have crossed over. You must remember that it is eternal day in the upper heavens.

Human life has cell phones to keep in touch with friends and family wherever they might be. In Astral life, there is the silver cord communications line. It is an invisible cell phone type apparatus that looks like a twisting turning rope. It is, actually, strands of vibration signals. You could stick your hand thru a silver cord connection and it would go right thru as though the cord were a ghost like form.

To access the 'phone system' between heaven and earth, you must go inward and upward to the center of the forehead where the spirit third eye exists. There is no dialing or punching in of numbers. You must picture there (with the third eye) the face of whom you want to communicate with. Like a child learning to use a cell or land line phone, you may have to learn to dial 911 first, the asking for your spirit guide's face to appear.

Just as humans are busy and sometimes don't answer their phones for various reasons, communications between you and those in the heavens will be the same. If the person you are trying to reach has reincarnated and has entered earth or other planet life in the form of a baby, you will not get an answer or a return call. If your spirit guide is extremely busy, you may be put on hold, especially if he has a communication that is more important. Sometimes, a spirit guide will send you a dream scenario return call in the night, as soon as he can get to it. Christ is a Master Guide. Think of all his followers and their many requests. He is an extremely busy spirit guide. Emergency calls are answered first. Your spirit guide master, or a fill in, may have a million emergency requests in a day. If you are asking him for funds to buy a new dress, when you have 30 perfectly good ones in your closet, you are on the bottom of his return calls priority list.

Be respectful when you use your silver cord communications line. Give your spirit guide time to work out communications between you and the deceased person you wish to speak with.

May 2

THOUGHT FOR THE DAY - There is war in the heavens between forces of light and dark. Dream communications are sent down in code to keep dark forces from intercepting crucial communications between Heaven and light being forces on earth that are traveling in human forms.

PHONING THOSE IN THE HEAVENS

Close your human eyes and then go inward and upward to the center of your forehead. Picture there the face of the deceased person, master, guide, angel, etc. that you wish to communicate with. When their face pops up, be quick to say what you want to say, as thought you were leaving a message on a cell phone or land line answering machine. Tell them in brief words what you are calling about. Then, ask them to return your call at their convenience. When your guide, or crossed over loved one's face pops out of the third eye position, open your human eyes and go about your business for the day, or to sleep if it is your night. Your call has ended for the present; you have left a message on heaven's answering 'machine'.

If you are not used to speaking with the dead (as humans refer to those who have crossed over) your answer will probably come down to you in the form of a dream scenario which you will have to decode. It may be the same night, or two or three weeks depending where you stand on their priority list.

(There is war in the heavens between forces of light and dark. Dreams are sent down in code to keep dark forces from intercepting crucial communications. No one can interpret your dream messages for you. You must take each item and word in your dream and assign it a code, what that item or word means to you.) Putting the word meanings together, you will decode your dream.

As you practice your between world communications, you will get faster and more experienced at it. If you have not become acquainted with your spirit guide yet, choose a master being and picture their face when beginning communications. A recently crossed over nun, priest, llama, rabbi, minister, choir director, Sabbath school teacher, etc. would be a good guide to start with. They will not have so many followers wanting their attention (tying up their astral cell phone lines.) You are basically a beginner, a preschooler in the communications department. Don't get frustrated.

May 3

THOUGHT FOR THE DAY – The Astral Shore/First Heaven is but a place of arriving and departure of Spirit Beings taking soul flights.

OUT OF BODY TRAVELING EXPERIENCES

Men have been conditioned with the idea that they can go to heaven when they die. At the same time, they have not been conditioned that they can travel to New York City, London, or Sidney, Australia when they die, or to other planets, in-between worlds, and other universes. Men have embraced certain ideas they feel are set in stone.

As man learns to exit his human form, he seems to want to focus only on going to heaven, and avoiding Hell. He wants to recline on clouds, visit with deceased relatives, and sit like a slave at a dictator master's feet forever. There is so much more to the heavens, its perfected masters, and the heaven's transportation system known as 'Soul Travel'.

A soul/spirit being on Earth can enter his portal of light at will, and then travel to the in-between worlds where ghosts dwell. Some of his deceased relatives he will find there. He can also travel forward and backwards in time like stepping into movies. He can also travel to other planets, as well as other countries and cities of his own planet, Earth. Heaven (First Heaven) is a destination, but not the only destination. The First Heaven is but a place of arrivals and departures, an airport or bus station waiting room of sorts. There are upper heavens, but only the perfected enter there.

Traveling to the Astral Shore /First Heaven is like taking a portal taxi to the bus depot. Once there, you watch other souls come and go, till it is your turn for departure to another planet or other destination. Earth men have just one goal, to reach heaven. Sitting on a bus bench for eternity would be the same as being astral homeless. True travel experiences come to those boarding the bus. The Astral Shore/First Heaven is but a place of arriving and departure of beings taking soul flights. You either take your flight, or miss it. The Astral Shore has its minor attractions, like going to the candy or pop machine. At the same time, danger lurks there. The Astral Shore is where souls return to the heavens for judgment. Light Beings (who have turned from the light and are awaiting judgment on the shore) are the pimp, thief, and pervert types found in Earth bus stations.

When you do manage to take your first soul flight/out of body experience, don't limit your thinking. Heaven is more than just a waiting room.

Masters like Christ live in the third heaven and above. If you want to sit at Christ's feet, you are going to have to perfect yourself. Otherwise, you are going to find yourself sitting on a bus bench on the Astral Shore watching perfected souls take higher flights.

May 4

THOUGHT FOR THE DAY - You have to breathe deep in order to levitate, the prelude to 'Time Travel' flight.

TIME TRAVELING CHILD

I time traveled for the first time when I was elementary school age, possibly eight or nine. I fell asleep, and then realized I was awake and in a farm setting where a group of pilgrim dressed men and women was chasing me with primitive wooden sickles, farm rakes, and hoes. In order to escape them, I started to breathe as deeply as I could. With each inhaled deep breath I began to levitate in a prone position. I rose in the air till I was out of their reach. Then, I traveled with lightning speed back into my sleeping form and woke up. I had traveled back in time to the days of the witch hunts.

I was a child who was raised in the heart of a large city. My family only left the city once a year and that was to travel fifty miles to visit my grandmother. I knew nothing about farm implements or tools. What I was familiar with was city life and the weekend comic papers. In the dream soul flight, I knew what the farmers threatening tools were. I also knew they intended to kill me, for being a witch in their thinking.

I never told my parents about the experience, for fear of them branding me as a child of the devil. My parents were extremely religious and held tightly to the belief that all religious experiences, not Pentecostal in origin, were of the devil. I wanted to be seen as good, not bad in their eyes. So, my being able to astral travel and time travel was never spoken of by me. I feared being branded demon possessed by them. Do you really know your child, the spirit being that he or she really is?

As an adult, I know that my human form does not have to be asleep to astral or time travel. It just has to be in a deep relaxed state of meditation. Relaxing, and breathing 'deep and slowly', is the prelude to 'TIME TRAVEL' flight.

May 5

THOUGHT FOR THE DAY – Messages from Heaven do not come down to dark beings. Their messages come up from their heaven, which is Hell. If a dark being receives a message thru a psychic, it comes from a dark being like them-self; one who is connected to the dark side.

PRISON PSYCHICS CROSSING YOUR PATH

People ask me the same question when it comes to psychics, seers, mediums, etc. They want to know how to tell if they are fakes or real. The answer, both the fakes and the real are real. It is their source that makes them so. There are standards of light and dark in the heavens, the between worlds, as well as the universe. The universal standards distinguish whether psychics are fake, dark psychics, or light, real psychics.

Those on missions from the higher heavens, working as earth mediums, psychics, seers, etc. will not read for darkness (dark beings), nor will they display the characteristics of dark beings. Messages from Heaven do not come down to dark beings. Dark soul's messages come from their heaven, which is hell. If they get messages from a psychic, it comes from a dark being like them-self.

For instance: A man is in jail for beating his wife and kids to death, murdering his neighbor, conning the business world, rape, terrorism, etc. Those are deeds a dark being/demon in human flesh would do. A light being would not be carrying messages from Heaven to him. Demons/devils/dark beings are not on the rescue list of the Masters of Heaven. They are not light beings, or citizens of the heavens. Children who kill kittens and birds for the fun of it are dark beings, as are child bullies.

Messages from Heaven do not come down to dark adult beings or dark children. Their messages come up from their heaven, which is hell. If they get messages from a psychic, it comes from a dark being like them-self.

There are church programs where groups go to prisons with the intent of saving lost souls. There is a difference between a lost soul light being and a devil. I have discussed in previous blogs how light beings sometimes gets their communication cords cut when entering earth life. Thus they are lost. Salvation/Rescue is for them. A psychic who chooses to read for the dark demons and devils in prisons, jails, etc. are dark themselves. Light does not embrace darkness.

Church groups who embrace dark, incarcerated beings are drawing hell to them. You mess with fire; you are going to get burnt! Individuals in prison are there for breaking the standards of right living in society. They are demons/devils/citizens of Hell. Those who read for them are citizens of Hell.

May 6

THOUGHT FOR THE DAY – Soul travel happens when human bodies sleep or they are in a state of meditation.

EXITING YOUR BODY TO SOUL TRAVEL

Have you ever sat up in a dream, looked down at your human body, and then climbed out of it to suddenly float upwards towards your ceiling and then out a window or door? That is the beginning experience of soul travel.

What you think is a dream, is an actual experience. More advanced travelers (MASTERS) can sit down in a chair in meditation and have the experience at will.

As soul travelers, it is a two way street/journey. Because we, as spirit beings, are on earth pursuing life missions and education, we cannot just soul travel to foreign destinations in the astral and remain there. We are on holiday, you might say. Sooner or later we have to return to our (sometimes mundane) lives on planet Earth.

Traveling earth in human forms is sort of like astronauts wearing space suits. Human bodies somewhat limit our mobility as soul travelers. However, they are the auto/vehicle that Divine Source has designed for us to move about in Earth's atmosphere. Returning to the Astral, our home atmosphere, we discard them. When out of human form space suits, we souls are free to soul travel.

Soul travel happens when human bodies sleep or are in a state of meditation. When the shut down sleeping or meditative state of the human form occurs, it is safe for the soul to climb out and return home to the Astral Shore/ First Heaven or elsewhere for little adventurous jaunts.

May 7

THOUGHT FOR THE DAY – The Divine side of us longs to be the gods we are, and pursue the things adult gods do, such as Time and Astral Travel.

MAN IS BOTH ANIMAL AND DIVINE

We humans are both animal and 'Divine Being'. As humans, thinking with the human brain, we tackle life with a survivalist mentality, one day at a time seeking food, shelter, etc. The Divine side of us longs to be the gods we are, and pursue the things adult gods do, such as Astral Travel.

I am writing this blog as a human, using everyday objects to do so, such as a computer and eye glasses on the end of my human animal nose. The god side of me has its own intelligence, as well as its own costumed body, hands, eyes, etc. A human walks on two legs. A god floats, levitates, flies, etc.

When the human body is awake, the human brain dominates and sets the course for its daily grind on Earth. When the human body sleeps or meditates, the god within awakens and dominates. Some humans willingly let their spiritual sides become the dominate force in their lives. They become mystics, psychics, seers, astrologers, monks, priests, nuns, ministers, spiritual writers, etc.

You might say in explainable, simple terms, that we inhabitants of earth are mixed, or half breeds. We are not purely human, nor are we purely god. We are gods traveling in human flesh, like a baby Kangaroo would travel in its mother's pouch. The mother Kangaroo is the transportation. The baby is the riding god. The human body, like the Kangaroo mother, is transportation. The spirit being traveling in human flesh is the god.

Earth transportation (human bodies) break down, and their engines die like automobiles. Dead human transportation bodies, like old autos, are sent to cemetery junk yards. Only the god within, that is driving the vehicle, is eternal. The god climbs out and moves on. If the mother Kangaroo should mysteriously die, it is the baby god Kangaroo that can climb from her dead form and move on.

When we discover that we are half god, we come into our divinity. At that point, we start to astral and time travel. If you are flying in your sleep, your god side is awake and exiting your human body at night.

May 8

THOUGHT FOR THE DAY - When you astral, or time travel, you exit your human form and leave it in a sleeping/numb/paralyzed state. When you return from your dream/meditative night adventures, you reenter your body and sometimes have to force it to wake up.

'I CAN'T WAKE MY BODY UP' DREAM STATE

Have you ever been asleep and realize that your body is in a 'NUMB' condition that you can't move? No matter how hard you try, you can't get your arm, hand, leg, or foot to move. You seem to be in a state of paralysis. After much trying, and efforts to tell your body to wake up, you manage to get a hand or a toe move. Slowly, the rest of your body starts to respond and then you awaken from your sleep. You have just reentered your body after astral traveling. The numb state is a common re-entry experience on earth.

When you return from your night adventures, you re-enter your body and sometimes have to force it to wake up. It is sort of like getting in a cold automobile in the winter time that has a weak battery. You have to crank the engine a few times before you can get its mechanical parts to turn over. Sometimes, you have to crank the engine of the human body to get it moving. Just as it takes a driver to get the auto's engine running, it takes the re-entry cranking of a soul driver to get the human body running again.

If you have had the above experience, you have had an out of the body experience and a re-entry into earth life one. Whatever you were experiencing before trying to awaken your body, was actual Astral Travel, Time Travel, In-between Worlds Travel, Planetary Travel, etc.

May 9

THOUGHT FOR THE DAY - When a spirit being exits his human form to astral or time travel, his human form slips into a numb state, like gums that have been numbed by a dentist.

PARALYZED NUMB IN DREAM STATE

This is a continuance of my last blog concerning the paralyzed state of human bodies when spirit beings are re-entering and waking them up.

I have a brother, who has all his dental work done without any numbing substance given him like Novocain in the gums. I cringe every time he tells me he is going to the dentist. Just the thought of getting a cavity drilled and filled without a numbing agent gives me the willies. I think he likes to tell me all about it, just to see me tense up and groan in reaction.

When a spirit being exits his human form to astral or time travel, his human form slips into a numb state as though it is tooth gums that have been numbed with Novocain. The body is in a very relaxed state, one that is numb or paralyzed. Sometimes, when a spirit being reenters its human body, it takes a few moments for the numbing sense to wear off, just as a numbing agent must wear off that was injected by a dentist in gums. Beings with no understanding of their ability to exit or re-enter their human forms, get frightened. All they know is that they are intent on waking their human bodies up.

If you have had the above experience, you (as a spirit being) have left your human form to astral or time travel. Before re-entering your human form, you assume you are dreaming. Perhaps, you visited deceased relatives or friends. Maybe, you traveled backwards or forwards in time to your childhood home, school, or church. Whatever your sleep state scenario was, it was an out of body experience that you labeled a dream.

May 10

THOUGHT FOR THE DAY – Spirit beings that enter earth life (with fully functioning silver cord communication lines) become earth's psychics, mediums, seers, etc.

WHO ARE PSYCHICS AND SEERS?

Some people tell me they never dream. Others dream, but can't remember them. Then there are the ones who dream, always remember, and see their dreams as guidance and visits from those beyond this life. Whether or not we remember our dreams has to do with whether we have our silver cord communication line to the heavens intact, damaged, or severed.

A person with a fully intact silver cord knows who he or she is in the grand scheme of things, both on earth and in the heavens. They enter dream and meditative portals at will and travel the universe and in-between worlds. They are psychics, mediums, seers, etc.

Damaged silver cord individuals are fuzzy in their attempts at communication with and soul travel to the heavens. As their cords start to heal, they start to dream travel, but don't necessarily understand what they are experiencing. They may also have a hard time remembering their dreams. As healing takes place in their silver cord, they become more aware of their status as a connected being of the heavens. They are the ones who need psychic healers, just as human bodies with broken bones need medical healers.

Severed silver cord beings have absolutely no communications available to them from the heavens, due to their cord being cut in to. If you accidentally cut a lamp cord into, the lamp will not light up. If you sever the silver communications cord of a Light Being, their communications with the heavens cease to be. They have no dreams, visions, etc. They have to 'believe by faith' that Divine Source, the heavens, the astral, angels, spirit guides, time travel, astral travel, ghost worlds, etc. exist.

You can judge the condition of your silver cord communications line by the above. Only the fully intact and damaged cord beings are able to exit their human forms while they live, travel the heavens in dream states, and then return to them and wake them up.

May 11

THOUGHT FOR THE DAY - Time Travel Portals look like round stars that have circling beams around them that resemble a series of moving pointed flower petals or saw blade teeth.

TIME TRAVEL STAR PORTALS

One of the first and easiest steps to experiencing 'out of body' travel is via interrupted sleep. The first part of your night's sleep is heavy due to human body exhaustion. The last hour or so is a 'reviving' from an exhausted state, a place that is half way between awake and asleep. That state is where the portals to the astral, the in-between worlds, and time travel are.

(Time Travel Portals look like round stars that have circling beams around them that resemble a series of moving pointed flower petals or saw blade teeth. Time Travel Portals look like round stars and have a circle of light beams around them that resemble a series of pointed flower petals or saw blade teeth. However, the petals/teeth are not physical objects. They are moving shapes of star light. When the round Time Travel star portal opens, two circles of starlight petal/teeth like beams will turn both clockwise and counter clockwise at the same time. In human thinking, when considering it, you would think it to be impossible. The turnings, two ways at once, are the controls for backwards or forward time travel.)

One way to start time traveling is to set your alarm clock for about three hours before you normally wake up. Get up, go to the bathroom, but do not drink or eat anything. After staying up an hour, return to the bed and doze off into your last short span of night sleep, which will not be deep sleep. It will be the half awake and half asleep state you will need to exit and re-enter your human form. During this time, when you suddenly find yourself walking around in what you consider to be a dream, you are out of your body. At that point, ask yourself, "Am I forward or backwards in time? Am I in the heavens, or peeping in on the life of a stranger?"

If you are walking around in your dream stark naked, you are beginning to astral travel. The spirit being within does not wear clothing unless he chooses to do so as a costume. He also does not have to wear a stark naked body costume that resembles a human. The spirit being within is actually an orb of light. If you enter an astral state and you seem to be just looking about like watching a movie, you are in an orb state. Clothing or body costumes are choices to wear when astral traveling.

I have a friend that has an interesting take on what to pack to wear on vacation. She takes her worst clothes, a set for each day that she is to be gone. At the end of each vacation day, she discards the set of clothing she is wearing in the hotel trash, thus making room in her suitcase for that day's souvenirs. When we enter the astral via dreams, we sometimes discard the day's human clothing.

Once you have mastered dream state travel, start to ask in your dream states to see deceased loved ones, masters, angels, or whoever you would like to visit in the other or in-between worlds. Eventually it will happen. Just remember that your spirit guide may need to organize the visitations. Be patient! The visits may not occur on the adventure in which you are experiencing. Usually, it will happen in future states of astral travel, providing the person has not incarnated for another lifetime on earth.

May 12

THOUGHT FOR THE DAY – Just as a dark sociopath being rapes women and children, charity rapists choose systems as their prey. They take what does not belong to them from welfare systems, food banks, church charities, friends, families, etc.

SOCIOPATH RAPISTS OF WELFARE, FOOD BANKS, AND DISABILITY SYSTEMS

Free will choice is given to each human on earth. You can choose to educate yourself, rise, and become a positive addition to society, or you can choose to be a user of society. Welfare recipients are users. They have no intentions of rising for anything other than to get out of their chair and walk to the mailbox to get free money and food stamps. A person who embraces/rapes a lifetime of welfare and disability systems is not a person of resurrection. They are not light beings.

Might I further add, Heaven is not a welfare state! Those trying to con others out of free finances and food on earth are considered to be dark beings/devils there. At the judgment throne they are recycled to earth (kicked out of heaven). They become part of the legion of darkness. They are not given second chances and cannot return to the heavens. They have been judged as demon/devil/dark being status.

Those of the resurrection are those who are taking baby steps, and advanced steps, toward being all they can be in earth life as well as in their spiritual life.

What does this have to do with our subject of astral travel? Light beings who have turned and embraced darkness (including the raping of social systems) return as far as the astral shore when their earth body dies. They wait judgment there, just like light beings returning to give account for their life missions. When you travel to the astral, you have to be aware that dark beings do lurk about there trying to cause havoc, before being permanently kicked out of heaven. Frightening people you meet in dreams are those dark ones.

For instance, on the astral shore you encounter a cousin whose human body died in the same car wreck as you. In Earth life, he/she was addicted to drugs, alcohol, and back street gambling. The cousin had abandoned his/her family and was eating in a soup kitchen daily, while trying to milk social systems for food stamps, low income housing, and free money. Every morning, your cousin stood on a corner with a cardboard sign begging, making people feel sorry enough for him/her to fork over free dollar bills. At night your cousin was a rapist of young men and women, and a thief. Working at a job was of no interest to him/her. That cousin was a devil, a dark sociopath being in life on earth. Don't expect him to be any different as he awaits judgment. If you choose to run and embrace him on the astral shore, he just might rape or try to assault you in some other form.

Do not attempt to contact deceased relatives who were dark beings, sociopaths in life. You will be sorry!

May 13

THOUGHT FOR THE DAY - Humans love to sing about flying away at the sound of a trumpet calling them to their long awaited rapture. However, no one has told them they have to go inward to catch their flight

HAVE YOU MISSED YOUR FLIGHT?

There is an old hymn that goes 'SOME GLORIOUS MORNING, WHEN MY LIFE IS OVER, I WILL FLY AWAY!' Humans love to sing about flying away at the sound of a trumpet calling them to their long awaited rapture. However, no one has told them they have to go inward to catch their flight. They think they will just automatically sprout wings and fly off into the physical sky somewhere. Their airport, named 'RAPTURE', is within.

The human body was not designed to fly, it does not have wings. It is the spirit being within a human body that is able to levitate and fly at lightning speeds wherever it wants to travel to, Flight starts with the stilling of the human body in either meditation, or sleep. The body must go to sleep in order for the spirit being to exit it for flight.

Day and Night is the dividing line between two existences. The human life form was designed to function during the day. The Spirit Being Soul within awakens and lives a separate existence during men's sleeping hours, the night. When the human form sleeps, the spirit being is free to climb out of the human body like it is a parked car in a garage. The bed is a garage for human body vehicles.

(When deceased human bodies are laid to rest in cemetery graves, they no longer have spirit beings in them. The Christian's believe that the 'dead in Christ shall rise first'. Bodies without souls in them are a waste of time to call forth. You have to remember that the Bible was written by archaic humans. Humans don't always get it right!)

Spirit Beings exit their human forms nightly and go about their business in the many realms of spirit. They return to their human forms every morning, just before the human form awakens. They are like earth men who go to work in the morning and then return to their homes at the end of their work day. Spirit Beings have work to do. Overtime working hours for them is when a human form meditates or naps. The Spirit being within does not keep the same hours that a human form does.

I, Jo Hammers the Mystic, am a spirit being who is traveling in a human form for a lifetime on earth. When my human vehicle is parked in its garage bed for the night, I am free to go pursue my other life and job in the heavens.

May 14

THOUGHT FOR THE DAY – When you stand up and become the god you are 'BORN TO BE', you may not get the approval of those about you. Become the god you were 'BORN TO BE' anyway.

GODS IN HUMAN FLESH

Now that we have discovered that we are spirit beings that are capable of climbing out of human forms to astral and time travel at will, it is time to look at the powers the spirit being within has other than astral flight.

When entering earth life/human forms, Divine Source bestows certain powers on each light being. The powers vary and make each incarnate an individual god in human flesh. From the beginning of time, man has believed in gods and goddesses, each displaying individual characteristics and powers. The Goddess of Love and the God of War are two. There were also gods of harvest, planting, moon, sun, water, fertility, etc. Today, masters of the heavens, who accept missions on earth in human flesh, also are god types with specific powers. My power is the written word. Yours may be composed music or cutting edge art.

I know a pleasant young woman who has two boys who have gone thru c-scouts and now are entering b-scouts. She became a scout leader, and progressed in the program along with her sons. She once told me that she was born to be a b-scout, because she absolutely loved every adventure and task they tackled. 'BORN TO BE' is the key to knowing who you are and what your specific powers on earth are. The young woman mentioned is a scout goddess of patience traveling in human flesh. You have to be a goddess of patience to deal with 12 little squirmy boys.

What are your powers on earth and in heaven? Only you know! Only you can display them. Only you know what you were born to be.

I was born to be a writer. I have loved literature and books from the time I entered first grade. We had no books at home. My religious mother thought books were sinful and a waste of time. She held to the idea that women were born to keep house, raise children, and nothing more. Until I entered junior high, I owned one little Golden Book titled 'Little Lulu'. I slipped around and purchased it with my lunch money on the way to school one morning. I had to keep my secret purchase hidden.

It is okay if you discover who you are born to be later than others. You can't help the limiting circumstances that control you during certain periods of your journey on

Earth, particularly childhood. The important thing is that you pursue your mission and use your powers once you discover them. Purchasing a secret book was my first step to becoming. After graduating high school and getting my first job, I started purchasing books. My mother did not approve. You may not get the childhood or adult approval of those about you. However, take steps and be who you were 'BORN TO BE'.

I knew at the age of ten that I would write a book someday. I was 'BORN TO BE' a writer.

On earth, a doctor is a god in the emergency room. A fireman is a god when he rescues a human from a burning building. A Chef is a god when he serves a plate of food that is perfection. An artist is a creative god with a paintbrush. I am a writer god dwelling in human flesh. Words are my power.

My goal is to share what I know about the heavens with those about me who have their silver cord communication lines severed or damaged. I do not intend to return to the home of the soul without taking one lost or fallen brother light being with me. Grab hold of my metaphysical robe's tail, if you need to! On Earth, I am Jo Hammers the Mystic. (My earth parents named me Jo Hammers.) In the Heavens, I am Master Barjoraven, a trumpeter of words.

May 15

THOUGHT FOR THE DAY – There is war in the Heavens. Earth is one battlefield. Some Light Beings entering earth life are soldiers/warriors.

ASTRAL HOME SICKNESS

Once we discover that we are Master Beings traveling for a lifetime on Earth in human flesh, we begin to understand our longing for perfect families, friends, children, houses, etc. As Master Light Beings, Earth is not our true home. We are from the Second Heavens and above where perfection is the standard. We cannot have perfection or peace on earth, because earth is a battleground (not a heaven). As weary soldier types, we sometimes suffer from homesickness.

Before many of us have discovered that we are heavenly soldiers in a war with dark forces on Earth, we have attempted to find perfect mates, children, family, homes, cars, things, etc., only to be disappointed at the lack of perfection in our lives. Peace and perfection do not exist on earth. However, we as master light beings still day dream about it, and desire it. We long for perfect Earth lives and to be perfectly loved like we are in the heavens.

Marriages between light and dark beings, traveling in human flesh, produce some of the fiercest battles fought on Earth. The being you once deceived yourself into believing was your soul mate, turns out to be a demon from the darkest of pits.

If you are longing for what you cannot find this morning, realize that you are a light being soldier who is fighting a war on Earth. Just like human soldiers, you will one day return home to those who love you perfectly. Till that time comes, you must take one day at a time on Earth and do battle with the enemy. You may have to eat spiritual food you don't like, sleep in pew trenches, and buddy up with new spiritual warrior friends which could be cutting edge books on becoming. Earth is a battlefield.

May 16

THOUGHT FOR THE DAY – Light Beings do not return to the home of the soul without taking at least one severed silver cord, lost, amnesia plagued, stranded light being with them.

ASTRAL THRILL SEEKERS

When damaged and severed silver cord beings stumble upon rescue masters who tell them that they are spirit beings who can step from human forms and travel the astral at will, the being enters a carnival, thrill seeking stage in spiritual development. They climb from their bodies and astral travel the heavens just to see what they can see and what mind boggling time travel adventures they can take. They become temporary thrill seekers, like teen riders on Ferris Wheels and other fast and furious carnival rides.

Crazed adventure seeking in the astral gets old as a spirit being matures, heals, and no longer has a teen thrill seeking mentality. At that point, he steps back and returns his focus to earth and asks what his purpose for living an earth life is. Hopefully, you are beyond the thrill seeking stage. However, if you are not, it is okay. We all have had our youthful moments, the basis of who we become. First kisses are remembered, just as first trips to the astral are remembered.

In adulthood, the human mind focuses on making a living, acquiring cars, household possessions, and frivolities such as boats, motorcycles, second homes, etc. Then, the human form starts to age and the human mind says it is time to downsize, or cut back to the basics in earth life. After all, at age 70 you might as well toss your hockey stick or ballerina tutu out. The human mind is forced to face the fact that it cannot take material possessions with it to the grave. Hoarders of things struggle with the letting go.

Back in the 1990s I read an article about the Dali Llama in which he said, "I have two watches that have been given me by others. I should give one of them away, because only one is necessary." The Dali is a mature Master Being who understands that the basics are all that is necessary as we travel our earth paths. (After 20 plus years, I cannot remember what publication I read about the watches in. However, his words stuck with me.)

What is necessary to sustain human life till a Spirit Being abandons it for good? The answer is simple, water, air, food, shelter, one set of clothing, and an environment to warm and cool you. Three sets of china are useless. Ten fishing rods are over kill. 27 shirts are ridiculous, as is 57 neckties. 27 pairs of hi-heels falls on the hoarding side of life, while going barefoot is on the other. Paying storage shed fees on useless stuff that should have been gotten rid of years ago, is a hoarder's refusal to move forward on his path to its next progression, or way of living. Hoarding is turning on your life path to embrace that which is behind you, which is the turning from the light to embrace a life of hoarding darkness.

A light being knows when to let go, when to get down to the basics, when to discard his final possessions, and when to lay down his human form. When we go home to the eternal home of the soul, we can take nothing from earth life with us, except the memories of missions and educational experiences accomplished.

My goal on earth is to share what I know about the universe and the home of the soul with light beings who have had their silver cord communication lines damaged or severed when entering earth life. I do not intend to return to the home of the soul without taking one lost brother light being with me. Grab hold of the tail of my Master's robe, if you are one of them. My robe is my writings.

On Earth, I am Jo Hammers the Mystic. My Earth parents named me Jo Hammers. In the Heavens, I am addressed as Master Barjoraven. I am a light being.

May 17

THOUGHT FOR THE DAY – The physical universe is made up of planets inhabited by both dark and light beings. Earth is inhabited by both dark and light beings traveling in human forms. The First Heaven is inhabited by both light and dark beings. You must judge those you encounter on earth, in the First Heaven, and on other planets by standards of light and dark, right and wrong.

TRAVELING THE ASTRAL SAFELY

After reading my writings to this point, I feel sure that you know there are dark beings as well as light beings on earth, other planets, and on the Astral Shore. Traveling via portals must be done with common sense. Be aware of anyone displaying the characteristics of darkness. Just as you judge humans on earth to be light or dark by their words, deeds, and actions; you must also judge those you encounter in portals, on the Astral Shore, and on other planets the same way. The only place of pure perfected beings is in the upper heavens which exist above the Astral Shore.

After entering a portal, listen to what spirit beings (sharing portals with you) are saying. Watch their body language. Dark shades of gray spirits (light beings that have turned from the light) return to the heavens for judgment via portals, just as light beings return to their homes in the heavens in them. Run from anyone purposely invading your space, using foul language, or trying to touch you inappropriately. Avoid scary scenarios on the Astral Shore that have obviously been constructed by dark beings that have not been judged yet. When you reach a certain degree of perfection, and you are allowed to travel to the second heaven and above, you won't have a problem. Dark beings, or fallen angels, are not allowed past the Astral Shore.

Just as you use common sense when traveling in your city at night, you must use the same common sense when traveling portals to the Astral Shore which is not a perfected place. The Astral Shore or First Heaven is a gathering place, a returning and disembarking place for both dark and light souls.

Shades of Gray/Fallen Angels have willfully chosen to embrace darkness on earth, as well as on other planets. Before being judged and kicked out of heaven for good, they see the Astral Shore as their last chance to attack, assault, rape, etc. light forces.

Ghosts are spirit beings that refuse to return to the home of the soul, or the disembarking location known as the Astral Shore. Ghosts wander about in a parallel world that is about three feet above the surface of the Earth. Sometimes, if we see them, they appear to be floating or walking on air. Actually they are walking on the surface of their world which is about waist high to us.

If you should choose to adventure into the world of ghosts, you must judge them as light or dark ones. Remember, they are spirit beings that have left their human and other planet forms, but are refusing to go to the Astral and face judgment for various reasons. A few spirit beings are so attached to their earth families that they refuse to go home without them. They wait in the ghost world for their earth families to join them before crossing. These beings may be dark or light. However, most ghosts are running from judgment and are gray spirit beings. If you encounter ghosts that appear dirty, have rotted teeth, or have maggots crawling out of them, they are dark being ghosts. If they appear smiling or pleasant, they are light beings who have not gone to the light yet, but have chosen to be earth bound, for family or other reasons.

Your family may have deceased members that were dark, sociopath beings when alive on earth. For your own safety, you should avoid them in portals, the ghost world, and in astral life. Avoiding is a safety tool. If you are a female, you would not hang out on earth with an uncle who tries to touch you or be inappropriate with you. Astral safety comes with the same common sense. Avoid deceased loved ones who were dark beings on earth. They are still rapists and abusers. They have not been to the Throne of Judgment and kicked out of heaven yet.

May 18

THOUGHT FOR THE DAY – Some dreams are actual astral traveling adventures your spirit being takes, after it climbs out of your sleeping human form.

ASTRAL WINDOW PEEPERS

You have become comfortable with the idea that you can exit your human form when it sleeps. In dream states, you are now visiting the Astral Shore. What you used to think was crazy dreams, has taken on a new meaning to you. You now know that your dreams are actual experiences/adventures of you a spirit being after it climbs out of your human form as it sleeps. Now, it is time to learn the laws of the heavens, and not break laws on the astral shore, while visiting there.

So, what are the laws of Heaven? One law is the same as on earth. Don't infringe on other beings' privacy, which means do not be an astral window peeper! Spirit Guides and throne judges, taking breaks in their offices, are not to be disturbed. You don't peep in tents of campers from other planets, etc. Peeping is illegal. You wouldn't want a window peeper viewing your private acts on earth. Respect is respect. Astral window peeping is the breaking of the law of respect.

When I was a child in the United States, back in the 1950s and before air conditioning, people left their windows open at night for cooling purposes. Everyone did it. My father got up one night, just in his underwear, and went to the kitchen sink to get a glass of water. It was a very hot night. The window above the sink was open. When he stepped to the sink, he saw a pair of eyes looking in at him. He immediately yelled at the pair of eyes. "You are a dead man! He then grabbed a knife and headed for the back door to pursue the man." Barefoot, my father was not able to catch the peeper. However, the peeper never returned. Getting chased by a barefoot man, in his prime, banishing a butcher knife was apparently detour enough.

They say most window peepers are teens. First time astral travelers are like teens. They are there for the thrill of peeping at all they can see, with no thought as to repercussions.

If you peep in a window in the astral, you are more than likely to get chased by a being that can outrun you in his bare feet. Being chased in dreams is sometimes the result of your doing something illegal in the heavens. Consider what you were doing in your dreams before being chased.

If you find yourself being chased in your dreams, it is possibly because you have wandered in and peeped into a scenario of dark beings doing business as they were awaiting judgment. When you first start to astral travel, you don't take into consideration where you should, or should not go.

May 19

THOUGHT FOR THE DAY – Loud vibrations interrupt communication between worlds. Noise is a serious weapon of dark forces.

KNOCKS ON DREAM STATE DOORS

Have you ever made a run to answer a knock at your door, stubbed your little piggy, and ended up with a broken toe? Are they ever painful, and not much a doctor can do except to buddy tape it to the next toe. My friend Amy experienced that unique experience a couple of days ago. She caught her foot and ankle on a chair leg. This experience happens in our earth lives, as well as in our astral lives.

Sometimes, spirit beings knock on our portal doors in dreams at night. We, spirit beings, jump up out of our human bodies and fly to open our portals to see who is visiting. Before we reach our portal doors/gates, we are jolted awake from our dream state by loud sounds coming from earth life. We then fly at lightning speeds thru the spiritual realm back into our human forms. We crash and fall haphazardly back into our human forms. Thus, stubbed spiritual toes happen.

Having missed a visit in the astral with a supernatural visitor, you wake up mad on the earth realm. Dark Forces are notorious for slamming doors, blasting stereos, tooting car horns, or making a baby scream at the top of its lungs, etc. Noise is vibrations. Loud vibrations interrupt communications between worlds. Noise is a serious weapon of dark forces. Your baby wailing could have been pinched or frightened by a demon warrior of darkness. Loud, pounding, rock or other music keeps sleep and heaven/astral states away, or at bay.

Know you are under attack by dark forces when your dream states are interrupted by loud noises.

May 20

THOUGHT FOR THE DAY - There was once a friendship gate between heaven and earth. The Garden of Eden was God's garden in the heavens that he walked in during the cool of the morning. The gate between heaven and earth allowed man (Adam and Eve types) to walk thru a friendship gate between earth and heaven. Today, we call them portals.

PERSONAL GARDEN GATES OR PORTALS BETWEEN WORLDS

Most people, starting to pursue spirituality, are obsessed by either having visitations from angels, or being able to astral travel. There is so much more to life outside the human body. Walking thru a supernatural, friendship Garden Gate to visit with a master is one of them.

Years ago on earth, when a neighbor put up a fence, he put in a small walk thru gate between his and his neighbor's property. They were called 'friendship gates'. There was once a friendship gate between earth and the Second Heaven Garden of Eden (God's garden that he walked in during the cool of the morning). Adam and Eve walked in that garden till they became fallen angel types, and were kicked out of it by God to walk and labor on earth. The friendship garden gate to the Garden of Eden was closed and locked, with Adam and Eve not permitted to return thru it. They entered earth life and lived as humans in human flesh.

There exists a fence between Heaven and Earth life. In that fence are many openings that we now call portals. Each light being traveling earth in human flesh has a personal gate that can be opened and the heavens peeped into. The gate is called the 'THIRD EYE'. That 'Peeping Gate' exists in the center of the human forehead, on the inside of the human head. It is accessed/opened/unlocked by the spirit being within.

The Third Eye is a 'Peeping Gate' for brief visits with angels, masters, guides, loved ones, etc. Going inward, while the human body is awake, you can look thru the Third Eye into the heavens. Your friends or masters' faces will pop up at the gate and you can hold short brief conversations with them (just as you would do at a friendship gate on earth where you say a quick 'How are you?" and would you like to join me for coffee later).

'Third Eye' friendship gates between worlds are for brief interactions and conversations with beings in the heavens. Psychics use 'Third Eye' friendship gates to retrieve information on a regular basis.

May 21

THOUGHT FOR THE DAY - Hell is a state of being. Your family or coworkers verbally assaulting you is a state of hell. If you enter depression over it, they have managed to cast you down into hell's dark pit.

DOES HELL DANCE LITERALLY WITH FLAMES?

My father was not particularly a religious man in his 20s. My mother was and attended church regularly. One night my father dreamed that he was in Hell and that flames were lapping painfully at his feet. Taking his dream literally, my father instantly became a pew sitter with my mother and had a conversion, as he called it. Sometimes it takes fear to bring about change in a being that has not taken any interest in his spiritual side, or inner being. Fear changed him!

Men fear the supernatural, pain, strange peoples, and

anything they do not understand. Going to a place called Hell is one of those fears. Down thru the centuries, men have developed theories as to what Hell looks like. The most popular is that it is a place where fires burn forever and that there are red demons and devils with long pitch forked tails that live and breathe to torture you. Hell, down thru the centuries, has become ingrained in the minds of humans as a fire burning place of eternal torment and pain, and that only bad, sinful people went there. Leaders of religious or social groups designated what was considered sin. Wrong varied from culture to culture.

Somewhere, in the Stone Age, a damaged silver cord light being (traveling in a human form) was sent a dream message by his spirit guide. In the dream, he was told to straighten up his act up on earth, or judgment was going to fall on him. That particular being, living in primitive state, feared wild beasts and the fire he cooked his meat with. In an effort to communicate with the dense, human mind using, primitive man; his spirit guide/angel showed him a dream in which he was standing in a pit of fire and being burned painfully to a crisp like a piece of burned meat, to get his point across. The Stone Age Man gave his fire dream place a name, calling it hell. He then shared his experience with others, scaring them with his tale of a place that you could go (if you didn't live right) that would burn and roast you like a piece of meat.

Hell is actually a state of being. Being cut off from God is a state of Hell. Suffocating in a bad marriage is a state of hell. Being raped or molested is a state of hell. Being beaten is a state of hell. Being bullied or verbally assaulted is a state of hell. Being put down by your family or coworkers is a state of hell. Hell exists, but it doesn't have literal flames dancing about you. Your rapist isn't a literal flame of fire raping you. Your bully isn't red or has a pitch forked tail. Your marriage bed does not burn literally like logs in a fireplace. Hell is a state of being, like an angel that is cut off from god. In my father's case, having his face turned from anything spiritual was a state of hell. It is the state of your mind that becomes a pit of hell.

Heaven and hell exist all about you on a daily basis. Devils and light beings, traveling in human flesh, walk about you on a daily basis. Devils in human flesh are not nice, and they are out to assault you in any way they can. Their tongues are their main weapon. Their words can send you down to a pit of hurt feelings, depressed Hell. Have you ever used the expression 'HE/SHE BURNT ME'?

Dreams of hell and flames of fire dancing is a scenario warning dream from your spirit guide that is trying to get you to cease something you are doing of a dark nature on earth. Scenario dreams have to be interpreted. They are not literal. Your spirit guide could show you flames of dancing fire. Your flames of dancing fire could actually be a situation where you are being verbally abused or burnt.

May 22

THOUGHT FOR THE DAY - When you leave your body to travel on sound waves, it is like following a pied piper. You are not your own, you are part of the sound and flow.

SINGING IN THE WIND

Sound is vibrations. Music is vibrations. Humming is vibrations. Human voices project vibrations of the vocal cords. The sounds that vibrations make can be a mode of communication, if meanings are assigned to the individual sounds.

When the wind is rushing over a landscape, it produces sounds according to whatever it brushes up against. Spirit guides in the heavens can attach meanings to the sounds and send rushing winds to deliver messages. A person in a state of meditation may hear voices in the wind speaking, chanting, or singing. Spiritual ears may also hear instruments playing along with the sound of the rushing wind.

Back in the early 1900s, my grandparents lived on a farm outside of Springfield Missouri. A trip into the city was about thirteen miles, an all day journey back at that time in a wagon. One summer day, my grandmother was outside doing some farm chores. She stated that she heard the most beautiful singing coming from multiple voices in a valley beyond their farm field. She said it was excited singing. Drying her hands, she walked across their farm field to see where the singer's voices were coming from. The music was riding a rushing wind and it drew her across the field like a pied piper. When she reached the valley, she realized that the music was coming from a brush harbor, a revival meeting of a group of Christians that she had never heard of, Pentecostals.

Fascinated by the Pentecostals' singing, shouting, and speaking in tongues, she took a seat on the back row, forgetting she was dirty from doing farm chores. The Pentecostals offered something supernatural that was not available to my grandmother in the traditional Methodist, Baptist, and Catholic churches of the area. It offered her the truth that she could walk and talk with god and have supernatural experiences with a being called the Holy Ghost. My grandmother converted. Her soul awakened to who she really was. Her awakening came to call as voices carried on a rushing wind.

My grandmother held Pentecostal prayer meetings in her home till the day she died. One of her sons became a Pentecostal minister. My mother was a Pentecostal follower her whole life, and had the gift of healing. Pentecostalism is my family roots religion, although I now see a much deeper experience.

On earth, I am Jo Hammers the Mystic. In the heavens I am known as Master Barjoraven. I am a trumpeter of words, pursuing my mission on Earth of calling you to rise from your human form. I am a voice of resurrection, a trumpet calling you to rise and walk a higher spiritual path.

May 23

THOUGHT FOR THE DAY – Some messages come down from the heavens attached to the sound of rushing wind.

A MINISTER'S WIFE SOUND TRAVELS

When I was in my twenties, my husband and I would travel for seven hours on interstate 44 heading for Dallas Texas to visit a relative. On the passenger side of our vehicle, the front window didn't have proper rubber stripping around it. The wind, as we drove down the highway, would come rushing in even thought the window was rolled up.

On a regular basis, when we made the long car trip, I heard choirs of voices singing in the rushing wind that was finding its way into the car. The voices sang "Holy... Holy ... Holy...!" The voices sang in rhythm with the rushing of the wind. As I listened to the voices and incredible music, I felt inner hands inside of me lift up in holy reverence. I was sitting in a car seat as a human. At the same time, I was aware that there was a being inside of me that was lifting its hands in reverence to the voices singing "Holy". I became aware that I was two people, not one.

I never told my minister husband about the singing voices for fear he would get jealous and go into a non speaking mode. When I had a supernatural experience like the above, he would get jealous and state that he didn't understand why I got spiritual visitations and not him. He claimed it should be him that god or angels talked to, not me. He was the minister. At the time, being young, I did not realize he was demeaning me. So, I kept my mouth shut about my many supernatural experiences.

It wasn't only voices singing "Holy"... that I heard. In dreams in the night, masters and angelic men of the heavens came to me. I saw events like 'the New Jerusalem coming down'. I saw heaven's gates and predictions of future events that were coming three days down the road in my life. The predictions came on a regular basis. If I saw it in my sleep, it came to pass.

I never questioned that I was hearing choirs of voices singing holy for two and three hours as we drove down the highway on multiple occasions, or my other supernatural visitations. I did question (as I matured) his jealousy, put downs, and demeaning of me. One day I discovered my true light being status. On spiritual wings I flew away to follow and sing with those in the rushing wind. The dark being I left behind still stands in his dead silence, not hearing or seeing anything.

Dark beings try to impersonate ministers and other spiritual leaders in order to infiltrate the ranks of light beings and cause what havoc they can. If you awaken as a light being and discover that you have linked yourself unknowingly to a demeaning being of darkness, spread your spiritual wings and fly away. God does not join light and dark. He says to flee from it.

May 24

THOUGHT FOR THE DAY – Demon warriors of Darkness are not interested in assaulting beings in human forms who have already succumbed to darkness. Why would they waste their time attacking a being they already own?

DEMONS WHO GO BUMP OR HOWL IN THE NIGHT

Humans fear bumps and noises in the night. They have a right to. Some night sounds are the voices of invisible dark beings that have not taken or entered human forms yet. Just because they do not have bodies to physically slap you, they can assault you or what is yours in other ways. Light Beings are the prime targets of dark demon warriors. They are not interested in assaulting beings in human forms who have already succumbed to darkness. They already own them. The drunk in the gutter is owned by darkness, as is the addict in a flop house. Gossipers' tongues are owned by darkness, as are the eyes of a peeping Tom. Gamblers are owned by darkness, as are sociopath rapists and murderers.

Next door to where I am writing, sits a brand new house

which is a secret drug rehab house. Single, rehabbed, female drug addicts and their children are given the opportunity to live in it for six months till they get a job and get on their feet. You would think the new home would be a safe haven for someone to start over. Instead, it is under physical assault, and not by humans.

Two weeks ago, a huge limb fell and landed on the front of the house where a supposedly rehabbed female slept. The insurance man was called and the roof and guttering fixed. Less than two weeks later, another tree limb fell striking the same place over the addict's bedroom, doing the exact same damage. The owner of the rehab house thinks she has just been unlucky as a property owner. The rehabbed female thinks her ex-drug dealer is climbing the tree at night and causing the problem. Neither wants to face the fact that they have been targeted by dark forces. Dark Forces wants its female addict back.

Angels can come down to us in or out of costumed, winged forms to assist us. Devils, or Fallen Angels, can come to us in or out of costumed forms to assault us. Demons out of human form can cause branches to fall, tires to blow, things to fall from shelves, light bulbs to shatter, etc. Devils don't come to assist us, like angels of light do. Devils come to destroy, frighten, and assault.

Exact repetition of assaulting events is a sign that it is dark forces causing the havoc, not Mother Nature. Dark Forces may howl in the winds as they travel the skies above you. You may be the target, or someone else may be! Beware of howling winds.

May 25

THOUGHT FOR THE DAY - A fine dividing line fence of sorts exists between Heaven and Earth. In that fine line of separation are many friendship gates. Today, we call those gates portals.

FRIENDSHIP GATES BETWEEN WORLDS

People are obsessed with wanting visitations from angels. There is so much more in the heavens to see than just an angel. One such phenomenon is Garden Gates. They are portals between worlds, or friendship gates between the gardens of the gods in the heavens and earth.

Years ago, when a neighbor put up a fence on earth, he put in a small walk thru gate between his and his neighbor's property. They were called 'friendship gates'. There was once a friendship gate between earth life and the supernatural Garden of Eden, God's garden that he walked in the cool of the morning. It was a gate between heaven and earth. Adam and Eve walked and dwelt in that garden till they became fallen angel types, and were kicked out of it by God. The friendship garden gate to the Garden of Eden was closed and locked, with Adam and Eve not permitted to return thru it.

There exists a supernatural fence between Heaven and Earth life. In that fence are many friendship gates that we now call portals. The name for one gate is the 'THIRD EYE'. That gate or portal exists in the center of the forehead, on the inside of the human body. It is a gate for the spirit being within to use.

The Third Eye is a portal gate for visiting astral friends, angels, and masters. Going inward, even while the human body is awake, you can look (as a spirit being) thru your psychic third eye/garden gate. Your crossed over friends faces will pop up at the gate and you can hold short brief conversations with them, just as you would do at a friendship gate on earth where you say a quick "Hello" . . . 'How are you?" and "Would you like to join me for coffee".

Friendship/Third Eye gates between worlds are for brief interactions with angels, masters, deceased loved ones, etc. Psychics regularly visit individuals, via the third eye friendship gate. Sometimes, neighbors on Earth will step thru garden gates for brief visits. Astral visitors are able to step thru portal garden gates and come to us for brief visits. People refer to these visits as visitations.

Visitations are not limited to just angels. Christ, Buddha, or other masters can step thru your Third Eye garden gate for a brief visit, if they choose to do so. Catholic saints can step thru gates and visit individuals, as well as famous deceased ministers, rabbi, nuns, priests, teachers, etc. etc. You must be a friend of those in the heavens to receive such a visit. The gods don't waste their time on devils and demons in human flesh. The gods, orbs, are light beings.

May 26

THOUGHT FOR THE DAY – Successfully completing missions or education assignments on Earth is the key that unlocks the gates to the Second Heaven's 'GARDENS OF THE GODS'.

TRAVELING TO THE 'GARDEN OF THE GODS'

If you have read my writings from the beginning, you

know that the First Heaven, or Astral Shore, is a disembarking place for souls returning to the heavens. A mixture of light and shades of gray spirit beings mill about there, as well as spirit guides, travelers from other planets, etc. Shades of gray beings have limited travel privileges in the heavens. Exploring the Astral Shore is their only allowed experience.

The Throne of Judgment, on the Astral Shore, is the major gate between the First and Second Heaven. It is a gate that is accessed or unlocked for a perfected light being that has just exited a human body that has died. On returning home to the Astral, the light being presents to the throne judge/gate keeper a list of his failures and accomplishments pertaining to his Earth life assignment. Acing assignments on Earth is a key that unlocks the gate, thus allowing travel upward to the Second Heaven where the 'Gardens of the Gods are.

The Second Heaven Gardens of the Gods are front or curb gardens, which are enjoyed by Master Souls returning home after work days on Earth and other planets. The Gardens of the Gods can have form like humans are used to seeing, or have a form that a returning master wishes to see it as. For instance, the Buddha sat beneath a tree in his earth life and sought enlightenment. He may have become attached to or especially fond of that particular tree. The Buddha's garden, in the Second Heaven, might have multiple Bodha trees and monkeys swinging in them. My idea of a garden would be filled with Weeping Willow and Formosa trees. Carnations (my favorite earth flower) would grow there and blue birds would nest in my trees. Some other person might like to see and enjoy a cactus garden with Joshua trees in bloom. Just as the neighbors on your street plant their front gardens according to their tastes; so do the masters of the 'Gardens of the Gods'.

Traveling to the 'Gardens of the Gods' is a third eye gate journey that can be taken in dream and meditative states. However, only aspiring masters will be granted gate entrance to walk and talk with the Second Heaven's masters in their gardens. Ask your spirit guide to get you permission to go there in your dreams or meditative states.

If you are granted permission to visit the 'Garden of the Gods', you have been granted permission to call on heaven's royalty. Be respectful and do not ask frivolous questions about soul mates or for help in getting that big boat or deluxe stainless steel refrigerator you have been wanting. It would be more appropriate for you to ask what you can do in the grand scheme of things to advance spiritual life on planet earth. If you ask weed questions, you might just get pulled up and discarded from the garden.

May 27

THOUGHT FOR THE DAY - In the upper heavens, light beings are orbs of light. They have no need for physical structures such as gas stations, courthouses, restaurants, halls of records, or mansions, as we know them on Earth.

VISITING HALLS OF RECORDS, ETC

Human minds only understand what they are familiar with. They relate to the animals of their planet, the color of skin of its inhabitants, and the physical structures (homes, schools, courthouses, halls of records, police stations, restaurants, etc.). When they travel on Earth, they have pre conceived ideas about the types of other humans they will see, as well as what the structures on their travels will look like. When the spirit being within a human form climbs out and travels to the Astral, he enters a lap over world that is partially heaven and partially what men with preconceived ideas think heaven should be. The Astral Shore/First Heaven wears costume forms of courthouses, halls of records, restaurants, etc.)

In the upper heavens, spirit beings are orbs of light. They do not have physical bodies. Also, they do not drive down to a county court house to pay taxes, or to a gas station for fuel. They have no need for restaurants, jails, or auto body shops. Only on the Astral Shore, or First Heaven, do physical structures such as a Throne of Judgment, mansions, gates, etc. appear. The structures appear in order not to confuse damaged or severed cord light beings who are returning home, still thinking as humans.

Lately, there is a trend for astral travelers to want to go to a Hall of Records to view personal charts for information as to their purpose in Earth life, or to find out who their soul mate is. (Soul Mates are perfect and perfection does not exist on Earth. Soul mates are awarded in the upper heavens to those who have sought perfection and enlightenment on earth and other planets.) The Astral Shore/First Heaven is a lap over world between earth and heaven. The Astral wears costume structures for those having preconceived ideas of what they want to see there. The Throne of Judgment and Hall of Records are structures created for returning severed silver cord light beings who are expecting to see them, due to being told they exist (preconceived ideas on earth). Physical structures are costumes that the Astral Shore wears, just as orbs of light put on winged angel costumes to appear to men. The Astral Shore, or First Heaven, will appear as damaged and severed silver cord beings expect to see it as.

Orbs in the higher heavens have no need for physical structures as we know them on earth. They function as a light society, a place of pure energy beings.

I, Jo Hammers the Mystic, am a spirit being, traveling for a lifetime on Earth in a human form. I have three forms in which I am recognized. On Earth, I am human. When my human body sleeps, I am a costumed orb who climbs out of my human body and travels the Astral. Beyond the Throne of Judgment in the upper heavens, I remove my human form costume and am known for the orb of light I am.

Gods come down to you in the same fashion. In the upper heavens, they are master orbs of light and energy. They enter earth life in human baby costume forms. Aging, they (orbs) exit human forms, but wear costumes of their former human body. They return to the upper heavens where they remove the human body costume and once more travel and live as orbs of light and energy.

May 28

THOUGHT FOR THE DAY – Human forms cannot access/enter Spirit Being's gates or portals. Human forms are like autos that get parked in garages at night. The home (Astral Shore or First Heaven) is entered by the spirit being that gets out of the human body car and enters its door.

HUMAN CREATED PORTAL GATES

Humans try to establish friendship gates, or openings, between worlds by using the human mind and voice to try to make contact. A Wiccan, who draws a circle on the floor and then draws a star in the middle of it, is using human intelligence to try to make a portal or gate open, that he has been told about. Somewhere, down thru the centuries, a Wiccan accidentally discovered the time travel gate, which is a circle with a star. What is missing, on the Wiccan's star, are rows of beams turning two ways at once on the edge of the circle which is the traveling forward and backwards in time. The wiccans circled star on the floor is the passed down experience by a spiritual seeker of the dark ages who had a Time Travel gate experience. Followers grew up about his/her supernatural experience.

Wiccans today draw the star and try to open it, but what they don't understand is the fact that the star can only be accessed by the spirit being on the inside of the human form. It is not an outside on the ground or floor experience. Human forms cannot access Spirit Being gates or portals. The Time Travel circle star gate is for spirit beings, not human forms.

The Native Americans also have a friendship gate, or opening, between heaven and earth. It is the dream catcher. Out of fear, they have placed a web in the center of their gate to keep dreams and astral visitors out. Their gate is a closed and locked one. Somewhere backwards in time, a medicine man or woman went within and upwards, and had a supernatural experience of a hole in the heavens opening. Dark beings, on the Astral Shore/First Heaven, who were awaiting judgment, returned to earth thru the hole frightening the Native American who had the experience. Myth and legend grew up around it. Those frightened of the unknown made dream catchers using their physical minds. They saw their original being's experience as a curse and not a blessing.

Another type of created friendship gate is the gypsy's crystal ball. Once upon a time, a gypsy peasant went inward and upward and experienced looking thru his third eye. For lack of a better way to explain it to his Dark Age friends, he stated his experience was like looking thru a ball of crystal into a land where the dead talked back to him/her. Followers of his experience took it literally, and started creating crystal spheres in an effort to recreate the experience.

Man's mind tries to create what he hopes will be gates to supernatural experiences. Time travel machines are an example. However, time travel is a gate within. That gate is only accessed by the spirit being that is traveling in a human form. It is not accessed by human forms. Prayers said by human lips are also manmade gates. Only prayers said by the spirit being within are heard in the heavens. Lip prayers are only heard out in the physical world outside the human form. (If you have not been getting your prayers answered, this is possibly the reason why.)

May 29

THOUGHT FOR THE DAY - Every light being has a mandate to pass on to at least one other damaged or severed silver cord light being on earth what they know about astral travel and the heavens before they cross over or return to the home of the soul. I, Jo Hammers the Mystic, am choosing to share with more than just one! To go home empty handed would be disrespect.

COSTUMED GHOST VEHICLE

On Memorial Day weekend, I left Springfield, Missouri with my sister to visit family cemeteries north of the city. The traffic was heavy and moving at speeds above the limit. I looked at my sister and told her not to drive above the limit, because there was sure to be multiple highway patrolman set up giving tickets ahead of us. About that time, a peachy beige, non-descript semi truck and trailer passed us and pulled into our lane ahead of us and then slowed to way below the speed limit. I mentally made note that there wasn't much in the way of signs or writing on the semi or the trailer.

"He is going way below the speed limit!" my sister (who was driving) stated.

"He is definitely going slower than the traffic about us." I replied, as cars zoomed past us and the semi.

"I think I will stay behind him till we are away from the city. We can't get a ticket for speeding, if we follow him!" My sister shot back. After pausing, she then added. "God help us, we don't need a ticket!"

So, we followed the semi truck that was moving down the highway at a constant slower speed. Sure enough, not more than a mile down the highway, sat a police car with a radar gun.

My sister glanced toward the patrol car as we passed and so did I. Then we turned our attention back to the highway and the semi we were following.

In shock, my sister asked, 'Where did the truck go?"

"Where did it go?'" I asked, twisting my neck and looking all about us. There was no place for it to have turned off. The semi had just vanished. The road was flat. We could see a mile or so ahead of us. We had not passed it and it had not pulled off on the shoulder. We had experienced a supernatural encounter with a physical thing that had slowed us down and prevented us from getting a ticket.

We know that orbs of light, or light beings, (some people refer to them as angels) put on winged, or non-winged costumes to come down and make appearances to heal, aid, or speak with man at times. The semi falls in the same category. The semi truck was a costume for a supernatural being to use, in order to aid us.

May 30

THOUGHT FOR THE DAY – If Christian people were presented with an opportunity to talk to their dead loved ones via a medium or psychic, they would get their holy tail feathers in a spin and be outraged. In reality, they go to cemeteries to talk with the dead every Memorial Day, not to mention on birth and death dates.

TALKING WITH THE DEAD

In the United States, it is Memorial Day Season (a time of observance for our deceased fallen soldiers). It has also become a custom to take flowers to the graves of deceased loved ones. You will see scores of humans, mostly Christian, standing at graves crying and bearing flowers, hoping that their loved one is down there listening. They are talking to the dead, but it is a one way street due to the fact that their loved one is not there. Spirit beings that once lived in human forms are not dead or buried. They returned to the Astral Shore/First Heaven when their vehicle form died.

If the same mourning, grave visiting, Christian people were presented with an opportunity to talk to their 'live' dead loved ones via a medium or psychic, they would be outraged. Their Bible says it is a sin to consult a seer, and that they should put to death such persons of the occult. That being said, they would also have to kill themselves, because they go to cemeteries to talk with the dead. They just don't get answers back.

When we are talking with the dead, we are talking with those who are having permanent out of human body experiences. If we would go within ourselves to speak with the 'live' dead, they would answer us. They can also answer us thru a medium or psychic who goes within.

May 31

THOUGHT FOR THE DAY - As light beings, we are responsible for our actions and what we produce/create for others to see. We are responsible for our path and the markers we leave on it.

ROTTING HIGHWAY 'DEATH' MEMORIALS

Living in the low income housing of my town is a mother who lost her elementary school age son five or so years earlier. The child died riding a skateboard out into traffic. The mother was not watching him. He was a gutter kid turned out into the streets to play with no supervision.

After the funeral, the mother and friends placed flowers against a light pole at that corner. Absent were crosses or other religious symbols. A few still return to the site and place an occasional stuff toy there. At the time, the creation of the street memorial was a nice thought and action on the part of those who knew him. Now, it is five years later and the flowers and stuffed animals left there are wind weathered, rotted, and filthy.

The mother continues to return to that spot and add more flowers and stuffed animals to the mess. In my opinion, the accumulated mess has now become a tribute to darkness instead of a soul that has crossed over. It is like his mother is now saying, "All you are worth to me is a bunch of weather beaten filthy stuffed animals and years of rotted, dust covered, fake flowers."

In our cemeteries, as a rule, flowers are left on graves for two weeks after Memorial Day to keep cemetery memorials respectful to those buried there. I personally would not want filthy fake flowers or nasty stuffed, heads falling off stuffed animals gracing my parent's grave. I loved my parents and still do. I respected them in life, and still do now in death. I am in agreement with the cemetery association that flowers should be removed when they have outlived their graciousness.

It is my opinion that the memorial to the skate boarding child has now become a disgrace, and should be removed by his mother. It is a matter of respect. Disrespect comes into play when the memorial is uncared for, or the mother expects someone else to clean up her hoarding mess. I question the woman's love for her son, as well as her status as a light or dark being. The now filthy memorial, lacking in religious symbols, doesn't show any respect to the dead or those in the neighborhood who are forced to look at it. Filth is a standard of darkness.

As light beings, we are responsible for our actions and what we produce for others to see. We are responsible for our path and the markers we leave on it. Dark beings litter their lives and paths. The mother's memorial has become a form of litter. The lack of crosses or other religious symbols also states that the mother is one of darkness.

If you put up a memorial marker to one who has crossed over along a highway (a path), be respectful enough to remove the memorial items when they have outlived their graciousness. If you do not, you are a litterer (one of darkness).

I, Jo Hammers the Mystic, am a light being traveling for a lifetime on Earth in a human form. My path and markers are my responsibility. Your path and markers are your responsibility.

CHAPTER SIX
JUNE

THE BOOK OF TWISTS & TURNS

June 1

THOUGHT FOR THE DAY - Soul mates do not exist on earth, because they are perfect. Perfection only exists in the upper heavens. Even there, Divine Source does the picking and joining of perfected souls. Unperfected, young, spirit beings and students do not mate in the heavens. Mating is for the perfected.

PURPOSE ON EARTH

What you are called to do on earth has nothing to do with occupations, soul mates, acquisition of houses, etc. What you are called to do on earth is to follow your spiritual path and to complete either an education or mission assignment. If you are following your spiritual path, things having to do with your education or mission will follow/come to you. Your occupation on Earth will relate to your path and creative talent powers. The individuals you come in contact with will relate somehow to your path. Possessions coming to you will relate to your path.

If your chosen earth traveling partner is totally uninterested in your personal path, you have chosen with the animal human mind and its attractions, not as a divine being. If your occupation pulls you away from your daily, divine spiritual path, you are in the wrong occupation and have made a human error choice. If your possessions do not reflect who you are as a divine spiritual being, you have made human mind purchases.

Your purpose in life, your spiritual path, should be in the forefront of all you pursue on a daily basis. Your occupation should reflect your divinity, as should your traveling companion and possessions. If you are called to be a missionary in a remote Eskimo igloo village, working your backside off making payments on a convertible, a giant stainless steel fridge, or an air boat for fishing the Bayou, is walking your destined path in error. Things, and the payment for them, can be dark chains preventing us from pursuing our destined Earth educations and missions. Human error choices in mates can also be dark chains.

June 2

THOUGHT FOR THE DAY - If a car wreck blocks the highway you are traveling, see your detour route as a destined twist or turn on your path. You may not know the reason for it, but see it as an arrow pointing you in a new direction for the moment. Pay attention to what you are seeing from your car's windows.

ILLNESS WAKE UP CALLS

Turning points are just bumps or forks on our life paths that cause us to look and travel in a different direction. They aren't always pleasant. When things are going well, a vacation traveler doesn't think about changing courses. Suddenly, a highway detour pops up which takes him down a bumpy, pot hole riddled, dirt road, before he is rerouted back onto the interstate. Forced to take an unplanned detour, his mapped out perception of how his trip should go is forcibly changed.

When you and I have detours in life, we are suddenly forced to take new routes and view the unexpected. Detour routes can be hospital stays, car wrecks, sudden job losses, divorces, deaths, etc. See your sudden life detours as signs of forced change delivered by the universe. If you are too comfortable to tackle and make needed changes, your comfort rug will be pulled from beneath you by your spirit guide. Life is about completing missions on earth, not about being comfortable. Perfection of the soul doesn't come from comfort.

Although I am a writer, art is my pleasure. I love to paint. Once, while taking a highway detour, I spotted an old abandoned farmhouse that called to me to one day return to paint it. Another time on a detour, I spotted a gorgeous gathering of at least a hundred sheep. Life's bumps sometimes lead us to pleasant moments. Other bumps may be ones that are physically or emotionally hard to deal with, such as the loss of a child.

Detours in life come without notice. I know a woman who fell seriously ill at age 29. She was rushed to the hospital and had emergency surgery. She had a section of her bowel removed because her appendix had burst. After surgery, she had a tube down her nose that pumped her stomach for days. All her family gathered in and kept vigil on a daily basis thinking she might die. Her husband, however, came to visit her for 15 minutes every other day or so. It took a serious, sudden, life threatening, bump to make the woman see that her husband was not the man she thought he was. In her hour of greatest need, he had practically abandoned her. She had to face the fact that she was off her path, and in a relationship with a dark being. A light being would never leave their earth traveling partner to possibly die alone. Abandonment is a trait of a dark being.

Sometimes lives and relationships are not as pretty as we think they are, or convince ourselves they are. It may take a serious bump on our path to make us see reality and move on.

June 3

THOUGHT FOR THE DAY - Marriage is one weapon used by dark forces to chain, take prisoners of war, and imprison the light.

HAVE YOU MADE YOUR BED IN HELL?

Hellish pits exist all around you on Earth. Dark beings/demons/devils travel in human forms, the same as Light Beings do. One type of Hell comes to call when a light being decides to join a dark being in human marriage. The light Spirit Being erroneously convinces him/herself that they can change the habits and behaviors that are not appealing of their mate choice. It doesn't work. Demons, devils, dark souls are what they are. They cannot be changed. They don't want to be changed. They are inhabitants of Hell who want to destroy light beings in whatever fashion they can. Marriage gives dark beings easy, legal access to verbally and physically abuse light beings.

There is war in the Heavens. Earth is one battlefield. Marriage is one weapon used by dark forces to imprison, or take prisoners of war. If you have made a marriage bed in Hell, rise up and walk away, never looking back. You cannot recycle a hellish bed of horror and make it one of heavenly roses. An abusive marriage is what it is, a dark union.

A dark force being cannot be the soul mate of a Light Being. Divine Light/GOD does not join light to dark. A light being's soul mate is another light being. A dark force devil's soul mate is a demon. Don't fool yourself into believing you can change a devil, or that you must stay in a mixed being marriage because God expects it. God/Divine Source is at war with Evil, not in leagues with it. If you have chosen to marry a devil from Hell, it was your choice, not God's.

There are other dark unions on Earth. Joining forces with business associates who clearly display under the table, questionable business practices will take you under. Befriending a prostitute will bring dark pimps to your door. Hanging out with a thief will bring the police to your door. Associating with child abusers, murderers, rapists, thieves, con artists, liars, etc. will bring you experiences to call that will not be pleasant. There is war in the Heavens. Darkness wants to destroy Light. Which side of the War are you on? Joining forces with darkness is being a traitor to the light. The act will turn you a shade of gray. Flee associations with dark beings traveling in human forms.

Traitors to the Light will be judged and kicked out of

heaven. There are legions of fallen angels/light beings that have been kicked out of Heaven and walk about on Earth in human flesh rubbing shoulders with you on a daily basis. Heaven and Hell exist side by side on earth. Are you married to a devil? Do you hang out with dark beings? Have you chosen a dark mate?

June 4

THOUGHT FOR THE DAY – Personal becoming (resurrection) is like climbing a ladder. Each rung is a learning experience. You must climb up and master each individual, spiritual, path rung as it comes to you. As you ascend, you become a master, a resurrected one.

QUIT SHAKING MY TREE HOUSE

Have you ever sat on the end seat of a row in a movie theater? If you have, you have put up with the ups and downs of those seated in the middle. As the man on the end, you have to constantly stand, so those in the middle seats can sneak out to get snacks, go to the bathroom, etc. All you want to do is sit peacefully and enjoy the movie from beginning to end. Those in the middle do not understand the significance of your desire to not be disturbed.

Your spiritual path is like a movie. You must meditate/pray/watch/sit in silence/etc. as it plays. As your path plays like a movie, you will be annoyed by dark beings who try to get up and down in your face on a daily basis. They will constantly try to interrupt your concentration on what is important. Your friend phones during your meditation/prayer time. She knows you dedicate that specific time to your spiritual life. She does it anyway. Your mother-in-law calls and demands a ride to the doctor. You have plans to go to the book signing of a famous spiritual writer. Your DUI brother calls from the county jail, demanding you leave your house of worship and come instantly to bail him out. Your sister calls begging you to take her kids for the day, saying she has a headache. In reality, you know she is having an affair and will use the time to meet her lover. She is asking you to embrace her darkness.

Dark Forces know when to attack you, make you stand up in annoyance as your movie plays. As you rise, you become aware that you cannot force your family members or friends to get their act together, sit down, and respect your desire to set aside time for your spiritual climb to enlightenment. What you can do, is sit on the front row where you don't have to give into their pettiness. Front row sitters in life are the enlightened ones who know how to navigate their paths peacefully, blocking out interference from those about them.

Five little boys build a tree house. One is a daredevil who climbs up its rickety steps to make sure it is sturdy and safe for the others coming behind him. The four on the ground start shaking the tree because they think it would be funny if they shook the climber from his high perch. If you have experienced personal resurrection, dark forces about you are going to do their best to shake you out of your spiritual tree.

June 5

THOUGHT FOR THE DAY – Mother birds kick baby birds out of their nice warm nests in order to teach them to fly. Spirit Guides kick the props out from under fledgling angels on earth that need wake up calls or flying lessons.

FALLING OUT OF BED

Have you ever fallen out of bed while sleeping? It is a definite wake up call. Other types of wake up calls come in just as surprising fashions. You get fired, robbed, or in an auto accident. Maybe your blood pressure or sugar spikes out of control. Then again, it might be something as simple as the heel breaking off one of your spikes, just as you are to get up to give a presentation of some sort.

'Falling out of bed' experiences prelude change. After falling out of bed, you don't sleep on the edge of the bed anymore. After being fired, you seek a new way of supporting yourself financially. A thief takes your Big Screen. You are forced to consider other media to entertain yourself. A drunk driver hits your car. You are forced to rely on friends, relatives, or public transportation, which limits the scope of where you can go. Health issues send you on instant diets. Broken heels cause you to embrace a barefoot moment. All change, no matter how big, little, or devastating, is a step in to your future and whatever it holds. Being comfortable, having everything going your way, is a stagnant position. Mother birds kick baby birds out of their nice warm nests, in order to teach them to fly. Spirit Guides kick the props out from under those on earth that need flying lesson wake up calls. The god in us comes alive when we are faced with forced change. We don't discover our flying powers as gods, till we are tested.

Are you the lightning striking in your world? Are you a god of lightning power? Are you the god of your body, telling it to heal itself? Are you a couch potato god, or one of knowledge who devours books? Is your god money, or are you a god who knows how to go out and make new money? We are gods walking about in human flesh. We are capable of creating hellish or gracious worlds to live in.

The man (who fell out of bed in his sleep) awakens, gets up and becomes a middle of the bed sleeping god. What kind of A 'Risen' god in human flesh are you?

June 6

THOUGHT FOR THE DAY - There are millions of individuals who smile, but work at jobs they hate. If a person hates their job, they are off their path, as well as holding onto a job position that belongs to someone else

WHERE DID JOE GO?

Have you ever been at work, when one of your fellow workers is suddenly missing? Furthermore, no one knows why or where he went? Poof, they were gone; somewhere between the coffee machine and the candy bar vending machine mid morning. After coffee break, the individual working next to you leans over and whispers asking, "Where did Joe go?" You reply that you don't have a clue. Later in the morning, you ask other workers. They are as clueless as you. Joe was well liked, had been with the company for some time, and appeared to be happy with his job. Did he get fired?

There are millions of individuals who smile, but work at jobs they hate. If a person hates their job, they are off their path, as well as holding onto a job position that belongs to someone else. There are a lot of smiling Joes lying in occupational graves, just waiting for an opportunity to escape. Joe was one of them.

Three years after your Joe disappears, you happen to run into him at some public event. Down deep, you are dying to ask him if he got fired. The once neck tie wearing, black suit Joe is now wearing chef's white, and frying catfish in a food truck. When you get the chance, you walk up to his moving outdoor cafe and ask him what happened. He smiles and asks you what has not happened to you. He then goes on to tell you that he walked away from an occupational grave, and has pursued what he is really called to do. His dream was always to be a chef.

Resurrections come when we make personal choices to return to, or pursue, our mission paths. It doesn't matter if office buddies try to crucify us for our choices, which might seem to them to be a step down. What matters is that we abandon our personal graves (occupations that we hate) and rise to be all that we can be in the field of occupations that we are called to work in.

Christ has risen! Joe has risen! Have you risen?

June 7

THOUGHT FOR THE DAY - Unnecessary things can be ripped out from under you by the universe, if you are refusing to leave a comfortable job and lifestyle to walk down your destined path.

GETTING FIRED FROM YOUR JOB

Getting fired is one of the most demeaning things that

can happen to a person. It is embarrassing and attacks your self-worth. However, for light beings traveling in human forms, it is but a road sign that points us on down our paths to what we are supposed to be doing. Getting fired is actually a forced severing of outdated or error choices. If you are not willing to walk on into your future, the universe will force you to do so.

Children are like spoiled men in comfy, well paying jobs. They will lay down on department store floors (and elsewhere) and throw serious, crying, temper tantrums when they are not given what they want. Mothers have to literally pick them up and carry them out of stores as they wail, cause a scene, and refuse to walk on their own two feet. The man in a comfy job (who gets fired) is like that child. He wants what he wants even though it might not be what is best for him. So, when he gets fired he lies down and cries and wails.

Workers place their worth on how much their job pays. Thus, many males who get fired from high paying jobs are devastated. They have built their life around the things that higher wages can buy. The same goes for women. However, being on your true path is not about things. Your true path's wealth is education, enlightenment, and the mastering of the particular mission that was assigned you in the heavens, before entering earth life as a student, master, or angel in human flesh. Things accumulated on your life path sometimes become stumbling blocks.

Without a hint of it coming, you lose your job. Then, on a diminished income, you can't make the payments on your convertible, boat, or house. Repossession happens and your path is twisting and turning and discarding things as you are forced to journey in a new direction. Unnecessary things can be ripped out from under you by the universe, if you are refusing to leave a comfortable job and lifestyle to walk down your destined path.

A friend of mine graduated with a degree in accounting recently. For four years of college, she worked at a fast food hamburger place to pay for her education. After she received her degree, she continued to work at the fast food place she was comfortable with, thinking she was going to move up to manager. One day, right after graduating, she was asked to pull a night shift rotation, which was a minor twist or turn on her normal life's path. On that night shift rotation, she got in a little spat with a barely out of high school night manager and he fired her. The day boss stood by the night shift manager and she was out the door, fired. She was devastated. In error, she had set her sight on being a fast food manager where she was comfortable, instead of starting up and owning her own accounting firm. She had gotten sidetracked by the dark manager position promise of her bosses.

Bumps, twists, and turns on your life path will come. Don't look at the events as devastation. Look at them as the hands of the universe turning you toward your true calling in life. Success in life is not money, things, pretty girlfriends, handsome boyfriends, fast cars, big boats, diamond rings, manager positions, big paychecks, etc. Life success is the continuous walking of your path toward being all that you can be (perfection) and the completion of what you (a student, master, or angel) came to earth for.

Bumps in the road of life are simply wake up calls that let you know that you have gone to sleep on life's high way. There is no need to crash and burn!

June 8

THOUGHT FOR THE DAY - When a skunk sprays your house, you are in hell and your nose is being tortured and burnt. Cat urine does the same. Hoarders of trash and animals are the gatekeepers of mini hells on earth. When they die, they set up dark trash camps on the Astral Shore, while they await judgment. The Astral Shore, or First Heaven, is a gathering place for returning light and shades of gray dark beings.

HOARDER HELLS

I know a teen that started purchasing things for her future, when she got her first job in a fast food restaurant. One summer, she discovered garage sales, and that her dollars would go further purchasing second hand items. After a few weeks of devoted garage sale purchasing, her mother's garage began to fill up with household items. The mom asked her daughter why she was buying certain things.

"Someday, I will buy a house and I will need all of these things."

That sounded reasonable, so the mother ignored the growing accumulation.

At age 22, the daughter purchased her first house. The mother was thrilled, thinking she was going to get her garage space back. However, the daughter never came for the accumulation of things that she had purchased as a teen. The mother eventually asked her daughter when she was coming for her things. Her reply was, "Mom, my house is new. That stuff is a bunch of junk. Get rid of it."

Hoarding for tomorrow, prevents us from enjoying the

basics of today. The teen would have been better off to have saved her money, or enjoyed Saturday afternoons at the movies. Our tomorrow is our returning to the home of the soul. We cannot take human life's hoarded collections of junk with us. It is time to get down to the basics of human life, down size, and pursue that which we can take with us, our spiritual discoveries. We cannot take with us the purchases we make at shopping malls, flea markets, garage sales, and shopping centers.

Collections are stumbling blocks, self made barbed wire fences that obstruct life paths. Once you have a collection, you have to spend your time dusting and caring for its items, not to mention insurance and physical protection to keep them from getting stolen. Guns, knives, and tools are such items to men. China, jewelry, and decorator knick knacks are such items to women. Once we have them, we lose focus on what is really important, our assigned missions on earth. Collecting is not a mission. It is a hang up. Choose to down size and focus on spirituality, perfection, and enlightenment, your true mission.

Serious hoarders are not light beings. They are unwilling to clean up and throw out that which is useless. Dark being hoarders enjoy the filth they live in, such as cat urine, months of trash in the floor, and so much clutter that they can't find their bed. Light Beings would never live in darkness filth. Light Beings would never live in a house with seven peeing/pooping dogs and nine cats that have sprayed till the smell of urine dominates every inch of air space, and burns the nose. Light beings embrace perfection, not filth.

Hoarders of trash and dozens of neglected animals are the gatekeepers of mini hells. Family or friends can clean their houses up temporarily, but it is not because the hoarder wants it to be done. Filth living hoarders are dark beings/devils traveling in human flesh. Their dark path mission is to create burning filth pits, just as light being paths is to create mini heavens.

June 9

THOUGHT FOR THE DAY – Just as a dark sociopath being rapes a woman or child; con artist rapists choose welfare, charity, and social systems as their prey. They take that which does not belong to them from welfare systems, food banks, church charities, friends, family, etc.

CHARITY RAPISTS

Free will choice is given to each human on earth. You can choose to educate yourself, rise, and become a positive addition to society, or you can choose to be a user of society. Welfare recipients are users. They have no intentions of rising for anything other than to get out of their chair and walk to the mailbox to get free money and food stamps. A person who embraces/rapes a lifetime of welfare or disability living is not a person of resurrection. They are not light beings.

Might I further add . . . Heaven is not a welfare state! Those trying to con others out of free finances and food on earth are considered to be dark beings/devils there. At the judgment throne they are recycled to earth (kicked out of heaven). They become part of the legion of darkness. They are not given second chances and cannot return to the heavens. They have been judged as demon/devil/dark being status and have been permanently kicked out.

Those of the resurrection are those who are taking baby steps, and advanced steps, toward being all they can be in earth life as well as in their spiritual life.

What does this have to do with our subject of astral travel? Light beings who have turned and embraced darkness (including the raping of social systems) return as far as the astral shore when their earth body dies. They wait judgment there, just like light beings returning to give account for their life missions. When you travel to the astral, you have to be aware that dark beings do lurk about there trying to cause havoc, before being permanently kicked out of heaven. Frightening people you meet in dreams are those dark ones.

For instance, on the astral shore you encounter a cousin whose human body died about the same time as yours. In Earth life, he/she was addicted to drugs, alcohol, and back street gambling. The cousin in Earth life had abandoned his/her family and was eating in a soup kitchen daily, while trying to milk social systems for food stamps, low income housing, and free money. Every morning, your cousin stood on a corner with a cardboard sign begging, making people feel sorry enough for him/her to fork over free dollar bills. At night your cousin was a pick pocket and a break in thief. Working at a job was of no interest to him/her. That cousin was a devil, a dark sociopath being in his life on earth. Don't expect him to be any different as he awaits judgment. If you choose to run and embrace him on the astral shore, he just might rape or try to assault you in some other form.

Do not attempt to contact deceased relatives who were dark beings, sociopaths in life. You will be sorry! Nightmares are dark encounters on the astral shore.

June 10

THOUGHT FOR THE DAY - How do you tell the difference between the true poor and con artist users of men and systems? The answer is a willingness to work.

Who are the Poor? Who are Leaches?

In the Midwest of the United States where I am currently writing this, the corners are barraged with men holding signs reading "Hungry... need help!" or "Homeless!" Several have asked whether they should see these men as charity cases and help them. A friend shared with me that she always feels guilty and gives each one a dollar or so. She doesn't give because she feels they have a real need. She just wants to make sure she is okay with her God. She sees her God as one of wrath who is out to get her for any small slip up.

I smile inwardly and shake my head. She is a divine spirit being traveling in a human body, capable of discerning men of light from men of darkness. Like a lot of humans, she hasn't discovered her divinity/ her true being yet. Thus, she gives blindly.

How do you tell the difference between the truly poor and those who are leaches on society? The answer is a willingness to work.

A friend of mine is a wealthy man who owns a construction company. Like my friend above, he feels guilty when he sees a man standing on a corner begging for money. Rather than have his God of Wrath be at odds with him, he came up with a solution. He stops and offers each individual a job for the day at minimum wage. Surprisingly, one out of a hundred and fifty might take him up. The others will in disgust tell him to take a hike, further adding that they make more money standing on the corner than he is offering. One was in a wheelchair and was offered the opportunity to just answer a phone for the day. Leaches come in disguises . . . beware!

The answer whether to give to those begging on a street corner is to first offer them work. If they are willing, they truly need your help. If you want to give them a few dollars and drive on, it is okay. The others are society' leaches.

June 11

THOUGHT FOR THE DAY - Help the poor woman or man who works, or is willing to work. The leaches of society will only use you.

WELFARE GUTTER RATS

Part 2 of who are the poor, and who are the leaches?

"What about women?" my lady acquaintance asked. "What about those in the food bank lines and on welfare?"

The answer is the same applies for women as men. Is a poor woman willing to work on a regular job to help get her- self out of the gutters of life? Working under the table and not turning it in is the abuse or rape of welfare and food stamps.

Some women choose to live a lifetime on welfare and government handouts. The food banks and other programs are simply them standing on the corners of life begging the same as the men. Their cardboard sign is the paperwork they have to fill out to get the free handouts. If you tell them about a good job that is available across town, they will more often than not tell you, "I can't do that! I would lose my welfare or food stamps." They prefer to be leaches on society, rather than contributing to society. They should not be considered as poor. Willingness to work distinguishes the difference between a poor woman and a gutter rat. Gutter rats and street corner beggars with signs are the same.

Help the poor woman or man who works, or is willing to work. The leaches of society will only use you. One who rapes charities will also rape you and your finances.

June 12

THOUGHT FOR THE DAY – To find your purpose in life, you must go inward. When the answer comes, it will be simple. You are a spirit being who is traveling Earth life in your current human form. You are on earth as a master light being on a mission, a light being student on earth for lessons, or a dark being on a mission to assault and use others.

THE DISCONNECTED WITH NO COMMON SENSE

A seventeen years old girl meets an older man in his thirties. He is very handsome, drives a nice car, and has all kinds of money. Thinking she is a smart girl, she snags and marries him (after he divorces his wife). She does not consider the fact that when she becomes 30, he will leave her for a 20 year old 'cutie pie' who flatters his ego like she once did. He will then leave 'smart girl' wife number two with no money and three kids to finish rearing. She did not have the common sense to run from him to begin with, and use her free will power of choice to choose more wisely. (Men can find themselves in the same situation, suddenly finding they are a divorced dad with three kids to rear and that his ex has cleaned out all bank accounts.)

Common sense seems to be one earth life lesson light being student beings are tested on. The 'cutie pie' third wife will wake up one morning to find that she is a nursemaid to an old man on a cane or in a wheel chair while her younger year dreams of being a flight attendant or a cosmetologist are long gone. The man in the wheel chair is no longer attracted to 'cutie pie, but needs her to wait on him hand and foot as he sits in his wheel chair. Also, in spite of his failing health, he is eyeing his third wife's niece who is staying with them briefly. Taking a spouse that does not belong to you, is a life lesson. Ace it by running.

The reason man has such a hard time finding his purpose in life is that his human mind looks on the outside of the human form for answers with his natural human thinking and its lusts, instead of questing on the inside. It is the spiritual being within that should make all life decisions. If the spirit being within is dominating, more perfect spiritual life paths will be chosen. By spiritual, I don't mean going to church or temple weekly and sitting on a pew for a lifetime. Pew sitting is not spirituality.

To find your purpose in life, you must go inward and quest for the answer. When the answer comes it will be simple. You are a spirit being who is traveling in your current human form. However, you are not that human form. You are on earth either as a master light being, a light being student, or a dark being. If you are a master, you are an expert in some supernatural field such as psychic healing. If you are a student, you are on earth for lessons. The womanizer in the story above is a dark spirit being traveling in a human form seeking to devour and destroy the lives and futures of women.

Only you can decide what your purpose on earth is. What it is will fall under one of three categories: Masters on missions, Student lessons, or Dark warriors. For instance, a person who loves to cook can be a student or master chef. At the same time, he can be a dark warrior, if he spits, urinates, or puts drugs in food he serves to the public or you in private.

I, Jo Hammers the Mystic, am an artist and a writer on an Earth journey. In the heavens, I am Master Barjoraven a trumpeter of words. I call men with the written word to rise and be all that they can be. I am a Light Being.

If a spirit being like me chooses to use his art and written words to project blood, gore, and stories of perversion, he will be a dark being, a dark Master of words from Hell. Many authors (who write about blood and gore and the brutal killing of others) actually would like to do the perversions they write about. Instead, they walk around legal boundaries and get by with the perversions by writing about them. They would go to jail if they physically committed assaults, murders, and rapes. In their perversion, dark beings legally entice men into joining them in their acts, by providing them reading material telling about how to commit the acts of perversion.

Authors who write only blood and gore stories and books are dark beings.

June 13

THOUGHT FOR THE DAY – You can stand at a grave and weep to no avail. Go inward to the position of your 'third eye' to visit with those who are deceased. They are spirit beings, not rotting corpses.

DYING YOUNG

Human bodies are designed to live to the age of 70. If a light being student, master, or angel traveling in human flesh completes his Earth life assignment early, the human body must die in some fashion because the spirit being within will exit and return to the heavens, the home of the soul.

People say, "Oh . . . he or she had so much potential and life ahead of them. It is such a tragedy them dying young." Not so! If a mission, or life, on earth is done, it is done. The death of the human form may be used as lessons for those left behind, but it is not the spirit being that has just exited it. For explanation purposes, the human body is merely a car left behind, abandoned.

People get hung up on visiting the graves of the dead. What they are visiting is an auto junk/salvage yard where human vehicles (like cars) are no longer capable of running anymore. They are junk heaps and the spirit being/engine life in them is no more. Human body vehicles give up their spirit drivers.

To visit deceased loved ones, you must go inward to where a third inner eye exists in the center of your forehead. Look with it for the face of your crossed over loved one (young or old) to pop up. Those who have died young will visit you there. Those who have died old will visit you there.

I, Jo Hammers the Mystic, am a spirit being, traveling in a human form for a lifetime on Earth. So are you. Those crossing over young are over achieving spirit beings traveling in human forms. They go home young because they have accomplished their assignments/missions sooner than the average man on earth. Those who die young, just park their human vehicle/cars, climb out, and return to their true home.

June 14

THOUGHT FOR THE DAY – If you let your light being god within awaken, you will be able to astral travel, time travel backwards and forward, have psychic knowledge, and make the world a better place just by walking thru it.

POWERS OF GODS TRAVELING IN HUMAN FLESH

If you have been reading my writings on a continuous basis since January, you have come to realize that you are a spirit being, an orb of the heavens, that is traveling for a life time on Earth in a human body. Your human body is just a vehicle (auto) that you drive. Perhaps you need to awaken your spirit being within and let it successfully drive your human car. Your human body is an animal and its mind makes decisions with survival as its main instinct. If you awaken your spirit being within and let it guide, you become a god, not an animal with base thinking and desires.

Human mind man has tried to dominate his daily walk and those about him. Before child abuse laws came into being in the United States, it wasn't uncommon for children to be beaten into submission with belts, switches, and physical hands. Human mind parents were gods of belts, switches, and assaults. Until the 1960s or so, men also beat their wives and got by with it in the United States. Kind gentle giants (gods and goddesses in human flesh) were rare during that period of time. The gods within were sleeping.

There are two types of spirit beings that travel in human bodies. One is dark devils. The other is light beings or orbs.

When a dark being devil/god awakes within the body of an animal human, he will beat a child to death. When the dark being within awakens in a human husband, he will abuse and beat his wife to death. The same goes for dark beings awakening in female humans. Earth men are fierce animals. When they turn control over to, or awaken, dark gods within, they become savages.

Human's power is whatever they can do to survive in their animal nature. The god within, whether dark or light, is the most powerful. When it awakens, goodness or evil is displayed.

What are the powers of light beings/gods within? If you let your light being god within awaken, you will be able to astral travel, time travel backwards and forward, master healing, have psychic knowledge, and make the world a better place just by walking thru it. Dark gods awakening will make Earth life a savage place just by walking thru it. Are you making the world a better place by just walking your path thru it, or are you leaving destruction in your wake?

The Pentecostals believe they have supernatural gifts such as: Prophecy, Word of Knowledge, Word of Wisdom,

Speaking in Tongues (other languages), the Interpretation of languages not their own, and a gift of helps (angels are helpers). Although they have not mastered the 'going away and coming again' like Christ, they are letting their powerful gods within dominate or somewhat have control of their daily walk, or path.

I am a light being traveling in a human form for a life time mission on Earth. So are you! The question is, "Are you a light being or a dark being?" Also, "Do you have an awakened god within or a sleeping one?"

June 15

THOUGHT FOR THE DAY – God moments are like attending barbecues. Prayer or meditation is the barbecuing. The tasting of the barbecue, his answering our prayers, is blissful to taste.

PRAYERS ARE LIKE BARBECUING

Spirit Beings get bored with everyday routines on earth, just as human minds get burnt out with repetitive daily experiences. When burn out comes, it is necessary to have a little change of scenery, to have a little fun to break up the monotony of Earth life. Humans have a tendency to invent fun, to relieve their boredom. They hold barbecues, play tennis, watch movies, play board games, etc.

There are some divine funs that cannot be planned or invented. They are blissful moments. For instance, you are holding your infant. The baby opens its eyes, looks up at you, and then smiles. He recognizes for the first time that you are his mother or father. That is a blissful fun moment.

In my younger days, I knew a man who could barbecue the best chicken I have ever eaten. He made his own barbecue sauce from ketchup, maple syrup, and garlic. He invented dining fun moments. However, the blissful moment came in the tasting of his barbecued chicken.

God moments are like attending barbecues. Prayer or meditation is the barbecuing. The tasting of god (communication with him and his presence falling on us) is the bliss, or fun moment.

What fun are you inventing as you travel your path? Will that fun bring you bliss, which is true fun? Moments spent connecting with the divine brings true rest, fun, and relief from boredom. You just have to plan the time to seek him. Seeking is invented fun. Receiving his presence is bliss fun.

June 16

THOUGHT FOR THE DAY - Have you ever considered that the sweet fast food worker that is waiting on you is actually a young light being angel in disguise?

SCOUTS AND ANGELS

My eleven year old grandson leaves for his first week of scout camp (without mom and dad) this weekend. He has never stayed anywhere for more than one night without his parents before. This is a milestone in his life, his first chance to function as a 'free spirited' boy that is becoming a man.

Light beings that are on Earth for education are similar to my grandson. Angel parents can just protect their young child angels so long. One day, the youth has to enter earth and other planet schools. Earth is sort of a scout camp school for young light being angels. They will have choices of paths to hike down and lessons to learn. The use of 'FREE WILL CHOICE' is the main education lesson for young angels and scouts to ace. My scouting grandson will be making a lot of 'FREE WILL CHOICES' this coming week, choices that his parents have made up to this point. Young angels traveling in human forms on earth will be doing the same. Occasionally, a young angel will get into minor mischief, just as a scout might. A young angel might throw a ball out of a closet just to see a human child catch it and be delighted, or he might blow his breath on a sleeping being just to see them swat in their sleep what they think is a bug.

One of the items on my grandson's list to do is to be able to put up his own tent. Light beings coming to earth must learn to work and build dwellings/homes for their human vehicle/body to be parked or housed in. My grandson (a picky eater) will have to make choices as to whether to eat things he is not used to eating, or starve. Young Light beings on earth have to work as humans to provide funds to purchase food to feed their human bodies. Choices of occupation have to be made by young angels. Have you ever considered that the sweet fast food worker that is waiting on you is actually a young angel in disguise?

My grandson will go down to scout camp and live in survival mode for a week. At the same time, a young light being angel will come down to Earth and tackle educational issues in his first scouting earth life adventure. The heavens are perfect! Earth is not. The young picky angel will eat the sorrows of life, whether he likes them or not. My grandson will learn to eat what is set before him.

Sometimes earth life is not pleasant and we have to sleep where we don't want to sleep, eat things we do not find pleasant, and are victims of the elements and the poisons of life. We will survive and be better for the experience.

June 17

THOUGHT FOR THE DAY - The mastering of 'FREE WILL CHOICE' is the major education course being offered on earth. Mastering Earth weekends is the test.

Weekend Dark Path Choices

In our time off, it is just as important to make good choices as it is during our work week. We should get enough sleep and eat healthy. We should go to bed on time and be on time for our weekend adventures. Free time is not to be used unwisely, wasted, or abused. The light side and the dark side exist in all facets of earth life, including weekend leisure.

If you are seeking perfection (the mastering of earth life's education and the move up to be a master in the heavens) you can't embrace out of control weekend darkness and expect to graduate. A hangover on Monday prevents you from giving your all to Monday's life lessons. Staying up to late on Saturday night prevents you from choosing to attend church, temple, etc. on Sunday. Eating eight plates of food at a buffet on Friday night, may spike your blood sugar out of control on Saturday making you deathly ill for the next week. We become what we embrace.

So, when approaching weekend leisure and its variety of opportunities, make choices that will not affect your education path and mission on earth. The mastering of 'FREE WILL CHOICE' is a major course being offered in Earth school. The weekend is the test.

With each weekend opportunity, ask yourself if you are choosing wisely as a light being. Unwise choices turn you to a shade of gray or worse. Getting drunk is a bad choice, as is over eating and failing to get enough sleep. Sleep time is the soul's chance to travel the heavens and other planets. A weekend of staying up all night in a cheap bar is no comparison to an astral dream trip to Mars, Venus, black holes of space, or forward and backwards in time while your human body sleeps.

June 18

THOUGHT FOR THE DAY- If you have a child or a baby that has climbed from his physical form and 'CROSSED OVER', realize that he/she has accomplished his/her mission on earth.

A CHILD OR BABY'S DEATH

My brother is in the hospital dying! Facing my sorrow with the human mind, I can experience his death in two ways. (1.) I can moan and groan (mourn) my brother's human body that I think will be placed into a grave to rot, with no spiritual understanding to comfort me. (2) I can go inward, step from my human form, and celebrate with the spirit being that has just permanently laid down his human body to return to the true home of the soul.

In spirit form, when my brother steps from his body for good, he will probably be amused at those mourning their loss and their self centered views of 'losing him'. Spirit Beings (who have totally abandoned their earth forms and are hovering before crossing over) can read human minds if they want.

A grieving mother (who has lost a child) in human thinking mode wails "Why has god let my child die?"

Just as there are laws of gravity and the assurance that the sun will come up and go down on a regular basis, life and death is also a law. We must abandon human forms to return to the heavens where we have no need of them. Bodies are just autos that we travel earth life in.

Some spirit beings are on earth for short missions. Babies and children who die 'young' are adult spirit beings that have been traveling in human forms on earth for short missions. When you go to visit them in the heavens (astral travel) they will be adults, not babies or children. However, adult spirit beings can put on children or baby costume forms to appear to you in dreams if they choose to do so to comfort you. Out of costumes in the heavens they are the equivalent of 30 year old adults.

So, my brother is dying. As a spirit being, I know that the laying down of the human form is a law of abandonment and a ritual act that must be performed. The abandonment of a human body to a cemetery grave is like sending a junk heap car to a salvage yard. The driver does not intend to go to the salvage yard with the wreck and remain in it. The spirit being within (the driver) moves on, and drives new forms on earth and other planets if he wishes (reincarnation). Reincarnation is the buying of a new car.

The stepping from a human form for the last time should be celebrated like birthdays. My brother is about to return to the Astral Shore/First Heaven and be free to visit with his true friends, family, masters, and acquaintances from earth life who crossed over before him.

As spirit beings, we are able to step from our human forms to celebrate with those who have abandoned their human auto bodies for good. The only difference between us and them is that we must step back into our forms because the law of death (abandonment of the human auto body) has not come to us yet. Our human body cars are not worn out wrecks yet.

If you have a child or a baby that has climbed from his physical form, realize that he has accomplished his mission on earth. Bodies have to die in order to free spirit beings driving them. Human forms have to succumb to illnesses, accidental deaths, or internal systems stopping. A spirit being cannot return home and leave a human body auto to idle forever. Early crossovers (babies and children) should be celebrated like a brilliant child who graduates college in two years instead of four.

I, Jo Hammers the Mystic, am a spirit being who is traveling on earth for a lifetime in a human form. In the heavens, I am a spirit being called Barjoraven. I am a trumpeter of words there. On Earth, I am a writer, and a reader and studier of all faiths.

My earth parents were spirit beings traveling in human forms. My earth mother in the heavens is a spirit guide. My earth father works in the hall of new souls where he cares for silver cord communication lines that are attached to new souls about to enter earth life. On earth, my mother was a housewife and devout follower of the Pentecostal faith. My father on earth worked in a railway tie yard and part time as a deputy sheriff. He too was a follower of the Pentecostal faith. In the heavens, they are not my parents. They are friends that I was commissioned to enter and live an earth life with.

June 19

THOUGHT FOR THE DAY – Christ was not sent to save devils, demons, and those who willfully choose darkness. He was sent to rescue light beings with damaged and severed silver cords, astral amnesia victims.

AMNESIA VICTIMS

Have you ever taken a vacation where there were no Wi-Fi, internet, or cell phone connections? Being cut off from what you consider to be civilization is a silent, lonely, disconnected, fuzzy feeling; the same feeling a spirit being experiences when he has his silver cord communications line severed when entering Earth life.

A severed cord being is cut off from all communications from the heavens when his silver cord communications line is severed on entry to earth life. With a severed communications line, a light being traveling in human flesh becomes one who walks about in a state of Astral Amnesia. He doesn't know his purpose for being on earth, nor does he remember his astral home, family, friends, occupation, and the experiences of everyday living in the heavens. On Earth, the severed cord light being becomes a survivor, instead of a light being on a mission. He is amnesia plagued and often becomes an atheist. Without spiritual connections, he does not believe that a Supreme Being exists.

Is there healing for severed silver cord light beings traveling earth in human flesh? It comes by faith alone. An atheist must believe there is a god, even though he has never seen one or will hear from one during his life span on earth.

Atheists, as a whole, are lost or clueless light beings on earth. Saviors will be sent to rescue them and help them to cross over when their human transportation vehicles die. Christ was sent to rescue/save the lost. His mission was to rescue damaged and severed silver cord light beings, not devils walking about in human flesh. The Christians have it all wrong. Devils and demons traveling in human flesh cannot be saved. They are dark forces. Christ's mission was to save lost astral amnesia victims.

You must remember that the Bible was written by human minds, not by third eye open, silver cord connected light beings. Christ's followers are those with damaged or severed silver cord communication lines. They are his mission.

June 20

THOUGHT FOR THE DAY - Individuals with two eyes (that you encounter in dreams) are spirit beings wearing costumes, not actually two eyed humans. A spirit being has one eye, a spiritual eye called the 'THIRD EYE'. The spirit being's third eye is located in the center of the forehead on the inside of the human form. It looks into the heavens, where your physical two human eyes look out into the physical.

BLIND PATHS

Learning to use your third eye is similar to getting glasses for the first time. You don't realize how really blind you are till you look thru the lens. The same goes for looking thru the third eye for the first time.

You must remember that you have three eyes for a reason. Your two human eyes are for looking out into the physical world/earth. Your human eyes do not have the power to look inward. Your third eye is for looking inward and upward. It is a spiritual eye or heaven's eye. It has the power to look about in the heavens and retrieve information from the heaven's many information resources, providing the silver cord communication line is not damaged or severed.

You, as a spirit being, are actually an orb of light. Bodies are costumes. Body costumes are worn on Earth, on the astral Shore/First Heaven, and sometimes in the Second Heaven and above, depending upon whether a light being might want to show off costume bodies from his travels (like a vacationer returning from a distant paradise such as Hawaii on Earth display colorful T-shirts). Individuals with two eyes in your dreams are spirit beings wearing costumes, not actually human bodies.

A blind path to a human on earth is the loss of his physical eyesight. A blind path to the spirit being that lives within a human on earth is the loss of his third eye communication line. Third eye communication is lost when silver cords are damaged or severed when a spirit being enters earth life.

If you dream of two eyed beings on the Astral Shore/First Heaven, you are encountering spirit beings (orbs) wearing human or other planet being costumes. The same goes for dreams of animals.

June 21

THOUGHT FOR THE DAY - There are grandparents who willingly babysit their grandchildren out of love, and can afford to do so. That is okay. A financially strapped grandparent being forced to do so is the act of a dark being parent. Children should not be forcibly placed in any home that cannot afford them. If done so, it is abuse.

STARVING HER NEWBORN

Occasionally, a friend of mine named Anne asks me if I can come to her work and give her a ride home. In good weather, she walks due to not having an auto or money for cab fare. Why is she so financially depleted? She has a grown, dark being daughter that has no intentions of working and dumps unplanned babies in Anne's lap and splits after they are born. Anne, a widow, has taken in three grandchildren to rear.

Why does the daughter dump babies on Anne? She thinks she can't live without a man in her life. When choices have to be made, she picks the man and dumps her offspring. Currently, Anne has three grand children living with her, one a newborn that is just a week or so old.

This morning, picking Anne up at work, she told me that she cannot afford the price of formula, so she is feeding the newborn 2% milk. She also said that she had nothing in the way of food to give her 13 year old granddaughter and five year old grandson except a can of vegetables to eat for dinner. Is it right for a grandparent to take children that she cannot afford to feed? If a grandparent takes, and then nutritionally starves a child, doesn't that make her an abusive slow killer? To starve a child's body is to kill it.

There are grandparents who willingly babysit their grandchildren out of love, and can afford to do so. That is okay. A grandparent being forced to do so, dumped on, is another thing. Anne cannot afford her three grandchildren, much less afford to send them to a legitimate day care, school, or in the future to college. If they stay with her, they will end up being high school dropouts and welfare gutter rats. The 13 year old has already slipped thru the cracks and is out of school. Love doesn't let children drop out of school, nor have their futures shortchanged by a lack of education. Grandparents have free will choice. Taking children that you cannot raise financially is doing them a great injustice, as well as being abusive.

Anne is off her path and in a dark place of holding onto what she should let go of. She is not old enough for social security yet, and her 30 hour fast food job barely covers rent and utilities. Yet, she refuses to see that the children in her care would be better off elsewhere (adopted out). She is starving her grandchildren of nutrition and futures by darkly holding on to them. Anne thinks she is showing love to her grandchildren by keeping them. Love doesn't starve children.

Love lets children be adopted into professional families who can afford to nurture and educate them. Love is letting someone raise children that will see they have opportunities to be all that they can be. Anne has become a shade of gray, a dark being who erroneously thinks her grandchildren are best with her. Anne's daughter started the cycle of darkness by abandoning her children. Anne has embraced the darkness by taking her children.

Welfare and food stamps do not give children social opportunities and bright futures.

Heaven and Hell exist side by side on Earth. Dark beings walk about in human forms the same as light beings. Dark beings want to make light beings a dumping ground, in order to interrupt their destined paths of being all that they can be. Light beings who accept being dumped on become shades of gray and start to venture down a path into the gutters of darkness. By holding on to her grandchildren, Anne has chosen dark gutter living. She is not a grandparent giving them a hand up in life. She is giving them a hand down into life's hells. Letting a 13 year old drop out of school is not love. It is damaging her future. That is the act of a dark being. Letting a five year old little boy eat a can of corn for dinner is not love. Stunting the growth of a newborn is the act of a dark being. Anne is starving and abusing her grandchildren. She just doesn't see it. She calls her abuse 'love'.

Not feeding proper nutrition to a new born, when an adoptive parent could, is the act of a dark being.

June 22

THOUGHT FOR THE DAY - Hell's pits are manned or guarded by dark beings traveling earth life in human body vehicles. Behind closed doors, hellish living conditions and lifestyles can exist for children. Their parents are dark, demon gatekeepers to Hell on Earth.

MY SLOB RENTER – a shared story

I am in the rental business. In one of my houses lived a woman who moved to my city in Missouri from New Jersey. When collecting the rent once a month, I was somewhat shocked to see that most of her possessions were always scattered on the floor. At first, I figured that her clothing and other items in disarray was due to her not having dressers, hangers, etc. She had left her furniture and possessions behind in New Jersey.

After my renter had lived in my house for a year, I gave her an inspection, which I do all of my rentals yearly. I was shocked to discover that she was a 'bon-a-fide' slob. Her clothing (clean and dirty) was piled and kicked around the baseboards of the house's three bedrooms as though they were meaningless to her. What shocked me the most was that she had piles of dirty and clean clothing kicked and mounded up against a water heater (a fire hazard)! Needless to say, I read her the riot act and told her to clean up her unbelievable mess or I was going to evict her. – The end of friend's story

So, . . . what does my friend's story have to do with personal spiritual paths, the subject I am writing on currently? It has to do with costumes, the clothing worn on a human body. In the endless piles of clothing on my friend's rental house floor, was costumes/clothing reflecting how her female renter lived her daily life. Weeks of dirty, stained undergarments, night wear, and very personal birth control items were on open display strewn about the floors for the world to look at. Some of the clothing reeked with alcohol. It was very obvious that the woman was a weekend bar fly, and possibly a prostitute who brought her Johns home. The renter, like all women, had one accessory that she loved. She had a passion for scarves. Even though she was nuts about them, they were strewn on the floors mixed in with the dirty and the clean garments. If the renter didn't respect the things she wore and loved, how could she respect and love the two children living in her man made Hell?

Light being Mothers don't let children live in filth. Loving, light being mothers are somewhat neat freaks and germ-a-phobic!

June 23

THOUGHT FOR THE DAY – We are given free will choice in earth life, clear up to the moment our human form takes its last breath. We can choose, with each breath, to embrace drama or inward and upward paths.

HOT SAUCE ON ICE CREAM

The nice part about earth life is that no two paths are the same. Watching others is like watching on going, walking and breathing daily episodes of human soap operas. The human mind seems to be fascinated with the good times, bad times, and loves of others, as they function as humans. People do crazy things!

Years ago, I had a friend who ate his brown beans on a slice of chocolate cake, instead of cornbread. That was dinner table drama, causing a few of his guests wanting to barf. Another friend of mine puts hot sauce on his ice cream. He also gets some weird reactions from those dining with him. Human soap opera drama comes in little packages, or major ones. The above crazy quirks of eating are not dark, just unique. All light beings have strange little quirks that make them unique or special. A dark eating habit would be the eating of human flesh, excrements, blood, or chemicals or foreign substances in food such as ground glass or motor oil.

On Tuesdays, an 80 year old man I will call Oscar, joins me at a fast food restaurant for coffee for the morning. He comes across as being a really nice, respectful man, except when it comes to his wife. He bends my ear concerning how much his wife mentally and physically abuses him.

Quote from Oscar, "She is one of the meanest women ever. She doesn't cook for me anymore or keep anything in the refrigerator for me to make a sandwich for lunch with. She gave away the lounge chair I sit in to watch TV, and now she has gotten rid of the TV."

Eighty year old Oscar loves to talk about his ongoing marital relationship drama. Considering his wife is also 80, there may be perfect good reasons that she is no longer cooking or shopping for food. There are always two sides to every soap opera. I suggested to him that he start doing the grocery shopping and the cooking.

"Oh no . . . I couldn't do that!" he replied, in shock that I would suggest such a thing.

Why Oscar's wife got rid of his chair and TV, who knows? Perhaps she is entering a state of dementia. Perhaps Oscar has been spoiled his whole life, having a wife who waited on him hand and foot. Perhaps he is not willing to walk down a new, necessary twist on the last leg of his life journey,

We are given free will choice in earth life, clear up to the moment our human form takes its last breath. We can choose, with each breath, to embrace flesh eating, excrement drama or quirky hot sauce on ice cream inward and upward paths.

June 24

THOUGHT FOR THE DAY – Americans complain about having to eat hamburger, when other U.S. citizens are eating steaks. Somewhere on Earth there is a father that is watching his family starve due to famine. He would give everything for the chance to buy one fast food hamburger and then cut it in pieces and share it with his wife and children.

PATH PROSPERITY/HOW RICH IS RICH?

Recently, I was in an unbelievably long line at a fast food counter. A man in his twenties struck up a conversation with me as we waited. He asked me what I did for a living. I replied that I was a writer and that I ate in that particular fast food restaurant at least once or twice every day because I did not have time to cook. (It is my choice to spend my cooking time writing.)

He replied, "Boy you have got it made! I would give anything to just be able to order my meals here from the main menu board, instead of the dollar menu."

I thought to myself, "Boy would I give anything for a plate of my deceased mother's chicken and dumplings, instead of this fast food."

Then it struck me how unthankful both of us were as we stood waiting to order. Somewhere there is a being starving in a country that is famine plagued, who would give anything for a dollar bill to buy a hamburger and then cut it in pieces and share it with his wife and children. Somewhere there is a woman making chicken and dumplings who is dreaming of getting to go out on the weekend with her husband to have a burger, a treat for them. Her husband works for minimum wage.

Prosperity on our paths is a state of the mind. You may be complaining for having to eat a bologna sandwich while the man across the street has no lunch at all to take to work. The man across the street is complaining because he is only able to eat two meals a day, while the man behind him on the next street can't eat at all, because he has cancer of the mouth. Prosperity where we are is a state of mind.

More prosperity coming to you is the result of being thankful for the prosperity you already have.

June 25

THOUGHT FOR THE DAY – To master our human world, we sometimes have to ask for assistance from the god within. We are two in one, both human and divine.

THE GOD WITHIN SPEAKS - A shared story

For three to four hours this morning, I searched for a new, small, red, fire engine toy I had purchased for my grandson for his birthday. I looked thru every drawer, nook, and cranny. I just couldn't remember (with my human brain) where I put it. Frustrated, I sat down in my rocker and decided to ask God where it was, after reminding him that I didn't usually lose things.

"God," I began, praying inside while biting my human lip on the outside in a frustrated motion. "I have heard of others asking you where lost things were and you giving them the answer. Would you show me exactly where this toy fire engine is?"

Instantly, possibly three seconds later, I heard a voice say inside me, "It fell behind the dresser!"

Immediately, I got up and pulled the dresser out. The toy fire engine had fell half way down and was stuck between the dresser and the wall. Was it a toy finding miracle, or a discovery that I was two persons in one?

People think of God as being far off in the physical sky somewhere, and out of the reach of man. The voice that answered me was within. I knew the divine being's voice was there within me. I just didn't have a name for the being and the voice.

After a few years, I discovered that I was a spirit being traveling in a human body form. I was two beings, not one. My human body was an earth being, thinking with a human brain. My spirit being within was a divine being who could retrieve needed information from the heavens and then speak to my human intelligence, telling it what it needed to know. I discovered that I was a god type being within and human without!

June 26

THOUGHT FOR THE DAY - Our human bodies are like cars. If we (Spirit Beings) forget to turn off our human engines at night, they remain active and are capable of having unexpected run away moments known as sleep walking or talking in one's sleep.

SLEEP WALKING & NIGHT TALKING

Three or four weeks ago, I was driving down a main street in Springfield, Missouri when a car came rolling off a side street in front of me in reverse. It crossed my road and backed into a ditch on the other side. Luckily, I was going slow and was able to slow down to avoid the runaway car that was going backwards. Apparently, the driver had left the standard transmission vehicle running, while running run up to a door to make a small delivery. Apparently, it slipped out of gear and rolled backwards.

Our human bodies are like cars. If we forget to turn off their engines at night, they remain active and are capable of having unexpected run away moments. Sleep walking is a body engine in idle that is running away. When the spirit being within exits the human body at night, humans sleep walk or roll out of sight into ditches. Waking up and finding your body in a different bed, house, or asleep in the hedges outside are runaway, sleep walking moments.

You have to remember that the human mind is not the mind of the spirit being within. The human mind looks out into the physical world and makes decisions about surviving it. The spirit being has a separate intelligence that looks upward into the heavens, via a 'Third Eye'. The spirit being is the driver of the human auto, just like I am the driver of a Chevy Cobalt. When a spirit being fails to shut down the mind of its human car at night, the human vehicle is left in idle and has the capability of rolling (walking) away and ending up in a ditch, neighbor's yard, or a strange bed.

Talking in your sleep is the same experience as sleep walking. Your human body auto has not been shut down by the driver within. Engines purr (talk) as they idly roll away (sleep walk) into ditches.

June 27

THOUGHT FOR THE DAY - A master like Christ answers directly to Divine Source (not to Christ or other masters). The New Testament Age is coming to an end. Modern masters will go away to the heavens and return again to human forms at will. Christ was like John the Baptist, a forerunner.

THE FACE OF GOD

There are master beings in the heavens equal in standing or status to Christ, Buddha, etc. They answer directly to Divine Source, not to Christ or other masters. A master who answers directly to the Infinite doesn't have to quote scriptures. They are divine spirit beings who have no need to expound earth men's writings. They are not human in need of bibles or masters to follow.

The books of the Bible were written by men such as you and me; and are full of antiquities, prejudices, and narrow views of the world, reflecting the paths walked during periods of time of their authors. They were written for their time and the customs of that time. Today is today! The revelation for today is that we are spirit beings traveling in human forms that have discovered our divinity within us.

Human thinking might say we light beings (traveling in human forms) march to the beat of a different drummer. We march to the pulse beat of the heavens. Human thinking cannot hear that beat. We don't embrace Dark Age thinking, writings, or antiquated religious rituals. We live in the now and embrace cutting edge thought. When we do not have a group to worship with, we make personal altars within

Master and student light beings don't embrace ancient human mind writings. We do not need to read and embrace archaic, human written books about a mythical God that was never seen by its writers. We light beings have seen and answer to the Infinite Power. Only blind human thinking needs a book written by archaic human thinking for a guide. We go within for guidance and communications between Heaven and Earth.

June 28

THOUGHT FOR THE DAY – Individuals from the Old Testament Age abandoned their religious roots and embraced the New Testament Age. It is now time to walk out of the New Testament Age and embrace what lies ahead in the New Age.

THE LAYING DOWN OF ARCHAIC BOOKS

Back in the 1940s and 1950s, our house was cooled by leaving the windows up and the use of electric fans. Air conditioning didn't become available in our neighborhood till the 1960s. Wakes were big back at that time. We were a huge family and I grew up with deceased family members being laid out in our living room for 24 hour wakes.

In the scorching heat of summer, the funeral home would open the caskets for display in our living room and then drape huge tablecloth size pieces of black lace netting over the caskets to keep the flies out. Back at that time, our fans (cooling system) was considered modern. The black lace covers were also considered modern.

Looking back, I shake my head and wonder how we survived those twenty four hour wakes, the scorching heat, and the flies. With droves of people arriving and leaving for the viewings, flies did make their way in. One person at the wake was always assigned to continuously wield a fly swatter. Thank God that air conditioning and funeral home viewings are now in style, modern.

Air conditioning replaced fans. The New Testament Age replaced the Old Testament Age. New Age writings are now replacing archaic Old Testament and New Testament writings. It is error to move backwards and embrace old religious rituals and thinking. You must move forward into a new age, just as individuals from the Old Testament Age abandoned their religious roots and embraced the New Testament Age. It is now time to walk out of the New Testament Age and embrace what lies ahead in the New Age.

Go within and find your inward path to God and all the mysteries of the heavens.

I, Jo Hammers the Mystic, have seen the face of God. He is like a great formless mist that moves across and thru everything. We are orbs of like and are like him. We enter and wear costume human forms on earth. We are not the forms. God once appeared to Moses as a voice in a burning bush. The bush and fire was a costume he wore. Human bodies are costumes. Animal bodies are costumes. Anything physical, such as a burning bush, can be a costume.

June 29

THOUGHT FOR THE DAY – When damaged or severed silver cord communication lines of a Light Being are healed, the being will walk away from the religion he was raised in on earth He will then pursue that which he was sent to earth to accomplish.

CROSSOVERS

When light beings enter earth life in baby forms, sometimes accidents happen and silver cord communications lines are damaged or severed. Until the communications lines are healed or repaired, light beings in human forms sometimes suffer from astral amnesia and travel earth life thinking they are human. They go to school and do the things other humans do. They will attend the churches, mosques, and temples of their earth parents. When they reach adulthood, they will take spouses and embrace the cultures that they enter life in. When their communications lines heal or are repaired by a healer/rescuer/savior, they instantly realize that they are not the human bodies they travel in. They automatically know that they are not Hindu, Protestant, Jewish, Buddhist, Catholics, Wiccan, etc. They know that they are gods or divine ones traveling in human form costumes.

In the new beginning, when a light being's cord heals, he rises on the inside of the human form he travels in, exits, and stands on the shores of time. He chants the sounds of heaven, the holy sounds of creation. He is one voice, or mouth pieces of the Infinite. He is a mini incarnates of the Infinite.

When damaged silver cord light beings first start to heal,

they learn to open portals and travel the astral in dream states. Excited about discovering that they are more than just human, they get lost in the thrill of what they can see and experience on the astral shore. When their cords are healed or repaired, they cross over from damaged communication lines thinking to divine thinking. At that point, they are no longer thrill seekers. They know who they are as light beings and their place in the heavens, as well as what their mission is on earth. They reclaim their divinity. In the moment of healing or awakening, light beings will walk away from the religions they were raised in on earth, and pursue that which they have come to earth to do. They will dump dark being friends and spouses they embraced in their astral amnesia states. 'Holy Joes' in Earth life are light beings!

Perfection is the standard in the upper heavens. Light Beings live by that standard. God/Divine sources demands that light beings turn from all darkness. They will obey that command when awakening, even if it means walking away from religions, occupations, earth parents, spouses, friends, jobs, family, etc. They will abandon any darkness they embraced while in Amnesia states. They straighten their twisted, bumpy, out of control life paths and walk away.

June 30

THOUGHT FOR THE DAY – Will you go home to the heavens empty handed? Will you have to explain there, why you have not been a savior to a brother light being who was lost, due to having a damaged or severed silver cord?

I AM MASTER BARJORAVEN – I AM THAT I AM!

I couldn't sleep very well last night. I watched a movie about the holocaust, and was appalled at the atrocities humans inflicted on each other as they blindly followed a sociopath murderer named Hitler.

Especially of interest to me, in the movie, were the trials, struggles, and abuse of an artist named Karl Weiss. To paint and draw is a power given to certain light beings when they enter earth life. The Germans broke Karl's artist hands when they discovered his haunting drawings of Jewish ghetto children. They attempted to destroy his god power. Karl died in a labor camp, but his drawings ended up in the Prague Museum. His power over came darkness and broken hands.

I haven't always understood some of the trials and struggles in my life, as I have painted and put my thoughts on paper. I am sure, like Karl, that my painting power creations will find their way to where they are of most use after I exit my human form. Karl was a witness thru his art of man's atrocities. My writings are a witness of what I have gleaned spiritually, as my damaged silver cord communications line has healed. My art now is on book covers and is currently being used as illustrations for my blog writings. What are your specialized divine power gifts? What are you creating to leave behind as a witness of the twists, turns, and broken hands on your life path?

My goal on earth is to share what I know about the inner heavens and home of the soul with light beings on Earth who have their silver cord communication lines damaged or severed. I do not intend to return to the home of the soul without pointing one lost brother light being toward home, and help him enter the light. Grab hold of the tail of my Master's robe, if you need to! I will lead you over. My robe is my writings.

On Earth, I am Jo Hammers the Mystic. My Earth parents named me Jo Hammers. In the Heavens, I am addressed as Master Barjoraven. I am a light being, a trumpeter of words. Hear ye the trumpet sound of the rapture, the catching away or stepping from human forms!

CHAPTER SEVEN

JULY

THE BOOK OF LIGHT AND DARK POWERS

July 1

THOUGHT FOR THE DAY – Angels can wear human body costumes, just as a little girl's paper doll wears paper dresses.

ANGELS ALL AROUND YOU

Angels walk all about you on a daily basis. They travel earth life wearing costume forms of humans, in order to speak with humans in a form that they understand. Humans are not spirit beings; they are animals. They understand and react according to what their eyes, smell, taste, touch, and hearing tell them exists. Humans expect angels and gods to look like them, or other animal life forms of their world. Human thinking may also expect angels to appear with wings like birds or possibly have legs like horses. To interact with humans, angels and other divine beings may wear human costumes.

New human parents use jibber language to speak with

infants to make them smile, angels use costumes to amuse or speak with infant man. In the Old Testament, God appeared as a burning bush to Moses. The burning bush was a costume. The human forms of Christ and Buddha were costumes that divine masters wore. Costumes are common for angels and gods to appear in when on missions on Earth. Divine beings in the heavens are actually orbs of light and energy.

Angels, in human flesh costumes, appear in all the religions and cultures of the world. They wear costumes of the animals and human forms of the different areas. Some divine beings are on earth on missions and others for schooling. When they are in human costumes, they will blend in with cultures to learn what they need to know and perform their missions.

Some divine beings, traveling in human flesh, appear as master orators calling men to higher levels of thinking. Others may be healers or comforters. Because they are divine beings, they will be kind and gentle of nature. The sweet little old lady who bakes everyone cookies for no reason could be an angel traveling earth in disguise. The gentle old man who gardens and shares his produce freely could be an angel in costume. The church prayer warrior might be an angel pursuing an assignment on earth. You entertain and rub shoulders with angels on a daily basis.

Dark beings, or fallen angels, also appear on earth wearing costumes of men. They will be cruel natured humans and live earth lives as killers, rapists, thieves, con artists, abusers, etc. Sociopaths are gods or angels of darkness. Earth humans refer to fallen angels as devils and demons.

Know who walks amongst you. Light being masters will

drip and ooze goodness. They will dress appropriately and display holiness of body, words, and deeds. To recognize holiness in an individual is to recognize that you may be in the presence of an angel or other divine being in human costume.

July 2

THOUGHT FOR THE DAY - Being 'caught away', or 'to rapture', is the climbing of a soul from a meditating/thinking human form. The soul seeks higher knowledge from the heavens, that which is beyond human mind intelligence. Being 'caught away' is the retrieving of 'out of the box' astral knowledge. The 'coming again' is a soul returning to the moment to use the knowledge in everyday human life. Using inspiration is the 'coming again'

THE POWER TO ASCEND

If you have been reading my posts from the beginning, you understand that you are more than just the human form you travel Earth life in. You also know that the crossing over between worlds is taking place on a daily basis by those who are 'going away' and 'coming again'. Light beings are climbing from their human forms and traveling to the astral and then returning to their human bodies that lay in beds sleeping. Christians refer to the event as the rapture. However, few Christians are acknowledging the 'it is a happening now rapture' for those who have awakened spiritual eyes.

The Old Testament Age gave way to the New Testament Age. John the Baptist was the New Testament Age's forerunner. Now, we are crossing over from the New Testament

Age to a New Age Dispensation. To cross over between dispensations, you must be caught away. Being caught away is the climbing of your soul from your human form as it sleeps or meditates, traveling to the heavens, and then returning again to your human form when it wakes up.

There are forerunners, prophets, and trumpeters of the New Age Dispensation. I am one of them. I am calling you forth, through written words, from your sleeping dead human form to rise, exit your human form, be caught away to the heavens and all it holds, and then return again. The 'catching away' is not for rotting, dead, human bodies. It is for spirits/souls that travel in human forms.

The Old Testament Age was an era of Dark Age, animal mind thinking. The New Testament Age called men to become out of the box thinkers when it came to accepting new religious thought. The New Age Dispensation is the call for spirit beings to abandon their human forms, travel the heavens, and then return to their human bodies.

When you realize that you can lay your human form down to sleep and then step from it to travel by light portal to the heavens and other planets, you become the 'Resurrection' or one of the 'Caught Away' throng. After traveling the heavens and returning to your human form, you become the 'Coming Again'. Those who accomplish the stepping from and returning to their human bodies become master Christs and Buddha of the New Age Dispensation. They are the New Jerusalem coming down.

I, Jo Hammers the Mystic, am a Light Being. I am a trumpeter of words, calling men to climb from their human forms and rapture. Hear ye your trumpet sound!

July 3

THOUGHT FOR THE DAY - The welfare gutters of life are hells that dark ones choose to dwell in on earth. Dark souls choose to live off of welfare, food stamps, charities, church food banks, social systems, friends, family, etc. They are demons who have no intentions of working, or adding to the advancement of light being society. They are gutter rat demons, life time rapists of social systems by choice. They are sociopaths. Raping systems is as bad as raping a woman or a child.

THE POWER OF DARK BEINGS TO DESCEND

Freewill choice is a power of both Light and Dark beings. White trash living in welfare gutters is chosen by dark beings. They are the gutter rat demons of society. They purposely choose to live off welfare, food stamps, charities, church food banks, social systems, etc. They willfully choose to not work or create a higher standard of life for themselves or their offspring. They produce more gutter rats like themselves. Light beings choose to educate themselves and their children. They think out of the box and seek enlightenment. Light beings settle for nothing less than being all they can be, and providing growth of soul opportunities for their children.

Heaven is not a welfare state. There are no freebee handouts there. Everyone works and everyone does their part to advance society, not degrade it. Lifetime welfare recipients on Earth are lazy dark beings, who have no intentions of getting out and working to provide for themselves or their off spring; much less add something to the advancement of planet Earth society. They aren't about to go to heaven or anywhere else that will require them to work for their daily bread!

Example of a gutter rat: a woman purposely has several children to obtain and keep a welfare check increasing in amount and coming in. One day, her children grow up and becomes of age. She suddenly finds she has no income. So, in true gutter rat form, she conveniently fakes a back ache and applies for disability to keep a freebee income coming in. She is a dark being.

There is no welfare in heaven, nor is there disability. All souls work for their light, position, and energy (daily bread). Gutter rats are exterminated there. They cease to be!

July 4

THOUGHT FOR THE DAY – Gutter Rat mothers raise their offspring in the welfare gutters of life. Angelic mothers choose higher paths for their lives and their children.

THE POWER TO PROTECT OR DESTROY

Recently, in a fast food restaurant, I met a 13 and a 15 year old brother and sister. They were clean and articulate. However, I could tell that the brother was in protective mode for his sister. It was way after midnight. I entered conversation with them and discovered that they stayed up nights in fast food restaurants, slept in a rented storage unit during the day, bathed in gas station restrooms, and did what they need to do to find food. What were the two young teens doing, living on the streets at such an early age? It had to do with the dark choices/power of their mother.

The mother of the teens was in jail for the selling and use of illegal narcotics. She was a gutter rat addict by choice. Before going to prison, she refused to tell her children who their father was, or if they had distant family somewhere. She chose to abandon her offspring to the elements when she was sentenced for years to jail. She purposely used her dark powers to abandon her children to the streets. She made no provisions for them. That mother is a gutter rat, a dark being traveling in a human form.

Mothers have a special supernatural power. That power is to nurture and protect, if you are a light being. That same power is to abuse and neglect, if you are a dark being. A light being will go over board to protect and raise well their offspring. A dark being will go over board to abuse and neglect their offspring.

Are you a dark gutter rat parent or a light being one? Were your parents dark or light? How about your grandparents? Gutter Rats are Gutter Rats, dark beings who enter earth life and travel in human forms, just as Light Beings do. Human bodies are transportation for souls, like autos or horses are for humans.

July 5

THOUGHT FOR THE DAY- There is a secret set of hidden stairs that you climb within. They are the stairs to enlightenment, as well as to the light or door of heaven.

THE POWER TO GET ANSWERS

Whispering prayers on the fringes of a football field will not get you the answers you need from a god, angel, master, or spirit guide who is up in the commentator's box. You have to go where the gods, masters, angels, and spirit guides are, if you want to be heard. They have more important things to do than to leave their assigned posts to answer your request for a bag of peanuts or popcorn from the concessions seller. After you learn to go where the gods are, you have to realize that there are some requests that those of the heavens will not fulfill. Even though you ask, there are some things you have to get or provide for yourself.

A very obese woman whispers a prayer asking for money for a surgery to remove hundreds of pounds of fat to give her a thin body. Diet food and plans are available to her at the corner grocery, but she is too lazy to use them. She wants a quick fix, the fat to be cut off instantly. She doesn't want to work for what she wants. The universe is not likely to answer her request. A dieting, obese individual asking for help will be heard by those in the heavens. She is willing to work for change.

Consider yourself and your world! Are there things that you are in need of that you absolutely cannot produce for yourself. Is it your opinion, that only gods or divine ones can help you? Are you in a panic, trying to figure out how to get up to the commentator box to ask for and receive help? There is a stairwell and a door to the heavens and the gods/divine ones who work there. You have to find the stairwell and the door to the commentator's box if you want help. That stairwell and door are within you. Some refer to the stairs as the climb to enlightenment. These writings are stairwell steps. To climb or not to climb is your choice. You must climb if you wish to open the portal or door to heaven.

For Power to call important things forth into existence in your life, you must go inward spiritually and upward to the position of the third eye in the center of your human forehead. Once there, look with your third eye for a portal of light. The light is the door. Beyond the door is where spirit guides, angels, masters, and gods are.

If you ask for path change, the items needed to accompany that change will arrive as fringe benefits.

July 6

THOUGHT FOR THE DAY – Only gods traveling in human flesh can look thru a third eye into the heavens. Human eyes cannot look into lands of the gods.

THIRD EYE SIGHT

Man has invented the telescope. With it, he can look with his human eyes out into the universe or natural sky and get glimpses of other planets, stars, suns, etc. What the telescope does not let him see is a desired, magical being god (someone to care about him) who has powers beyond that of animals to help him. Man is an animal. He thinks with an animal brain. However, he desires to be more than an animal. Man becomes more than human when a divine light being soul enters him at conception and becomes the driver of him, like he is an automobile.

Man has two human eyes. The spirit being driver within man has an eye all its own. It is referred to as the third eye/gypsy eye/god eye and exists in the forehead area inside the human head. That eye is not used to look out onto the Earth plane. The 'THIRD EYE' looks into the heavens, the home of the soul. The 'THIRD EYE' is a mystical telescope of sorts. Using it, a spirit being within can look into the heavens and view whatever they wish to see, including multiple heavens, stars, moons, planets, spirit guides, deceased loved ones, etc. The 'THIRD EYE' is a powerful magnifying glass that can see things that are light years away. 'THIRD EYE SIGHT' is a power of gods traveling in human flesh. A human not having a light being/divine one traveling in him and driving him is merely an animal.

You are human and divine if you have a spirit being that drives your human form.

July 7

THOUGHT FOR THE DAY - Are you in need of something and frustrated with patiently waiting? Remember, your spirit guide has to work change out. He will not hurt or rob Peter to pay you, Paul.

THE POWER TO CALL FORTH

For Power to call things forth into existence in your life, you must go inward and to the position of the third eye in the center of your human forehead. Once inward and centered; look with your third eye for portal or astral Lights. Then, picture yourself receiving or doing whatever it is that you have need of. If you need a path change, picture a fork on your path. The picturing is like sending a video of your desires to your spirit guide. Once you quit picturing, return to human brain thinking and go about your earth day. Your earth life path will slowly start to change. At first you will see small changes and then proceed to larger ones. Your spirit guide has to work change out, without interrupting or invading the space and paths of others.

The powers of the universe (including the power to call things forth) are for use by light being souls, not the human brain and its limited animal thinking. It is the spirit being/soul within that has access to heaven's powers. The animal brain is interested only in day to day survival. When you start to think higher /spiritual/paranormal/religious/ enlightened thoughts, you switch from animal thinking to soul thinking.

Once you learn to switch from animal to soul thinking, and within, don't get hung up asking for earthly material possessions. Calling forth powers are for path changes, not physical items. Physical items will come to you as they are needed on your path that is changing. Calling forth unnecessary frivolous possessions is a waste of time. Frivolities weigh you down to single moments. They are like boat anchors. For instance, you ask the universe for a yacht, because you envy the one your boss has. With the expensive adult toy come insurance, payments, and way too many friends and family wanting to borrow it, or invading your weekends. Your frivolous request calling forth a yacht becomes a curse to you. Ask only for things that are useful on your forward moving path.

The 'calling forth' power is available to light beings. It is not available to dark beings/fallen angels in human forms. Dark power is the opposite of Light Being power. Light beings call forth good things. Dark being steal and destroy.

JULY 8

THOUGHT FOR THE DAY – The time for retribution

for evil done you is not up to you. Karma angels wait and use just the right moment to Karmic whack your enemies. The same Karma angels will whack you for misdeeds you do to others.

THE POWER TO RETURN CURSES ON THE WIND

Ill feelings/ill will/curses are vibrations, just like spoken words are. Bad vibrations/curses ride air waves like radio signal vibrations, waiting to connect with a receiver. Curses are vibration words of damning that are spoken out into the universe with power behind them. We can return curses sent to us in the same fashion. We must use powerful words to turn curses and send them back to their sender. Returning curses is like returning an unwanted letter.

Humans as a whole are not very tall. Like radio signal towers, the human form must have height to successfully return curses. The human form must be above the surface of earth or floor where feet reside. Returning curses is a wind or higher atmosphere act. If you are in a house or an apartment, stand on top of your bed, chair, dining table, etc. to make your human signal tower taller. If you are outside, go to the top of a picnic table, a slide, or anything that has feet of its own to keep your feet off the surface. A bridge is fine as well as up in a tree. The bridge has feet and the tree feet roots. Standing on top of a vehicle will work. It has four tires which are feet. To return curses, you cannot be the feet of your tower. You must be the top, the higher the better.

Once you have taken position on high ground, making yourself the top of a signal tower, take in a very deep breath. Then, blow the air out slowly but forcefully, while stating in thought, "I return to you . . . the curse you have tried to assault me with. May the curse now fiercely rotate as a tornado of wind and return to you, its creator, as a karmic slap."

When the last of the deep breath of air is out, do not take another till you fashion two of your fingers in the form of scissors. Cut the wind connection from your mouth as though you were cutting an invisible rope. When you have cut the wind connection, then you can breathe. If you breathe in before cutting the connection, you suck the curse inside of you. You will then become very ill, depending upon what the components of the curse were that was sent you.

Illnesses that cannot be explained are curses, especially when they are lung or respiratory based. Curses are breathed in.

JULY 9

THOUGHT FOR THE DAY – Neglect is the willful abuse of oneself, people, animals, daily chores, and things necessary for healthy living. Neglect is a power of dark beings/demons in human flesh.

THE POWER OF NEGLECT

Neglect is a power of darkness. Its manifestation can be seen in many forms. Some dark beings do not mow their grass or wash their clothing. Some neglect personal hygiene, willfully letting their body odors offend noses of those in their presence. Others neglect aging parents, children, animals, jobs, housework, etc. Neglect is abuse. Those who abuse are not light beings. The power of neglect is a power of devils/demons/fallen angels/darkness.

I have a childhood friend that lives in another state. I haven't seen her for at least thirty years. She recently wrote me a letter complaining that Social Services was called by neighbors who complained that her 92 year old mother (who lived alone) was being neglected. After an assessment by social services, my childhood friend was informed that she had three days to get her mother into a nursing home or they were charging her with neglect of a parent. Apparently, my friend's bedfast mother had at least a dozen dogs and over 20 cats living in the house. The mother's hair hadn't been washed or combed for at least a month. Trash and animal feces were wall to wall. My childhood friend went on and on in her letter complaining that social services was sticking their nose in where it didn't belong. Like social services, I was horrified that my friend would let her bed confined mother live in such conditions.

My childhood friend is an only child, and lives a half block from her mother. Her mother, a lifelong real estate investor and landlord, owns two city blocks of mortgage free rental houses. Money for nursing care is not an issue. Since my friend did not live at a distance, there was no excuse for her mother's living conditions. My friend willfully chose to neglect her mother and let her live in filth. Neglect is a power of darkness.

After reading my friend's letter, I cringed at the thought that I had been friends as a child with an angel of darkness. Looking back, I do recall her encouraging me to do little things that were not kosher at the time. Dark children do try to get other children to do things that are unacceptable. A dark child may encourage a friend to write on the wall, stomp a bug, rock a bird, steal, lie, etc. When the friend gets caught, the dark child yells, "I didn't do it!"

There is war in the heavens, and earth is just one battlefield. We rub shoulders everyday with those of darkness. You can judge individuals to be light or dark by their fruits. The fruit of willful, long term neglect is a sign that an individual is one of darkness.

July 10

THOUGHT FOR THE DAY – The refusal to let children become who they want to be is the 'calling forth' of hell into their lives.

THE DARK POWER TO STIFLE CHILDREN

Just as light beings have power to call forth positive change and experiences into their lives as they travel on earth, dark beings have the power to call forth gutters to travel earth life in. Gutters are mini hells. The choice to live welfare and low income housing lifestyles is the entering into life's gutters. In calling forth that hellish lifestyle for yourself, you also take those about you to that hell. Children enter gutter hells holding the hands of dark being parents.

The refusal to let children become who they want to be is another type of hell that parents impose on their offspring. For instance, I know a young man who dreamed his whole life of entering the air force and making a career of it. His father was hung up on football and insisted the kid play all thru junior high and high school, instead of entering the high school ROTC program. The father demanded and got his wishes, but the son lost his dream. During his senior year of high school, the son had a serious football knee injury. The knee injury prevented him from being accepted into the air force after graduation. Now, the son works as a janitor. There are parents who call forth hell into their children's lives by insisting they embrace and become that which they are not.

Abandoning children is also the calling forth of hell into children's lives. Many children are reared by grandparents on social security that cannot afford to do so. Drug addicts and alcoholics are bad about dumping their children on someone else to rear, not caring who. If they were light beings, they would nurture their children, keep a roof over their head, give them religious roots, and plan for college educations for them. Dark being parents willfully call forth hell into their children's lives.

Are you letting your children become what they are destined to be? Are you providing a heaven or a hell for them to grow up in? Are you a light being who provides for your off spring, or are you a gutter rat who has chosen to live in welfare gutter hells?

July 11

THOUGHT FOR THE DAY - Choosing to believe that there is a heaven, without proof or memories, deems an individual one of the light. They live by faith, where intact communication cord light beings live by divine direction from the heavens.

THE POWER TO LET GO

Love is a standard in the heavens, an educational course that student light beings must master. Student light beings enter earth life sometimes accidentally having their communication cords with the heavens severed. When this happens, students forget who they are and live human lives with the human brain in total control. Divine love is forgotten, as well as memories of home life in the heavens. Heaven becomes a storybook place like the North Pole workshop is to Santa Claus. Heaven becomes a fairytale place that severed beings hope exists.

Sooner or later, all of us will have a loved one get ill and be about to die. If we have severed communication lines, we may desperately want to hold onto our loved one, thinking earth life is all that there is. Out of love and fear, we hold on to them seeking experimental drugs, operations, etc. We try desperately to keep them alive and safe from oblivion. Our dying loved ones are like little birds about to leave the nest and take their first flight. Our hands are like nests. We can close our hand on our little birds, refusing to let them take flight, or we can let go and let them fly away to freedom. Holding on to a bird that is about to take flight is an error or dark choice. Letting them go is a light choice. Letting go is extremely gut wrenching for those with severed communication lines to the heavens. They must believe by faith that their loved one is going to fly away to a better place, like the mythical Santa Claus does.

Choosing to believe that there is a heaven, without proof or memories, deems an individual one of the light. They live by faith, where intact communication cord light beings live by divine direction from the heavens.

I am sitting in the hospital watching my brother slowly die as I write this. In the next bed is a heart patient who collapsed in the car he was a passenger in. I just listened to him tell his nurse a story about seeing a light when he collapsed. He told of seeing a tunnel like object that's outside structure wall was similar to the texture of an ear of corn. He said he looked into the kernel structure tunnel and saw its inner walls turn from yellow to red. Then a bright light appeared at the far end of the tunnel. He was about to step into the tunnel when he suddenly popped back in to his human body, opened his eyes, and realized that he was in an ambulance racing down the highway toward a hospital. Paramedics had performed CPR on him, bringing him back to life. His going home to the light of the heavens was interrupted by strangers (paramedics) trying to hold on to him. He was a bird about to take flight. Paramedics stifled or refused to let him go.

Modern medicine is good, but at the same time it interferes with the scheduled flights of light beings returning home to the heavens. Modern, CPR techniques bring back life/souls to a human body, just so that same human body can eventually suffer the pain and pangs of human death all over again. In a way, it is a form of abuse. There are sociopath killers who choose to torture and strangle their victims to the point they quit breathing. Then they bring them back to life so they can repeat the killing. Those sociopath murderers are dark beings. Are modern CPR givers heroes or sociopath abusers and killers? The sociopath killer and the CPR giver cause human bodies to live again and pull souls back to earth life to reside in them. Both cause human bodies to have to die more than once. Killers strangle and bruise necks. CPR givers break ribs and bruise chests.

July 12

THOUGHT FOR THE DAY - When a mentally challenged human body baby smiles, it is due to the light being, observer angel within being amused.

POWERS OF THE MENTALLY CHALLENGED

There is a special order of light beings/angels that enter earth life as observers. They enter earth life traveling in human flesh, just as other divine ones do. However, they need a slow lifestyle, to observe one family or small group of beings for a period of time. They are laid back travelers who are not allowed to interfere with the faster lifestyles and events of those they watch. Observers let the human mind of its host dominate while they spend their time observing. They are side seat drivers you might say.

Human parents get angry with their gods when mentally challenged children are born to them. They shake their fists at the heavens and demand answers as to why they are cursed with a less than perfect baby. They don't realize that they have been blessed with a special type of human being that is host to an observer angel/light being. Human parents only zone in on the slow mind of the human baby born to them. They think that their god has given them a lemon.

Challenged children do take more care and have physical breakdowns. Like automobiles, they are constantly in need of care and repairs. I have a friend who owns a quirky car. Her temperamental auto is always stranding her, refusing to start when she goes to the grocery store. For some reason, she has to let her vehicle sit 20 minutes after she comes out of the supermarket before it will start. Mentally challenged or slow children are quirky like that. They will have their moments when they need some down time. Sometimes they will just refuse to get up and go (do what you want them to do). Just as my friend's car stalls at times, mentally challenged children do the same. The challenged children have a legitimate reason. They have an observer angel within that needs still time to do their work.

(Note: If your mentally challenged child is physically abusive, curses, and causes continuous havoc in your life, he does not have an observer angel within. He may be the host vehicle for a dark being. Dark beings/fallen angels travel in human flesh just as light being angels do.)

The power of the mentally challenged is that they are host vehicles for observer angels. Feel blessed if the universe has taken enough interest in you to send you an observer. Were you praying and asking for an angel baby?

July 13

THOUGHT FOR THE DAY – Light being students become masters by perfecting their power gifts.

THE POWER TO PLAY INSTRUMENTS BY EAR

When we enter Earth life, we are given special skills or powers to help us glide easily along on our individual, specialized paths. For instance, some individuals have a gift to play instruments by ear. They cannot read music. Those with the ear gift play from the time they are children, never having any formal music training. The gift is a power.

There are supernatural power gifts that we enter earth life with such as playing an instrument by ear. Then, there are perfected/mastered power gifts. Those who study and advance in their particular supernatural powers become masters. One who plays an instrument by ear is a student. One who has perfected his music skills is a master.

What special power have you entered earth life with? There are powers to cook, paint, write, compose, love animals, nurture children, carpentry, etc. Cooks go to school and become master chefs. Crayon drawing children grow up, study art, and become master art teachers and master museum curators. Animal lovers become master veterinarians. You have a power. You become a master when you study and perfect your power. Power gifts are given to students who are sent to earth to perfect their gifts.

I play the piano by ear. When I was a child, a Baptist church pastor heard me play and offered to give me free piano lessons if I would become their church pianist. I was nine at the time. My parents were of a different faith and refused the lessons; letting their religious beliefs stand in the way of my opportunity to study and become a master pianist. Parents can be hindrances to children with gifts. It is very important to let children study in the fields they are talented in.

What are your supernatural powers? What are the powers of your children? Have you mastered yours? Are you letting your children take advantage of opportunities to start the mastery of theirs? Opportunities for mastering powers don't always come in predictable ways. Be open to opportunities for yourself and your children.

JULY 14

THOUGHT FOR THE DAY - When man's divine side

sleeps, he is an animal. When man lets darkness awaken in him, he becomes one of darkness, a devil.

THE POWER TO CLOUD MAN'S THINKING

There is a spirit being soul that sleeps within man. It awakens only when the human brain decides to seek and discover whether God or an afterlife exists. Seeking is a supernatural power available to man's human brain. When man's animal brain makes the choice to ignore his 'power to seek', his spirit being soul within sleeps. When man's divine side sleeps, he is an animal that walks a fine line between heaven and hell. His other choice is to turn to darkness and let those of darkness enter and control.

Those of darkness are fallen angels who have been kicked out of the heavens for various acts. Those fallen angels have waged war against the heavens and those of the light. As an army of dark ones, they seek to entice and get human thinking to step over the dividing line into lower or dark thinking. For instance: A human seeking the light will read philosophical and religious literature. A human not seeking spirituality will choose porn and other magazines of darkness.

Earth is just one battleground in the universe. Human bodies are like army tanks that light and dark beings enter and do war in. Most war on earth is hand to hand combat, or the daily rubbing of dark and light at school, in the workplace, etc. War on earth is daily life. For instance: In the workplace, dark fellow workers and bosses will curse you, demean you, back stab you, fire you, etc. Soldiers of light will encourage and praise.

The power of clouding human minds is one battle technique that dark forces will use. If a fallen angel/devil in human flesh can keep man and his human brain bombarded/clouded with dark ideas of immorality, porn, prejudices, etc., he cut cause animal man and his brain to step over the dividing line into darkness.

July 15

THOUGHT FOR THE DAY – One of a light being's goals on Earth is to roll back clouded thinking for others. Clouded thinking has to be cleared up, in order for higher thought to be understood.

THE POWER TO MAKE CLOUDS ROLL BACK LIKE A SCROLL

There are many ways a human mind can become clouded. Pollution of thought is one. Just as some humans toss litter out their car windows littering and clouding the beauty of a landscape, others toss litter and garbage out their mouths in the form of gossip. Gossip clouds the thinking or landscape of the human mind.

Parents, who openly speak forth words of gay bashing, skin color hatred, religious prejudice, and other forms of bigotry in front of children, litter or cloud their offspring's minds. Ministers/priests/rabbi/monks/etc. who give narrow view talks from the pulpit declaring that they are the one and only church, cloud the minds of the gullible. Politicians are notorious for trying to cloud the thinking of voters in their favor. To run another candidate down is a dark act of clouding. A teacher who plays favoritism to the elite of her class clouds the thinking of the poor child making him think that he is worthless.

To roll back the clouds or scrolls for another person, you must point them toward education, wholesome ways of living, and their endless possibilities. A child or adult can rise and look into the heavens thru a rolled back scroll. They can become enlightened in thought with help. They can climb beyond human brain thinking to divine thinking. Dark beings help a child or adult to descend in thought to the dark pits of prejudiced and bigoted hell.

Back in the early 1950s, I would walk a few blocks to go visit my Aunt Golden. Most of my family considered her to be a little straight laced or stiff in her thinking. To me she was the voice of all that was good and decent. On most occasions that I visited her, she would always speak the same words to me.

"Jo . . . I want you to always remember that good girls don't smoke, drink, or curse."

My aunt's stiff, straight laced words have influenced my choices and actions for a lifetime. I do not smoke, drink, or curse. Her repetitious words to me concerning 'pure living' rolled back the scrolls of right and wrong to me, when I was a child. I have always made efforts to make good choices, out of respect for her. There have been times that I have goofed up. When that happens, I always remember my aunt's words which encourage me to stand up, center myself on my path, and keep walking toward the light and pure living on earth.

Are you rolling back clouds and scrolls for a child in your circle of family and friends, or are you darkening/hazing their minds with words of dark prejudices and bigotry.

July 16

THOUGHT FOR THE DAY – Some of the populace from the Old Testament Age abandoned their religious roots and embraced the New Testament Age. It is now time for the enlightened ones to walk out of the New Testament Age and embrace what lies ahead in the New Age.

THE POWER TO LAY DOWN ARCHAIC BOOKS

Back in the 1940s and 1950s, our house was cooled by leaving the windows up and the use of electric fans. Air conditioning didn't become available in our neighborhood till the 1960s. Wakes were big back at that time. We were a huge family and I grew up with deceased family members being laid out in our living room for 24 hour wakes, many in the extreme temps of hot summertime.

One August, it was 102 degrees when the funeral home brought a casket and body to our home for a wake. After positioning the casket in a corner, he opened the lid to display the upper torso of my grandfather. After straightening the clothing on my grandfather's corpse, he draped a huge black lace spread over the casket that was like a tablecloth. It was to keep the flies out. All of our windows in the living room were up due to the extreme temp. We had fans going, but they did not help much. They were just blowing hot air. However, fans were the latest in cooling systems for our area. The black lace cover to keep flies out was also considered modern.

Looking back, I shake my head and wonder how we survived those twenty four hour wakes, the scorching heat, and the flies. Even though our house had window screens and a door screen, droves of people arriving and leaving did let flies in. One person at the wake was assigned to wield a fly swatter for the wake. Thank God that modern air conditioning has replaced fans and funeral home viewings are now the modern style.

Just as air conditioning replaced fans, the New Testament Age of the Holy Bible replaced the Old Testament Age of the Holy Bible. Modern writings are now replacing New Testament writings. We are entering a New Age of Modern Thought. Just as it would be ridiculous to go back and embrace sweltering wakes with fans, lace covered caskets, and flies. It is also error thinking to hold on to past archaic writings. The Old Testament writings are like going to a sweltering wake where a casket has no lace covering and flies are crawling all over a corpse. The New Testament writings are like going to a wake where there is a lace covering over the casket, but the flies are still there and crawling all over you and those viewing. The New Age of Modern Thought is the abandoning of old wake ways altogether. Air conditioned viewing, without flies, is a type of modern thinking, or New Age Thinking.

You must now choose whether to move forward into a New Age or embrace the black laces and flies of New Testament living. It is now time to walk out of the New Testament Age and embrace what lies ahead. Those left behind will be those who do not move forward and out of the past. The Jewish religion is the past. The Protestant and Catholic religions are the black laced caskets that are about to be abandoned. New Age Thought is air conditioning and sensible viewing. Don't be left behind swatting flies and reading archaic writings.

July 17

THOUGHT FOR THE DAY - Humans have a power. It is free will choice. Supernatural powers belong to the light being, divine one, god, etc. that enters and travels in a human body. Human bodies are vehicles or cars for the gods.

THE POWER TO WALK ON WATER

Man has powers on earth, due to the light beings that live within. When the human mind listens to its divine being driver within, it can use the powers of its divine one. Walking on water is one of those divine powers.

Man can walk on water when it is frozen. He has learned to make ice or frozen water. Professional ice skaters walk and skate on water (frozen water) regularly in ice shows. Millions of people watch the phenomena on television when ice dancers compete on ice. Just as man learned to freeze water into ice for walking on, it is discovering how to use divine powers that makes it possible for man to perform miracles. The creating of a machine to freeze ice so man can walk on it is a miracle.

In the New Testament of the Christian's bible, Christ walked on water and invited a disciple to join him in the act. No machines had been invented yet to freeze water. When we lay down in sleep at night, our souls exit our human forms and perform all sorts of feats in the land of what humans blow off as gas dreams or nightmares. However, in dreams or out of body states, we are able to fly, levitate, walk thru walls, swim when our human body does not know how, and walk on water or clouds if we choose. Our powers are within.

Christ was a divine being traveling in a human form

called Jesus. Jesus was human and limited to the things that his human body could do. Christ was the soul driver of the human vehicle transportation called Jesus. The vehicle man named Jesus was aware that he had powers within and he let the divine soul within have control and be the driver of his vehicle. It was the divine one within that created the miracles we attribute to Jesus Christ. Just as creative souls today use their ideas to create methods of freezing water to walk on, Christ made the liquid water a surface that he could walk on back in that time period.

As human animals with animal brain thinking, we must have faith in ideas that come down to us from the divine ones that live within us. If we create with those ideas, we learn to walk the impossible in life. We create the impossible. We become the impossible. What makes some men masters and gods in human life on earth is the fact that they let the spirit man within be the driver, the creative force.

Our god powers may be somewhat different from Christ's. Instead of water walkers, we may be computer inventors or Moon and Mars walkers. Each god or light being traveling in human flesh is on a mission and has certain powers to use on his journey. Your powers within may be different than the man standing next to you. Have you bothered to ask your spirit being within what his powers are? Mine sends me words to put on paper. He is the miracle worker, a trumpeter of words. Human me is the typist.

July 18

THOUGHT FOR THE DAY – Your specialized miracle

working powers will be according to the field that your talents are in.

THE POWER TO TURN WATER INTO WINE

In Christ's time and in archaic times, ice was something that was available only in the winter. Today we have freezers and can make ice whenever we please. We have the power to take a physical thing like water and turn it into another form. Things that were considered miracles in the Old Testament and New Testament ages have become ordinary happenings today.

Light beings, coming from heaven and traveling in human forms, have powers. They have advanced or divine knowledge as how to change the physical make up of things. Light beings can invent with or use their powers, if they don't interfere with the path or progress of a single human, or of humanity as a whole. Their power cannot be used to change the physical make up of things to harm mankind. Creating freezers to make ice for cooling and storing food is acceptable. Creating boxing gloves for one man to hit and bruise another with is not. Some modern things have been created or invented by dark beings or devils traveling in human flesh.

A light being cannot use his powers to turn sugar into heroin for a drug dealer. Divine beings cannot turn pieces of metal into prison cell keys for career criminals. They cannot use their powers to make a willfully obese, food gulping person into an instant skinny model. What light beings can do is change that which will advance the thinking of mankind. Light beings can create cures for disease, write books of encouragement, turn frowning faces to smiles, invent machines that can turn water into ice, build canning factories that can preserve food to feed thousands, etc. With the advancement of the ages, divine ones use their powers for changes that are pertinent to that day. Christ turned water into wine at a wedding feast. There was no place to run out and get more. Today, you could just send someone out to the corner convenience store for some back up wine from their cooler.

Light beings are on earth today to create miracles that will take us into the future. Turning water into wine today is a waste of time for light beings, because it is already easily available. Christ also once walked on water. Today, freezing machines turn water into ice, and men walk or skate on it daily. Today's and tomorrow's miracles will be advanced and different from those of biblical days. Also, they will be manifested according to what powers each light being possesses for his particular mission on earth and other planets.

Powers of light beings are different and specialized. I am a writer. My power is words. I cannot create advanced electronics. That is not what I am on earth for. You may be a master chef. The preparation of gourmet food is your power. Cooking is not my power. I eat in a café every day. Your neighbor's power might be singing or playing an instrument. You may not be able to carry a note in a bucket. Each man can create miracles like Christ, but the miracles must be according to his powers or talents. Work a miracle today using your special powers/talents.

July 19

THOUGHT FOR THE DAY - Have you ever called a

friend and said, "Come go with me!" Calling forth or raising the dead is that simple. However, it is up to the dead whether they want to rise and go with you or not.

THE POWER TO RAISE THE DEAD

Who are the dead? There are three types according to human thinking. There are the dead bodies and brains that lay rotting in graves supposedly waiting for a resurrection, souls who have moved on to the heavens abandoning their human forms, and humans who are alive in body but walk about dead spiritually.

When the spirit being that travels in a human body steps from its human form, the host animal body dies. The death includes the human brain. Both body and brain rot and decay. The animal human form and brain has no chance of resurrection, unless the spirit being that has just abandoned it, decides to return to it for some reason.

Medical science has figured out how to raise the dead thru CPR. To some degree they are successful in making the human animal form live again. However, the sad part is that CPR only brings back the human animal body so that sooner or later it can suffer illness and the pangs of human animal death all over again. CPR cannot make a man live forever, nor can CPR cause a soul to return to its animal transportation vehicle. The brain dead are those who live physically, but do not have souls/spirit beings within. CPR givers say to human forms, "Come back to life, so you can be ill again and suffer death's pains again in the future."

There is the calling back to life of the human body and there is the calling back to the body the souls that once traveled in them before death. CPR can call back the human body but not necessarily the soul or divine one that traveled in it. The brain dead are soul free.

July 20

THOUGHT FOR THE DAY - Powers exists in the upper heavens that are unfathomable to human thinking. Being in more than one place at one time is one of those powers

THE POWER TO BE MULTIPLE PLACES AT ONCE

Humans wear clothing or costumes on earth that reflect their tastes and who they are. When a spirit being/soul climbs from a human body, he still has the tastes that he had while traveling in a human body. Returning to the Astral/First Heaven, a soul/orb may choose to wear a costume of the human body and its clothing that he has just exited. The costume is a memory projection.

Costumes worn in light portals and on the Astral Shore/First Heaven are sort of like T-shirts that earth vacationers bring back with them from Hawaii or other vacation paradises. Costume bodies and clothing worn by spirit beings returning to the heavens are projected costumes, vacation T-shirt souvenirs you might say. The spirit being's actual discarded human bodies lay rotting in graves on earth.

When a spirit being leaves the Astral Shore/First Heaven to enter the upper heavens, projected costume bodies and clothing is discarded. The orb soul steps from them. The spirit being soul at that point returns to being what he truly is, an orb of light and energy. As an orb, he is not limited in what he can do. Without a human body to weigh him down, an orb can travel the universe and be in four or more different places at one time. He can also travel backwards and forwards in time and be in several dispensations of past and present time at the same time. It is not unusual for an orb to travel to the four corners of the earth and appear in all four corner destinations in the same blink of an eye.

Powers exists in the upper heavens that are unfathomable to human thinking. Being in more than one place at one time is one of those powers. An angel, who visits you wearing a purple winged human costume, may also appear to three other humans around the world without wings and dressed in the colors of the rainbow. In Buddhist writings, there are masters who could be in two places at once. I am telling you that there are divine master orbs that can appear 'four or more' places at one time. Don't limit your thinking when it comes to considering what divine ones are like and can do.

If an angel should appear to you, ask him if you are the first, second, third, or fourth human being that is seeing him in that blink of an eye moment in time.

July 21

THOUGHT FOR THE DAY - Time stands still when you get lost or deeply involved in something you are enjoying. Sleep is one such pleasure.

THE POWER TO MAKE TIME STAND STILL

Have you ever heard someone say, "The time just got away from me!" or "Where did the time go?"

Time slowing down or speeding up is a power that accompanies moments of human bliss. 'Lost in time' is an expression describing the phenomena.

A master spirit being may choose to exit his human form and return to the heavens for a short period of time for various reasons. To do so, he can let his human body vehicle fall into a dozing or sleep state. He can then step from his human body transportation to pursue what he needs to do. It is like a human getting out of his auto and leaving it turned on, but running in idle while he runs into the convenience store for a quick purchase. After taking care of business in the astral, a master spirit being can return to Earth and awaken and further drive his human body vehicle.

When a master being returns to a human body, the body awakens and may say, "Boy . . . was I sound asleep. What time is it?"

You then proceed to tell him that he only dozed off for a moment or so.

He may reply, "Wow . . . I feel like I have been asleep for days!"

During a brief moment of human sleep, a master being within may climb from his human vehicle and take a few days, weeks, or years off for astral business, vacation, or down time. Masters can stretch time when out of the human body to accommodate their needs. They can make moments in time stretch for themselves and stand still for humans.

The human brain does not have the power to make time stand still. It is spirit being/soul that lives within that has that power.

July 22

THOUGHT FOR THE DAY – Words can bless or destroy! What comes out of a human's mouth denotes whether he has a light or a dark soul being within.

THE POWER OF WORDS

Much has been written about the power of demeaning words used to shatter the self esteem of others. A parent tells his child he is stupid. The child believes the parent and enters a pit of hellish depression thinking he isn't as smart as his siblings or others about him. A man tells his wife that she is ugly, worthless, fat, etc. With each berating assault of words, the wife sinks lower into a dark pit of believing she is nothing. The power of words can be used by dark beings to destroy.

The power of words can also be used to empower. A stranger tells you to have a nice day. You smile and return the greeting. We all want pleasant or nice days. The foundations for some pleasant moments in time are built by others. Your friend tells you how much he enjoys reading the poetry you write. You feel elated. He has built you up. We all want admiration for our accomplishments. A light being uses his power of words to lay pleasant foundations for others to build on. There is power in words. How we use them designates us as either of the light or the dark.

There is war in the heavens. Earth is one of many planet battlefields. Light and dark beings enter earth life to do battle. Light beings will say nice things to you and others in an effort to bring heaven down and into being on earth. A dark being will criticize and demean, causing hell to appear. Which side of the battle are you on?

July 23

THOUGHT FOR THE DAY – Man has the power to multiply, or turn one dollar into two. Those who are aware of and use the power turn every endeavor into financial gain.

THE POWER TO MULTIPLY

Have you ever met a man who could take a dollar and turn it into two? You have probably watched an individual like that embark on a financial quest, fall into a smelly pit, come out smelling like a rose, and carrying a handful of green backs. That same man can walk in the front door of a black tuxedo type business in rags and exit in black tails. He has mastered his power to multiply. He can take the impossible and turn it into possible.

Man has the power of free will choice. Those who have the power to multiply take that power, choose well, and then use their power to multiply to turn the ordinary into extraordinary. For instance: A man with a bad knee can look at a twisted, fallen tree branch and see it as a walking stick. He gets his pocket knife out and proceeds to fashion it as such. In doing so, the branch becomes valuable. The man does not have to purchase a walking cane, so the price of the cane stays in his pocket. He prospers from his powers of free will choice and to multiply. A woman goes into her kitchen and discovers that she has just a little flour, grease, and milk. She uses the power of free will choice to turn the ingredients into something else that is more valuable. She makes biscuits from the flour and grease and gravy from the milk. She uses her power to multiply to create from nothing a meal that will feed her family. After the meal, she lets her cat lick the plates clean. She further multiplies what she has to feed the cat. The cost/money for one meal of food for her family and cat food stays in her pocket. She is that much richer than when she began.

Children use the power to multiply in play. They put their imaginations to work and turn simple items into toys. Pots become drums to beat. Brooms become ponies to ride. Cardboard boxes become houses and forts. The creative child multiplies what he has. As a result, toy money stays in the parent's purse and the child increases the wealth of his family by the price of his created toys.

The financially drained in life are those who do not use their powers of free will choice and to multiply. They squander their finances to purchase everything they want, instead of using their power to multiply. Thus, they decrease their wealth instead of increasing it.

July 24

THOUGHT FOR THE DAY -- Miracle wine manifests for those who embark on spiritual journeys.

THE POWER TO TURN WATER INTO WINE

Water was contaminated in the days of Christ. There were not purification systems for water. Instead of drinking water, the people of that era drank wine as an alternative. Wine was their equivalent of purified water.

Christ used a power to turn unpurified drinking water into wine. He used his power to supply a drinkable liquid that would not make a group of wedding guests ill.

Today, we have modern gods in human flesh who have

created systems to purify drinking water. Water treatment plants are modern miracles. They purify water to quench the thirst of millions. Masters traveling in human flesh, light beings like Christ, have created, invented, and worked miracles in the water purification field.

There is a wine that is not a liquid, and it quenches the thirst of the soul (the spirit being living within a human form. That wine is spiritual thought, or living waters. The miracle wine that is not a liquid manifests for those who embark on spiritual journeys. That supernatural wine is enlightenment, the wine of gods. All master spirit beings, traveling in human flesh, have the power to take thoughts and turn them into supernatural enlightenment, wine of gods for others.

Humans get hung up on trying to turn drinking water into alcohol (wine). The power of turning water into wine (alcohol) is not given to those who just wish to make alcohol. The power to change the physical make up of things is given to those who will use the power for the betterment and safety of humans and other earth life forms.

The creators of water treatment plants or the diggers of clean wells use their power to change the physical make up of things correctly. They use their powers to purify. Spiritual leaders, who pour forth living water thought, produce the wine of the gods for their followers. They use their power correctly.

July 25

THOUGHT FOR THE DAY - Human attraction is a trick of nature to keep the animal, human body reproducing.

THE POWER OF OLD MAIDS

Human attraction and the mating process is basically an act of nature to keep the human species reproducing. The brain of the human species is an animal mind, and it makes decisions about whatever crosses its path and its need to feed and shelter itself to survive. Reproducing and surviving are animal brain's two main goals. The human animal brain is not the intelligence of the spirit being that lives and travels in a human form.

The human animal body is like an automobile. Spirit beings or souls are drivers. The soul has separate intelligence, as well as separate vision. The human animal body eyes are like the headlights on a car. The spirit being or soul's eyes are those of the driver. The soul has the ability to use its eyes to look out on earth as it travels, or into the heavens where focused human headlight eyes cannot.

Master light beings enter earth life as souls. They enter conceptions and travel in human form vehicles/autos. Master soul beings have already lived many lives on earth as well as other planets. They understand the workings and attractions of human bodies, their transportation. They understand that human bodies have a built in need to reproduce. As masters, they are capable of short circuiting attraction and reproduction quirks. Old maids who focus on religious education and spiritual occupations are master beings. They are on serious earth journeys and have no time or desire to satisfy the animal reproduction quirks of the human body.

Back in the 1950s, I had a childhood friend named Norma. She absolutely knew that she was called to be a church pastor. During that era, lady ministers were not accepted in the male dominated clergies of the United States. That did not stop or hinder Norma. She went to work as a waitress at fourteen and used her wages to rent a building and start a storefront church. Her dad built pews and a pulpit for it. In spite of male animal thinking at that time (women were to be kept barefoot and pregnant), she became what she dreamed of being, and chose not to marry. Reproducing and mothering an animal human form was not what she was called to do.

In human animal thinking, Reverend Norma was looked down on as a pitiful, lonely, old maid. In higher thinking, she was a revered soul who did not need an animal man to lean on, or to give her permission to work, create, preach, or fill a position that was considered to be a man's.

The old maids and bachelors in your life could be masters traveling in human flesh, if they are seeking spiritual paths.

July 26

THOUGHT FOR THE DAY – Those who handle stress well are master tight rope walkers. Those who fall off their high wire (have break downs) do not have that talent.

THE POWER TO ASK FOR HELP

Earth life has many types of balancing acts. Each has its own type of stress. Some people handle their individual type of stress well. Others do not. Stress reduces some men to tears, causes them to climb into bottles of alcohol, lands them in psych hospitals, and sometimes suicide attempts. Those who handle stress well can walk a fine line and still smile and see the bright side of every situation. Those who embrace the overwhelming darkness of their situation, step from the fine line of sanity, they fall into many forms of darkness.

When a man has a lot on his life plate, he becomes a life circus tight rope walker, trying to balance his many stressful life situations in an effort to survive. A single mother raising several children, having aging ill parents to tend to, and holding down two jobs to pay bills is a woman with a balancing act. A father paying three children's way thru college, alimony to two ex wives, and secretly about to file bankruptcy is doing a balancing act. A child hiding from bullies at school, working for his one daily meal in the school cafeteria, and goes home to endure nightmare abuse from alcoholic parents is a child tightrope walker. What causes stress or tight rope walking is not the same for everyone.

Some humans have the talent to be actual circus tight rope walkers, most humans do not. The power to be a circus performing tight rope walker is a rare one. Tight rope walking thru life challenges that are stressful cannot be handled by some. Yet, thru bad investments, marriages, and assaults by others, many individuals find themselves on a life high wire trying to walk and balance the impossible.

Invisible light beings who come to earth on specific, hard to accomplish missions are tight rope walkers. They are souls/angels who are capable of handling the stress of serious planet balancing acts. The invisible keepers of the four corners of the earth are supernatural tight rope walkers. If Earth should go out of balance, life as we know would be over. Like keepers, some men can balance the elements and forces in their busy lives. Others cannot and flirt with a fall from their tightrope and a not so nice landing or ending.

It is okay to ask for help when your life plate is too full. Asking for help or turning part of your responsibilities over to others is okay. It falls under the power of 'Free Will Choice'.

July 27

THOUGHT FOR THE DAY - Ghosts have powers. Some are light powers and some dark, depending on whether the spirit is a light being who has not traveled to the light yet, or a fallen angel/one of darkness that is hiding out in the Land of Ghosts.

THE POWER OF DARK BEING GHOSTS

There is a Land of Ghosts, a place of mists that floats just above the earth plane. Sometimes its mists overlap earth. The ghost world is so close to the surface of the earth that its inhabitants can step thru the overlapping mist into earth life. In reverse, souls exiting the Earth plane can step thru the overlapping mists into the Land of Ghosts, an in-between world. The Land of Ghosts is not a holy or pure place. It is basically a hiding place for dark and light souls that do not want to cross over from earth life to heaven or hell for various reasons.

Because the Land of Ghosts and Earth have surfaces that overlap, inhabitants of the ghost world can reach thru or step thru the mists to haunt or interact with humans. Dark being ghosts will use their dark powers to enter earth life to annoy and assault humans. Light being ghosts are usually lost in the mists due to severed silver cord communication lines. They are unaware that there is a light they must travel towards to reach the heavens. So, they reach thru or step thru the overlapping mists to try to get the attention of humans to ask for directions. Sometimes, lost light beings do not know that their human bodies are dead. They will step thru the overlapping and take up residence in houses on earth and be frustrated when humans living in them do not see or hear them. They will then do odd things to get human's attention like moving things around or knocking them off of shelves.

Dark spirit beings/souls who have exited human forms are fallen angels or devils. The entrance to their heaven (hell) is a down portal beyond the land of ghosts. Fallen angels/devils/demons choose to hide out in the Ghost World rather than descend into the darkness of their heaven.

There is a third group of ghosts called 'Shades of Gray'. They are light being souls that are running from judgment, the evaluation of their missions on earth. Some are goof offs who did not complete or take their earth missions seriously. For that reason, they are shades of gray. On the Astral Shore, shades of gray beings are sent back to earth after evaluation for second earth life times to get their missions right. Shades of gray souls may hide in the Land of Ghosts to avoid repeat lifetimes on earth.

Earth's legal systems can put a human body to death for crimes such as murder. However, they cannot put to death the soul of a dark one. Humans do not have that power. When legal systems put the human bodies of sociopath criminals to death, their dark soul just exits and looks for new human body conceptions to enter and travel in. Only the divine of the heavens can cause a dark soul to be destroyed and sent to the 'Land of Cease To Be', a cemetery for souls.

Killing a sociopath's human body on earth is opening a gate for him to escape punishment and live again. He will enter the ghost world and then start looking for a new human body to travel in. Some call the rebirth of a sociopath dark one as possession.

The power of dark being ghosts is that they can continuously live again in new host bodies, unless they are hunted down and destroyed by those who are at war with them in the heavens.

July 28

THOUGHT FOR THE DAY – The veil or mist of the ghost world distorts projected images of ghosts that are reaching thru or stepping thru it. Dark soul ghosts will project/appear as wild animals or blood covered dismembered beings with black holes for eyes.

THE POWER OF PROJECTION

The veil or mist between Earth and the Land of Ghosts is thin and like a piece of fabric that you can see thru. It is similar in density to a woman's nylon stocking, except that it is not beige. The veil between worlds is a misty gray. The mist or veil can only be seen on earth when a ghost soul thrusts body parts into it or steps thru it.

Bank robbers have been known to pull a pair of ladies panty hose down over their face for a disguise or mask when entering a bank to rob it. The filmy net distorts their facial features. The veil or mist of the ghost world distorts the projected images of souls that are reaching or stepping thru it to interact with man.

In my younger days, I had a homeless 14 year old friend who took up residence in an old abandoned, falling down farm house on the edge of my town. All he had in the way of luxuries was a mattress thrown on the house's bedroom floor. One Sunday afternoon, he reclined on the mattress to read a car magazine. Immediately, he heard fierce growling that sent cold chills thru him. He sat up quickly, thinking he had left a door or a window open, and that possibly a rabid dog had gotten in. To his shock, a wolf's neck and face suddenly projected itself thru the plaster wall into the room. The distorted, filmy wolf's head was growling and showing its fangs. My friend experienced a dark being projection in an animal form. Needless to say, my friend exited the farmhouse in haste and never returned.

The paranormal exists. Worlds that man is not familiar with overlap earth life. Beings exist that man and his human brain are not able of understanding or controlling, such as ghosts who have the power to project themselves in various forms thru the mists.

July 29

THOUGHT FOR THE DAY - In the land of 'Cease to be' there is no resurrection.

THE POWER OF GATE KEEPERS

There are gatekeepers/portal keepers who prevent dark spirit beings from entering the realms of light in the heavens. Those guards are armed with a weapon called 'CEASE TO BE'. With that weapon, they can cause sociopath souls to cease to exist.

Demons and devils are not allowed on the astral shore, or in the heavens. They do not have the right to stand before judgment on the Astral Shore, nor are they given travel permission to enter the upper heavens. The reason is that they are fallen angels who have already been to judgment and kicked out. There is no returning to the heavens for them. If they try to do so, their fate is to 'cease to be' at the hands of gate/portal keepers. The last thing a demon/devil/fallen angel wants is to 'cease to be'.

Heaven is not a place of second chances for fallen angels.

July 30

THOUGHT FOR THE DAY - Prayer is shared conversation, ideas, requests and compromises between two beings (one on earth and the other in the heavens). It is not a mumbo jumbo, childish beseeching of 'give me-give me-give me' for me and mine.

THE POWER OF PRAYER

Prayer is conversation between two beings. The power of prayer is when the two individuals can come into agreement with each other as to what is to be done about various needs.

A little boy, dirty from digging fishing worms, runs into his mother's kitchen hungry. He smells cookies that have just come out of the oven. "Mama . . . Mama, may I have one?"

"Not till you go wash your hands!" She replies.

We ask the masters of the heavens for cookies. Sometimes we have soiled spiritual hands. Spirit guides/angels/masters with the cookies (answers) may tell us to go wash first, or give us other instructions in order to receive.

The little boy, in the above story, could refuse to wash his hands and walk out without a cookie, or he could compromise with his mother and do what she asked to receive one. The 'coming into agreement' is the key to getting prayers answered. If your spirit guide/angel/master asks you to do something before receiving, it is up to you to decide whether a cookie answer is important enough to clean up your spiritual act.

Two eight year old brothers decide to build a car to enter a soap box derby. They both have ideas of how the end product/car should look like. One wants to use dad's lawn mower tires for wheels. The other wants to use the rollers off his mother's roll-away bed. They must reach a mutual decision, a compromise on which wheels will be the fastest. Both sets of wheels roll. One brother wants to use his mom's round pizza pan for the steering wheel. The other wants to use the front tire from their sister's tricycle for a steering wheel. The brothers must come into agreement as to which one will steer best. One brother wants to paint the soap box derby car blue, the other wants it painted red. Again, a compromise is necessary. For the soap box derby car to be built, the two brothers will have to talk, compromise, and come into agreement over the various aspects of the construction. Neither will be particularly happy when their idea is not the best one. However, it is the end product that is important, a car that just might win the derby.

Prayer is like building the soap box derby car. You are one builder, and your divine one/spirit guide of the heavens is the other. Unless the two of you come into agreement as to what the outcome/answer will be, your answer will not be constructed.

All of us pray prayers that will not be given a 'yes' answer. Sometimes, divine ones/spirit guides just straight out say, "No!" That would be like a mother telling her little boy, "Sorry, these cookies are for the church bazaar and I must have each and every one. I have committed myself to delivering each one. There are no spares."

Man grieves the loss of their loved ones who die. Praying for a loved one's soul to stay on Earth when his mission is over, will receive a 'no' answer. To ask in prayer that he be allowed to remain on earth in his ill human form is error. Letting a loved one go is like the little boy and the bazaar cookies. If he is in tune with his mother, he will understand that she needs every cookie for the bazaar. If he is self centered, he will demand one anyway. Telling those in the heavens that you can't live without a cookie/your loved one is being a demanding, temper throwing, self-centered little boy. When the Divine needs his cookies, ne needs them for his bazaar. Don't demand something that is not yours to demand.

A soldier and you (a soldier) go to the battlefield. The soldier has been in the military service a month longer than you. He completes his tour of duty and is getting ready to return to his home country, leaving you behind in a war zone. Having bonded with him, you pray for him to remain with you in the war zone, because you do not feel you can survive without him. Prayers to extend the missions of others are error prayers. When the tour of duty for a light being in a human form is over on earth, be kind and him go home in peace. Wish him well. Tell him that you will be joining them shortly when you have finished your own mission. Perhaps, God will send you a new companion/buddy to pal up with on earth till you complete your mission and cross over.

You have prayer power! Pray to a divine one like he is your eight year old brother, not a stuffy great uncle who lives a hundred miles away and has no interest in your derby car ideas. Present to your spirit guide or divine one your ideas, but also consider his. What you get from prayer is determined by the demands or respect you show.

July 31

THOUGHT FOR THE DAY – Men fear what they do not understand. Humans dream of seeing angels and going to a mystical someday heaven, but fear those who dare to say angels walk with us now and heaven has come down and the portals or gates to it are within.

THE POWER TO SAY, "I AM THAT I AM".

For those of you who do not know me, I am a light being soul that is traveling for one lifetime in a human body on Earth named Jo Hammers. On earth, I am a writer and artist. In the heavens, I am a soul called Master Barjoraven. In the heavens, I am a trumpeter of words. Words are my power on Earth as well as in the heavens. "I am that I am!"

You are either a dark soul or a light soul traveling on earth as well. Your human body is a vehicle, transportation like a car. Knowing that you are a soul and that your human body is just a mode of transportation, you can see yourself for who you truly are and say, "I am that I am!"

Actions determine whether you and I as souls are light or dark. Example: Porn magazines and movies will be read, watched, and relished in the minds of dark beings. Religious literature and philosophy will be read and studied by those of the light. Using this example as a guide, you can judge your own actions. You can determine which you are, a dark devil soul or a light angel soul of the heavens. You are what you are. I am what I am!

I, Jo Hammers, am a mystic, seer, psychic, writer, and artist. I am also Master Barjoraven, a light being soul that is traveling for one human lifespan in a human body called Jo Hammers, am on an assigned mission to earth. I am a trumpet calling humans to rapture in thought. Words are my power. What is your power? You know yourself better than anyone!

CHAPTER EIGHT
AUGUST

THE BOOK OF HEALING

August 1

THOUGHT FOR THE DAY - There is no ball bat or scissor wielding gods who will come down to you in your obesity and get rid of the 50 pounds of fat you willingly opened your mouth to put on.

BALL BAT CURES

Humans want a 'Baseball Bat Carrying' God, who is willing to come down and instantly fix their self made everyday problems and health issues. They want easy fixes. Buckling down and fixing one's own created problems, or health issues, is too hard.

An obese man eats himself into a dark pit of hell. To get out, he must climb out with the same teeth he used to eat himself down into it, eating one bowl of lettuce at a time. It is easier for the obese man to run to a god or healer in hopes for a fast fix. He wants that fix delivered like fast food restaurant burgers and fries. I am here to tell you that losing weight doesn't work that way.

Diet pills are another 'quick fix' choice that man makes in hopes of instant weight loss gratification. When that doesn't work fast enough for him he prays for a god to come down with a giant pair of belly fat scissors and instantly cut off 50 lbs, while he sits eating a bag of chips, three candy bars, and drinking a quart of soda. The scissors act is a type of many surgeries available today for overweight. The continued, indulgent eating after surgery is an act of irreverence that just might get you a Karma slap from the god or divine one you prayed to. You may have sudden complications, and then die from the ordeal.

If Christ, Buddha, or any other Divine One would knock on your house door at this moment, would you invite him in and serve him three day old leftovers from your refrigerator? After starting a diet or having surgery, having secret stashes of soda, candy, and chips is the same as having a refrigerator full of leftovers. You are the god of your life. Are you eating healthy gourmet, or are you eating trash food?

The simple solution, or easy fix, for obesity is to push oneself back from the table and eat a minor amount less until the weight drops off. There is no ball bat or scissor gods who will come down to you in your laziness and get rid of the 50 pounds you willingly opened your mouth to put on.

I have a friend who weighed close to 400 pounds a little over a year ago. She decided on an easy fix, and had lap band surgery to cure her obesity. For a period of about six months, she did okay as she recovered from the surgery (too sick to eat). However, she didn't do the work to change her eating habits during that recovery period. Now, she is back to the weight she was prior to the surgery, due to candy, chips, and soda.

Human bodies die from obesity, alcoholism, drug addiction, soda addiction, sugar addictions, tobacco addictions, lack of exercise, over exertion, as well as quick fix diets and surgeries for belly fat. The infinite's way for getting rid of human body obesity is for you to use your teeth to eat low calorie food one meal at a time like it is a ladder rung. You must climb the ladder to a thinner self with your teeth.

August 2

THOUGHT FOR THE DAY - If man chooses well, he is capable of living on earth as a god in human flesh.

HEALTH IS A CHOICE OF GODS

Man's greatest power is choice. He has to choose the heaven or hell on earth he wishes to pursue and dwell in. If he chooses well, he is capable of living earth life as a human god.

If man chooses dark ways and gutter living, he will experience the low class, hellish tortures of gutter life. Drug addiction, obesity, alcoholism, and being homeless are gutter existences.

Heaven and Hell exist side by side on Earth. Gods, divine ones, light beings, angels, devils and demons travel in human flesh and rub shoulders daily on Earth. Both the light and the dark beings choose to be who they are. Which have you chosen to be? You do have the power of free will choice. You have the choice to be an addict. You have the choice to be an alcoholic. You have the choice to be fat and ruin the health of the human body vehicle you travel in. You are your choices. Your choices deem you either one of the light or one who is embracing darkness. If you are a dark one, it is because you have made the choices that make you one.

Free-will choice is a power of spirit beings traveling in human bodies. They can choose well for their self and family members, or they can choose to embrace gutter living. A mother choosing to rear her child for a lifetime on welfare and food stamps and in low income housing is an example of a dark being thrusting her offspring into hell, the gutters of life.

August 3

THOUGHT FOR THE DAY – The human body cars we travel in have automatic systems. Self diagnosis and healing is one.

THE SIMPLENESS OF HEALING

It is late evening, and several children are out chasing fireflies. One child skins his toe while running barefoot. Bursting into tears, he runs to his mother for comfort and climbs up onto her lap. She kisses his inured toe to comfort him, and then proceeds to bandage it.

"Run back out to play now. Your toe will be fine in a day or so." She says to her child, as she eases him off her lap.

The mother knows that coddling him will only make him cry longer, and that he will miss out on the late evening fun.

Believing his mother (that the inured toe will be okay in a day or so) the child runs back out into the late evening shadows to continue what he was doing before skinning his toe, chasing fire flies.

Christians run to Jesus (a mother type healer) for comfort. To them, kneeling or bowing their heads is crawling onto his lap. As they cry (pray) he comforts and assures them everything is going to be okay in a short time. Afterward, they rise from their knees (get off their divine one's lap) and go back out into their adult worlds to work/play.

Refusing to get off your divine one's lap, or the returning to it, is what hinders healing. Doing so is unbelief that your mother type's words of comfort and instruction were true. Healing begins when you run back out to play in your adult world. Unbelief is when you return to the mother's lap for a repeat performance.

It does not matter what your religious persuasion is. The mother's lap exists for you. Go to your divine one for healing help. Then run back out to play in your world.

We are spirit beings on Earth, traveling in human forms for a lifetime. Our human bodies are our vehicles or autos. My human body vehicle has the ability to self-diagnose and heal itself. Yours does to! The healing function will work until the soul within a human form exits to returns to its home in the heavens. At that point, the human body car's self healing function will shut down and work no more.

August 4

THOUGHT FOR THE DAY – Souls of men do not die,

they crossover to resume their former soul lives in the heavens. Only animal bodies die. Man is an animal.

A VISITATION FROM ONE JUST CROSSED OVER

My brother Ralph was very, very ill from failing kidneys and years on dialysis. After over three years of suffering, he died. I was glad for his suffering to end, yet at the same time cried. After 24 hours of tears, (not for him, but for my loss of his presence in my Earth life) I crashed and fell sound asleep. He came to me in a dream.

In my dream state, I looked out and across a lush, green grassed hill. A hundred feet or so in front of me, sitting in a sparkling, white spa-like tub filled with bubbles, my brother waved and smiled the biggest smile I have ever seen him give. He then waved wildly at me, making sure he had my attention, because an angel had a towel and was trying to get him to get out of the tub of bubbles so those coming after him could have a turn. He ignored the angel's attempts and kept waving to me wildly and smiling. I know he was trying to tell me that he was okay, and that he was in a spa like paradise where angels were attending to his needs. As a soul crossed over, he was not ill.

When I woke up, I had to smile. My brother had chosen to hold up the line of souls that were crossing over so that he could get a message thru to me back on earth. The dream came two days after his death.

August 5

THOUGHT FOR THE DAY - Human bodies are vehicles, autos for souls to drive.

HEALING 'S LIMITS

The human body and its mind were created by Divine Source (a type of auto manufacturer). Men call that source God, Allah, Infinite, Supreme, etc. Divine Source installed in his automobile creation (man) the power of self healing. He did not install the automotive function/power to heal others, just him-self. Each human being vehicle is unique and programmed to meet its own needs.

A scratch, sore throat, or puncture wound from a mosquito or splinter in man heals. Man's built in self healing function activates and takes care of the situation. The self healing function ceases only when a soul leaves its human body transportation and goes home to the heavens. Autos on planet earth are repaired by auto mechanics. Human autos have self healing mechanics and medical persons who try to heal bodies by cutting, probing, and administering drugs. A human body transportation mechanic known as a doctor is limited. It is up to the human body's self-healing function to kick in and make the doctor mechanic's efforts work. If it is a soul's time to cross over, his human transportation will die. His self healing function will shut down and cease to work.

Every human body has an appointed lifetime of however many years and human days its inner spirit being needs to accomplish his assigned on Earth. Just as automobiles are given 3 or 5 year warranties, human body warranties are good for the days a soul needs to travel in it.

Babies and children die young because the spirit beings/souls in them have completed their short missions on earth. Not all masters or angels come to earth for 70 or 80 years. Some come for a few months, and others an Earth year or so.

Human bodies are vehicles or autos for souls to drive. When your old Ford or Chevy wears out, it goes to a salvage yard. When a human body vehicle wears out, it goes to a cemetery salvage yard.

I purchased a new car, a few years back. It was the smallest and cheapest vehicle put out by a particular United States car maker. It was not made to last for years like more expensive models. Its life expectancy was probably a hundred thousand miles or five years. At the time, I just needed short term transportation, like some souls just need short term transportation in human baby or child vehicles. I called my short term ride automobile 'Little Betsy'. You may have called your human baby or child (a transportation for a soul) 'Little Jack' or 'Baby Sarah'.

Vehicle bodies are not who we/souls are! We are spirit beings who ride in and drive human vehicles. The driver of your Jack or Sarah was a soul. In the heavens, Jack and Sarah are possibly adult master or college age beings. Should you pray for them to visit you in your dreams to let you know they are okay, don't be surprised if they come to you in an adult or college aged adult form costume. That is who they truly are.

Supernatural healing is available to human forms, as long as their drivers (Souls) need them for transportation. When it is time for master beings to return home to the heavens, the power of the human vehicle to diagnose and heal itself ends. Doctors can try to jumpstart and recall spirit beings to such vehicles, but death will still eventually occur. To call back and prolong the suffering of the human vehicle so it can suffer the pangs of death again is error. Dark beings abuse human bodies by trying to call back souls, making their human bodies relive the pains of death over and over and over again.

August 6

THOUGHT FOR THE DAY - When it is your time to go, your body will quit self-healing itself.

APPOINTED TIME

A male member of my family became ill suddenly. In efforts to save him from failing kidneys, doctors put him on dialysis. Also, his body was losing blood. The doctors did not know where his blood was disappearing to. In desperation to keep my family member alive, doctors gave him multiple pints of blood over a period of three or so years. After three or so years of dialysis, exhaustive invasive tests, blood transfusions, etc. he died. Modern medical science only succeeded in prolonging his illness and the suffering accompanying it. The male member in my family had an appointed time to die and modern medicine made a three or so year guinea pig out of him.

Humans using human brain knowledge cannot heal. Unless the self healing system in a human body kicks in, the human body will die. It was my family member soul's time to go (cross over to the home of the soul) when he first became ill. His years of agony afterward were doctors trying to imprison or chain his soul to earth life. His soul kept trying to escape life chains. My family member was given life saving measures more than once. Being forced to return to an ill body is an act of darkness. Today, there are dark criminal sociopaths who will strangle a victim to death, just so he can revive the victim and watch him or her die and suffer the pains of death again, again, and again. That is sadistic. Hospital and medical personnel, that revive the dead over and over again, do the same thing. Who says that all medical workers and procedures are of the light? Sadistic is sadistic. A sociopath is a sociopath.

When it is your time to go, your body will quit healing itself. You must be kind to your human body and not make a medical guinea pig out of it. It is not a scary thing to step from your human form. It is a day of celebration when you return to being who you really are, an orb of light soul. Earth life is like an astronaut wearing a spacesuit. You are limited in how much you can do. Free from your human body space suit, you as a soul can levitate, fly, travel at the speed of light, etc. Journeys to Earth by souls/orbs is exciting, and at the same time confining because of the human body space suits.

Space journeys have to end sooner or later. Souls like to go home to the heavens, just as astronauts like to return to earth. Just as an astronaut must abandon his space suit when returning, a soul has to abandon his human body spacesuit. Forcing souls to remain in ill body space suits so that medical science can experiment on them is a form of torture.

My family member was a master being of the heavens. He was a soul that wore an earth body space suit for 71 years, as he explored life on planet Earth. Now, he has discarded his human body space suit and returned to the heavens, his true home. He has managed to free himself from the limitations of his human body space suit, as well as from the probing, poking, cutting, and prolonged suffering inflicted by others.

August 7

THOUGHT FOR THE DAY - Mother's don't put cookies in dirty hands. Instead, she might slap the dirty hands of a child reaching for one.

REQUIRMENTS FOR HEALING

All of us have had family members that have been ill with colds, flu, diabetes, blood pressure, broken arms, rashes, ear infections, etc. Even though they have illnesses, we cannot reach out and use our self healing systems to heal them. They have their own healing systems and must learn to use them when body functions go wrong. What we can do is approach the Infinite for answers, as to how we might assist them as they heal. Sometimes the answer is as simple as making someone a cup of hot tea, or reading to them as they stay in bed and self heal.

A little boy, dirty from digging fishing worms, runs into his mother's kitchen hungry. He sees cookies straight from the oven. "Mama . . . Mama, may I have one?"

"Not till you go wash your hands!" She replies.

The little boy is a type of you and me. The mother is the Infinite or God. To get what we want, we must present our request to her. Then we must let our Mother/God type tell us what to do in order to get what we want. In the little boy's scenario, she told him to clean up before she would give him a cookie.

Those about us who are ill will have to find their cookie moment with their God. They may be asked to perform acts of obedience, like the little boy washing his hands, in order to get their cookie, or self healing system activated. An obese person might be told to eat bowls of lettuce instead of sacks of donuts. One with high blood pressure might be told to lay off the salt and change to a less stressful job. A child might be told to quit disrespecting his parents. We are light beings traveling in human form vehicles. If we choose dark ways of living and eating habits on earth, our automatic healing system is turned down, or shut off by the gods. All religions have their divine being.

You cannot activate the healing system of another, if they are not in alignment with what their Mother/God desires of them. Mother's don't put cookies in dirty hands. Gods don't bestow cookie healings into the hands of willfully dirty beings. Instead, gods might slap dirty hands, and tell them to go wash.

August 8

THOUGHT FOR THE DAY – When spiritual or psychic blindness is healed, the god within you wakens from a sleeping or comatose state.

HEALING FOR THE PSYCHIC EYE

Did you know that you have three eyes, not two? Your third eye exists in the center of your forehead, and it is your divine or psychic eye. Your two human body eyes look out into the physical world and keep track of what is going on there. Your inner third eye looks inward and then outward in to the invisible realms, heavens, hells, and in-between worlds. The third eye is the one that sees angels, deceased loved ones, dream worlds, astral shores, faraway places, forwards and backwards in time, and other supernatural phenomena.

You are a spirit being, a soul that is traveling in a human form for a lifetime on earth. You are the spirit being or god within, not the human vehicle auto you travel in. You are a god in human flesh, although you may be or have been a sleeping god up to this point. In order for the god within you to awaken, you must start to seek a spiritual path. Reading this book makes you a seeker who is stepping onto a spiritual path to acquire higher understanding. It does not matter what religious persuasion you step onto your path in. When you start to search for understanding (enlightenment), your third eye (god eye) opens.

Spiritual or psychic blindness is healed when the third eye opens. It is an awakening from a spiritual comatose state.

August 9

THOUGHT FOR THE DAY - Human eyes are not soul eyes. Lip prayers are not soul prayers.

SOUL PRAYERS OR LIP PRAYERS

When night sleep or meditation relaxes or numbs the human form, the spirit being within awakens and can climb out. Meditation or prayer is like using sleeping aids. The human body must become silent and relaxed in order for the spirit being/soul within to awaken and leave the human body to take astral flights to the heavens to take care of spiritual business.

Human lip words/prayers are just engine noise that is heard in the heavens. The human body is transportation for a soul. Its sounds are just car type noises. Human lip prayers are the moans and groans of a human type car engine, not the language of a soul driver. Flowery prayers from pulpits spoken by human lips are just moans and groans. True prayers are spoken by the spirit being that lives within.

To get prayers answered, you must relax and shut down your human form vehicle. Then, you go inward to the center of the human body forehead where the eye of the soul exists. That eye will open when your human body vehicle sleeps or relaxes. The soul eye looks into the heavens. Human eyes can only look out into the physical world. Human eyes are not spiritual eyes. Also, human lip prayers are not spirit being/soul prayers.

Are you saying human prayers or soul prayers? It makes a difference when you are asking to be healed or for major requests to be heard.

August 10

THOUGHT FOR THE DAY - Just as the sun shines soothing rays of heat upon humans; rays from the portals of heaven shine forth healing.

HEALING FOR ASTRAL INJURIES

On Earth, when walking alone at night, one doesn't as a rule walk into dark tunnels, underpasses, or alleys alone. We are aware that there are dark, sociopath individuals that hang out in secluded places waiting to rob, assault, kidnap, or possibly murder the unsuspecting. Portals to the afterlife can be stalked by dark beings looking for victims. Demons and devils cannot enter the light portals, but they can lurk in the shadows surrounding them. The Ghost world is one shadowy place that exists outside the light portal gates of the First Heaven.

Like light beings, dark beings pop or step from human forms at death. They then can choose to travel as far as the light portals to the heavens. Because they are fallen angels that have been kicked out of the heavens, they are angry with those of the light and seek to harm them. Assaulting light beings that are heading for heaven's portals is their focus. One of the most common assaults by dark souls is the severing of 'Silver Cord' communication lines. On earth it would be the equivalent of cutting a throat. The cutting of cords leaves light being souls with astral amnesia, the equivalent of an earth child who cannot remember, hear, or speak . . . or an aging adult who suffers stroke and cannot remember or speak.

Those who get assaulted in the shadows outside of light portals have healing available to them. Entering portal lights is the equivalent of stepping thru the doors of an emergency room in an Earth hospital. There are healers beyond portal lights whose duty is to tend to returning souls who have damaged silver cord communication lines.

There is war in the heavens between those of the light and those of darkness. Earth is a battlefield, as well as is the heavens and other planets. Portal entrances are a prime target for dark assaults in the war between those of the light and those of darkness.

August 11

THOUGHT FOR THE DAY - Souls with severed or

damaged silver cord communication lines must feel and grapple to find their way to the light of the Astral Shore. They cannot see it, when they exit human forms. Because they are blind, sometimes they get lost and wander off into the Land of Ghosts.

HEALING FOR SEVERED COMMUNICATION LINES

When the third eye is open, seeing light portals and communication with those in the afterlife is instantly available. Opening a third eye is like turning on a television or computer. Both television type story scenarios and computer type information is available. The third eye can check out the news or the weather in the heavens or other planets. The third eye sees all, where human eyes are limited to what exists directly in front of them.

Atheists do not believe in gods, masters, angels, or other divine beings. The reason is that their communication line has been severed, possibly when they entered earth life into a new conception. Silver cord communication lines are attached to the third eye of souls. Because they do not have a spiritually functioning third eye that is open to look into the heavens, they choose not to believe in that which they cannot see. Angels to them are like a fairy tale Santa or Tooth fairy. The third eyes of atheists can be healed, if they manage to make their way to light portals after exiting human bodies. Sometimes, rescuers from the heavens are sent for them. Spiritual third eye blindness caused by others (the severing of cords) is forgive-able in the heavens.

There are healers for damaged souls. They do their thing as healers just inside the portals of light. Lost or blind souls with damaged silver cord communication lines must seek and find their way to a portal of light and step thru it in order to be healed.

August 12

THOUGHT FOR THE DAY – Humans, as a whole, are only interested in receiving healing for their human bodies. They ignore their need for healing for their inner man.

HEALERS … HUMAN AND DIVINE

On earth, you wouldn't call a waitress or a food chef to come work on your car. You would call an auto mechanic, a specialist doctor for cars. When you are in need of spiritual help or soul healing, you have to request of the correct type of healer from the heavens for your particular soul ailment. If you need a silver cord communications line healer, you don't call an aura healer or a karma healer/remover specialist. Healers in the heavens are specialists, just like there are specialist doctors on Earth.

Out of a human body, a soul is an orb of light and energy. When in human form, an orb will emanate a body covering of light that is known as an aura. Third eye psychics can see the colors of auras as well as if there are breaks, cuts, or scrapes in them, like humans get paper cuts or broken skin from various small accidents. There are specialist astral healers who deal with aura/halo breaks.

Human, third eye open psychics can see damage to auras, but they cannot heal them. Souls must exit human forms, travel to astral light portals, and step thru the portals in order to find and use the services of an aura healer.

A practicing psychic on earth is similar to a paramedic. A human paramedic will say, "Yes, you definitely have a nasty cut that needs stitches .You have got to go to the emergency room." A practicing earth psychic paramedic type might say, "Yes . . . you definitely have a nasty break in your aura. You need to get to the astral shore emergency room to have an aura healer work on you."

As a being that is two in one (both human and a divine soul), you must decide whether you need a human doctor for your human body or an astral healer for what ails your soul.

August 13

THOUGHT FOR THE DAY - Astral stalkers (dark beings, demons, fallen angels, etc.) can put on the costumes of fierce animals, if it makes them appear more menacing to victims. Dark stalkers want to frighten soul travelers who wander into the in-between worlds. One in-between world that exists between Earth and the Astral Shore/First Heaven is called the 'Land of Ghosts'.

MONKEY ON A CHAIN

I met a man (in his late twenties) whose human body suffered from epilepsy. He would fall in the floor, have seizures, and display other characteristics of his ailment. He told me that when he seizures and looses consciousness of his existence as an everyday human person, he is suddenly on the end of a long chain, and it is secured to his neck like he is a dog. A fierce laughing monkey holds and controls the other end of the chain, and has dominance over him. The monkey twirls him in fast, terrifying circles with his whole body lifting off the ground, like he was a kite caught up in a fierce twisting and spinning tornado. The sadistic monkey laughs at him from the beginning to the end of the experience, when his human body quits having its seizure. He also told me that the same 'monkey and chain' experience is repeated every time he has an epileptic episode.

The soul that lives and travels in a human body does not have epilepsy. Epilepsy is a disease or malfunction of the human body. It is sort of an electrical malfunction, like an automobile will have a wiring harness or electronic brain go bad. The man's 'monkey with a chain' experience was a separate experience that happened to his soul when it is thrown violently out of his human body by his body's epileptic shaking. Once out of the human body, his soul was being repeatedly assaulted by a dark, astral stalking demon.

Demons/devils/fallen angels are astral stalkers. Because they are sociopath dark beings, they sometimes get obsessed with stalking and assaulting certain individuals/souls. Also, they can put on the costumes of animals, if it makes them appear scarier. Astral demons/devils/fallen angels are dark soul orbs, just like you and I are light being orbs when we leave deceased human bodies. The monkey costumed demon stalker was obsessed with the epileptic man for who knows what reason. Obsession leads to repeated attacks by dark soul human sociopaths on earth as well as by out of body demon sociopaths in the astral.

Be aware of your surroundings when you exit your human body to soul travel, just as you would pay attention in dark alleys or bus stations on Earth. Awareness keeps you safe.

August 14

THOUGHT FOR THE DAY - Even though a human body has a built in power to heal itself, it also has an appointed lifetime according to how many years a light being needs to travel in it to accomplish his mission on Earth. The human body has a preset time to shut down, or die.

WHY DO CHILDREN GET SICK AND DIE?

The human body and its intelligence were created by Divine Source, a master orb of energy and light. Humans call Divine Source 'God'. Divine Source has installed in his creation, man, a power. That power is 'self healing'. He did not install that individual power in man to use to heal others. The power is limited to man's own human body.

Even though a human body has an automatic power to heal itself, it also has an appointed number of days to live on Earth. The appointed days are according to how many years, months, and days a light being soul needs to accomplish his appointed mission on earth. The human body is transportation for a soul, a type of automobile. A baby or child's body dies young, because its light being soul driver has completed its short mission on Earth. The bodies of those who die young are like rental cars. They are for short term use.

Souls travel in human bodies till their missions on Earth are completed. When their journeys, missions, or educational assignments on earth are over, they shut down their human vehicles and exit them. The shutdown to baby and child engines come in many forms (illness, accidents, SIDS, etc.) When human body transportation vehicles are turned off, soul drivers exit them and return to the heavens. The great lighted portal that souls travel toward (after exiting the human body) is a porch light of home.

August 15

THOUGHT FOR THE DAY – If we listen to our spirit guides in the heavens, we eventually learn their language.

MASTERING HEAVEN'S LANGUAGE

My neighbor John told me an interesting story about his dog understanding the English language. One morning, he had been in his garage working when he realized he needed to go purchase gasoline for one of his gas powered tools. He looked all about for his gas can, but couldn't find it. In frustration, he went inside to ask his lady friend if she knew where it was. His dog followed him inside. John then proceeded to ask his lady friend if she knew where his gas can was. His dog immediately turned and left the house. A minute or so later, the dog came back carrying the gas can by its handle, in its mouth.

If a dog (that doesn't speak human words) can understand (master the English language) and retrieve a gas can just by listening to a conversation; it is possible for us to master communications with our Spirit Guides (John types) in the heavens. We are capable of being more than human animal dogs?

I am sure that John gave his dog a treat for his intelligent act of helpfulness. If we attempt to master the language of the heavens, I am sure that our Spirit Guides will treat us for our future gasoline can moments of helpfulness. What do you want as a treat from the heavens . . . healing maybe?

August 16

THOUGHT FOR THE DAY - The soul within a human form does not lay down with its body in a coffin at death. The soul is eternal and will take flight to the heavens to continue its true life as a light being when its human body dies. Only damage to or the severing of silver cord communication lines will hinder a soul from returning to the heavens.

CHRIST WAS A SOUL HEALER

There are two types of healing. One is for the human body and one is for the soul that travels in a human body. The human body has a built in function called 'self healing'. The second is divine healing and it is for the soul driver of the human body vehicle. Divine healing for the soul comes from a rescue healer light being. That healer/rescuer practices his craft just beyond the portal light entrance to the Astral Shore.

The human body is like an auto. It has to be polished, fine tuned, fed, given its fluids, and rested occasionally to keep its parts from overheating. If a human body is given proper nutrition, fluids, and sensible care, the human body's automatic healing system will kick in. When a human body auto refuses to heal itself, it is because it has not had proper care, or it is breaking down because the soul within has completed his Earth mission and is about to exit. A comatose state is an example of a soul abandoned human vehicle.

Humans get out of their autos at times, leaving them running in idle. Perhaps the drivers are just going to make a quick trip into a convenience store for a snack. Their auto runs, but they are not in it. Human bodies in comatose states are cars that have been left in idle. If souls do not return to them, they (like an auto) will eventually run out of gas and die.

Light being souls have one major medical problem that they are in constant need of healing and surgery for. That medical issue is the damage to or the severing of their silver cord communications line. The severing or damage happens when a soul is in the process of entering a human baby vehicle at its conception. Fallen angels try to destroy or cut communication lines between a soul and heaven. It is an act of war. That medical problem can only be repaired and healed by astral healer surgeons.

Christ was a rescuer and a healer. The beings he healed were not demons and devils. They were light beings who had lost their way due to having damaged or severed silver cord communication lines. He descended from the heavens to rescue and heal the lost of the light. Christ was not sent to rescue fallen angels, demons, or devils traveling in human bodies. Christ was not on a mission to save and turn monster sociopaths into light beings. Murderers, rapists, and con artists are fallen angels, forces of darkness who have already been judged and kicked out of the heavens. There is no rescue or salvation for them.

Christ was sent to Earth to rescue the blind, those whose communication lines to the heavens were either cut or severed. The Christian religion has been created by human thinking followers and is based their ideas and tales of Christ's feats. When a divine one leaves us and returns to the heavens, we need something to hang on to. Religion is the result.

Christ was simply a rescuer, a healer from the heavens who was sent to earth to travel in human flesh and to heal silver cord, communication line blindness. The miracles he performed were due to him having an open third eye and a direct line to those in the heavens for whatever assistance he needed. Christ was not the only healer or rescuer in the heavens, just as there is not just one human doctor available for all the peoples of the earth. Healer/rescuer light beings are sent to the souls of all the peoples in all religions and cultures on earth that are in need of silver cord communication line restorations. You might say that Christ the rescuer/healer was a 'lineman'.

August 17

THOUGHT FOR THE DAY – You must remember that you are 'two in one'. You are human and divine and can be healed two ways. 'Self healing' is for the human body. 'Divine healing' is for the soul.

UNDERSTANDING DIVINE HEALING

Mental health problems are the medical issues of the human brain, not the divine mind/intelligence of the soul within. The human brain mind looks out thru two human eyes at the physical world, and is either happy or sad about what his earth life is all about. The third eye of the soul looks into the heavens and is either happy or sad about spiritual path. Depression is one type of breakdown of the human brain mind. Walking away from spiritual paths or missions causes soul mind breakdowns.

There are two types of healing available. One is automatic 'self healing' for the upkeep and repair of human bodies.

The second is 'divine healing' for the soul, the driver of the human body vehicle. Divine healing for souls comes from the heavens and is delivered by rescue healers. Christ was one.

Human doctors cannot heal. They can only cut, experiment, and poke pills down your throat in hopes that your human 'self healing' function will kick in. Ministers and religious figures cannot heal you spiritually. All they can do is bombard you with words and poke their religious theory down your soul's throat, hoping they can change your spiritual thinking. You must remember that you are 'two in one'. You are human and divine. Both have predestined, distinct ways of being healed. One is the human 'self healing' function and the other is the 'divine healing' for the soul function. Divine healing for the soul gets it back on track spiritually.

Souls are spirit beings that travel in human forms for lifetime missions on earth. Human bodies cannot die (no matter how sick they are) till the souls traveling in them have completed their Earth missions. You are a soul traveling in a human body. You cannot exit earth life till your soul's mission is complete. If you are thrown from your human form by perhaps a jarring accident, you can re-enter your human body to complete your mission.

New automobiles get in accidents and are dented. Still, they are drive-able. Human bodies get their share of dents and dings. However, they are still drive-able till their driver souls decide it is time to abandon them and send them to a salvage yard cemetery.

August 18

THOUGHT FOR THE DAY - Entry into human life by light beings or dark souls is a diving and swimming process. Souls from the heavens jump or dive into human baby body conceptions from the Astral Shore, as though new human conceptions are swimming pools. When more than one soul jumps into the same conception, you have Schizophrenia.

SHARING HUMAN FORMS

In the Astral, crazy things happen at times, just like they do on earth. On Earth, a distracted cook might put two cups of milk into a recipe when it only calls for one. A distracted waitress might bring you two menus instead of one. A distracted nurse might give you an overdose. An auto mechanic might put an extra quart of oil in your car. On the Astral Shore/First Heaven, equally as crazy things happen.

Keep in mind that dark, gray, and light beings roam the Astral Shore awaiting judgment for their deeds and missions on earth. Dark beings there are new fallen angels. Shades of gray there are light beings that have goofed off on earth and not completed their missions. Light beings are those who did not waver from their paths or missions on Earth. All await their turn to have their accomplishments on earth analyzed or judged.

So, the Astral Shore or First Heaven is a dwelling place of dark and light beings, like Chicago or New York City. In the cities on Earth, there are hospitals and obstetric floors where babies are born. On the Astral Shore there are halls of souls where souls wait to be birthed into human baby conceptions. You might call the Astral Hall of Souls the obstetrics ward of the heavens. From there, souls jump, dive, etc. into human baby body conceptions, as though human conceptions are swimming pools.

Remember, both dark and light souls exist on the Astral Shore. Sometimes dark beings will sneak into the Hall of Souls to escape judgment by attempting to dive into new human conceptions. Shades of gray souls may also try to escape their judgment in this fashion. When that happens, more than one soul may dive and enter the same human baby conception. A human child might have a devil and a light being within, if this happens.

When you have a variety of souls trying to take up residence in the same human conception, crazy things can happen. It is sort of like two little boys racing to try to get the last horse on the merry go round. The fastest, a light being, hops on first. Then a devil jumps on the back and puts his arms around the light being. Then, to their dismay, a third little 'shade of gray' boy grabs the tail of the horse and flies in the wind. Three souls have taken control of one horse. It is possible for a light being, a shade of gray being, and a dark being to all dive and enter the same human conception. However, the light being is the only one that is supposed to be in the human conception. The other two have sneaked on board, like 'stowaways' on a ship. Three souls travelling in the same conception is diagnosed by doctors as 'Schizophrenia'.

When multiple souls enter one human body, the stronger of the souls will dominate and be the driver of the human vehicle. The others will war with each other for dominance when the driver soul sleeps.

August 19

THOUGHT FOR THE DAY - Human bodies can use a built in function called 'self-healing" to heal their human bodies. However, they cannot use that power to heal the soul that drives them like they are an automobile. Divine healing for souls comes from the heavens and is administered by light being healers.

SOCIOPATH SOULS

Legal systems can sentence sociopath killers to death for their crimes. However, earth legal systems and its human executioners do not have the power to put a soul to death. If the human body of a sociopath is put to death, its dark soul just steps from the dead body and enters the in-between worlds to look for another body to possess and travel in again. A sociopath on Earth today was a sociopath in back generations, in a different human body. The dark being today has just chosen a new mode of transportation, like humans choose cars when their old one has worn out.

Sociopath dark beings are fallen angels. Divine Source kicked them out of the heavens. Now, they are at war with Divine Source and those of the light. There are guardian light beings in the invisible worlds that are charged with the destroying of fallen angels' souls. They have a weapon that is similar to a laser, and it is called a 'Cease to be'. When guardians point and fire their laser weapon on dark sociopath souls, they cease to be. Only the laser like weapon can put a dark sociopath soul to death. Human gas chambers and electric chairs cannot.

Fallen angels do not have access to the powers of the heavens that Light Beings do. They cannot heal. Instead, they destroy. When a sociopath soul enters or possesses a new human body, it will start to turn it to a hideous state. The first part to turn hideous will be the mind or brain of the human body. Perversion of thought will be the first tactic used by a dark sociopath/fallen angel to torture a human being with. The fallen angel will inflict mental illness. By turning the human mind to darkness, its light being soul driver will abandon it.

August 20

THOUGHT FOR THE DAY – Life time Gutter Rats (welfare and charity leaches) are dark beings.

GUTTER RAT AND DISABILITY FAKERS

Those who receive welfare and disability benefits can never be healed of body or soul, because they have to claim to be ill n order to receive their freebee benefits. If you claim to be sick, you draw illness to you by the law of attraction. Gutter rats and disability fakers use free will choice to choose freebees instead of health. They willingly choose gutter living. They, by their choices, are dark beings.

We are our choices in life. We can choose to work, educate, and create good healthy lives for ourselves, or we can choose to be gutter rats (welfare and disability types) that embrace illness and gutter living every day. The taking of freebees and food stamps hinders healing, financial success, and the bliss of being able to pay for one's own food and life style.

There is war in the heavens. Earth is one battlefield. Military forces of Heaven and Hell have set up camps on the surface of planet Earth. Welfare gutter life and its freebees are a hell camp. Humans willingly enter that camp of darkness and take up residence with its fallen angel soldiers. Heaven's military camps are inhabited by those willing to work, educate themselves, own homes, and pursue higher standards of living and spirituality. They are light beings.

August 21

THOUGHT FOR THE DAY – A shaman has dual powers. He can talk to those who have crossed over and he is a master healer.

SHAMAN HEALING

Those who know they are spirit beings traveling in human forms understand that there are healers available just beyond the entry portals of light on the Astral Shore. That is where the 'doctor offices' are for heaven's healers and rescuers.

Healing is also available on earth from master healer light beings that have descended and are traveling in human forms. Those healers are master light beings, and they will work as shamans, witches, seers, mediums, etc. of all cultures and countries. Master light beings/shamans will display a common characteristic. They will all be cutting age thinkers.

Spiritually blind men, unbelievers and skeptics, have always feared what they did not understand. In their fear, they have not wanted to admit that a human, other than themselves, might have more power. Thus, in their selfishness and blind states of thinking, they embrace censorship, bigotry, prejudices, closed minded thinking, etc. They try to avoid or destroy what they do not understand.

The spiritually blind have created a word to describe that which they fear and do not understand. That word is 'occult'. They have created the word as a demeaning one to brand anyone not embracing their narrow viewed religious persuasions. They use the word 'occult' to fence themselves in and everyone else out. They see their religious circle as being the only true fellowship or church of god. It is a ridiculous concept when you think that their particular religious group/church might not have but 250 members. The Earth is a huge planet and light being masters are sent to all cultures, religions, and countries. Light being masters usually work as shamans, seers, witches, etc. on earth. Christ was an out of the box thinker and rubbed the religious persuasion of his world raw. He was a shaman, a healer.

Shamanism is a spiritual practice where a follower goes inward and attains an altered state of consciousness (the stepping from one's human form) in order to encounter and interact with those of the spirit world. They relay messages or healing information to those needing it on Earth. A shaman enters into a trance state during a ritual and lets those of the heavens speak thru him. He talks with those in the afterlife who have exited dead human forms on earth. John the revelator was a shaman.

According to blind human thinking, a shaman talks to the dead. However, the dead he talks to are not dead. They are eternal souls who are alive and have crossed over. Blind men's thinking wants to brand a shaman as evil, or occult. Actually, those doing the branding are the evil ones. They seek to stamp out the arrival of light and the divine on earth.

August 22

THOUGHT FOR THE DAY – A shaman can help heal unbalances in nature, as well as in human bodies.

SHAMANS & BALANCE

Shamans are master connected ones, communication officers that are receivers of messages for souls traveling in human forms on earth. They can also convey messages to the heavens for souls who have damaged or severed Silver Cord communication lines. Shamans are master healers of souls, silver cord repairmen, and communication experts. One of the main assignments for Shamans is to heal Silver Cord communication lines that have been damaged or severed by dark forces when certain light being souls entered Earth life. He heals those who do not know that they are light beings. When you are cut off from the divine/god, you do not know that you are a light being.

(Silver Cords are like telephone lines, except they are composed of a supernatural gray mist that can be seen thru and walked thru. The cords are connected to light beings entering Earth life, but are not confining or binding like a dog would be if her were to be put on a chain. Silver Cords can be walked thru, like radio and other type of signals/vibrations that are in the air on Earth.)

Shamans in altered states of consciousness can enter numerous realms/dimensions beyond earth to obtain solutions for problems afflicting countries, cultures, communities, etc. on earth. A Shaman knows that restoration of balance in nature cures some physical world problems such as drought and starvation. He also knows that balance restored in a human body eliminates illness.

A shaman has dual healing powers. He can heal the balance of elements on Earth and in human bodies. He can also heal communication problems that exist between Heaven and Earth by repairing silver cord communication lines. A shaman is a healer and a communications expert.

August 23

THOUGHT FOR THE DAY - Pentecostal believers who let a 'Holy Ghost' speak thru them are channels or shamans.

PENTECOSTAL SHAMANISM

The followers of the Pentecostal religion believe in an infilling of a 'Holy Ghost'. He is a comforter who descends in soul form, enters them, and speaks thru them. They let the 'Holy Ghost' speak thru them, thus becoming channels or shamans. Holy Ghost is a nick name for the one they channel. It is not a proper name.

My human father nicknamed me 'Hot Foot' when I was a child and my sister 'Angel'. Because my family's last name was Hammers, one of my younger brothers was nicknamed 'Hammerhead' by his classmates. 'Holy Ghost' is a nickname for a light being, and is not a proper name. The Pentecostals' light being spirit guide (nicknamed the 'Holy Ghost') actually has a proper name in the heavens, but few Pentecostals have bothered to go within and ask him what it is. On Earth, my nickname is 'Hot Foot'. My proper name is Jo Hammers. In the heavens, my proper or divine name is Master Barjoraven. Do you know what your proper name is in the Heavens? Do you know what your light being spirit guide's name is?

Pentecostals have made some strides forward beyond other religions in embracing the supernatural. However, there are grater strides to be made. One simple one is for them to know their Holy Ghost's proper divine name.

Supernatural healing is another power that Pentecostals embrace. They lay hands on each other and pray for divine healing. The stride forward for them would be to learn that there are two types of healing available, one for the human body and a separate one for the soul. There is a built in 'self healing' function in the human body. It will kick in and work as long as man does not abuse his body.

Dents and dings to the human body come from minor accidents on earth, such as catching your toe on a rocker and breaking it. Self healing will kick in, but there may still be some scarring or the toe may point in slightly a different direction than before. Kid's scraped knees are dents and dings. Wrinkles are due to sun exposure and cavities are due to sugar consumption or the failure to brush. Teeth are not healable. Wrinkles are permanent. Self healing will not heal the man who continues to eats sugar, in spite of him being a diabetic. Self healing will not make the fat of an obese person disappear, just so he can over eat himself into that state again. 'Self healing' activates and works for the human that respects his body.

Pentecostals cannot lay hands on a human head and heal a divine soul. Healers for souls are masters and they perform their art of healing from the heavens. Occasionally, a master healer will descend to Earth to travel in a human body and perform his art for awhile. Keep in mind that divine healers have mastered earth life and are advanced souls in the heavens. Few Pentecostals are master healing shamans. Most are just believers. It is easier for a Pentecostal to approach a healer asking for healing, than it is to become a healer. Pentecostals are basically interested in being channels for their spirit guide, the 'Holy Ghost'.

The third area that Pentecostals have become shamans in is their belief that they can channel a gift called 'speaking in tongues'. They believe the tongues are messages from their 'holy Ghost'. The unknown tongues they channel are possibly different language messages of souls that have just crossed over from the various countries of Earth. Newly crossed over souls try to get messages back to those they have left behind. Keep in mind that not every soul that has just crossed over is light. There are shades of gray and newly fallen angels that have crossed over and await judgment. They too want to send messages back.

Shamans do not need to slap human body hands on an individual's head to heal them. A shaman speaks healing. When he does, it will sound like a rushing wind.

August 24

THOUGHT FOR THE DAY - A Hindu priest or priestess may channel information from their deities concerning spirits who are troubling a human with symptoms of physical or mental illness. The Hindu medium will prescribe ritual actions to get rid of the pestering spirits.

HINDU HEALING

Simple practices of divination are common to Hinduism. Every Hindu wants to know if his wish in life will come true. Yes and no answers to such questions may be revealed by any of a number of Hindu practices. Plucking grains between thumb and finger from a pile, and then counting them to see if they add up to a wanted or agreeable number is one. In the west, we guess number of jelly beans in a jar in contests. The guessing of the number is the same as the guessing of rice grains plucked.

People of all cultures, religions, and countries assign luck and non luck to certain numbers. Unlucky might be the day your child died. Lucky might be the number of the day you got married. It is the believing in the number that makes it so. We pull to us what we believe deeply about (The Law of Attraction). In the United States, a young girl will pluck the petals of a daisy for answer as to whether a boy loves them. As she pulls petals off one by one, she will state, "He loves me . . . he loves me not". The last daisy petal can be lucky or unlucky.

A more elaborate mode of Hindus communicating with divine powers is possession. A human's mind and voice is thought to act as a vehicle for a Hindu deity's mind and voice to be projected or heard. A Hindu priest or priestess becomes a channel and is able to provide more complex answers than simple yes and nos. He may relay information about crossed over spirits who are annoying certain humans with symptoms of physical and mental illness. The Hindu channel will prescribe certain ritual actions to get rid of the annoying curses. Practical Hinduism is greatly concerned with maintaining mental and physical health.

You should study the healing practices of all religions. Why? There are keys to enlightenment, perfection, and healing for body and soul. Christians refer to them as the keys to the Kingdom of God. One key is hidden in every religious persuasion around the world. It is up to you to be open minded enough to seek and find them.

August 25

THOUGHT FOR THE DAY - Enlightenment comes with being open minded and thinking outside of the box. The box may be your church and its narrow minded beliefs.

ANCIENT HEALING MASTERS

Followers of Buddhism and Christianity pour over ancient writings/holy books in an effort to find keys to possessing supernatural powers and doors to other dimensions and the afterlife of the soul. What they don't do is lay aside yesterday's archaic thinking and writings in favor of going within to find cutting edge spiritual thoughts that are in alignment with what is happening spiritually today. Reading about ancient ones miracles is fine for entertainment. However, man must experience and embrace what is happening in the world of religion and spirituality today, if he wants to awaken his soul and become more than just being human. He must be a forward thinker.

Enlightenment and advanced cutting edge thoughts come with seeking. Dwelling in the past is a waste of time. You cannot re-invent the radio, toaster, or microwave. They have already been thought about and invented. You cannot seek and find yesterday's enlightened thought, when it has already been reached and shared in books. To be a current master you must think out of the box and create that which has never been thought of before. Christ was a master light being yesterday. You are capable of being a master light being like him, only of today. He walked on water. Today, you freeze it and skate on it, and let others skate with you.

What could you do with water that would be a miracle today? I turn boiling water and instant coffee into a hot brew. Instant coffee was unheard of in Christ's day. Someone dared to think outside of the box and create it. What could you do to advance the understanding and practice of miracle healings today? I am writing about the subject. This book of writings is my miracle, and what I have been sent to earth to accomplish. If this book's writings increase the spiritual knowledge of just one person, I am a successful master. I have worked a miracle.

Buddha is legend to have had more super powers than any other being in his day. He could travel through space, as well as dive in and out of the earth. He had the power to be in multiple places at the same time conversing with people. The Buddha could increase the size of his human body to be as big as a giant or small as an ant. He could walk thru mountains. Also, he could travel to the heavens to inform Gods and Masters there of his realizations, and then return to earth. Today, we call 'travelling to the heavens' as stepping from our human bodies to travel the astral and visit with our spirit guides. Buddha was a miracle worker in his day.

Human minds put up mental fences to protect themselves from what they fear and have no understanding of. They erect fences around their choice of masters, holy books, and archaic thoughts. Providing no gates for today's masters to enter is their downfall. There are master teachers today, just as Christ and the Buddha were ones for their day.

You cannot eat yesterday's bread alone. Sooner or later it is going to get stale. Reading instruction pamphlets on how to operate an early 1900's toaster will be of little value to you in this current microwave age. You must advance in spiritual thought with the movement of time.

All religions on Earth are acceptable paths for seekers to start their spiritual journeys in. Eventually, if they are serious seekers, their path will wind in and out of all religious persuasions as they seek for the keys to the Kingdom of Heaven. One key is hidden in every religion. To understand healing and how it works, you must stay on and follow your winding path.

August 26

THOUGHT FOR THE DAY - When dark beings are bombarding you with verbal abuse, they are inflicting you with mental illness.

SICKNESS IMPOSED ON YOU

Assaults by darkness can cause health issues for human bodies, and the assaults can come in various ways. For instance: you enter a restaurant that serves buffet style. The man standing in front of you is using the buffet utensils to serve him-self. Before getting in the buffet line, unknown by you, he has made several trips during the day to the restroom and has never once washed his hands. In serving and filling your plate, you handle the serving utensils the man used. The dark being devil in a human body has successfully assaulted you. He has passed germs, viruses, and who knows what to you. Your body then has to have its 'self healing' function activated in order for you to overcome the germ, virus, or whatever he has assaulted you with.

Dark beings will assault you in other sneaky ways. They may spit in your food, or urinate in the coffee pot at work. Out in the public he may sneak illegal drugs into what you are drinking. A light being must always beware of the situations he moves about in, and the possibility that darkness may choose to assault him. There is war in the heavens. Fallen angels/dark beings are at war with the light. Earth is one battlefield. If you are a light being, you are their target of war.

The worst imposed illness is the one dark spouse beings inflict on their mates. A man that bombards his wife daily with demeaning words will eventually see her enter a depressed, nervous breakdown state. Mental illness is a sickness of the human brain. When your human brain can't think straight, you cannot find your way inward to let your soul take control to get you out of the depressed mess you are in.

Depression is mental illness, a dark hellish inflicted pit that only your soul can help your human brain to climb out of.

August 27

THOUGHT FOR THE DAY – Master healers are available in all the religions of the world. They travel in human flesh, just as you and I do. Prayer chains are successfully created when healers join forces.

SUCCESSFUL PRAYER CHAINS

Healing cannot be had by one human slapping his hands on another human's head. A human body is just a human body, and it does not have the power to heal anyone. The human body is like an automobile. Automobiles need drivers. Human bodies need drivers. Healer Light Beings are souls that reside in and drive human vehicles.

Just as earth humans work at all sorts of occupations, those coming here from the heavens also have different occupations or assignments. Not all light beings coming to Earth are healers. I am a trumpeter of words. You may be master of fine cuisine, while the person standing next to you is a financial genius. Not every light being is a healer. Each light being on Earth should automatically know what his supernatural gifts are and focus on them. I am a trumpeter of words. I cannot make a gourmet meal with my writer's pen. A gourmet cook cannot write a book with their rolling pin. Financial wizards cannot heal you with a dollar bill, and healers have no powers to make money. If you are seeking help with healing go to a specialist.

Churches in the United States have developed what they call 'Prayer Chains'. Using modern telephone systems, every member in a church is called in a round robin fashion when a member is ill. Each church member is a link in the chain and they know who they are to call after they receive a request to pray. For instance, the pastor calls you, you call me, I call Jane, and then Jane should call the pastor back to complete the circle or circuit. This concept is great, if every member in the prayer chain is a light being healer. When you include non healers in the chain, you break the circuit. Prayers of this nature do not get answered for that reason. Short circuiting a prayer chain is like hanging up a telephone half way thru a conversation.

Dark beings will join church prayer chains just to be circuit breakers. They will purposely not pass on prayer requests, much less pray for them. Healing Prayer chains are only successful if its links are light being healers.

I have a grown nephew who has experienced healing due to a prayer chain. When he was about two he came down with a fever that could not be explained and he ended up in the hospital. He was clammy, sweating, and too sick to sit up. The family gathered in his hospital room because he was expected to die. Both sets of the grandparents were there consoling his parents. In desperation, the elders from his mother's church, The Reorganized Church of Jesus Christ, were called. The elders circled my nephew's bed, took his hands, and then each other's hands. They became a prayer chain circle of connected hands. The elders closed their eyes and prayed. When the elders concluded their prayer, my nephew instantly sat up in bed and went to playing. He was well.

The prayer chain type miracle happened due to a supernatural circuit formed when the elders joined hands, closed their eyes, and went within. When they went within, it was no longer humans praying. The elder's souls in unison were requesting of the heavens a miracle for the toddler. The elders all just happened to be light being healers.

August 28

THOUGHT FOR THE DAY – There are some humans who turn to religion, even though they have never had any religious or supernatural experiences. They choose to believe by faith that an afterlife exists and that other humans besides them have been endowed with certain supernatural powers like healing. They go to those healers when in need. They are spiritually blind, but walk by faith.

HEALING FOR SLEEPING SOULS

There is one type of healing that is the most important. That healing is the curing of spiritual blindness of souls. Spiritual blindness happens when a soul's silver cord communication line is severed by dark forces when the soul is entering Earth life. Without a functioning communication connection to the heavens, a soul sleeps in its human vehicle. The sleeping is spiritual blindness.

Human eyes look out into the physical realm and the human brain makes decisions about what to eat, where to sleep, how to stay warm, etc. The human brain makes survival decisions for the human animal body. The soul that enters and drives a human body vehicle makes decisions as to spiritual matters and is the receiver of correspondence from the heavens. When a soul's silver cord communication line is severed, the soul sleeps. It is cut off from all supernatural experiences.

There is healing for severed silver cords. It comes at the death of the human body. The sleeping soul will be rescued by a master healer who will escort him to the light and then thru it to where he can have his silver cord repaired. He will not know that he is a divine light being, till his cord is repaired. He has spiritual blindness, a form of astral amnesia.

August 29

THOUGHT FOR THE DAY – On other planets, divine ones can walk the skies on air, just as Christ on Earth walked the sea on water.

HEALERS WHO SKY WALK

It is foolish to think that Earth humans are the only living, intelligent life form that exists in the universe. Just as there are intelligent human beings on Earth, there are intelligent life forms that exist on distant planets, moons, & stars. Traveling in some of those alien life forms are healer light beings on missions.

Native Americans refer to certain construction workers who walk about on tall sky scraper metal structures as 'Sky Walkers'. It is very possible their descriptive name for the workers originated from some ancient, Native American medicine man having had an encounter with a visitor from another planet. Perhaps he saw an alien visitor walking across the tops of trees, or stepping from one Teepee top to another, or just walking high in the air. Just as Christ walked on water on Earth, master alien light beings may be capable of walking on air. Thus, they were called 'Sky Walkers'.

Astronauts, human and alien, strive to interact with each other and visit each other thru the use of spacecrafts. However, light beings that travel in Earth human vehicle bodies and Alien ones can travel between planets in split seconds when they step from their life forms vehicles. Portal travel for souls is at the speed of light. The same light being souls that travel today in human bodies on Earth can also, in the future, enter other planet life forms to do missions. Healer light beings on Earth today may have been a 'Sky Walking' healer on another planet in the past, or will become one in the future.

Light Being Healers from the heavens are sent on missions to all planets, stars, moons, etc. To think otherwise is to label your-self as 'slow in thinking' or 'mentally challenged'.

August 30

THOUGHT FOR THE DAY – Whether human bodies receive healing is determined by appointed times for light beings/souls to complete missions on Earth. We do have appointed times for our human bodies to die.

WHEN HEALING IS NOT AVAILABLE

Human bodies have a 'self healing' function that is built in. It will operate till it is time for the soul driver of the human body to exit and return permanently to the heavens.

A soul, exiting a human form, is sort of like you pulling in your driveway after a long work day. You shut your car's ignition. Your engine dies. Then you get out of your car and make your way to the front door of your home and enter. You have abandoned your vehicle.

You and I are souls, drivers of human vehicles. Earth is our work place. When our missions/work on earth is complete, it is time for us to go home. To do so, we must get out of our human vehicles and walk toward the light and enter our heavenly home. 'Self Healing' is one function of our human body vehicle that shuts down when the human engine starts to die.

Souls entering Earth life are on missions. Some missions

are short and some are long. On short missions, souls will shut down their human body vehicles in infancy or early childhood. Baby and child vehicles are sort of like temporary rental cars for souls on short journeys on Earth. Souls that are on long term missions on Earth will travel in their human bodies till they are elderly. The human body's 'self healing' function will shut down in a baby, child, or elder when a soul has completed his mission. When 'self healing' shuts down, a human body gets ill, collapses, and enters a comatose state. The body then dies.

You as a human may die young, or you may die old. The length of your human lifetime will be determined by the length of your soul's mission. Healing for your human body is available, but only for the time your soul chooses to travel in it to complete his mission on Earth.

August 31

THOUGHT FOR THE DAY – There is a time to pray, and then comes a time to stand in expectation.

HEALING RAIN

A Native American medicine man needs rain to refresh his dry desert, and to fill the watering holes that are about to dry up. He proceeds to do a rain dance. Afterward, he stands still, shields his eyes with his hand, and peers into the distant skies looking for rain clouds.

"Why are you bothering to pray for the impossible? It never rains here!" Gawking bystanders ask, as they shake their heads in disbelief.

The rain dancing medicine man ignores them. He is determined to let nothing interrupt his focus or dedication to receiving. As he stands in expectation of rain, a small cloud appears in the distant sky. Then the little cloud multiplies and the sky is filled with thunder clouds. All the disbelievers run for cover as lightning streaks the sky and thunder clouds burst, showering the desert floor with much needed rain.

You must be a rain dancer, when you are in need of the impossible. If you need healing, do a healing dance. Then stand in expectation, looking into the future for your gulley washer outcome.

I have a Pentecostal friend who has a metal skeleton of an umbrella that has no silk top. When she needs healing, she gets the skeleton umbrella out, opens it, and walks about with the topless frame over her head. People laugh at her. However, she is a firm believer in a religious concept called the 'latter rain, the end time out pouring of the Holy Ghost. She prays for healing rain. Then, she carries the skeleton umbrella over her head as a sign to her god that she is expecting latter rain healing to fall on her (not around her as it would if the umbrella had a silk top covering).

Rain dancing for healing comes in many forms. Do you have a healing rain dance that gets the attention of your god?

CHAPTER NINE
SEPTEMBER

THE BOOK OF DIVINE POWERS

September 1

THOUGHT FOR THE DAY – We are gods, divine beings, who travel in human flesh. Human bodies are like space suits to us. Earth is a planet we have chosen to inhabit. Dark beings have also chosen to war for its surface.

THE POWERS OF GODS IN HUMAN FLESH

The simple, invented, retractable pen I use seems insignificant in comparison to greater inventions such as computers, microwaves, and cell phones. However, somewhere in the world there is a factory worker, a human doing what he may see as a mundane job assembling pens like mine.

When you think about my pen, you have to acknowledge the fact that someone was technologically intelligent and creative to have been able to design it, make its ink flow smoothly, and makes its retractable mechanism parts work. Scientists and inventors are gods in human flesh. There are other gods in human flesh that are producers.

Producers work on factory lines. It is their mission in life on Earth.

We are gods/light beings/souls/guides/supernatural beings traveling on Earth in human body spacesuits. You, a divine soul, have a special power! I have a special power. I am a creator, or trumpeter of words. Your neighbor may be a healer, while your best friend is a factory worker. You may be a chef and your brother an auto mechanic. What we are passionate about working at is our power. Gods would not be divine, if they were all cookie cutters of each other. Individuality is power! When you possess a creative power that others do not, it makes you powerful. An auto mechanic to me is on the same level as a medical doctor. I call him to heal the ailments of my automobile, and I pay him dearly . . . much more than the fast food worker who cooks me a burger. He is a powerful god in human flesh to me, because I am not a 'doctor of wrenches'. I am a 'trumpeter of words'.

Do you take the time to acknowledge the importance and powers of each god that is traveling in human flesh in your work and social circle? To embrace gods is to have combined powers.

September 2

THOUGHT FOR THE DAY - It doesn't matter how primitive a culture, there are the brilliant, high IQ individuals who invent the unbelievable, study the stars, dream dreams, are psychic, and see themselves as souls, not humans.

Culture proclaimed gods

In the days of the pharaohs there lived a beady eyed man who had a long skinny, pointed nose that hooked down looking like the beak of a bird. Those about him laughed and referred to him with de-meaning intent as a bird. When the bird man came into his own and his brilliant inner mind produced cutting edge thoughts for his day, he was proclaimed by the less intelligent as a god.

It doesn't matter how primitive a culture, there are the brilliant, high IQ individuals who discover and invent the unbelievable, study the stars, are psychic, and know they are more than their human body vehicles. In primitive thinking, only gods could dream, have visions, and travel the in-between worlds and the many heavens. Today, we have a better understanding of astral traveling, psychic powers, and paranormal phenomena and powers.

So, in the time of the pharaohs lived a man with a pointed, bird beak nose that was declared a god traveling in human flesh. He was portrayed in drawings as a male figure with a bird head. His name was Troth.

Troth was a human that had a brilliant light being soul traveling in him on Earth. Troth was a god in human flesh, but not in the way that the Egyptians saw him. He was not a bird god. He was a god of cutting edge thought, who just happened to be traveling in an ugly human body that had a long, skinny, hooked, nose.

September 3

THOUGHT FOR THE DAY – You are attacked in public by a mad man. To get away from him, you bite him. In pain, he lets go of you and runs away. If a primitive culture artist watched your assault how would he describe you? Would he declare you to be a god because you overcame evil? Would he then paint you with a wolf head, because your side teeth are a little long, looking a bit fang like? Would he even bother to consider that you are a soul traveling in a human body, and that your powers are there, not in your human, fang like teeth?

WHAT IS YOUR DIVINE IMAGE?

You and I are orbs of light and energy that travel earth life in human vehicles. If our spirit being within is awake, we are gods in human flesh. When our souls sleep, the human brain takes over and man functions in animal, survival mode. Man lives to eat, drink, and reproduce, he is an animal.

I am a writer who daily carries a lap top computer in a cloth bag. I wear a black hat most days, a simple clothing preference. On my nose I wear black rimmed glasses, and my face has numerous moles on it. If an artist in the day of the pharaohs was to draw me, how would he portray me? Would I be a bumpy faced human with dark circles (glasses) around my eyes? Would the artist picture me as a god with a magic box in a bag? Would he think I kept my head covered (black hat) in order not to lose black magic out my head? Humans with sleeping souls create themselves gods from what they understand, what they have seen or been told exists. Winged, or no wings angels is an example.

How would a primitive culture, human artist describe your human features, as well as your inner soul uniqueness or powers? How do you describe yourself? Do you see yourself as human, or human and divine? If you see yourself as just human, your soul is asleep.

September 4

THOUGHT FOR THE DAY – Buddha had a follower who walked on water. Christ walked on water after him. Peter of the New Testament was also a water walker.

WATER WALKING GODS

Have you ever had multiple, hindering, roadblock circumstances happen in one day's time? Such experiences will bring out the 'water walker' in you. Only faith in your ability to tackle the impossible can get you thru certain trying times.

Example: Your alarm clock fails to go off. You wake up 45 minutes late. You enter a panic mode and hit the floor running, performing your morning rituals in lightning time. Then, just as you are about to go out the door, you take a quick glance into the hall mirror and discover that you have on one black and one lime green sock. Also, your necktie has serious coffee stains on it. Reaching the garage, you discover that you have a flat tire. In more panic, you force yourself to fix the flat in record time. Burning rubber leaving your garage and driveway, you head for work. At the first corner, a car wreck is blocking its use. Backing up quickly, you turn around and take a different route. A quarter mile down the new route, a patrolman pulls you over for speeding and delays you 20 minutes while he writes you a ticket. Then you drive off in a reasonable speed till you are out of his sight. Then, you speed up. As you drive like crazy in a foul mood, your stomach growls. Because you hadn't had breakfast, you swing thru a fast food drive thru window for coffee and a breakfast sandwich. Grabbing the sack from the hands of the girl at the window, you squeal your tires pulling out of the place while trying to open your sandwich. In doing so, you knock the coffee over and it guns down your pant leg burning you. A few explosive words escape you as you try to regain your composure and drive. A block down the road, you finish unwrapping your sandwich and discover that the fast food girl gave you someone else's cheap sandwich, instead of your expensive special order. Your whole morning goes that way, and gets worse when your boss threatens to fire you for being late. That is a day when you must find an inner power to walk on water.

Buddha had a follower named Sariputta. He was one of two major male disciples or followers of the Buddha, and one who was ahead of his time in wisdom. In the Theravada tradition, he is one of the most important disciples of the Buddha. Like Christ and Peter of the Christian religion, he walked on water. He did so, before Christ did.

Water walking gods are able to get where they want to go, in spite of hindering circumstances in their physical world. Are you a 'Water Walking' god?

September 5

THOUGHT FOR THE DAY - A poet's sweet words of love jump off a written page. Your heart turns flip flops and then you shiver. He has caused your human earth to shake.

THE POWER TO CAUSE EARTH TO QUAKE

When you discover that you are a god traveling in human

flesh for a lifetime on Planet Earth, you suddenly realize that you have powers. One power is to cause quaking of human earth flesh, as well as the surface of Planet Earth. How you use your powers to make 'earths' quake, can either be positive or negative.

A great spiritual leader/minister/orator gets up and gives a soul stirring speech causing your human flesh to tremble and then break out in goose bumps. That speaker's power of speech made your human earth flesh quake. A soprano gets up to sing. When she hits a particular high note, it sends chills down your spine. Your frame reacts by giving a sudden shake. The soprano has caused your human earth to quake. A poet's sweet words of love jump off a written page. Your heart turns flip flops and shivers occur. He has caused your human earth heart to shake.

Just as there are gods with powers in men that can cause human earths to shake, there are also demons and devils in men that can do the same. A devil man in an outburst of verbal spousal abuse can cause a frightened, crying wife to shake. A dark teacher can cause a student to shake by threatening to send him to the principal for something he hasn't done. A boss can reduce you to tears and shaking by berating you, or firing you. A pedophile father can cause his children to lay awake and shake at night in fear of him entering their bedroom. Dark gods in human flesh use the power of fear to cause human earths to quake. Also, they can make Planet Earth quake/shake by dropping bombs.

Earth is a school for some light beings traveling in human flesh. Some of them, being students, have teen mentality and sometimes do stupid stuff that makes men quake. Back in the 1930's and 1940's, it was a common practice of teens at Halloween to sneak up on outhouses and turn them over with their unsuspecting users in them. Stupid pranks like that cause human earths to quake. Just the thought of suddenly being upside down and having feces and urine dumped all over me makes me shiver/quake as I write this.

September 6

THOUGHT FOR THE DAY – Some beings traveling in human flesh on Earth are students. Learning to use free-will choice wisely is an Earth school lesson. To master free will choice, students have to experience the results of both good and bad decisions.

THE POWER TO BE STUPID OR MAKE BAD DECISIONS

Back in the early 1900's most graves were hand dug by family members or friends. It was not uncommon for my father or brothers to be asked to man a shovel to dig a grave. In the 1950s my father was appointed to help dig the grave of his mother.

My father's parents got a divorce back in the 1940s, due to my grandfather's infidelity. He died before my grandmother and was buried in the family cemetery. Fifteen or so years later, my grandmother died. One of her children asked "Where do we put mom . . . in another cemetery or next to dad?"

My father and his siblings were at odds with each other as where to bury her. Half said their mother would not want to be buried next to the man she divorced. The other half wanted her to be buried next to him, showing family unity in spite of the separation. The minister, who was to officiate, convinced my father and his siblings just to forgive, forget, and bury their parents together. After all, he said, they were both asleep in Jesus and would not know they were in twin beds (caskets) beneath the earth anyway. So, my father and his siblings prepared to bury their mother next to their father.

My father and his cousin were appointed to dig the grave. A Chestnut tree, heavy with nuts, was at the foot of the grave. As my father and his assistant made efforts to dig the grave, they ran into a shelf of limestone and serious roots about two feet down. They were not able to dig past them. My father, a non-explosive expert, got the bright idea of using a stick of dynamite to loosen the rock and major roots. They proceeded to a farmer's house where they got a stick. Then they returned to work on the grave hole, all smiles thinking they were genius.

My father's cousin hid behind a tombstone about 50 feet from the grave. My dad lit the long fuse on the dynamite stick and then dropped it into the hole and ran. He took refuge behind another tombstone. The dynamite went off. Rocks flew, the ground shook, and every nut and leaf on the Chestnut tree fell off. I can just imagine how many deceased human bodies shook in their caskets beneath the ground. Stupidity of men can sometimes cause physical earth and human earth to quake. Luckily, the grave of my dad's father with stood the blast with only one corner of his damaged casket showing. My father and cousin quickly put dirt back to hide it.

A conversation was overheard after the grave closing when my family revisited the grave taking a sibling who had missed the funeral due to his auto breaking down.

The late arriver, who had visited the cemetery a couple of days before to mark the grave for digging, asked," What happened to the Chestnut tree? It has died over night."

Another sibling replied, "I told you they would fight down there. The poor Chestnut tree has been accidentally killed by them."

My father, in a stupid moment, caused a tree and multiple bodies in near graves to shake or quake. Stupidity is forgive-able. The purposeful hurting or quaking of others or Planet Earth is not.

September 7

THOUGHT FOR THE DAY - You have to lay down the present, in order to pick up the future!

THE POWER OF BEING A FORWARD THINKER

Forward thinking is a power! It is a pioneering power. Pioneers of enlightened thought discover new heavens of intellectual and spiritual plateaus. Forward thinkers are modern day prophets, masters in their particular field of expertise. There are master bowlers, just as there are master violinists, or orators.

Forward thinkers in the field of advanced thought are gods/masters of knowledge. Parents who choose not to fully educate their children, letting them drop out, are backward thinkers. They are forces of darkness, plunging their children's minds into darkness. Willingly letting a child drop out of school is a power displayed by devils.

Devil gods in human flesh are backward thinking individuals that cling to the past and assault anyone not agreeing with their archaic ideas, holy books, and beliefs. Preventing light to shine in others is like an electric company refusing to let you have electricity. The Amish are past embracers, as are those who refuse to read anything but the King James Version of the bible, and similar other archaic holy books of various religions.

Censorship and burning of books is an example of backward thinkers, as is keeping your children home when there is a visiting evangelist at your church that doesn't share your beliefs. Perhaps, the visiting minister says angels have no wings, and you are dead set that they do. 'Nit picking' is a power of darkness.

My readers ask for insights on how to walk forward into the Future of advanced thought. They desire to be gods of forward thinking. To discover higher truths, you have to lay aside the old, outdated teachings of your ancestors, as well as their holy books. You must think for yourself, and embrace cutting edge thought and books being written by modern day gods of the pen. At the same time, you must not see yourself as above the individual who is just starting his journey and still needs his church and holy books to lean on. There will always be beginners just as there will be forward thinkers.

Cutting edge thought is the power of forward thinking gods in human flesh. Forward thinking gods are the inventors, creators, writers, artists, composers of this very moment. Tomorrow is another day and you must make another trip to the bookstore for the advanced thoughts of tomorrow. Seeking enlightenment never ends. Masters of forward thinking are writing about spiritual issues for this moment in time. You are standing in this moment in time. Are you lost in the past by choice, or are you thinking yourself into the future. The New Testament Age replaced the Old Testament Age. Now, it is time to move into the New Age. It will replace the New Testament Age.

Seek enlightenment! Be a 'forever' forward thinker. Be a master today and tomorrow. Thinking 'outside of the box forever' will carry you continuously into the future away from darkness.

September 8

THOUGHT FOR THE DAY – A boy cries wolf over and over, tricking his friends into coming to his rescue, when he has no need. When a wolf actually appears, the boy cries wolf but his friends do not come. He is a trickster. Karma whacks him in his time of need by letting him be eaten by a wolf. A human man borrows money over and over from his friends, saying he is going to use it for some specific need. Instead, he buys cigarettes, drugs, and alcohol with it. His friends catch on to his deceit. When he has a legitimate need, his friends do not come to his rescue. Karma whacks tricksters by alienating their support systems.

THE POWER TO AVOID KARMA WHACKS

Humans are animals like dogs and cats. They use the thoughts of their human brains to survive, feed them self, and to reproduce. The human brain is a survivalist and a self centered thinker. Sometimes, human thinking gets man in trouble with the 'Keepers' of earth and its animals. Karma whacks are used as discipline to force a human animal to rethink his error steps and actions in life.

Example of a Karma whack - A man does not pay his utility bill. The gods of thunder and lightning at the utility company send him written warnings that he is in error for not paying his bill. He pays no heed and continues in his error of not paying. The gods at the utility company have spoken, made their demands, and have given the man a chance to rectify his error. The man ignores the gods as the utility company. A Karma van leaves the utility company. It pulls up in front of the man's residence. The van's Karma god gets out with a huge wrench and shuts all the man's utilities off. The man has been Karma whacked. To avoid future whacks, he must pay his old bill, late fees, put up a hefty deposit, and not be late on future bills.

Some Karma whacks are for actions that have been done in secret. A gossip may die from a Karma whack of cancer to the tongue. A man who kicks animals or children may develop diabetes and Karma will see to it that he loses his kicking foot. A car salesman who lies and sales junk autos as reliable ones; may get Karma whacked by one of his own junk cars jumping out of gear and running over him. What a human sows, he will reap. The reaping is karma.

Man has the power to avoid Karma whacks. It is a simple power. Make good decisions, harm no one, pay what you owe, and walk in integrity. If you do those things, the gods of Karma will leave you alone.

September 9

THOUGHT FOR THE DAY - We must know what powers are available to us at a moment's notice.

THE POWER TO THINK & SURVIVE

Moving from power to power is like crossing a small stream, stepping from one stone to another. Each step we take in Earth life may require a different power in order to successfully move forward and reach our destinations and goals. Each stepping stone we take is a different disaster, tragedy, loss, accomplishment, spiritual height, etc.

When I was young, I worked in a men's clothing store. A man, twice my size, asked me to retrieve a pair of pants from a low shelf for him. When I stooped to get them, he immediately pulled a crow bar from his long shirt sleeve and knocked me in the head. Before getting hit, I was in need of the power of an expert salesman to make a commission on the pair of pants that I thought I was about to sell. After getting hit, I needed a different power, one to empower me to think and survive. As gods traveling in human flesh, we may need more than one power in a minute, an hour, or a day's time.

As I was falling to the floor, I immediately knew that if I tried to fight him, he would beat me with the metal bar and possibly kill me. So, when I hit the floor, I lay lifeless with my eyes closed, in hopes he thought he had knocked me out. Thinking is one of the great powers of man. My thinking power saved my life. He immediately headed for the cash register and started cleaning it out and then started stuffing things in sacks. I did not move or open my eyes till I heard him head for the front door. In my thinking, I figured he could not carry me, stuffed sacks, and the cash from the register. My thinking was correct. He was out of the front door of the store in possibly three minutes. I survived with five stitches, and still have a groove in the back of my skull from the impact of his crowbar.

We are gods in human flesh with a variety of powers available to us. The 'Power of Thought' is the activator for other divine powers, such as the 'Power to Survive'.

September 10

THOUGHT FOR THE DAY – Choosing to use your coping powers to survive is up to you, just as crawling into a deep dark hole of depression and choosing not to use them is.

SURVIVAL POWERS

You may never come in contact with a being who takes a crowbar to you. However, there are other weapons that darkness uses that you will need survival skills/powers to get past or overcome. A gossip's tongue is a crowbar. Someone stealing your ideas is a crowbar. Someone preventing you from advancing in your career is a crowbar. Someone stealing your client is a crowbar. A parent or spouse demeaning you is a crowbar. Crowbars come in many forms and are carried by dark beings.

You have powers to overcome. In current time, those powers are called 'coping mechanisms'. Choosing to use your coping powers to survive is up to you, just as crawling into a deep dark hole and not using them is.

'Karma whacking' is a power of gods. Those who watch out for you will deliver recompense to those inflicting evil on you. For instance, if I am hit over the head with a crowbar by a thief, the thief somewhere down the line will have his personal items stolen and he will be hit over the head with some object. A Karma whack will return to the thief in a similar or harsher form.

You have powers to survive the assaults of darkness. Think and use them.

September 11

THOUGHT FOR THE DAY - Thunder and lightning warnings are given, followed by Karma retribution.

THE POWER OF THUNDER AND LIGHTNING

As humans, thinking with animal brains, we walk our daily life paths greeting each other with a simple "Hello!" or "How are you?" We speak pleasantly in tones that do not provoke, or offend the ears of those we are speaking to. We raise our voices only when it is to emphasize points, or as an outburst at assaulting words being said to us. Survival instinct tells us to be nice, in order to keep our place in our culture's social pack of wild animals.

How we react to the physical or mental abuse outbursts of others is a choice. One person will bite their lip to keep from saying something they shouldn't to someone who has just demeaned them in public. Another will take a deep breath and count to ten. Your friend may spin about on his heels and walk away. The above coping mechanisms are 'self control' powers. We have the power to choose how we will react to adversity.

You are two in one. You are both human and divine. Your human brain has choices as how to react and survive. The soul within is different. Your soul is a light being and soldier of the heavens. The soul is at war with darkness. You, as a light being soul, have the power to 'Thunder and Lightning' at injustices.

Thunder is the power of words, spoken or written. Gods of Thunder tell the world of the injustices that human brain thinking inflicts. Lightning is the raised voice of the pen and voice. Thunder and Lightning calls human thinking to be accountable for its outbursts of darkness.

September 12

THOUGHT FOR THE DAY – Angels will appear in spotless clothing, ooze goodness, convey messages from the heavens, and speak of what their mission is on Earth. They may also wear the same clothing every time you encounter them, which is a costume. In the heavens, angels are orbs of light and energy.

THE POWER TO RECOGNIZE ANGELS

I drink coffee on Wednesday mornings at a fast food restaurant called McDees. Routinely, I arrive there about 7, eat my breakfast, chat with other writers who gather there, and write a little. After a year or so of the routine meeting and chatting with other writers, you get to know the light and the dark sides of them. Like all social groups, there are some members of the group who are safe to socialize with, and others of a dark nature you avoid.

An older white haired man shows up at the restaurant just after I do. He is not a writer of words like me. He is an orator, a speaker of powerful words. He is an extremely kind and gentle old man who seems to be always watching over us, and encouraging us to do good with our days. I have nick named him 'Angel Man'.

'Angel man' never fails to say grace before eating. Afterwards, he sits, smiles, and says nice things to anyone paying him any attention. He always speaks of what a great day it is, how good God is, and what he intends to do in God's service for the day. He does not enter into conversations about the weather, politics, or anything normal human males speak of, such as sports, women, or automobiles. He is a holy man!

'Angel man' is a divine being traveling Earth in human flesh. He is on a mission, and speaks of nothing else. His power is kindness and words of doing well for those about him. He always tells about his weekly outings to a local nursing home where he sings, visits patients who have no families, and helps feed the elderly. At McDees, he is a witness to the goodness of his god. He is a Trumpet Angel.

'Angel man' is always spotlessly clean and wears the same set of clothing year round (rain, snow, sleet, or scorching heat). His clothes do not fade or age. The restaurant staff and customers are oblivious to the fact that they are entertaining an angel unaware!

September 13

THOUGHT FOR THE DAY – Know your family, friends, and coworkers by the words of their mouths. Those of the light speak positive words. Those of the dark speak negativity.

NEGATIVE POWERS

Have you ever met an individual who was absolutely negative about everything?   Negative people never feel that anything good is going to come to them. No amount of talking can change their mind on the subject. They also believe that everyone is out to get them, use them, or abuse them in some way. Nothing ever goes right for them. When they get their minds off of themselves, they look about their physical world and only see the bad things that are happening there. They seem totally oblivious to anything good going on in their lives, or in the lives of others.

Examples of a negative thinking person: A fellow employee gets a much deserved promotion. You have a negative thinking co-worker that insists the one that was promoted got the job just because he or she was the boss' pet. Your sister and her spouse have tried for ten years to have a baby. Suddenly, your sister is pregnant. Your negative co-worker declares that your sister must have played around on her husband to get pregnant after that many years. You bake banana bread and take it to the office to share, just for the sheer joy of it. Your negative co-worker tells everyone (behind your back) that you are the worst baker ever, and that your bread gave her indigestion.

Negative people see, feel, and say that something is wrong with everything. They live in a constant world of negative storm clouds. Their tongues, like tornadoes, are twisters that are intent on cutting negative paths of destruction.

Gods of darkness as well as gods of light have powers. Negativity, the power to destroy with the tongue, is a power of darkness. Those who display nothing but negative words and vibes are demons/devils traveling in human flesh. Flee from all evil! Don't pal around with evil thinking humans. Don't car pool with them. Don't set yourself up to be their victim one day.

September 14

THOUGHT FOR THE DAY – Curses are word vibrations spoken out to ride moving air/winds. Gods and angels of light have the power to return curses on the same winds they arrived on.

THE POWER TO RETURN CURSES

The air about you is filled with vibrations. They are the result of industrial machinery, men's voices, cars, and electronic signals from radios, cell phones, and televisions. On Sundays, churches have sound systems that fill the air with projected vibrations. Outdoor sporting events, fairs, concerts, carnivals, and stock car races project vibrations or noise. Vibrations are riding the air waves all about you on a constant basis. Some of the vibrations are good, some are annoying, and others can be a curse sent to you from a specific point.

I heard a psychic recently state that no one can put a curse on you. That is not so! Curses are broadcasted, forcefully projected vibrations sent out into the atmosphere from the mouths of dark ones/enemies. If you tune into the sounds of curses, like a radio tuning in radio programs, you are immediately affected by them. Thru the ears, you let a curse's vibrations/sounds enter you.

Gods, masters, and angels of light traveling in human flesh have the power to return curses on the wind. To do so, they must stand on the highest physical point available to them. In your apartment, it might be standing on a bed or kitchen table. In the desert, it might be sitting on top of a camel or the top of a safari vehicle. The key to returning curses is going to the highest point in your world to do the returning. Once standing there, take in a deep breath of cursed vibrations and hold it. Then slowly and forcefully blow the air back out picturing it returning to whoever has sent it to you. When all the air has left your human lungs, use two of your fingers as though they are scissors. Put the finger scissors to your lips and cut the exhaled breath as though it were a giant rubber band. The cutting will let the vibration curse snap back like elastic or rubber band material to where it came from.

There is war in the heavens between angels and fallen angels. Fallen angels send curses. The power to return curses is a weapon of light beings or angels of light. All light being souls, traveling in human forms on Earth, have this power.

September 15

THOUGHT FOR THE DAY - You have two bodies. One is human and one is a copy, or costume of the human form. The costume body is worn by the soul when it has stepped from a sleeping human body to astral travel. There is one difference between the human body and the soul's copy cat costume body. The soul costume has a third eye in the middle of its forehead. Why? It is to accommodate the mystical third eye of the soul that humans cannot see.

THE POWER TO RAISE THE DEAD

In the inner and upper heavens, souls are eternal and ageless beings that are orbs of light and energy. In the afterlife, a soul can choose to wear a costume of its former Earth or other planet bodies. The costume an orb chooses can be toddler age up to 30 years in human appearance.

On Earth, orbs of light and energy travel in human bodies like they are cars. When souls exit human bodies, they wear a costume of their earth body. You have heard stories how a man dies on an operating table. In shock, he floats up to the ceiling, and then looks down at his dead human body on the operating table below. He looks at his hands and body of the form he is floating in. That body is a carbon copy or copy cat costume of his dead body below. He discovers that he is a soul who lived in the human body below.

When a human body dies, a soul steps or floats from it, to return to the home of the soul. In some instances, a soul may be told to return to their body that it is not their time to cross over yet. That soul will return and dive into his human body. Once there, the soul will activate his dead human form's self healing function. He will raise his human body from the dead. Souls have the power to raise the dead.

Returning to a dead human body and reviving it is one use of the 'Power of Resurrection'.

September 16

THOUGHT FOR THE DAY - If you befriend a 'Saint', you automatically have a friendly door that will open, allowing you to also be friends with your saint's friends in the heavens, including God.

THE POWER OF BEFRIENDING A SAINT

In high school, you had a circle of friends that you paled around with. Each friend varied in gender, personality, dress, and taste. They were human like you, but not like you as an individual. Angels, in the heavens, are all alike, due to all being angels. As individuals, they are not alike. They each have likes and dislikes, have different ways of expressing themselves, and have different ways of appearing to man on Earth. Individual angels are like two individual little girls on Earth. One little girl will embrace the color pink, while the other loves the color purple. Saints in the heavens are all saints, but they too are individuals with different likes, dislikes, and powers.

In the heavens, a leader of one group of saint friends is nicknamed God. His friends also have nicknames (St. Luke, St. Paul, St. Matthew, etc.); the saint friend nick names are plays on the names they were known by as humans on Earth. They are not the actual heavenly names of the saints. On Earth, my human body was named Jo Hammers. In the heavens I am a soul that has a name. That name is Master Barjoraven. On Earth, my father nicked named me 'Hot Foot'. In the heavens as a soul, I am sometimes called the nickname 'Jodi'. Members of God's social group of friends have heavenly names, as well as nicknames given them by humans. St. Paul is a nickname for a man named Paul.

God's friends are sent to Earth on missions. When a friend of god leaves for earth, he does not, as a rule, take his social circle of friends with him. That would be like a human taking his exercise or book club members to work with him. When one of god's friends enters earth life, he has miracle powers that humans do not. If you encounter and befriend one of these holy ones, they remain your friend when they return to the heavens. Like any true friends, you can ask them for favors. One of those favors is to intercede to god for you.

There is more than one god or master being in the heavens that has a circle of friends, just as there are many leaders and groups of friends in an Earth high school. Buddha is the leader of a spiritual circle of friends in the heavens. The Great White Spirit of the Native Americans has followers, friends in the heavens. Christ has followers in the afterlife, as does Mother Teresa.

It is okay for you to choose, embrace, become friends with, and pray to a saint who has returned to the heavens. Prayers are simply you asking your friend for help with something that you cannot accomplish on your own. I have a neighbor who can fix anything. I often ask him to help me with little things that I have no skills to fix. He is my friend. He helps me. In return, I am there for him. He has my friendship loyalty. Wearing a saint medal is one way faithful followers of a saint show their loyalty to them.

September 17

THOUGHT FOR THE DAY – Stripped stark naked, you are capable of starting over and providing the basics of life for yourself. Water, food, and shelter are those basics. The ability to think and create what you need is the 'boot strap' power of naked gods.

BOOT STRAP POWER

In the United States, we have an expression that goes 'Pull your-self up by the boot straps'. What it means is that an individual, who has hit bottom financially or emotionally, can stand up and thru inner will start over again. He can create the basics (water, food, shelter) for himself and move on up the ladder to success from there. A 'boot strap' individual doesn't sit down and die in his financial and emotional disaster. In spite of his predicament, he chooses to stand up and start over. He digs down deep and creates a new world from scratch.

Example: A husband and wife are on vacation in a big city in a far away state. They basically have their car and a suitcase of clothing each. The wife has her purse and it holds all her ID, money, makeup, toiletries, etc. The fiftyish woman, raised in an orphanage, does not have a job, family, children, or friends back home. She has always been a housewife at her husband's insistence. The husband has been the woman's world up to this point.

The husband has been in a foul mood all morning. The wife does not know why. He starts 'nit picking' her, as he drives. They get in a heated quarrel and the abusive husband pulls off the freeway onto an off ramp. He reaches across the woman and flings her car door open. He then literally with his foot kicks her out of the car onto the pavement where she falls flat and struggles to get up. He then yells, "You are history! I am divorcing you!" The husband then speeds off with the passenger door flopping, before she can get back in. The wife has been abandoned without suitcase, purse, shoes, and her eyeglasses which she had placed on the dash when they were quarreling. Her only possessions are the shorts and T- shirt she is wearing. This is a woman who will either sit down in the gutters of life and give up, or pick herself up by the bootstraps and create a new world to live in.

The woman has basic needs to start with. She needs water, food, & shelter. On the shoulder of the off ramp lies an empty plastic water bottle. She picks it up and then walks to a gas station. She washes the plastic bottle out in the restroom, and then fills it with water from the lavatory. She has pulled herself up by the bootstraps and provided for herself one of the three basic needs of life, water. Leaving the gas station, she spots a covered bus bench in the distance. She walks barefoot there, enters, and sits down. She has provided another basic need for herself, shelter. As she sits pondering her situation, city bus riders come and go carrying soft drinks and snacks. She watches what they throw away in the trash next to the bench. She then feeds herself for the day off of their discarded chips, candy, etc. She has provided for herself the third basic, food. One small step at a time, she will continue to pull herself up by the boot straps and provides for herself. She is a creator who has tapped into her 'Come Back' or 'Boot Strap' power.

When life taps you on the shoulder roughly, sending you spiraling down unexpectedly into the gutters, don't just lay there in despair and die. You are a divine soul that is perfectly capable of thinking and creating a new world to live in.

September 18

THOUGHT FOR THE DAY – Atomic power is the energy source of gods, not human blood.

IS THERE POWER IN THE BLOOD OF JESUS?

Jesus Christ was two beings, not one. He had a human body, and a spirit body that he returned to the heavens in. Both of his two beings had power sources.

Jesus the human had blood for a power source to run his

human body. The blood carried nutrients to feed his human body. It was blood, the same as you and I have coursing thru our veins.

Christ, the Spirit Being/soul who was traveling in the body of Jesus, was a divine orb of energy, a master light being. In the heavens, Christ the Light Being soul is a supernatural being. Human brains have decided to call him the 'son of god'. The main thing to remember is that Christ is not human. As a soul, he is an orb of light and energy, and that orb does not have human blood.

Christ came down and entered a human baby named Jesus to live a lifetime on earth traveling. The human body Jesus was transportation for him, a vehicle. The name Jesus was the name given his human body by his human parents. Christ was two in one. He was both human (Jesus) and divine (Christ). As a human, his body could be injured and its blood spilt. As a light being, his light and energy source (not blood) could not be destroyed by human hands or spears. Christ was two in one. He was human and divine.

Humans think there is power in the blood of Jesus. That is error thinking. The power of the Jesus/Christ duo is in the Spirit Being Soul that drives or lives within the human vehicle Jesus. Jesus' blood is like the oil you put in your automobile. It keeps your car running, but it won't keep you the driver running. Christ was the power source, the driver of the human body vehicle called Jesus. Christ did not have blood. He had a divine source of light and energy that fueled him.

Men waste their time worshiping the blood of Jesus. The soul that traveled in his human body (Christ) was an orb of light and energy. A soul has no blood. It has a different life source. Divine beings like Christ the soul have atomic power coursing thru their beings, not human blood. Christ the Soul was not Jesus the human vehicle car he drove. You, a soul, are not the human body vehicle you drive. You are not that human vehicle's body or blood. You are light and atom energy powered.

September 19

THOUGHT FOR THE DAY – Future destinies are reached by walking, not sitting and dozing.

THE POWER TO CREATE YOUR OWN DESTINY

Creating your future starts with a dream, a plan. Calling your dream into physical existence starts with taking the first tiny step towards building/creating your dream. Fantasizing about someday starting accomplishes nothing. Dreamers, with couch potato mentality, are lost causes who become the failures in life.

Suppose, you want to write a novel! The first step is to write the first word or title on paper or in a computer. Then you must proceed to take step two and outline or write the first paragraph of the first chapter. Dreaming about writing a novel, but not taking the first and then the second step toward producing it is fantasizing. The power to create your destiny is accomplished in the same manner. You must quit fantasizing and take the first step.

I know a well known author who starts her novel writing process with a first step of picking her book character's names. She does it in a very unusual way. Her first step is to open a phone book with her eyes closed. Still, with her eyes closed, she then lets her finger fall on the phone book page that has opened. Whatever name her finger lands on becomes her first character's name. She then repeats the process for five names. No two novel writers' first step may be the same. What matters is taking the first step.

I have a brother who never functioned well as a student in school. He was a chronic hooky player who dreamed of becoming a salesman. One day, he walked away from high school life, borrowed an old pickup, and headed south where he purchased a pickup load of cantaloupe. Then, he returned to the Midwest and sold it. That first truck load of cantaloupe was his first step toward becoming who he knew he was destined to be, a salesman. After the cantaloupes, my brother sold load after load of fruit and progressed to other items. That first load was his first step to living his dream.

My brother, now in his retirement years, buys out estates of antiques and sales them. He lives in one of the wealthiest areas in our city, and is richer than any of his college educated siblings and other family members. His continuous success has been due to a continuous willingness to take first steps over and over, buying a new load. (Note, I am all for education and would cringe if my grandsons dropped out of school. However, there are some individuals who have destinies that are beyond normal boundaries.)

What is your dream? Have you taken your first step toward achieving it, or are you just a couch potato that is sitting and fantasizing? You have the power to create your dream! Take the first step. The second step will not appear till you take the first.

September 20

THOUGHT FOR THE DAY - There is nothing wrong with a friend giving you a couch, table, car, clothing, or shoes . . . as long as it is not their trash.

THE POWER TO CHOOSE & RECEIVE

Everything in your world, good or bad, was once just a thought in some creative person's mind. If that person was a light being, they invented or created fine things like the microwave, air conditioning, eye glasses, soap, hot chocolate, or toothpaste. If the creative person was a dark being, he created such things as gas chambers, slave whips, porn movies, date rape drugs, cigarettes, etc. Look about you and make note of the light being or dark being created items in your world. Each item you own was once just a thought. Also, consider that your possessions have been drawn to you by your dark or light desires and choices.

Example – You find yourself in need of a simple thing like a couch. Perhaps you are a dorm student or a newlywed who doesn't have one. You think/project out into the universe that you would like to have a couch. A friend calls offering you their old couch which is thread bare, has holes in its cushions, fleas from their dog, and ten years of hair and pet dander from their cat. One couch leg is missing and your friend uses a can of veggies to hold up leg corner. If you accept the ratty couch, you let poverty enter your life. To wait for a better couch to come to you is a prosperity or positive choice. There is nothing wrong with a friend giving you a couch, kitchen table, car, clothing, shoes, etc. . . . as long as it is not their trash.

The Christian's Bible says to flee from evil. Face it, the

above thread bare, flea infested couch is one evil you should definitely flee from!

September 21

THOUGHT FOR THE DAY - You are a walking and talking force field, like a magnet. You draw to you what you think about. Thoughts are your 'turn on' switch to attract that which you desire.

THE POWER OF GENERIC PRAYERS

Sometimes we have to ask the universe for things that are not available in our little corner of the world. When in need of the unobtainable, it is important to be exact when you put in your request. If you don't, the universe will send you a generic brand.

For instance, if you walk up to a friend and ask, "Will you give me a lift?" Your friend can interpret your request in various ways. He could scoop you up, and then boost you up thinking you want something from the shelf next to you. Then again, he may go to his garage and get a jack to loan you. You wanting a lift or ride to town may not cross his mind. To get what you want from your friend, you must be precise in your request. This would be a request that is in more detail. "Would you drive me in your car to town to 'Pam's Flower Shop' and let me get out in front of her business' front door?"

The more detail you add to requests of spirit guides and angels, the closer you will get to what you really have need of. You may be between pay checks and say a simple prayer asking for food. That is a generic request. Angels or spirit guides may let you encounter a neighbor who is on his way to the dumpster with leftover birthday cake from a party he had three evenings prior. You stop to chat and he says, "I was about to throw this away, would you like it?" Food has come to you. Whether or not you accept your answer to prayer is up to you. However, second choices (answers to prayer) are never given.

When you prayed for food, you should have asked more in detail, such as this "Please send me nutritious food!" Had you been a little more specific, you might have been offered a sack of apples or a jar of applesauce the neighbor was about to discard in the dumpster. If you pray generic, you will get generic. How you describe what you want from the universe is important. When praying for nutritious food, had you added vegetables, the jar of applesauce offered you by your neighbor could have been a can of vegetable soup. You get what you ask for from the universe.

Besides being a writer, I am an artist who loves to paint outside in the summer. One spring, I put out a simple (generic) request into the universe. "I want to paint all summer!" I painted alright. The universe let all the paint on my residence, and a couple of rentals I own, blister and peel. It took me all summer to scrape and paint the three houses. The universe gave me what I asked for. I got to paint all summer.

You have awakened to the fact that you have the power to pray for and get what you need from the universe. Be a wise 'master of requests' and don't ask entirely for things. When you leave Earth and return to the home of the soul, you cannot take things from Earth with you. A wise master asks for higher thoughts, advanced states of consciousness, educational opportunities. Wealth in the heavens is knowledge. Knowledge you can take home to the heavens with you. Asking only for things on Earth will let you return to the heavens someday 'empty handed'.

September 22

THOUGHT FOR THE DAY - Choosing companions in life is like choosing autos. We must choose wisely, or we might be stuck with a pretty or handsome face that is a lemon. Choose companions by the purr of their spiritual engines.

THE POWER TO CREATE HEAVEN OR HELL

Man has one super power. That power is 'Free Will Choice'. With that power, he can choose to walk in heaven on Earth, or in dark gutter hells. Man walks a fine line, and he can choose to step off his fine line by making positive or negative choices. Drug addiction and alcoholism are negative choices, as is choosing companions for their beauty and not compatibility.

Example: A family man with four kids needs to purchase an auto. He goes to a car dealership after saving for two years for a down payment. Once there, he looks at four door family cars and then super expensive, two door, sports cars. The man is not single, nor is he rich. His car choice will have to serve him for at least five years, maybe more till he gets it paid for. He has to make a decision whether to choose wisely a car that is in his budget and family friendly, or a two seat sports car with payments that are totally out of his price range, not to mention that his four kids can't fit into it. He walks a fine line and must use his power of 'free will choice' to enter car heaven or car hell.

Choosing companions in life is like choosing autos. We must choose wisely, or we might be stuck with a pretty face that is not compatible with our spiritual path and mission in life. Pretty or handsome human faces can be masks for dark pits of Hell. Compatibility is the wise choice that men/women should make. A sports car companion may not be what is best for you.

If you have (by choice) made your bed in Hell (married a sporty demon), you can rise, flee hell, and find your fine line or path again. God does not chain light beings to darkness. He is at war with darkness.

September 23

THOUGHT FOR THE DAY – He who disciplines a child in anger embraces darkness. He who controls his anger and disciplines in peace is a Light Being.

THE POWER OF SELF CONTROL

The Christians have a god who at times is angry and sends fiery destruction upon his followers in fits of rage. Their god throws them out of gardens, sends plagues, and kills those who do not follow him to his exact liking. Their angry, vengeful god expects his followers to be absolutely perfect.

Why should followers of a deity be perfect, if their god is not perfect? On Earth, we put raging killers in prison for life, or to death. Those who assault in anger are given jail or prison time. If a deity expects perfection from his followers; then he should be the role model for that perfection.

Is it possible that there are dark gods out in the universe that some of us mistakenly worship, believing them to be god? Darkness is darkness! Light is light! Devils are devils, and Gods are gods. What are the characteristics of the god you serve? Is he a dark being or a light being? Does he expect more from you that he expects from himself? Is he there in your time of need? Do you feel slighted by your god when you ask for something good like healing? Is it possible that you are worshipping a dark, angry, vengeful, self centered dark being that will kill you if you don't jump when he says jump or follow him blindly? Does your god expect more perfection from you than he is willing to display himself? If he tells you not to be angry, then he should not display anger.

The Power of Self Control is a perfection power. Biting one's tongue, or counting to ten, are common self control practices. As a young child, we start to learn to control our speech and actions. We have our mouths washed out with soap when we curse. If we bite another child or hit, we are disciplined. We are students of perfection. When we reach adulthood, we have mastered, hopefully, the 'Power of Self Control'.

The Power of Self Control is a learned power, and is a beginning step toward perfection. Those who fail to learn the lesson of self control become the sociopaths of Earth society. Ask yourself if there are sociopath dark beings/gods in your heavens? To know, you must judge the individuals you encounter by which side of the fine line dividing dark and light that they walk. Light side beings choose to practice self control and live responsible lives. Dark side beings choose to be vengeful, angry, sociopaths who prefer the gutters of life. Which side of the fine line dividing light and dark do you think your vengeful, angry, killer deity embraces? Self control is perfection. The lack of self control is sociopath darkness. Being angry is not self control! Anger is not a characteristic of perfection!

September 24

THOUGHT FOR THE DAY- If you purposely destroy your body by eating too much, smoking, using drugs, and drinking alcohol, you are committing a slow form of suicide.

THE POWER TO SELF HEAL

Healing Power is available to humans in two forms. One is healing for the human body. The second is healing for the spirit being/soul that lives within a human body. Healing for the human form comes in the form of a built in immune system of cell healers. Healing for the spirit being/soul comes from the heavens in the form of divine healer orbs that attend to and repair the communication silver cords of spirit beings traveling in human flesh.

The human body is built to heal itself. If the body gets a scratch, healer immune cells make their way to the damage and heal it. The human mind is responsible for activating the immune system. If a human brain thinks itself sick (hypochondria), the immune system will not function. Error thinking shuts the system down. If the same human brain thinks itself well, the immune system will activate and go to work healing the human form. Human doctors can cut, probe, patch, and prescribe. However, the human form will not heal itself unless the body's built in self healing function is activated.

Example: A child in summertime play falls and scrapes his big toe. In tears, he runs to his mother and crawls upon her lap in distress and pain. She kisses his boo-boo and assures him that his injured big toe will be fine in a day or so. In faith that the words of his mother are true, he gets down and runs back out and plays in spite of still having a bloody toe and some pain. In a few days, his big toe does heal and the pain goes away.

As adults, healing for our adult boo-boos comes in the same fashion. We have the free will choice to run to religious leaders (mothers) and to ask for healing prayers and comfort (mother kisses). If we believe in the words of healing prayed and comfort given, we must run back out into our adult worlds to play, even though we still have our boo-boos.

Man's human body has a certain number of days appointed for it to live on earth. The number of days is predestined, according to the number needed by the soul within to complete his mission or education assignment on Earth. Keep in mind that the human body has to die when the spirit being within returns home to the heavens. Certain illnesses are built in to end the life of a human body when it is its soul's time to go home to the heavens. A sudden heart attack and death is one such function.

Some illnesses that kill human bodies are due to the free will choice of man's brain. Free will choice types of illnesses are slow forms of suicide. Humans kill themselves slowly with food, cigarettes, alcohol, drugs, etc. When that happens, the soul is thrown from the human form before its mission is completed. It is sort of like you slashing your own car tires. The soul will go home early, and be given a new human vehicle to complete his mission in.

September 25

THOUGHT FOR THE DAY - People commit suicide to free themselves from the results of former bad choices. Apocalypse or the end of time comes to some humans in the form of suicide.

THE POWER TO APOCALYPSE

The 'Power to Apocalypse' is the power to self destruct. Suicide is self destruction. Drugs, alcohol, over eating, etc. are slow forms. Human beings shorten their appointed years on Earth by indulging in addictions. The power to apocalypse is a 'free will choice', and an error choice. The reason it is a bad choice is that it denies a soul its transportation to complete its mission.

Some men, who are physically ill, choose to die rather than wait for their illness to kill them. They make that decision using their human brain. They use their power of 'free will choice' to kill their own human vehicle engines.

Back in the 1940s, I had an uncle I will call Vance. He was happily married and had two little girls toddler age. Everything seemed to be going his way. Uncle Vance lived in a Garden of Eden, or Utopia life on Earth. He and his wife were happily married. Then, my uncle made an error choice and his paradise turned into a downward spiral descent into hell. He had a one night stand with a bar fly. Afterward, his wife became ill and had to go to the doctor. To her shock, she was told that she had a serious venereal disease. My aunt knew that the shameful disease had been passed on to her by her only sex partner, Uncle Vance. She went home, packed her bags, and left on the afternoon bus while my uncle was at work, taking my two toddler cousins with her. She left him a note telling him about the shame of the disease she had gotten from him. Uncle Vance went on a few weeks drunk before he was sober enough to go to the doctor. To his shock, he was in the advanced stages of a life threatening venereal disease.

Uncle Vance eventually found out that my aunt had caught a bus to California. My uncle decided to catch a bus to California and try to convince my aunt to forgive him and take him back. She refused. Despondent, Uncle Vance returned to Missouri penniless and ill. One late evening, he showed up on my parent's doorstep and asked to stay. By that time, all of our family members knew of his infidelity and the contagious disease he had.

My parents, with six of us children at home, refused him. The disease he had back then was feared, like aids would be in future years. I recall my mother telling my father, "There is no way that your brother is going to sleep in my beds and possibly give his shameful disease to one of our children and possibly kill one of them or us!"

My uncle left our house and walked away into the evening shadows. A week later, he left his billfold on a bridge in St. Louis, Missouri. He jumped to his death in the raging river below.

Uncle Vance chose to kill himself, before his illness killed him. He chose to apocalypse or self destruct.

We are souls traveling in human bodies. When we as souls sleep, the human brain takes over and makes decisions for the human body. It is the human brain that has the 'Power to Apocalypse' or self destruct.

September 26

THOUGHT FOR THE DAY - What happened to the human body of Jesus? It eventually decayed and rotted, like all human corpses do after death. Jesus' body was human, not divine. It was the Christ spirit/soul within Jesus that was divine.

THE POWER TO EXIT HUMAN FORMS

At night, while sleeping, have you ever floated above your body and looked down at it? If so, you (a soul) have stepped from your human form. Christ stepped from his human form on the cross. He went away as a soul and then returned. If you have floated above your human body, you have experienced what Christ did.

Many stories have circulated about patients (who have died in intensive care units or during surgery in hospitals) who suddenly find themselves floating above their bodies and watching medical personnel trying to revive their deceased human forms below. As 'out of body' floating souls, they look at their hands, feet and body. They look exactly like the ones below on a surgery table or hospital bed. The souls, floating above their human bodies, are wearing costume bodies that look like their human bodies below. Souls are actually orbs of light and energy.

There is another circumstance in which a soul will lift and leave the human form. It is in dreams. When you float or fly in dreams, you are out of your human body. The experience is called astral travel. When you are tired of soul flight, you can return to your human form, enter, and then force it to awaken.

Other resurrections of the soul from the human body

happen. One comes when the human mind starts to search for spiritual knowledge and understanding. The soul of the seeker awakens, letting human thinking soar in thought. Being caught up to the heavens and seeing visions come in this manner.

Man is not one life form. He is two. One is a human animal, and one is a divine being soul that lives and travels in the human body. The soul, a separate life form, can exit its human body vehicle like it is an automobile. Men on Earth have automobiles they ride and travel in. However, men on earth don't drive or live in their cars 24 hours a day. They park and exit autos when arriving at work, or when getting home in the evenings. A soul, stepping from its human form vehicle, is like that. It has a life beyond the vehicle it drives. A soul has a heavenly/astral home and family there to interact with. Souls can park and leave human vehicles, when they desire to be home or interact with friends and family in the astral.

When we step from our human forms to take astral flights to our homes in the heavens, we are the 'going away". When we return to and get back in our human forms, we are the 'coming again'. Christ was a soul who could 'go away' and 'come again'. We are souls that can step from our human bodies to 'go away' and then 'come again' to them. The rapture or catching away is taking place as you read this, one awakened soul at a time. Awaken to your powers, don't be left behind.

September 27

THOUGHT FOR THE DAY - Unexplainable orbs of

light appearing in photos, or floating and dancing about you, may be alien souls from other planets.

THE POWER TO SEE ALIENS

Don't limit yourself to thinking that life exists only on Planet Earth. Life exists on all planets. Some life forms can be seen with the human eyes and others are invisible. Just as you are a soul that is currently living a life in a human body on Earth, you can also live as a soul in alien life forms on other planets in the future.

The 'Power to See Aliens' is twofold. Human eyes can see alien life forms, if those forms travel by space ship to planet earth, or vice versa. As Earth life forms, human animals, we view them with our human eyes. Human eyes can also see alien souls. Alien souls can be seen when they are out of body or astral traveling. They appear on Earth as orbs. Human eyes can see them floating and flitting about as spots of light at times, and sometimes in the photographs they take. Cameras catch shots of orb figures that human eyes sometimes can't see.

Just as there are light and dark souls traveling in human bodies on Earth, there are both light and dark souls traveling in the life forms that are on other planets. You must judge alien visitors by the same standard of light and dark as you do humans and light beings on Earth. If an alien visitor tries to assault, do harm, or kill you, he is a dark soul.

Alien souls from other planets can travel to planet Earth via astral flight. It is not necessary for an alien orb soul to enter a life form on his planet and then travel via spaceship here. It is quicker and more comfortable for an alien soul to fly here as a soul. On a soul astral flight, an alien soul can travel from the outer realms to here in less than 30 seconds of Earth time. When they arrive on Earth, they will float about as orbs of light taking in the sights like a human being on vacation. Alien souls/orbs may enter your home just to get a peek at you and your lifestyle. You may have already had encounters with alien orbs, and have not realized it.

If you wish to see aliens, look for orbs of light floating about you, or for them in the photos you take.

September 28

THOUGHT FOR THE DAY - God appeared to Moses in a burning bush. The burning bush was a costume he wore. To be able to see God is to recognize the forms/costumes he chooses to wear in order to communicate with you.

THE POWER TO SEE GOD

There is a power that exists that controls the universe. Human thinking likes to call the energy source God, and bestow on him a human likeness and personality. Some men see their created god image as an angry old man with a white, flowing beard. The true power of the universe is an orb of intelligence and energy that is composed of billions of elements smaller than the atom. Supreme Power does not have skin, flesh, and bone like Earth's creatures. He is light and energy. Man, in his limited thinking, has created costumes he expects him to appear in. The angry old man with the flowing white beard is one.

God appeared to Moses as a burning bush. The bush was a costume. Apparently, Moses related to bushes or God would not have appeared to him in the costume of one. Supreme Power/god knows that the men of cultures and religions on earth are different in how they dress, as well as speak different languages. Using costumes, Supreme Power visits man in forms he understands and speaks to the people of the different cultures in languages and forms they understand. He can appear wearing the costume of a Buddha, a monk, a nun, a holy man, a priest, an animal, a white buffalo woman, a mother Mary, a burning bush, the pages of a book, etc. All are correct sightings of him.

God/Supreme Power can walk and talk with you in the costume form of a stranger who encourages you to be all that you can be. He can also wear the pages of a book for a costume. If written words speak to you, it is God talking to you. If beautiful words of music stir your soul, it is God talking to you. If you want to see god, you have to recognize the costumes he chooses to visit you in.

September 29

THOUGHT FOR THE DAY - A happy marriage is a Heaven on earth. A bad one is Hell!

THE POWER TO CREATE PARADISES

In the Christians' bible, God decided to create Earth and creatures to inhabit it, a utopia paradise. We humans would like to do the same. With our human brains, we dream of paradise vacation spots in far-away places. After a few years of dreaming, we may make the choice to buy a cottage somewhere in the mountains or on the beach and make it our private utopia. That is about as close as humans can get to creating like god. Humans are somewhat limited in the size of what they have the power to create. God created a planet. Man creates a cabin on a tiny piece of land.

Planets are out of the ability of humans to create. However, creating good marriages, friendships, family bonds, working relationships, etc. is. A happy marriage is a Heaven on earth, a paradise. Having friends that walk and talk with you and are there for you is a paradise experience. Having those about you love and respect you is a heaven. That is what every human dreams of creating; perfect 'Garden of Eden' experiences.

The opposite of the above is self created hells on Earth. Drug addiction is not a paradise. It is a hell on earth. Alcoholism is not a paradise existence. Marrying the wrong person creates marriage beds from hell. Hells are created, just like paradises are created.

I have a male cousin that chose to embrace alcohol consumption as a young teen of 14. He became a serious teen alcoholic and was hanging out in seedy bars before he reached 21. When he was drunk, he would get in fist fights. One night in a bar, he got in a fist fight with another lush and beat him to death. Family rumors say that he beat the other drunk to death with a whiskey bottle. My cousin, like all humans, had free will choice. He chose darkly and then spiraled downward into a dark hell that he could not climb back out of. He lived and died in a self created hell on Earth. Hell is now for some humans, just as paradise is. Heaven and Hell exist side by side on Earth. Human thinking becomes the gatekeepers for both.

Create a heaven to live in. Be the god of that paradise. At the same time, visit other gods in their created heavens.

I have a friend who is a gourmet chef. Her kitchen is her paradise. I am at bliss visiting her in her heaven and sitting at her table eating what she has created. Heavens can overlap.

September 30

THOUGHT FOR THE DAY – Suicide causes an early bird flight home for a soul. A human committing suicide is like the kid at summer camp who hates his camping experience and goes home mid-week. The kid's parents may be disappointed in him, but they don't put him in their fireplace back home and burn him forever in its fiery hell. His camping experience is just an unexpected death they deal with.

THE POWER TO CATCH A SOUL FLIGHT HOME

By now, reading my writings, you should know that you are a spirit being, an orb/god/angel/soul traveling in human flesh. Also, you should have the understanding that Planet Earth is just a vacation destination, work place, or school of learning for a soul. With this knowledge, you are also aware that you will one day exit your human body, take an astral flight, and return to the heavens, the home of your soul when your appointed time to do duty on Earth is over.

You, as a soul, have the power to complete your mission on earth, whatever it might be. However, your human body vehicle (car) is capable of having breaks downs (nervous break downs) on the highway of life. Mental illness, nervous breakdowns of the human vehicle, causes men to kill themselves, thus ending their life of usefulness as transportation for a soul. A human who slashes the tires of his own car is a type of a human brain breaking down. The slashing of the tires is like a man cutting his wrists to bleed to death.

When a human brain has a nervous breakdown and suicide results, the soul does not die. When that happens, the soul takes a forced flight home to the heavens.

Sometimes a soul volunteers to come to earth on a mission and on arrival finds Earth life deplorable. A soul has the right or power to say I refuse to wade around in this mess down there. My son-in-law is a vegetarian. If someone sent him to a third world country where he was expected to butcher chickens if he wanted to eat, I am sure he would catch the first flight home. When a soul comes to earth and says no way, he has the right to abandon his mission. When doing so, he will stop the function of the human form he is traveling in, like turning the key off in a car. A human heart attack is a key turning off the life of a human vehicle.

On Earth, not every human is cut out to be a survivalist who lives in a tent. One night of sleeping on rocky ground and being eaten alive by mosquito causes a non camper human to head for the nearest plush motel. Student souls on earth, on educational assignments, sometimes pull this. They are like the kid at summer camp who goes home mid week. Human bodies that die unexpectedly in their preteens and teens have been shut down by student souls, who can't hack private school on Earth.

You are a soul traveling for a lifetime in human flesh on a mission or educational assignment on Earth. You have powers! One of those powers is the right to catch a soul flight home, if earth life doesn't suit you. However, if you are a student soul, you will eventually have to return to Earth and travel in another human body to repeat your lessons.

Many human children repeat kindergarten because they are not mature enough to move on to first grade. Not all kindergarten age light being souls are mature, or prepared for higher learning. Parent souls in the heavens sometimes travel to earth to retrieve young failing souls and take them home. They do so to give their off spring some additional time at home to mature. Eventually, the same little souls will be re-enrolled in soul kindergarten classes on Earth. When soul parents retrieve these little souls, their human body vehicles are shut down.

Human children that have died young may have had kindergarten age souls in them that could not handle their beginning Earth educations.

CHAPTER TEN
OCTOBER

THE BOOK OF THE DEAD

October 1

THOUGHT FOR THE DAY - Humans communicate thru words and body language. In the heavens, spirit beings have silver cord communication lines of advanced intelligence and memory.

UNDERSTANDING ASTRAL COMMUNICATIONS

To understand how to communicate with those who have crossed over, you must understand their communication system. Also, you must understand that souls are not human. They are spirit beings, orbs of light and energy. They do not communicate or function like human bodies do.

On Earth, humans communicate thru words and body language. In the heavens, spirit beings have silver cord communication lines of advanced intelligence. The cord looks like a twisted, spiraling gray rope that can be seen thru. It is a misty cord structure that you can walk thru or stick your physical hand thru. It is transparent and ghost like in appearance.

Sometimes, when a spirit being/orb is entering Earth life into a new conception, silver cords are damaged or severed. When this happens, the soul may lose memories of its former life as an orb in the heavens, his associations there, and his occupation or status. At the end of a soul's appointed days to travel on a mission on Earth, a severed or damaged cord being may need to be rescued and escorted back to the heavens by a savior/rescuer. A severed cord being has no memories or divine connection to help him return there. He has a form of astral amnesia. Christ was a rescuer, a savior.

Severed cord beings/souls have no memories or inclinations that they are anything but human. Damaged cord beings have some vague inclinations that a heaven exists. Undamaged, fully connected silver cord beings/souls are your psychics, seers, mystics, etc.

You have heard Protestant Christians declare, "I was lost, but I was found!" They are souls with damaged or severed cords that are being healed, repaired, and rescued by silver cord repairmen from the heavens. Christ was a healer, a rescuer. His followers are damaged and severed silver cord accident victims that he was sent to rescue, sort of like him being an astral paramedic.

A quip from the Protestant hymn, 'Amazing Grace'. . . "I once was lost, but now I am found . . . Was blind, but now I see!"

October 2

THOUGHT FOR THE DAY – If you purposely ask for a visitation from a dark, sociopath deceased relative or friend, you are asking for a mental and physical assault from a demon.

CONTACTING EVIL

Consider the personality of the person that you are wishing to contact in the afterlife. Were they a religious, spiritual person before death, or were they one who lived to do evil to the bitter end? Being truthful with yourself about your deceased loved one is a must before attempting to contact them in the afterlife.

Dark, sociopath beings do not travel to the light of the heavens after the death of their human body. Dark beings have their own heaven to return home to which is called Hell. The doors or gates to their hell are on Earth. They do not have portals of light. Sociopath dark doors are many. Some are opened when men become drug addicts, alcoholics, killers, rapists, etc. Other sleeping doors are mystical, and they must be called on to open. Calling forth darkness will not bring you the soul of your dark deceased loved one. Possession, obsession, addictions, unspeakable horrors, and physical calamities will answer your knock.

Fallen angels are the gate keepers of hell. Demons/devils are fallen angels. When these dark souls choose, they can enter Earth life by possessing the form of a new conception. They then become the rapists, murderers, and pedophiles of Earth society. When their human forms die, they become dark gatekeepers of hell. No matter how much you loved a deceased dark family member, you should not try to contact them in the afterlife, unless you desire some sort of hellish experience to call on you.

Man can arrest, sentence, and put to death the human body of a dark sociopath killer or rapist. He cannot kill the dark sociopath's soul. It lives on and becomes a gatekeeper to hell as it waits and watches for another body on earth to enter. When you knock on hell's door, a devil will open it and embrace (possess) you. There are no friendly handshakes.

October 3

THOUGHT FOR THE DAY – You jump into your car for a quick trip to the corner convenience store. Student light beings jump into new conceptions for transportation as they pursue educational lessons on Earth. Human babies die young because their student driver soul is only on Earth for a short educational assignment.

NEWLY CROSSED OVER SOULS

Are you having trouble communicating with your friend or loved one that has crossed over? If so, it is probably a silver cord problem. Sometimes, they are damaged or severed. When this happens, communications between the heavens and Earth are static ridden or don't get thru at all.

If your deceased loved one has a fully connected, silver cord, he will usually get back to you within three days of his exit from or human death on earth. He will be accessible right away for a visitation, and it is usually him that contacts you, not you him.

The quickest way for him to get a message back to you on Earth that he is fine in the afterlife, is in a dream. Because there is war in the heavens between forces of darkness (fallen angels) and the forces of light (light beings) the dream he will appear to you in will be in code. That is to keep dark forces from intercepting messages and using them against light beings that are still traveling in human bodies on Earth.

Interpreting dreams is like playing the game of charades. Your loved one who has crossed over gives the clues to you in a dream concerning his health and well being. You must take the clues in the dream you receive and interpret them. No other human can interpret the clues in your dream for you. You must guess according to what items in a dream mean to you. Books on dream interpretation are a waste of your time. For instance, I hate the color red. To me the color red would mean something I hate is about to come to me. My mother loves the color red. To her it would mean that something she loves is about to happen. You must set your own meaning (according to your likes and dislikes) to what colors, items, places, pets, and people who appear as clues in your dreams.

Dreams are the simplest communication method used by crossed over loved ones to contact you quickly. Dreams are in code to protect souls on Earth from assault by fallen angels, forces of darkness.

October 4

THOUGHT FOR THE DAY – Spirits do not die, they crossover to resume their lives in the heavens.

A VISITATION

My brother died recently. His human vehicle was very,

very ill. His kidneys had failed and he had been on dialysis for close to five years. After years of misery and suffering, he died. We were very close and my grief overwhelmed me. After crying 24 hours of tears, (not for him, but for my loss of his presence in my Earth life) I crashed and fell sound asleep. He came to me in a dream.

In the dream, I stood on one side of a river and he appeared on a lush, green grassed hill just beyond me on the other side. (There is a veil between worlds. The river is a type of that.) My brother was sitting in a sparkling, white spa-like tub filled with bubbles (like those in a bubble bath). He smiled the biggest smile I have ever seen and waved wildly at me, making sure he had my attention. He was not sick. He was enjoying himself in the bubbles. An angel stood next to the spa tub holding a towel. The angel was trying to get him to get out of the tub of bubbles, so those who had arrived after him could have a turn. He ignored the angel and kept waving to me wildly and smiling. My brother, in a dream, was trying to convey to me that he was okay and in a spa like paradise where angels were attending to his needs. He was not ill. He was well, clean of his diseases, and happy!

When I woke up, I put aside my tears. My brother had managed to get a message back to me via a dream that he was in paradise. Note . . . the human body of my brother had been cremated prior to the dream. Our souls live on after death on Earth, and they can choose to wear human costumes of their former bodies to appear to us in. If they visited us in pure form, they would be a ball, or orb of light.

October 5

THOUGHT FOR THE DAY – An orb returning to the heavens will wear a costume of his human body at first. The costume is like a vacation T-shirt that a human will purchase and wear after trips to distant paradise beaches.

Costumes Worn By Souls

A man having surgery dies. He pops out of his dead corpse body and floats up to the ceiling wearing a costume body of his human one that lies below. The costume body that the soul is floating in is an exact copy. When Christ went away after being crucified, he was wearing a costume of his human body. He also returned in that costume body to appear to and speak with his disciples. Afterwards he left them in his costume body. Christ's human body had scars from being crucified. His costume body, being an exact copy, also had the scars.

Suppose you have a child that dies. In grief, you ask your god to let your child get in touch with you in a dream or a visitation. You want to know that he is okay. Keep in mind that your child is now a soul, and his soul was a member of heaven's light being forces before he entered Earth life. Because the soul of your child is an eternal light being, and ancient of days, he may not want to put back on the costume of your dead child, in order to communicate with you. The adult soul of your child could appear to you as an orb of light or in any costume he chooses, which could be a costume of one of his previous human bodies on earth. An adult that appears to you in a dream in an ancient Eskimo, Egyptian, or African body costume could be your child.

What a soul wears in the heavens is his choice. To wear or not wear a body costume is his choice. Appearing to you in his true heavenly form, as an orb of light, is also his choice. To wear the body costume of one of his former lives, like an old T-shirt, is also his choice.

October 6

THOUGHT FOR THE DAY –Souls can speak to you thru things. Moses entertained a divine being speaking to him from a burning bush. I speak to you thru words on a written page. After crossing over, I might speak to you thru a scroll of words that rolls down from the sky. Keep an open mind as to what an angel or other divine being may speak to you thru.

ANGEL & DIVINE BEING VISITATIONS

Physical (on Earth) visitations from keeper, costumed, light beings are rare. Those types of visitations mark special events happening around the globe. Winged angel costumes are common forms for them to appear in. They appear in the costumes that man understands, or has assigned meanings to. Keepers of the four corners of the Earth and Light Beings are delivers of messages and protectors. Should the Master Christ decide to return to the Earth to speak with someone, he will put on a costume body of Jesus a former incarnation of his. Christian followers would not understand him appearing in the costume of a Buddha, although that would be ok. Divine souls in the heavens are orbs of light. They do not have physical bodies to travel in there. They travel by atomic power at the speed of light. So, the divine ones will put on body costumes to appear in.

Moses was visited by a divine being wearing a costume of

a burning bush. A light being in a winged angel costume appeared to the two women at Jesus' tomb. Ezekiel saw a wheel in a wheel, which could have been a costume for a light being. Moses, the women at the tomb, and Moses were key figures in history. The three's physical visitations from light beings were for reasons.

On my mother's death bed, for a month previous to her dying, a being came to her in the costume of a blond haired woman who stood at the foot of her bed. The blond woman would slap her foot and tell her to rise. There was no one in my mother's house during these happenings but me and her. A death angel or a light being in a costume human body form had come to help her cross over, . . . a death angel. My mother's human body was embalmed and buried. It was her soul that the being had come for.

Now, with advancement in understanding of how orbs in the heavens move about on Earth, we know that souls of our crossed over loved ones and friends can return to earth in different forms and walk about us in costumes. We brush shoulders with them on a daily basis. However, humans who are not seeking a spiritual path are blind to that fact, and that they are entertaining angels/orbs unaware.

Consider your day to day surprise encounters with what you may have previously considered just nice humans. Are you having encounters with angels? Have your deceased loved ones returned and are wearing the costumes of the nice humans? Souls/angels/gods/light beings/etc. choose the costume they wish to wear when coming to Earth. How they appear is not up to you!

October 7

THOUGHT FOR THE DAY - Pedophiles, spouse abusers, murderers, bullies, con artists, abusive bosses, pimps, etc. are examples of hell's gatekeepers on earth. They are walking gates.

ONE HEARTBEAT AWAY

Where is Heaven? Surprisingly, the Astral Shore/First Heaven is just one heartbeat away from earth. Earth is like a suburb to it, as well as is the in-between worlds. The Land of Ghosts is an in-between world. Hell is the Land of Fallen Angels. You enter its gates on Earth, thru the enticement of dark beings in human bodies. A pimp enticing a young girl to become a prostitute is an example. He is a gate or portal to hell.

There are portals to take to heaven, hell, or the in-between worlds. Men using their human brains make decisions to walk on the dark side of life, thus becoming hell's gate keepers. Men using their soul intelligence go within the human body and discover their light portal to the heavens. Souls that are afraid to face judgment for failed missions on Earth ignore the light portal and enter the gates to the in-between worlds, one of which is the 'Land of Ghosts'. They are fugitive souls. Light being souls who hide out in the ghost world because they do not want to leave loved ones behind, are also fugitive souls. From the ghost world, fugitive souls can haunt or interact with Earth life.

You are not the human body you travel in. You are a soul. If you want to travel to the heavens or the in-between worlds, you must go within to find the portals and gates to those destinations. You as a soul are not your human body transportation. You are just the driver of it. The human brain makes decisions concerning the human body vehicle and its survival on Earth. The human brain concentrates on getting enough to eat and drink, shelter, and its reproductive urges. The soul's intelligence kicks in and makes all decisions concerning soul/spiritual survival.

Close your eyes. Go in thought inward to the center of your human body forehead. There you will look about with your third eye, the eye of the soul. Turn inside your human body vehicle and look towards the back of your human skull. It will become like a movie screen. Lights will start to flash. That is where you will find your viewing portal. When the lights start to flash ask your spirit guide, angel, or deity for the soul of your deceased loved one to appear to you. This is the beginning. Keep in mind that souls are orbs of light. They do not have to appear to you in the costume form of the human body they once traveled in. If you are seeing flashing lights, you are seeing orb souls. With practice, you will be able to see and hold conversations with your orb guides and those who have crossed over, providing they are not on new missions to Earth.

The Christian's promised 'Catching away' is happening now. It is souls stepping from sleeping/dead human bodies to travel the heavens. Their 'coming again' is their returning to their human bodies and awakening them to continue their travels or missions on Earth. You can be like Christ. You can master the 'going away' and 'coming again'.

October 8

THOUGHT FOR THE DAY – When trying to speak with those who have crossed over, remember to speak and call forth with the voice of your soul within, not your human lips.

VIEWING PORTALS

Your soul's eye is the one that is able to see heaven. It exists inside you in the location of the center of your human forehead. It is most commonly called the 'Third Eye'. It is with the third eye/soul eye that you have the power to look into the heavens and in-between worlds. Awakening your third eye awakens your divine powers.

You, as a human brain, are ready to let your soul awaken. You have relaxed your human body thru meditation, and have gone within. When you manage to get within yourself, you have moved from human brain thinking to soul thinking. As a soul, you will start to see flashing lights. The lights are orb souls starting to interact with you. At that point, you can start asking the flashing orbs to bring to you the soul of your deceased loved one or friend. The asking has to be done with the mind of the soul, not human lips. If you ask with human lips, you will be back to brain thinking and actions without. When you first start portal viewing with your soul's eye, visitations may not last more than 5 to 10 seconds. Some of the souls you will know, and others you will not.

There are many souls on the Astral Shore who are trying to use viewing portals to get messages back to their loved ones on earth. They want those left behind on earth to know that they are alive and well. At the point you start seeing and conversing with souls you do not know, you become a channel (a postman for messages). It is up to you to accept the job or not.

When faces start to flash, ask quickly for your loved one to appear to you. Keep in mind, that they have just returned to the heavens and may not be quite sure how to use the viewing portals. You must be patient with them, and them with you. Some crossed over loved ones may have damaged or severed silver cords that have not been repaired yet. Their confusion as to how to send messages to earth via the viewing portals may seem as daunting to them, as contacting them is to you. Be patient.

October 9

THOUGHT FOR THE DAY – We all cling to certain memories that were pleasant to us when we were young. Man collects things that are associated with those memories. Ghosts do also.

ROLLER SKATE WEARING GHOST

My grandson, when he was two and barely talking, kept seeing a man named Gene in his closet. My grandson was barely able to talk. He kept telling us that Gene had wheels on his feet. Visitations from Gene lasted for about three years. A few years later, my grandson's father checked back into their home's paperwork and found that the original owner of their home was named Gene. Years later, in a casual conversation with a woman who lived in the neighborhood, I was told that the former home owner loved to roller skate.

Young children and dogs have psychic ability to see into the Astral and the Land of Ghosts. Souls, that have just entered earth life to travel in infant human forms, still have memories and third eye connections to those they leave behind on the Astral Shore. As an infant grows, the soul within becomes comfortable, and his memories lessen, so that he can move forward and tackle his mission or education on earth.

When we go to our 9 to 5 jobs on earth, we do not stand about. We have a job to do and it requires our concentration. We tackle our work day, full steam ahead. When we enter Earth life, we do the same. Memories of those at home on the Astral Shore are laid aside and forgotten for the moment.

My grandson at age two, probably still remembered his family on the Astral shore and needed psychic comfort from them as he adjusted to Earth life in his human body vehicle. In his need for psychic comfort, it is possible that Gene was sent him. It is also possible that Gene was an earth bound spirit who just refused to leave the earth house he loved and his roller skates.

We all cling to certain memories that are pleasant to us. As a teen, I loved riding the school bus. The thirty minute ride home gave me time to visit with my friends after school. At the end of my senior year, looking back, I can see where it was the teens on the bus that I was bonded with, not the general population of school mates who just said Hi and Bye in the halls. Had I, as a human, died, I might have chosen to exit my body as a soul and get on that school bus every evening with my former friends after school. Had I done so, I would have been a Gene in my closet, the school bus.

Ghosts appearing may choose to project his memories of

happy times and carry happy projections of a pet parrot, dog, basketball, ball bat, doll, work tools, rolling pin, etc. Had I died and chose to haunt a school bus; I probably would have carried a stack of books. Also, I had a huge red purse as a teen. I would also probably have projected my memory of it also as part of my ghost costume. Souls are actually orbs of light and energy. Clothing, objects, and situations are projected costumes of memories.

October 10

THOUGHT FOR THE DAY – The Garden of the Gods is a peaceful, lush, green paradise where gods (wearing costume forms) will walk and talk with master souls that arrive via meditation or dream portals from Earth or other planets.

SEEKING AUDIENCES WITH MASTERS

There is a mystical Garden of the Gods, a place that souls can travel to while their living human bodies sleep or meditate. In this garden, you can walk and talk with the masters of all times, providing they have not reincarnated for another human lifetime on Earth, or on another planet. The mystical Garden of the Gods is located in the Second Heaven. The Astral shore (place of judgment) is the First Heaven. Only those passing judgment for their life missions are allowed to travel upward from the First Heaven to the Second where the garden exists.

The Garden of the Gods is a peaceful, lush green paradise where gods (wearing costume forms) will walk and talk with light being souls that arrive via meditation or dreams from Earth or other planets. The Garden of Eden on Earth was created in the likeness of the Garden of the Gods. The Garden of Eden was a private garden. The Garden of the Gods is a public garden used by all light being gods, masters, angels, etc.

In the First Heaven there is a gate that lets light being souls enter and exit the Second Heaven Garden of the Gods. Only light beings travelling the astral are granted entrance into the garden. If you, traveling in dreams to the astral shore, are denied entrance, it is because you have embraced some form of darkness, making you a shade of gray or dark being. The judgment seat, on the astral shore, guards the gate to the Second Heaven. Fallen or shades of gray angels can only travel as far as the judgment seat in the First Heaven which is an imperfect place due to fallen angels returning there for judgment. The Second Heaven and the Garden of the Gods is the first perfect heaven. You will find no fallen angels there.

So, what does the garden have to do with you contacting friends or family? If you have a deceased loved one or friend that was a major religious figure such as a guru, priest, minister, monk, saint, priest, rabbi, etc., you will need to travel to the Garden of the Gods to make contact with them. Divine Ones do not mill about on the Astral Shore waiting for judgment. They are gods or perfected ones. On returning to the heavens after missions, they by pass judgment and immediately enter the gates of the Second Heaven, a place of rest and refreshing. After a time of refreshing, perfected ones travel upward to the upper heavens, to where their homes are. If you request an audience with a master in the third heaven and above, he will have to come down to you. He may choose a dream or a visitation on Earth to speak to you.

When wishing to speak with one of the gods or perfected ones, you must travel portals to the Astral Shore, and then make your way to the gates of the Garden of the Gods. There you must request to be allowed to enter for an audience with the divine one of your choice. Because you are astral traveling in a costume of your human body, the divine ones in the Garden of the Gods will put on and walk and talk with you in costumes that you understand. However, when they speak with you, the lips of their costume forms will not move. You will hear the words, but you will see no lips moving.

October 11

THOUGHT FOR THE DAY – The third eye (psychic eye) does not look out into the natural universe, like human eyes do. The psychic third eye looks inward and upward into the heavens. Man is two in one. He is both human and a divine soul. He has a total of three eyes, not two.

JUDGING PSYCHIC READINGS

A friend drops in for a chat. You may offer them a cup of coffee and then sit down at the table across from them to converse, or sit on a couch next to them to talk. As a rule, humans like to face each other when they hold conversations. Even sitting side by side on a couch, we can turn our necks and face each other to speak. Rarely do we stand behind someone's back and try to hold a conversation. So it is with encounters from those from the afterlife.

Visiting souls from the heavens want your attention. They will expect to speak with you face to face. If you go to a medium or psychic for a reading, and she tells you that she sees your dead loved one standing behind you, she has contacted those from the dark side. Devils and demons will stand behind you in the shadows. Light beings will face you or stand next to you, like two friends sitting on a couch to chat.

Some mediums are limited in the information they can retrieve from the afterlife. If your psychic is not a master soul, a perfected one, he or she cannot look for crossed over souls that have entered the upper heavens. Unperfected souls (traveling in human bodies) can only look about on the Astral Shore or in the land of ghosts for your deceased loved one. Unperfected or shades of gray mediums are not allowed in the Second Heaven and above. They don't have psychic viewing privileges for the Second Heaven and above.

Dreams are the simplest way that your deceased loved ones and friends can use to send back scenario, movie like messages to you. Dreams are sent down by spirit guides who work on the astral shore. A psychic is not needed for that form of communication.

October 12

THOUGHT FOR THE DAY – Ancient man's brain wanted to see angels and gods that looked like him. He also decided that his divine ones had to fly, to make them above and more powerful than man. Most modern humans embrace the same thinking and the gods that were created by human thinking in ancient times.

VISITS FROM THE GODS

Men with sleeping souls think only with their human brain. That intelligence is animal and interested mostly in day to day survival and reproduction. A human doesn't usually awaken his soul till a death or some horrific tragedy happens to him. When the human brain cannot solve his problems, he goes within and seeks to find if there is more to life than being a human animal and if there is a mystical being somewhere that will come to his rescue. When man starts to question life after death and the possibility of inner gods and heavens, his soul awakens.

In ancient times, only birds could fly. Airplanes and kites had not been invented yet. So, man fantasized about flying the skies and created himself some super hero gods who could. His created gods could do what man could not. At the same time, he gave them good and evil powers in the tales of fiction he told about them. Ancient man had not discovered yet that dark souls and light being souls traveled in him and his fellow man. Camels are beasts of burden for men, as are donkeys, horses, llamas, etc. Animal man is a beast of burden (an auto) for souls.

Divine, perfected beings move about you every day, traveling in human forms. They rub shoulders with you in the subways, malls, sports events, supermarkets, schools, etc. Some are light being souls from the heavens. Others are fallen angels, or dark souls.

Perfected Light Being Souls come to earth to function as Master teachers of advanced knowledge and spiritual understanding. Master writers, artists, teachers, musicians, doctors, philosophers, orators, etc. can be perfected ones. A man who writes only about horror, rape, murder, animal torture, and the shedding of another's blood is a master of darkness. He is not a light being. What a master creates deems him either dark or light.

October 13

THOUGHT FOR THE DAY - Man expects to see supernatural beings in forms that his human eyes understand. He fears what he hears or sees that he does not understand. The witch trials and burnings in the United States are examples of men fearing what they did not understand. New Age Thought (those thinking outside the box of mainstream world religions) is what men fear today.

THE WITCH OR GOD BURNERS

A miniature poodle would not fit in with a pack of wild, wolf type dogs. The bigger, carnivore dogs would kill the tiny domestic dog and possibly eat him. There are times when divine ones must enter Earth life and appear wolf like in order to pursue missions amongst human wolves. Human wolves will attack and kill humans not like them. The Salem witch trials and burnings are an example of this.

Once, when living in the hills of Missouri, I watched a pack of wolves chase a German shepherd down in a farm field. They killed the German shepherd. Light Beings, on missions on Earth in human bodies, do not want their human bodies killed. They need them for transportation. So, they have to blend in with human wolves for survival.

Gods need a certain amount of incognito when walking the earth. If they appeared in true orb form, human wolves would fear them and call for government armies to try to destroy them, calling them aliens. If a god put on the costume of an angel with wings and appeared on

Earth, men would panic thinking the end of the world had come. Some humans would welcome a light being in an angel's costume. Others would crouch in fear. Atheists would think they were being invaded by aliens and call out invasion forces. So, gods enter ordinary human forms to perform missions in.

Many of these gods in human flesh live lives as relatives and friends of ours. Because they are light beings, they are loving individuals that we form great attachments to. When they die, the loss of them is traumatic. If we are not silver cord connected spiritually, and have no understanding how souls take astral flights back to the home of the soul, we grapple for ways to contact them to see that they are okay. Mediums, psychics, seers, etc. are the gifted ones we go to today. Human religious wolves would burn our current connected ones, if they could get by with it. There will always be witch burners, those who do not understand anyone that is not of their social pack of wolves, their religion.

Have you ever considered that the nice person who lets you get in front of them in the checkout line could be a god in disguise? How about the nice little lady that you do not know that hands you a tissue at a funeral and then disappears? What about the kind stranger that stops on the highway and changes a flat for you? Gods in human flesh display kindness, goodness, joy, laughter, smiles, etc. They travel in human flesh.

October 14

THOUGHT FOR THE DAY – Traitor, light beings return to the Astral Shore at the death of their human forms. It is there they are judged, lose their light being status, and become fallen angels or devils.

TRAITOR SOULS

The Astral Shore is like a giant air port or train station waiting room. Returning souls to the Astral make their first stop there, where they wait till it is their time to be judged or held accountable for their earth missions. If you pass judgment, you get a ticket to continue your journey to the upper heavens or to other planets.

On Earth, there are light beings that turn to darkness becoming traitors. When their human bodies die, they return to the Astral Shore the same as those who have aced their Earth missions. At judgment on the Astral Shore, they are weeded out and not allowed passage to other planets, the upper heavens, or beyond. They are kicked off of the Astral Shore because they have become fallen angels.

The Astral Shore is the dividing line between light and darkness, good and evil. Traitor souls are kicked off the fine dividing line into darkness. Hell is the dark place that is the heaven of fallen angels.

October 15

THOUGHT FOR THE DAY – There are gods and heavens besides ours. Man's human brain limits how far his soul within can travel, by his narrow or expanding thoughts.

OTHER GODS & HEAVENS

Man's limited thinking sees his universe consisting of

planet Earth, the Ghost world, and the Astral Shore or First Heaven. His limited world has human and animal inhabitants and his heaven has angels and one god. The Christians, after Jesus, have added a divine being to their list, a son for their one god. The deities of other religions are not considered at all. The human brain is an animal brain and it is very narrow in its thoughts.

It is the mind of the soul that considers all possibilities and thinks out of the box. Animal man has put himself in a box and does not think beyond it. If we truly want to be successful on Earth and in our afterlife, we must let our soul do the thinking. Advanced thought and ideas come to the soul, not to the human brain that is interested in basic survival, the need for food, shelter, water, and reproduction of its animal kingdom.

Why limit yourself to being an animal. Let your soul awaken and think from there. Why not travel soul portals to the Astral Shore and then take other portals from there to the North Star, Neptune, or Pluto? Communication with an entire universe of life forms and travel to all stars, suns, and planets are available to us, if we let our soul be the driver of our human vehicle.

An awakened soul mind does not need a psychic or medium to escort them and their wallet on a journey to the outer limits of astral travel, or to the heavens to visit with loved ones that have crossed over. Astral soul flight is available to all awakened souls.

October 16

THOUGHT FOR THE DAY – A Shrine Story - A lady

dressed in gray with something glitzy on her head appeared to three children herding sheep. The eldest was an eight year old girl. The Lady in gray gave the children three secrets. The third secret was concerning certain religious figures dying. The deaths did not happen, so the third secret was a lie told the children. The gray lady also encouraged the children to flagellate or harm their bodies. Do light beings story to children? Do light beings/angels ask children to harm themselves? No . . . those are actions and demands of evil ones, devils. Devils/fallen angels try to appear and trick humans into thinking they are light beings.

MOTHER OF GOD OR FALLEN ANGEL

There are many accounts of individuals having spirit beings appearing to them in costume forms of ghosts, angels, divine beings, etc. The above story is one. I find the story above to fall into the category of 'Fallen Angel' or 'Devil' visitations.

The Lady was dressed in gray, a color that is half light and half dark. Fallen angels are light and dark. The eight year old girl wanted to keep the lady's appearance a secret. We tell our human children about 'stranger danger' and to never keep encounters with strangers a secret. In our modern culture, we have learned that pedophiles tell young children not to tell, that something will happen to them or their family if they do.

The second thing about this shrine story that bothers me is that the lady apparition asked the three children to do penance, acts of reparation, and to make personal sacrifice. After the event, the girl and two very young children who were with her, wore tight cords around their waists, performed self-flagellation with stinging nettles, and abstained from drinking water on hot days. Those are actions a sociopath would demand of children. We have child abuse laws and agencies today that would be outraged at that demand. Child abusers are not angels or divine beings of light.

If a dark being/fallen angel can appear, wearing a glitzy crown and costume, to get a child to self abuse themselves, they are successful as a dark, astral sociopaths/devils.

October 17

THOUGHT FOR THE DAY – When a year of private school on Earth for a soul is completed, summer arrives and school is out. Student souls return to their homes in the heavens for a season of summer. A failed student soul will be forced to attend summer school. He will return to Earth or go to some other planet private soul school for a makeup course.

NOT HEARING FROM THOSE CROSSED OVER

Have you ever considered that you, a soul, have lived previous lives on Earth and other planets in bodies other than the one you now travel in? Once upon a time, we souls were all student light beings. I hate to say it, we were failing students or we wouldn't be doing repeated lessons.

A woman marries a man who beats and abuses her. She manages to get out of that union only to choose the same type again. She is making a trip around the same mountain of abuse over and over. She didn't learn her lesson the first time, to choose differently, so she does a repeat course. Men who enter the business world and have one failing business after another, are also doing the round the mountain repeat thing. A child who is repeatedly punished for not taking out the trash is a 'round the mountain' student. Loaning money to friends over and over and not getting it back is a repeat life lesson. Are you a student trying to ace some repetitive crazy life lesson?

If you have a friend, or family member, that seems to be always making the same mistake over and over, they are probably summer school students. Students learn from having to take repeat courses and tests.

If you have been trying to contact a deceased loved one or friend in the afterlife, and are having no success, it might be due to the fact that they have reincarnated on Earth or another planet for summer school.

October 18

THOUGHT FOR THE DAY - Have you ever looked into a 6 month old baby's eyes and felt shocked because you saw your deceased uncle, brother, child, or mother looking back at you? Your deceased one is alive, he has reincarnated.

SUMMER SCHOOL FOR GOOF OFF SOULS

Have you considered that the soul of your deceased loved one may be back on Earth and sleeping in a new infant in your neighbor's, arms? In my last writing, I discussed failing student souls and how they have to do makeup courses in summer school on Earth. The difference between their last year soul journey and summer school is that they will be traveling in a different human form.

Have you ever looked into a 6 month old baby's eyes and felt shocked because you saw your deceased uncle, brother, or mother looking back at you? If baby suddenly smiles at you, your decease loved one is incarnated in there and happy to see you. The soul within the human baby form still has some memories of his former life in the heavens and on earth; that includes some memories of you.

Until a baby reaches the age of one, its former memories of heaven and other lives are not erased. However, at the age of one, as a baby starts to learn to speak, his memories of his former lives are erased. The reason being, a reincarnated goof off soul needs a blank slate to live his repeat lessons on.

Check out the eyes of the baby faces born to you, your family, friends, and neighbors. There is a good chance that your deceased goof off family member or friend has returned to you. You have the privilege of 'talking to your dead'.

A very young child (a stranger) is learning to talk. He yells, "Hi!" to you in a supermarket or mall. He could be having vague memories of you from his former Earth life where he was your friend or family member. In the present, he has reincarnated, just not in your immediate social circle. The brief encounter is your spirit guide's way of letting you know that our crossed over friend or loved one is okay. Accept your visitation and then move on.

October 19

THOUGHT FOR THE DAY – Earth, the Land of Ghosts, and the Astral Shore are inhabited by both light and dark beings. Your protection, when astral traveling those areas of the universe, comes with smart thinking and choices.

LOOKING FOR DECEASED LOVED ONES

When the human body dies, the soul in it steps out and floats upward and about for awhile just above its earth body. After a few moments, the soul will start its journey toward the light, a portal or gate to heaven. Between a soul's deceased human body and the portal exists the in-between worlds. One of those worlds, and the most accessible, is the Land of Ghosts.

Light beings (that have turned to darkness and shades of gray on earth) purposely try to get lost in the in-between worlds. They fear facing judgment for their lifetime of misdeeds on earth, and of being kicked out of the heavens. So, they try to stay clear of the portal of light and create dark existences and scenarios to occupy in in the Land of Ghosts. The Land of Ghosts is inhabited by souls that have not crossed over.

You are in inconsolable grief, due to a friend crossing over that you did not get to say good bye to. You are doubly concerned because he has not tried to contact you in your dreams. Determined to hear from him, you decide to leave your body, while it sleeps or meditates, and go look for him in the afterlife. Being a seasoned astral traveler, you know that Earth, the Land of Ghosts, and the Astral Shore are not perfect places, you must take precautions.

Just as you would not walk down the back alley in a big city ghetto on Earth after dark, you are wise not to do so in the Astral or in-between worlds as well.

A sociopath murderer on Earth is not satisfied with his last kill, or the seven before it, he is a dark soul that has the continuous mentality of wanting to do it just one more time. When he crosses over to the Astral Shore, his killer tendency is still there. He will create dark scenarios on the Astral Shore or in the Land of Ghosts for some unsuspecting, astral travelling soul to wander into. Sociopath souls can be light beings who have embraced darkness on Earth. They will be on the Astral Shore to face judgment for turning from the light. A devil soul that has stepped from human flesh will be found stalking the highways of the in-between worlds. Portals to Hell, haunting, and darkness are found there.

Awareness is your protection as you travel the Astral Highways and the in-between worlds. Willfully walking into an Earth swamp of hungry alligators is tempting fate. Don't tempt fate in the Land of Ghosts or other in-between worlds. Remember that portals to hell exist there.

If after much searching in the in-between worlds and on the Astral Shore, you do not find your friend, accept the fact that he may have already reincarnated on Earth and is living a new life as a baby or a young child.

October 20

THOUGHT FOR THE DAY – Human mothers, who refuse to believe that their child is a sociopath, becomes shades of gray due to their mindset. Darkness rubs off!

DARK SOUL CHILDREN

Everyone likes to think that their deceased loved one, especially a child, has gone to a forgiving heaven where they are changed and okay. Parents want to believe that their deceased children are happy, sane, and free from any dark urges they displayed on Earth such as the killing of small animals, being bullies, etc. Human parents see and love their child with an animal, human brain instinct, not the divine intelligence of their soul.

Children's human bodies have light being and dark being souls traveling in them, just as adults do. Just because you have a child, it doesn't mean that they are a light being. A sociopath dark being, traveling in a human child's body, is what it is. Ministers have preached many adult and child souls into heaven that have actually been lifetime devils in human flesh.

I have a friend whose son has been in and out of drug rehabs and jails for years. It doesn't matter what she does, or what program she pays for, he always returns to his chosen dark world of drugs and criminal activity when her back is turned. She is blind to the fact that he is a dark being. My friend needs to walk away from him, and concentrate on those in her family that are light beings. Instead, she focus' on her dark son. In doing so, she has turned from the light and is embracing darkness. She has squandered her finances, love, and time on a devil in human flesh. Currently, her dark soul son is back in jail for about the tenth time. Before this incarceration, he hooked his younger brother on drugs. The mother, by holding her dark son close, made it possible for him to ensnare one of her other children. She let evil enter her world and attack her family.

Once human children are adults, we have the free-will choice to continue to be there for them, or to walk away if they are dark. If you have a child with a dark soul that dies, do not try to contact him in the afterlife. You will regret it. Dark souls do not love or have allegiances.

October 21

THOUGHT FOR THE DAY – Have you considered that your deceased loved one is not in Heaven or Hell? Perhaps, he may be forward in time backwards in time. He may be time traveling.

TIME TRAVELLING TO FIND YOUR DECEASED LOVED ONE

If you decide to exit your human form while in meditation or sleep, don't think that the ghost world and the Astral Shore or First Heaven are the only places your deceased loved one has flown away to. Once a crossing over soul travels to the light, he is capable of stepping thru a turning clockwise and counterclockwise portal that will let him time travel.

If you learn to time travel, and go backwards in time, you and your loved one or friend may not recognize each other. The reason is that the two of you will be traveling in orb form and that you may be taking a journey backwards to a moment in time when the two of you had not been born yet. If your loved one or friend was in a different human body back then, he will not recognize you because you were not part of his world back then. He may see you as a stalker or a nuisance intruder.

Haven't you had strange people pop into your earth life briefly that were absolute nuisances? The most common today is religious, pamphlet toting, door knockers. Others might be a new neighbor who is constantly borrowing things from you, or a waitress who continues to stand at your table and talk, even though you are eating? One day you say, "Enough is enough!" You don't open your door to the neighbor or door knocker and you quit eating in the waitress' restaurant. Time traveler nuisances want to converse with those in the past and the future as much as possible before their time in the time travel portal expires. In doing so, they are seen as nuisances or stalkers. Time travel forwards into the future is the same.

The Time Travel portal has two circles of light beams, one on top of the other. The two circle structures turn clockwise and counter clockwise at the same time. When stepping thru this portal, you must state whether you want to go forward or backwards in time. If you do not state either, you will just end up feeling lost in a place you might call a confusing dream of past and present events.

Some souls who are in the process of crossing over decide to hide in the past. They are afraid of facing judgment for their life missions. These hiding souls are in the human bodies walking about you. They may find comfort in the collecting of things from the childhood of the life they have just exited. Antique dolls and toys are common things for hiding souls to collect.

October 22

THOUGHT FOR THE DAY – Portals to the Ghost world and in-between worlds exist between the Earth's surface and the Astral Shore. When learning to astral travel, the lying position in a bed or on the ground puts you in a position to accidentally enter the ghost world, or in-between worlds, first.

HOW TO EXIT YOUR BODY

For those of you who are new at going within and letting your soul step or float from your human body, I am going to talk about the experience. The first step is to choose a chair or sitting position in which you will be comfortable. The reason for a sitting position is that it allows your soul to travel to the highest point of your, the head region, to exit from. When you take off your jeans or dress pants at the end of the day, you step from their waist or top. Exiting any other point would be difficult, if not impossible. So it is with the human form for beginners.

Astral Portals of light loom about three feet to ten feet above the surface of the earth. Portals to the Ghost world and in-between worlds exist between the earth's surface and the portals. A lying position in a bed or on the ground puts you in a position to accidentally enter the ghost world first.

After you have sat down in a comfortable chair, move your attention down to your toes. Stretch, wiggle, and then relax them. Then move your attention to your lower legs, move the knees and the legs about and then relax them. Move on up the thighs doing the same. Next, do your fingers, lower arms, and upper arms using moving and relaxing techniques. Let each body part rest unmoving in a comfortable position when you are thru moving and relaxing them. Work and rest the muscles in your lower and upper abdomen and then relax them. Then twist your neck from side to side, and then relax it. Last do your facial features and scalp. The human body must be at rest for the soul to exit.

Completely relaxed, close your human eyes and let all of your body parts rest in a limp, non-moving state. Look about inward and realize that you are inside your human skull looking at the front of your human forehead and the backs of its two human eyes. You are looking with your soul eye, better known as the 'Third Eye' Turn within your human skull and look at the center of the back of your human head. Then turn your soul's eye's focus slightly upward. You will start to see a light. The light will be a portal to the afterlife.

(Every direction the soul turns within the human head will cause different portals to appear. There are portals for the four corners of the earth and elements. There are portals of the gods, death portals, rescuer's portals, time travel portals, etc. There is not just one great white light to travel toward when you exit your human body.

Feel yourself starting to float and head out of the top of your human head towards the light you see in the back of the human skull. That will be your personal portal to step thru or view thru.

Lights will start to flash as you look with your soul's eye. Faces may start to pop up here and there as you concentrate on your experience. Keep in mind that souls in the afterlife are orbs of light. If you have tiny orb like structures popping and flitting about you and then disappearing, it is out of body souls checking you out. At this point in your experience, you must ask for whom you wish to speak with. This is where your spirit guide will be. Also, requests to time travel are made here.

After speaking with a spirit guide, or stepping thru the light onto the Astral Shore and taking a look about, you suddenly will snap backwards. With lightning speed, you will travel backwards and re-enter your human body. Your human eyes will fly open, and your third eye will close. You may feel tired. Just as if you had worked a 14 hour day or had driven hundreds of miles returning home from vacation.

October 23

THOUGHT FOR THE DAY - The reason for dreams being sent in code scenarios is so that dark forces cannot intercept and use transmitted information to change the course of history.

DREAM VISITATIONS & MESSAGES

When night falls and our human bodies relax in sleep, dreams come to us thru silver cord communication lines. The dreams are sort of like amateur short videos made for us to view by friends. The only difference is, in a dream scenario video, you will be an active actor or observer standing and watching in it.

When you receive a dream message scenario, you must interpret it because it will be in code. The experience is like playing a game of charades. Your spirit guide is the sender of a dream video. The clues are different segments of the dream. You, on Earth, are the guesser and interpreter of charade dream clues. Some humans are good at the guessing game, others are not. When totally unable to guess the meaning of received dream clues, humans may turn to psychics or mediums for help.

The reason for dreams being sent in charade code is so that dark forces cannot intercept and use transmitted information to change the course of history. Dark forces want to confiscate and use personal information of the light to cause havoc. If a dark one/devil/fallen angel can come in possession of private information, they can use it to change the course of the war between the dark forces of hell and those of the heavens.

For instance, you just don't understand why your father was so abusive to you when you were a child. You have spent a lifetime in therapy trying to get past your memories of what he did to you. Your therapist convinces you to forgive him. So, you decide to enter the Astral World to find him and tell him so. Traveling to your portal, your spirit guide stops you and tells you that your father is not in the heavens. He also tells you to return to earth, and wait for information concerning your father's whereabouts. You return to earth and your human body.

A day or so later, your spirit guide sends you a dream in which your father, in a burning house, not only tries to rape you, but your sisters and neighbors. The dream is showing you that your father is and was a dark sociopath soul, and that his abuse was inflicted on others besides you. Then your dream switches and an entirely new segment starts. You see yourself in your therapist's office and you are dumping him as your doctor and then running from his office. The dream changes again and in a third segment you see yourself purchasing a particular item to turn your failing business around and make it successful.

Your spirit guide has sent you a dream post warning you that both your father and therapist are dark beings/devils/fallen angels and that you should run from them. Your spirit guide is also showing you that your father is not in heavens. The burning house represents hell. (Hell is the heaven of fallen angels.) The vital information about a new business in the dream is a tack on for you, and the most important part of the dream. If you don't receive and act on the purchase information, your business venture will fail. If dark forces can intercept that important information, they can keep your information from you.

If dark forces can intercept vital information and hide it from you, they have managed to assault you.

October 24

THOUGHT FOR THE DAY – Perfected ones (gods and masters) in the upper heavens have private portals to Earth and other planets. The special ones are the equivalent of the president of the United States who has his own private jet.

GODS TRAVEL PRIVATE PORTALS

There is not just one bright light to travel toward, when you exit your human body in death, meditation, or when sleeping. Many gates or portals exist. Knowing which portals are available for your use is important. It will make your initial astral experiences more pleasant. For instance, if you want to 'Time Travel, you definitely don't want to take a subway portal to the in-between worlds or to the hell of Fallen Angel's. Just as you need a map on earth to travel across the United States, you will need a general idea map of the Astral to travel it, and its surrounding realms, successfully. I am attempting in my writings this month to map some unknown portals for you.

Perfected Ones (Gods and Masters) have private portals to enter earth life, speak with man, and then return to the heavens in. Gates between worlds are for brief encounters or visitations. When god appeared to Moses in a burning bush, he was visiting earth via a brief encounter portal. Brief angel visitations are via visitation portals. These special portals are like private penthouse elevators in apartment houses or business buildings that are not for public use.

Sometimes the Perfected Ones (gods and masters) decide to walk and live briefly amongst men. They are the penthouse types of the soul world. They will have private gates or portals to the heavens. However, their gates will be invisible to the human eyes of man. Only souls can look at the invisible and see the visible.

October 25

THOUGHT FOR THE DAY – A soul putting on a human body costume is similar to an astronaut putting on a spacesuit, or a paper dress that little girls put on paper dolls.

PORTALS AND COSTUMES

All light beings souls are connected. We are not beings with physical bodies like animals on Earth. We are orbs, or balls of energy and light. In orb form, we communicate with each other without having lips that move and vocal cords that vibrate like those of humans. We do not have lips. When we speak with each other, it is done so telepathically, or via a 'silver cord communication line' if one of us is on a mission on Earth or another planet.

As balls of light, we do not have human forms. However, should we need to appear to a human in a form that he will understand; we will put on a human body costume. It is sort of like an astronaut putting on a spacesuit. However, we are not the spacesuit or the costume. A human after a visitation might tell you, "He appeared and talked to me, but his lips didn't move." His lips didn't move because the body was a costume, sort of like paper dresses that little girls put on paper dolls.

Souls on other planets travel to the Astral Shore and upper heavens the same way we do. They step from whatever life form they are traveling in and return to being an orb of light and energy that can travel at the speed of light. As a ball of light and energy, they take astral soul flights home to the heavens. The souls of deceased loved ones on Earth return to the Astral Shore/First Heaven in this fashion.

The Astral Shore or First Heaven is like an enormous train station or air port waiting room. Exit ramps from there are portals to the universe's many planets, black holes, stars, moons, etc. Those same portals can be used for return trips to the astral shore.

Space ship travel is an antiquated form of travel between planets. Portal travel only takes minutes to get you to the Astral Shore, and then on to whatever planet you wish to visit.

October 26

THOUGHT FOR THE DAY – Certain life forms on all planets are transportation vehicles for orbs or souls. Any intelligent life form, that has the mental possibility of seeking spirituality, acts as host transportation for divine souls.

ENCOUNTERING HORNED BEASTS

Many strange beasts, seen in visions by men in the Old and New Testaments, were actually costumes worn by soul travelers who were returning to the Astral Shore from other planets. Humans, having no concept of beings that look different from them, try to make them into mystical beings that need to be interpreted. In actuality, they are just life forms that are different than what we have on earth. Costumes of the beasts are just like T-shirts that earth human travelers wear returning from vacations. A soul from Earth traveling to the Astral Shore will wear a human animal costume and he will encounter horned beast, flying dragon, unicorn, and other animal costumed souls there.

When John, of the New Testament, was caught up in the spirit and saw a horned beast, he was actually astral traveling and viewing a costume on a soul from another planet. Not understanding what he was seeing, John tried to make the beast an interpretable thing. You have the power, via astral travel, to take portals to planets that have horned beasts and wild things beyond your imagination. John was an astral traveler. However he had no understanding of soul flight or costumes. So, he just tried to interpret with his human brain what he thought his divine being was trying to tell him about his situation on Earth. Clergy, with human brains, are still trying to interpret John's horned beasts and being caught away today. John's 'visions' cannot be interpreted because they were just encounters with astral travelers on the Astral Shore. What he heard was just conversations amongst them. His being caught away was interpreted as a magical moment. It was just simple soul flight to the heavens that every man's soul is capable of.

Cherubs are another example of a different type of costumed form that souls wear while traveling via portals. They are human looking, except their bodies have wings and they do not age past the age of five. Cherubs are life forms on other planets, just like we humans are animal life forms on Earth. What makes cherubs or humans divine, are the orb souls that travel in us. Cherubs, horned beasts, and humans are animals of different planets. Leprechauns, fairies, and other little mystical beings are souls astral traveling in the costumes of the little people they live in on other planets.

Traveling by man created spaceships to the moon, stars, or other planets is not available to common man on Earth. Soul Travel to the planets of our universe is available to you, and at lightning speeds. Go within and travel to the Astral Shore. Once there, take a portal to whatever planet you wish to visit, as you vacation or look for the soul of your deceased loved one or friend.

When the soul of your deceased loved one does not return to you after death to give you comfort in dreams, etc., there is every possibility that he has incarnated (took up residency in another life form) and is living a new life on Earth or another planet. Go where he is, take a soul flight. He is just one heartbeat away!

October 27

THOUGHT FOR THE DAY – Sociopath dark souls travel in human forms, the same as light being souls do. When their human body dies, they return as souls to their heaven which is called 'Hell.

DUMPING DARK MOUTHY SOULS

When you are a teen, spring break days off is anxiously awaited. Adult humans look forward to vacations. When teens or adults go on vacations, they meet new people on the beach or vacation golf course. After vacation and spring break, those acquaintances are rarely ever seen again.

When I was a sophomore in high school, I was invited to go horseback riding with a girl named Marvis on a spring day off from school. The day was pleasant, and the horse was agreeable. However, Marvis and I just did not click friendship wise. I was a quiet reserved person and she had a mouth that talked non- stop. After the one afternoon of horse riding, we went our separate ways and blended in with different groups of high school friends. Marvis and I graduated high school together, but we traveled in different student circles before graduation. Now, it is 50 or so years later. Occasionally, I think about Marvis and our one shared afternoon of bad conversation and riding horses. However, it is not enough of a good memory to make me spend the time to look her up.

Families are groups of beings like and not like Marvis. There are some family members that appall us with their mouths, while others are interesting conversationalists. Some relatives we will keep in touch with, while others we will avoid for a lifetime. Souls in the heavens are colorful and different as well, especially on the Astral Shore where both light being and dark being souls await judgment.

There are many reasons why human relatives don't click with each other. Sometimes it is because one has a light being soul as a driver of the human vehicle, and the other has a dark being soul as a driver. If you a soul leave your human form to travel to the Astral Shore looking for the soul of a deceased dark soul family member, you are likely to be assaulted by that dark soul. Out of human bodies, that dark being is no longer a human family member of yours. Human bodies do not go to heaven or to the light. Only souls do. Human bodies do not go to judgment and then to hell. Dark souls do. (Dark souls are fallen angels).

On earth you may be forced to ride horses for one human lifetime with a mouthy, verbally abusive family member. When that lifetime ride (relationship) is over, you do not need to continue to be horse riding, buddy souls in the heavens. It is okay to dump or not keep in touch with family member souls that you had nothing in common with, or those who abused you. Don't feel guilty if you need to dump family member souls in the afterlife that are mouthy, dark soul sociopaths,

October 28

THOUGHT FOR THE DAY - If you decide to travel to the Astral Shore to look for one of your crossed-over loved ones, expect to endure weather elements. Dark souls create tornados, hurricanes, disasters, dark alleys, and astral dark nights to exist in as they await judgment. A light being soul crossing over will create the opposite on the Astral Shore.

SURVIVING THE ELEMENTS AS YOU ASTRAL TRAVEL

Have you ever dreamed of a deceased loved one and they were standing in a hail storm, or you were with them on a sinking ship in a hurricane? Weather conditions exist on the Astral Shore, just as they do on earth. The elements/weather conditions are created by dark and light being souls that are returning to the afterlife.

Heaven to one person is sleeping on fluffy clouds, while to another it might be sitting in a rocking chair and basking in the warmth of the morning sun. Children are taught that heaven is a place where angels fly about in blue skies watching over them. An Eskimo child might be taught that his deceased grandfather has gone to build snow shoes or snow mobiles for Eskimo angels. The elderly dream of a tropical heaven where the cold of winter does not cause their bones to ache. Coffee is my love. I might fantasize about a heaven that is a restaurant where my coffee cup is kept full and steaming hot. Weather conditions are fringe benefits for those who want them. The benefits are scenarios created by those returning there.

The owner of a trucking company gave Christmas gift certificates for hams to all its employees a couple of years ago. The owner did not take into consideration that he had some employees who were vegetarians and that his Jewish drivers didn't eat pork. To the ham eaters, it was a great fringe benefit. To the others, it was a dark fringe benefit. Elements on the Astral Shore are like the hams. They have different meanings to those awaiting judgment for missions there.

We are gods traveling in human flesh who are capable of creating heavens and hells both in earth life and on the shores of the First Heaven. When you are astral traveling, you may not appreciate some of the elements you encounter. One soul will create a sunny beach to sit on, while his neighbor may create an igloo to take shelter in while it snows like crazy. I love a rainy day. I have fond memories of my father and me walking and talking in the rain. When I cross over, I might create a rainy day scenario to enjoy my memories of my father in. We are gods and have the power to create when we are in soul state.

The Astral Shore is an un-perfect place where both dark and light spirit beings rub shoulders as they wait their turn for judgment. Just as light beings will create elements, dark souls will do so also. A dark soul will create scenarios with killer tornados, devastating hurricanes, etc. If you see death, injuries, blood, or disfigurement of souls in a scenario, you have encountered a dark being. Light being souls who embraced dark lives on Earth will exist on the Astral Shore. They will be given fallen angel status at the judgment and be kicked out of the heavens. If you wander into one of their dark element scenarios, turn and flee. Don't go looking on the astral shore for a deceased loved one if they were a dark being on Earth. You are just asking for trouble.

Light souls create mini heavens on the Astral Shore to dwell in as they await their turn at judgment. Dark being souls will create mini hells to exist in and try to ensnare you to become one of them. It is sort of like a last temptation.

October 29

THOUGHT FOR THE DAY – Being a Spirit Guide is an occupation in the heavens. Your guide has a home and a life beyond his astral job of guiding you. Respect his privacy, time off. When he doesn't answer his silver cord phone, his office is closed. Leave a message with his switchboard helper who has a face or a voice that you will not recognize.

GUIDES AND KINDERGARTEN SOULS

Traveling to the Astral to obtain information from your spirit guide is like a kindergartner going to the school library and asking a librarian how to find the kindergarten reading section. Spirit guides are helpers.

When a human kindergartner advances and finishes elementary school, he moves on to complete high school, college, master, and doctorate degrees. When his education is completed, he no longer needs a helper. The same goes for astral or soul students. Fully educated, functioning souls on earth in a human body or in the heavens as an orb, have no further need for librarians, teachers, and spirit guides.

The time will come when you (a soul) will master going within, traveling light portals, and exploring the universe. You, a student soul, will graduate. Your spirit guide may soon slap you on your astral back and say, "Good Job! You are on your own now!" Then you must face your adult soul world and ask,"What next?"

Once out of boot camp, human soldiers on Earth do not need anyone to hold their hand in combat or to carry their riffles. Once you are out of soul boot camp, you must hold your own hand, and carry your own load (mission). Souls who are students on Earth need psychic teachers and spirit guides. Those who have graduated their Earth, private school, astral educations, fly the skies alone.

Once you, a student, have mastered portal and astral travel don't get up-set if you have an occasional spirit guide substitute. Spirit Guides take an occasional day off from work to take care of personal business, just like workers do on Earth. Respect his need for some down time. Make friends with his replacement.

October 30

THOUGHT FOR THE DAY – Humans walk on two feet to travel. Souls fly at the speed of light.

TRAVELING GODS

Orbs of light and energy in the heavens do not need airplanes to fly in, cars to ride in, or bodies to walk about in. They travel by atomic thought waves. In split seconds, they can think of somewhere, and then be there in seconds. Orbs of light are not weighted down by human bodies in the heavens. We, as gods in human flesh, must learn how to free ourselves from our heavy, human, animal forms, in order to astral travel as the orb gods we are.

When we meditate, enter dream states, or lay our human bodies down in death, we suddenly exit our human forms and become the gods or orbs of light that we truly are. In soul or orb state, we can travel to the heavens, in-between worlds, or other planets in seconds. We can visit with friends all around the universe in a period of time that would be considered a cat nap to a human. Also, we can travel backwards and forward in time. We are only limited in what we can do when we are on Earth. Our limit is the weight of the human body.

We have a soul that has a mind that is separate from the

human brain. We are two beings in one. We are both human and divine. We have a human brain and a soul brain. We have a human body and an orb of light body. When the human brain dominates, the soul sleeps. When the soul dominates, the human brain and body sleeps.

October 31

THOUGHT FOR THE DAY – To enter the presence of gods, guides, and angels, you must go within. That is where the veil between worlds exists.

THE THINNING VEIL BETWEEN WORLDS

Old Testament Jewish priests needed to prove that they alone had god's ear, to protect their position in the religious culture of their day. So, they created a man-made curtained/veiled sacred room and designated it as a 'Holy of Holies'. Then, they convinced their followers that only they could enter the sacred place without being killed by God. The priests had no clue that a real 'Holy of Holies' and a real veil existed, that separated god and man. The real veil was within every man, even the ones they were trying to keep out of their man made holy place.

The priests knew that they couldn't let ordinary men enter their man made holy place. Why? Their followers would find out that the priest's man made holy place actually had no power, nor was occupied by God. They had to keep men out of their creation, and they used fear tactics to accomplish that. The priests brainwashed ordinary man into believing that they would die if they entered.

Religious cult leaders of different faiths today try to convince followers that they are the only voice of god and the only door to him. They are modern day 'Holy of Holies' con-artist priests, equivalent to the Jewish priests of the Old Testament.

Does a real veil exist between worlds? Yes it does! The veil between worlds is the eyelid that closes over the third eye (psychic eye) of the spirit being or soul within man. When the eyelid of the third eye is fluttering, preparing to awaken, the veil between worlds is thinning. When the psychic eye opens, the veil between worlds is rent.

CHAPTER ELEVEN
NOVEMBER

THE BOOK OF PROSPERITY

November 1

THOUGHT FOR THE DAY – You complain about having to eat hamburger, when your friends are eating steaks. Somewhere there is a human that is starving in a famine on Earth. He would give almost anything for the possibility to buy one fast food hamburger, cut it in pieces, and share it with his wife and four children.

YOU REAP TODAY PAST CHOICES

You have free will choice. Your current prosperity or poverty is the result of your yesterday's choices. If you are living today in the ghettos today, it is because of your poor choices to move there yesterday. If you are living a life of prosperity at this moment, it is due to your yesterday's wise investments.

"What about a man in a famine" you ask. "Is he reaping his choices?"

A man living in a famine country has free will choice. He chose to stay in his land of the famine as food shortages started. He could have made the choice to relocate to another part of the world before famine hit, or to stock his food supply for long term use.

Our circumstances, wealth, and poverty are the result of our yesterday's choices. For instance: Unpaid rent last month will get you kicked out in the street this month. An unpaid utility bill last month will leave you shivering and your teeth chattering this month when the utility company turns your utilities off. If you spent every penny you earned last week on beer, cigarettes, and frivolities, this week you will not have the money to buy food. You will go hungry. You are living today the results of your free will choices of yesterday

Make good choices now, if you want your tomorrow to be better than your current one. Make the choice to save your money and get out of the ghettos of life, if you don't want to be living in the ghettos tomorrow.

November 2

THOUGHT FOR THE DAY – You are the creator of your Heaven and Hell. You are the one who chooses to walk in low places or heavenly places. You are the god of your life.

IS YOUR GOD IGNORING YOU?

One of the great disappointments in the lives of faithful, tithe paying, church going humans is when they really need their God to meet a desperate need, and he seems to ignore them. The faithful then enter 'let down' states of depression. Their overwhelming disappointment may be due to the death of a child that their god didn't heal, or no helping hand in a financial disaster. The church goers prayed for help, but no help came. Thus, they enter a state of thinking that their god does not give a damn.

Why do men's gods ignore them? Why do their gods seem to rain on their parades when they are at their lowest points and in desperate need? The reason is that the god they have been taught to believe in does not exist. The old man in the sky, with a long white beard and an angry temper, is a human created god.

Example: If I draw a super hero on a piece of paper, and then devote myself to worshipping and believing in that image, I am going to be disappointed when he doesn't come to my rescue in my hour of need. That is the way it is with gods that have evolved down thru the ages in various religious persuasions. Their super hero gods have been drawn with words of persuasion upon the minds of men.

In the heavens there is Supreme Energy. It is similar to air that moves in and out of all living things. When Divine Energy (atoms) chooses to take shape, it becomes one big orb of light and energy, or individual orbs of light. Supreme Energy can divide and become many divine beings or gods. It can also re-absorb its individual manifestations and become one Supreme Energy being again. Individual orbs (manifestations) are like toes, fingers, ears, etc. of Supreme Energy. Even though the individual manifestations of Supreme Energy have evolved and taken their own form, they are still god. They are manifestations of him. They are not children or offspring of god. They are parts of god that have become individual gods. Those individual gods are souls. You and I are souls, thus we are gods in human flesh. Is god ignoring you? If so, it is you ignoring yourself. Get busy as a god and create the financial miracles you are in need of. You created your financial fortune once (before disaster hit). You can do it again!

Human bodies are not divine. They are transportation for orb souls to travel earth in. We souls drive human bodies as though they are automobiles. You and I, if we are orbs or manifestations of Supreme energy, are capable of taking care of our own problems. We are god in human flesh. Also, we must understand that Supreme Energy (god) re-absorbs his manifestations to become one with him again at times. Souls of children return and are reabsorbed by him. Children's souls become part of Supreme Energy, which was what they were to begin with.

Supreme Energy exists in pure form above the 8th Heaven. In the lower heavens, Supreme Energy's manifestation orbs can wear costumes, if they choose. Winged and non-winged angel forms are costumes.

November 3

THOUGHT FOR THE DAY - You are the god in your world and the only god that is going to come to your rescue.

YOU ARE THE GOD OF YOUR WORLD

Free-will choice is our god power to accomplish what we wish on Earth. We can make good choices and create heavens to live in, or we can use free-will choice to create hells. Bad jobs and abusive marriages are two examples of free-will choice hells.

You are a god in human flesh. It is your choices that make you a god of light or a god of darkness. What you have chosen to create in the past is now your current god reality. If you chose to create a one room shack type lifestyle yesterday, that was your choice. Today, you sit in that simple lifestyle. If you chose in the past to work hard, make money, and now live in a penthouse, you are the god who has created your current experience. If in the past, you chose to fill out a welfare application instead of a job application, youth current gutter lifestyle is what you have created as god of your world.

What powerful free-will choices are you making today that will affect your lifestyle tomorrow? You are the god in your world and the only god that is going to come to your rescue. Friends on Earth and spirit guides in the heavens can lend you a helping hand, but it is up to you to take the help and make it work for you. For instance: As your friend, I can send you a cake mix (an idea), but it will be up to you to bake the cake (create with the idea).

Man has failed to trust in himself as a god. When he learns to trust in his powers, he can create some very unique and beautiful heavens to live in. I love art. When I am walking thru an art museum, I am dwelling in a personal heaven. I create that heaven for myself by getting up and traveling to the museum, paying for my ticket, and entering. I go to my heaven. I don't wait for my heaven to come to me.

I have been over eating. This morning, I ate just a banana for breakfast with black coffee. I have chosen to create a thinner heaven for myself. I must do the work now, to live in a thinner heaven tomorrow. What are your problems in Earth life? You are capable, or have the power, to fix them. Your god power is free-will choice.

November 4

THOUGHT FOR THE DAY - Men of darkness will stand in food bank, clothing bank, and welfare lines to afford themselves a living they don't have to work for. Men of light are creators, gods in human flesh, who work and create financial heavens for themselves and their families.

CREATIVE GODS or WELFARE DEVILS

Heaven is not a welfare state. It is a working society. If you wish to go there (on Earth or in Heaven) you must work and create. There are no free-be handouts, like welfare systems that dole freebees to the con-artists and dark leaches of society. If you want to live in Heaven on Earth or in the astral heavens, you must work for it. Those on Earth, who choose to live lifetimes on welfare checks and food stamps, are dark beings. Dark beings choose dark lifestyles.

Food bank charities just enable those of darkness to exist another day without having to work for their daily bread. If you give a dollar to a man who won't work, you have turned from the light and are embracing darkness. Have you ever considered that it takes devils to create freebee charities and welfare gutters?

Welfare living is a low class/no class gutter experience. If you help a person to live in the gutters of life, you are a devil. Gods of light demand that their families, followers, and friends create and work, not take from society. You can turn from dark charity thinking.

If a man should need welfare assistance, he should only take it for the length of time that is needed to fill out applications and obtain any type of work. The assistance time should be limited to no more than 30 days. There is a dividing line between light and dark, heaven and hell. 30 days of assistance is the line. Those of the light should not cross over the line and contaminate their own light by supporting, housing, or feeding those not looking for work.

Enabling darkness will be held against you when you cross over. That includes handing out dollars to street corner beggars with signs. It also includes being the social worker who writes welfare checks to women who have been on welfare all their lives.

November 5

THOUGHT FOR THE DAY – Dark beings want to trample on the finances of others and social programs to get where they want to go in life. They are the ones who willingly default on student loans, etc. after getting there. They want something for nothing.

STUDENT LOAN DEVILS

Just as there are light and dark beings in all walks of life, the education system is no different. You have the dark users of handouts, and the light beings that are willing to work, create, and be all that they can be. A man, or a woman, that has worked for his education is a light being. If he has taken out a student loan, he will pay it back first when he enters the work force. He has integrity.

Students being sent to college by their parent's finances can be either light or dark. If they goof off and spend their parent's money partying, they are dark beings (welfare types). If they study hard and graduate in three years instead of four, so as not to be a financial burden to their parents, they are light beings. Shades of gray are those who coast thru college, just doing what they have to in order to appease their parents who are sending them.

Total Student loan recipients are the leaches, or welfare receiver type students in society. They want an education the easy way. Once they graduate, they get all upset because the government wants their loans paid back. They are dark, couch potato type students who chose to ride the welfare train for a student lifetime.

When the party is over for college students, the working student is prepared for his future. He has paid for his education and probably has a new car paid for. The couch potato student loan individual faces financial bankruptcy, because he does not want to work and pay back what he has borrowed. His life as a dark being catches up with him, when the government demands their money.

Heaven is not a welfare state. You work for what you have and become. Student loans cater to welfare personalities.

November 6

THOUGHT FOR THE DAY - Holding on to rising coat tails pays off.

TAKING SOMEONE TO THE TOP WITH YOU

Fast food empires have been built by forward thinkers in human flesh. They were built by simple men who took an idea and ran to the top with it. Along the way to the top, the fast food god provided a good living for his family. He took them with him on his journey to the top. They rode on his coat tail. By supporting him and his fast food restaurant idea, his family will eventually inherit his fast food empire. Holding on to rising coat tails pays off.

The fast food man took others, besides his family, to the top with him. There were managers, crew chiefs, cooks, and counter helpers that held on to his coattails and he rose to success. Think about all the jobs that fast food has provided to teens, giving them their first chance to make money.

I have coffee every morning in a local fast food restaurant. Last year, two of its employees graduated college and moved on to better jobs in the professional world. One became an Accountant, and the other a teacher. They had worked their way thru school, paying for their educations with fast food wages. Their fast food god owner had let them work and ride his coattails.

You have an idea that could be an elevator headed for the top of the financial world. As you implement your idea, you have the ability to take people along with you to the top. If you have a student who works for you along the way, goes to college, and then enters the profession al field, you have given someone a hand up. You provided the job, finances for him to rise on.

November 7

THOUGHT FOR THE DAY - By the power of 'Free Will Choice' we pull poverty or prosperity to us. Every financial choice in life has a negative effect or a positive outcome

PARTYING DESTROYS YOUR TOMORROWS

Every human can think, and then use his ideas to create or not create. A poor woman can purchase a bag of fabric scraps at a garage sale for a couple of dollars. Then she makes the choice to cut and create a magnificent quilt from them which she turns around and sells for a couple hundred dollars. She has used her god power to think and create from what is available to her. When she sells the quilt, she is the price of the quilt wealthier than she was before. Betsy Ross chose to take her fabric scraps and create the United States' first flag. She has gone down in history for doing so, a wealth that does not have a price tag on it.

By the power of 'Free Will Choice' we pull poverty or prosperity to us. Every financial choice in life has a negative effect or a positive outcome. For instance, if you take your week's wages and squander them on the weekend for cigarettes, alcohol, drugs, etc., you will reap the effect of an empty wallet the following week, with no money to eat on. If you squander a month's wages, you will not be able to pay your rent or mortgage payment. Your landlord or mortgage company will eventually evict or foreclose on you for your bad financial decisions.

Our wealth tomorrow depends on how we invest our dollars and ideas today. The investing of your ideas and dollars in partying, drugs, alcohol, frivolous living, etc. will bring you gutter living tomorrow. Men standing on street corners with cardboard signs begging have been poor investors. Poor investors have embraced the dark side. Do not help them. Embracing darkness will turn you to a shade of gray light being. Help only those who are working and walking toward the light. Give them a hand up if they need it.

November 8

THOUGHT FOR THE DAY – If you should win or inherit a large amount of money, you should use your powers to think and create a way for your winnings to increase. A man who squanders his money is not wealthy. He slowly becomes a loser with every frivolous purchase.

LOTTERY LOSERS

Lottery winnings and inheritances are fleeting wealth, a momentary gain in your hand. The receiver becomes a poor man again the minute he starts to squander or spend the money. Thinking to invest the money, and then spend only the interest (minus one dollar interest to be saved) makes the individual an ever progressing wealthy man.

People dream of winning the lottery. They see themselves using the financial gain to buy two or three fancy cars, clothes, jewelry, fishing boats, etc. Also, they see themselves giving certain amounts to family and friends who are down and out. Other parts of their windfall, they will give to charity or their church. They create a spiral down into a new kind of poverty.

I read somewhere that within 5 years most lottery recipients have run thru their winnings and are broke again. Their cars and boats are old and starting to break down. Designer clothes are worn out and jewelry pawned. Their chosen church and charity programs will do nothing for them. Fair weather friends have abandoned them. Family members hit bottom again and are mad because the lottery winner won't give them more money, dollars he no longer has.

If you should win or inherit a large amount of money,

you should use your power to think, and then create a way for your financial gain to increase. Then spend only the interest on your new wealth, after taking a small amount of the interest and adding it to the original financial gain. You should never spend every dollar that comes into your hands as earnings. By continuing to save a dollar more, you become richer and richer and richer. The squanderer becomes poorer and poorer and poorer, even though he looks like a rich man at the moment in his designer clothes and fancy cars.

Choosing to squander or become wealthy is a daily decision. You choose to be a poor man or a wealthy man with every dollar you earn or spend.

November 9

THOUGHT FOR THE DAY - Gamblers brag about how much they win at casinos or cards. However, they never speak about how much they have lost in previous years before a win.

DOORS TO FINANCIAL ADDICTIONS

When I grew up, there were mom and pop corner grocery stores. The one in my neighborhood had a gum ball machine that sat in prominent display on the counter next to the register. In it were colored gum balls as well as a handful of gum balls that were speckled. The regular colored gumballs were a penny. If you put your penny in and you managed to get one of the speckled balls, you were a winner and could have a 5 cent candy bar. Every kid in the neighborhood put in way more pennies than their eventual won candy bar cost. The speckled ball idea was created by dark minds to addict children to gambling at an early age. The speckled gum balls were a hook.

A man, using his earnings to buy love from a lady of the night, is like the child who puts his pennies in the speckled ball machine. He develops an addiction for speckled ball ladies that take his money, but never pay off in true wealth or love. He squanders more of himself, than he ever gets from the speckled ball relationships. When his money is gone, the possibility of candy bar love from his speckled ball ladies' disappears.

Gamblers like to brag about how much they have won at casinos or cards. However, they never speak of how much they have lost to reach the point of the one big win. They don't speak about how many times their children went hungry because daddy gambled away the grocery money. The children gamblers above spent possibly 25 pennies to get one 5 cent candy bar. The same quarter could have bought 5 of the same candy bar, back at that time.

Church ladies who sell chances to win a quilt are dark beings who are encouraging church members to gamble. Office pots are gambling. Poker is gambling. Betting on horses is gambling. Betting on sports game outcomes is gambling. Betting on whether someone's baby is a boy or a girl is gambling. Flee from darkness' addictions.

November 10

THOUGHT FOR THE DAY – Thinking, making choices, and taking one step at a time will take you wherever it is that you want to go.

DREAM WEALTH ACHIEVED

I have a cousin named Ralph who, as a teen, dreamed of living in Alaska. His mother was dead, and his father was a drunk who let him fall thru the cracks and eventually out of high school in the foothills of Missouri. At age 16, Ralph's chance of coming up with plane or bus fare to Alaska was zilch. My cousin did not have anything going for him, except a dream.

What Ralph did was use his mind to think and create a way to obtain his dream. Ralph came up with the idea of signing onto an Alaskan fishing boat as a cook. Working in that capacity, he knew the boat would feed and house him in a corner of the world that he wanted to live in.

Ralph hitch hiked from Missouri to the state of Washington. From there he caught a ride on a small tourist fishing boat heading for Alaska. Once arriving there, he did find a boat that hired him as a cook. Ralph spent 20 years in Alaska as a fishing boat cook. His dream at sixteen was not to be a cook. It was to live in Alaska. He did so, on a fishing boat. He made his dream come true by making choices.

What is your dream? What can you do, taking one small step at a time, to make your dream a reality?

November 11

THOUGHT FOR THE DAY - Gods of light demand that their followers work, not take from society. Devils encourage and train their followers to rape society's good will.

WELFARE SYSTEMS ARE CREATED BY DEVILS,

NOT GODS

Heaven is not a welfare state. It is a working society. If you wish to go there and reside there, you must work and do your fair share. There are no free-bee handouts like Earth welfare systems dole out to the con-artists and leaches of society.

Earth welfare systems and charities enable those of darkness to exist another day without having to work, giving them free time to sell drugs, drink, watch TV, and plan havoc they can inflict on society. Have you ever considered that Dark Forces/Devils create welfare systems, charities, food banks, and ghetto hells? Devils create social system hells for their own dark forces to live in.

Welfare living is a low class/no class, hellish gutter living experience. If you enable/help a person to live a lifetime in the gutters of life, you are the devil who is creating and providing him a hell to dwell in. Gods of light demand that their followers on earth work, not take from society.

If a man does request help (welfare assistance), it should only be taken for the length of time that is needed to obtain work, and that limited to 30 days. There is a dividing line between light and dark. 30 days of assistance is it. Those of the light should not step over the line and accept assistance beyond the 30 days. Children of those who refuse to work should be taken by the courts immediately at the end of the 30 days and be adopted out.

Enabling darkness will be held against you when you cross over. There is war in the heavens between light and dark forces. Don't be a traitor to the light by financing and embracing social systems that enable dark forces to be couch potatoes that do not work for their daily bread.

November 12

THOUGHT FOR THE DAY – Financing our path and lifestyle on Earth must be done with integrity, in order to keep our status as a being of light.

WEALTH OR ILL GOTTEN GAIN

There are dark and light repercussions for every word, deed, and step we take in earth life. As light beings we have a heaven's standard of light and dark that we must measure ourselves by. If we go home to the First Heaven some day as a stained, shade of gray being, we will be forced to do a repeat lifetime in a karmic situation. What we have chosen to do to others will be done to us. If we totally embrace darkness, before returning home, we will be kicked out of the heavens. We will be deemed fallen angels.

Financing our path and lifestyle on Earth must be done with integrity, in order to keep our status as a being of light. For instance, we cannot sell drugs or prostitute ourselves for money. We cannot enter business relationships with dark beings. We cannot steal what belongs to someone else to increase our wealth. We cannot hock our sister's engagement ring, leaving her wondering what has happened to it. We must create our human wealth without harming another being, or the human vehicle we travel in.

It is time to start taking steps toward becoming a wealthier human than you are in the present moment. Your first step will be to ask your guide for an idea to use to create honest money. Then you must take the idea and create with it. Along the way, with every decision, you must weigh it against heaven's standard of light and dark.

Example: A dark man may rob a bank as his first step

toward becoming wealthy. A Light Being might choose to learn all he can about the banking business, perhaps taking a teller position to begin with. Moving up a business ladder with integrity is in agreement with heaven's standards. Stealing is not!

You become your choices. What you have tomorrow in relationships, health, and wealth will be the result of today's choices. Rob today, you will be in prison tomorrow. Drinking and eating nothing but sugar foods today will bring diabetes to call on you in your tomorrow. Marry a dark individual and you will be a victim of his abuse one day. Choose well, measuring all choices against heaven's standard of dark and light.

November 13

THOUGHT FOR THE DAY – Wealth is different to every individual.

TAKE YOUR FIRST STEP TOWARD WEALTH

One morning, I decided that wealth, to me, was being able to afford to drink coffee every morning in a restaurant, and have a waitress pour it for me. Also, I decided that wealth was always having a tip to leave the waitress.

My discovery of what wealth was to me was eye opening. After my eye opening experience, it was up to me to embrace my coming wealth. So, I took the first step. I took my last dollar and went to the local cafe and ordered my first cup of coffee (calling my wealth into existence). Action pulls new wealth to you. From that day forward, I have had money to live my wealthy, coffee drinking dream.

Wealth is different to every individual on planet Earth. However, the first step to achieving is the same. Think about what wealth is to you. Then take the first tiny step toward achieving that wealth. Afterward, keep taking daily steps. If you quit stepping, your wealth will cease. Steps forward are like magnets. They draw daily new success and wealth to you.

A painting doesn't just occur. An artist first thinks about the subject he wishes to paint. Thinking brings ideas to the artist from his spirit guide. Then the artist must take his first step as a creative god in human flesh. He must pick up his drawing pen or paint brush. Finished paintings are wealth to artists. His future wealth will be new paintings.

November 14

THOUGHT FOR THE DAY – If you ask for generic from the heavens, that is what will come to you. 'Tweek' your prayers, if you want designer.

What Goes Up Must Come Down!

If you throw an apple into the air, it must come down due to the law of gravity. When you go inward to where your soul is, the same law applies. As a soul, you throw an apple request up and it will come back down due to the law of gravity. However, when a soul's apple request comes back down, it will be in a different form. The apple request becomes an apple answer.

Inward thoughts are the same as prayers. Whatever you think about inwardly will fly upward to the heavens, and then come back down to you wrapped in the law of attraction. Ideas and things will start to come to you. You are the god of your world. You must take what the law of attraction gives you and create your god lifestyle with it.

When you think or make requests inwardly, be specific what you are in need of. If you send up generic requests, you will receive generic answers. If you send up wealth requests, you will receive ideas as how to make money. If you ask simply for a dollar, a sand dollar from the ocean might show up on your path as you walk home. The dollar is a generic request. The sand dollar is a generic answer. If you ask for a five spot, five pimples or imperfections might appear on your face. If you ask your spirit guide for stock, you might receive a cow, a couple of sheep, and maybe pig or two. If your ask generic, you will get whatever your words mean to your spirit guide.

When you ask the heavens for help, be specific as to what kind of help you need.

November 15

THOUGHT FOR THE DAY- Wealth does not come from working at a job you hate. Misery is the reward for walking a path that is not yours.

WORKING AT A JOB YOU HATE

Partially why humans don't prosper is because they settle for jobs that are not in alignment with who they want to be in life. When humans settle, they quit pulling to themself that which is right for them.

When you work at a job that is not right for your path, you are taking a job away from someone that is right for the position that you have settled for. You become a road block to someone else's wealth. Purposely becoming a road block makes you a shade of gray light being. Hurting another light being in any fashion will turn you into a shade of gray.

Two young male friends, just graduating high school in a small town, apply for the same position in a local fast food restaurant. (We will call them Tom and Clark). The town is so small that this is the only local position available.

Tom dreams of sailing around the world. He does not really want the fast food job, but he needs money to get by on till his day dream ship comes in to sail him away to what he really wants out of life.

Clark wants to build and own a fast food restaurant someday. He wants the local fast food job for experience and to learn the ins and outs of the business. On his application, he simply states that he is interested in learning the fast food trade.

Tom lies on his application, stating that he has always dreamed of managing that local fast food restaurant. The aging owner of the local restaurant gives Tom the job, thinking he has found a kid to help him manage his restaurant. Tom is totally out of alignment with what he wants out of life by taking the job. You don't sail around the world in a fast food restaurant. Joining the Navy would have been a better choice for Tom.

Clark leaves the small town, after Tom darkly sucks up the fast food job. He takes a similar fast food position in the city. Clark is still on his path. He has just had to take a fork in the road that was caused by someone else. Have you had forks on your road?

Once your educations years are over, you must ask yourself what your adult dream is. Then you must choose a job that will be in alignment with that dream. Achieving your dream is wealth. Making money at a job you hate is poverty.

November 16

THOUGHT FOR THE DAY – Bad marriages are like tow trucks with wrecked vehicles in tow. Light being tow truck souls cannot pursue future missions with permanently chained dark tag-a-long spouses in tow. Bad marriages are types of tow truck chains.

TOW TRUCK MARRIAGES

Getting married is a human brain choice, not a soul choice. The human body and brain have a built in function that causes them to want to reproduce. Society adds the legal need of a license, ball and chain. When initial attraction and dividends end, humans sometimes find themselves in marriages they don't want to be in.

You must remember that a human body is transportation for a soul. It is not a soul. The human body is like an automobile, and a soul is its driver. When the soul is asleep at the wheel of its human auto, the auto idles or lives just as a human animal. Mating and reproduction are animal functions.

When a soul driver awakens, it sometimes is in shock to find that its human vehicle has another car in tow, like a tow truck pulling an auto. When a soul is awake, it knows that it has a soul mate in the heavens, not on Earth. The soul also realizes that its human body is chained in marriage to another vehicle with a dark devil soul in it. Then the light being soul will go to war with the dark being soul in the other human body, in an effort to flee darkness.

Human marriage is a tow truck experience. When a tow truck unhooks from the experience, a rape of personal wealth/finances happens. Alimony checks are payments to dark tow trucks.

NOVEMBER 17

THOUGHT FOR THE DAY – As a light being, your word is your integrity. If you ask for something specific from the universe, there are no returns.

EMOTION INVESTMENTS

The Law of gravity says that what goes up must come down. You throw a ball into the air and it immediately comes back down for you to catch. Emotional inward cries are like balls. They are thrown up into the astral skies, and just like a ball, they will fall back down to you. However, things thrown into the inner skies come back down in a different form, just as prayers sent up come back down as answers.

Emotional cries can be positive or negative, and their form coming back down may be positive or karmic. For instance, you go to bed in a bad mood. Then, in an emotionally negative state, you say the following inward as you fall asleep.

"Go ahead . . . just give me another crap day tomorrow." You mumble sarcastically. Then you fall asleep from negative exhaustion.

Your careless words spoken into the inward ethers will come back down like this: You awake the next morning to your alarm clock sounding thirty minutes late. In a rush you get in the shower, only to discover that you are out of soap and shampoo. You reach for your towel and accidentally drop it into the toilet. When you go to get dressed, you either get a run in your stockings or can't find your belt anywhere. Entering your kitchen, you try to make coffee. The coffeemaker gurgles and spits, but refuses to brew. So it goes till you get into your car and head for work. You are having a crap morning. On your way to work, you have to take a detour due to construction. You run thru the fast food window and they give you the wrong order. When you arrive late at work, your boss chews on you. Your whole day goes like that, including having a stress migraine when you return home for the night. That is a crap day! When you dared the universe to go ahead and just send you another crap day, your spirit guide did just that. What you sent up came back down.

What does the above example have to do with finances and wealth? You become wealthy or poor according to how you ask for help with finances. If you look up to the inner heavens and tell your spirit guide that you will be happy forever if he will just send you the finances to buy a set of golf clubs or a designer purse like your neighbor. Your spirit guide will always take you at your word. He will send you the number of dollars for the item you asked for and then expect you to be happy because you said you would be, even though you don't have a clue where you are going to come up with money for the rent or utility bill. I will be happy is like telling your spirit guide "Amen", an ending that states you will not be in need of further financial help. Your spirit guide will hold you to your 'Amen' word. After all, you are a light being. Your word is your integrity.

Look back at your life path and consider the frivolous things you have asked for, and how you asked for them. Your current poverty could be your own doing.

November 18

THOUGHT FOR THE DAY - When you have asked amiss for friends (generic) and have received a can of dark, dirty worms, it is best to dump the worm individuals, trash the can experience, and move on. Next time, ask for 'Name Brand'.

Attracting Poverty Relationships

We all have high school classmates that we haven't seen since graduation. Students just go different directions and lose touch. In big city schools, some students we never know to begin with. They are just faces we pass in the hallways on a daily basis. In our later adult years, former high school friends and faces try to hook back up with us for walks down high school memory lane. Some we remember, and some we don't, especially in big city classes.

I believe in the law of attraction, and that we attract wealth, relationships, and friends to us according to our thinking. Last week, I was feeling a bit nostalgic. I asked the universe to let an old acquaintance get in touch. My request was generic and I got a generic return. An acquaintance from high school, a face l I did not remember, wanted to renew our old friendship. I didn't have a clue who she was. She however, said we were friends in high school. After we spoke a few times, she set about trying to tell me how much of a sinner I was, and that her religion was the only way to heaven and my spiritual choices were all wrong. Basically, she tried to stuff her religion down my throat. I had to laugh and then have a serious talk with my spirit guide. I asked generically for any old high school acquaintance to get in touch. My spirit guide sent the nearest old high school face individual to me. I pulled her and her craziness to me, because I asked generic. The Law of Attraction brings to us that which we ask for, whether it is light or dark of nature. Because she put down other religions, she was a dark being.

Had I taken the time to think about my nostalgic request, I should have asked for by name the old light being friend I wanted to hear from. When you have asked generic and have received a can of worms, it is best to dump the worm individuals, trash the can experience, and move on.

Good friends are wealth. Narrow minded friends are poverty. Cans of worms are hells.

November 19

THOUGHT FOR THE DAY – Picking up one penny sent to you by the universe can cause domino effect wealth to fall your way.

KEYS TO WEALTH

All of us have been out and about and spotted a penny here and there on floors and the pavement of parking lots.

Some people step over them and others take the time to pick them up. It is how you view the penny that makes it found wealth or a waste of time.

I once heard a rich man give a speech on found wealth. His main point was that if you pray for wealth and a penny suddenly appears on your path, you have been presented with a key to further wealth. If you step over the penny, you reject the key that the universe has sent to you. You become in that moment, either a penny richer or a penny poorer.

I took the speaker's 'Pennies from Heaven' speech seriously and decided to pick up the next penny I spotted on the ground and see what the key to wealth experience would bring me. Keep in mind, that wealth to me is being able to have coffee every morning in a restaurant and tip the waitress. So, over the next year, I picked up found pennies and placed them in a tea cup on the window sill in my kitchen. Along with the pennies, I found an occasional nickel, dime, and quarter on the ground. The hardest pennies to pick up were the ones I found in restrooms where they had slipped from people's pockets in the stalls. However, I did so knowing that if I didn't, I was denying keys to wealth. At the end of the year, the tea cup was full.

One morning, I poured my tea cup of pennies and coins out onto my kitchen table to count them and give them a monetary value. One penny became a keepsake. It was minted my birthday year. Another was a hundred year old penny that was worth more than a penny. The other pennies and coins were enough to purchase three morning cups of cafe coffee and tip the waitress.

Wealth comes to us according to what we see wealth as.

Keys to wealth come daily. Keys can be pennies on the ground, ideas for businesses or investments, or even a little voice telling you to use coupons for your purchases. Wealth is built on the use of keys.

November 20

THOUGHT FOR THE DAY – The 'Law of Attraction' will bring to you items and ideas to be used to increase your wealth. It is up to you to invest and make those items and ideas grow. You are the money making god or squandering devil of your world.

TURNING A DOLLAR INTO TWO

This is a shared story from a friend.

I have two brothers that have been in a competition to be the wealthiest their whole lives. My brother Gene has always been jealous of my brother Rob. Why? Rob seems to have the gift of turning nothing into dollar bills. Rob does not know that Gene has always been jealous of him and his greater wealth. Gene lives a flamboyant in your face lifestyle, and appears to be wealthier. He drives cars he can't afford and lives in houses he can't make the mortgage payments on. To the world, Gene looks wealthy, but probably doesn't have two or three hundred dollars to his name.

Rob loves to buy and sell. He started out by purchasing a load of cantaloupe when he was sixteen. He sold the load on a street corner for a profit and immediately went south for another load. As Rob matured, he started dealing in antiques and then buying out estates. You never know what beautiful or exotic odd thing you will find in Rob's home. You have to enjoy his home treasures in the moment, because he will have them sold for a profit by the next weekend.

My brother Gene died a few years ago. In death, his family had to borrow money to bury him. He exited life as a poor man, not the rich one he put on a phony front of being.

I once asked Rob what his secret was for making money. His reply was, "Never hold onto any item thinking it will make you a bigger profit in the future. If someone offers me one dollar more than I have paid for an item I let it go. My dollars are continually making dollars. If my money is tied up in dusty someday items, my dollar bills can no longer produce for me. At that point, I am out of business. The dollar I make on an item today, may turn into fifty tomorrow, and thousands down the line. Money tied up in a dusty someday item is a waste of my current moment to make money."

Wealth doesn't come from hoarding. Wealth comes from creative releasing.

November 21

THOUGHT FOR THE DAY – Take a dollar bill in your pocket and ask those in the heavens for an idea of how to stretch it to feed six. If an idea comes to you, then those in the heavens are hearing you. Next ask for an idea to increase your financial wealth.

TURNING NOTHING INTO SOMETHING

A winter blizzard has hit, trapping a woman in her house the day before she is to purchase groceries. She goes to her cupboard and finds that she has only about three tablespoons of flour in it. She goes to her refrigerator and it is empty, except for about 2 cups of milk. She checks her bread box and finds a half a loaf of bread. As she ponders her lack of food, a knock sounds on her door. A stranded family of six asks for shelter for the night. Their car has broken down. Our woman's food problem has grown worse. She will now need to feed dinner to six strangers plus her-self.

The woman goes within and asks for a miracle idea of how to feed her unexpected guests. Her asking is like throwing an apple into the air. A return apple idea comes down to her. She then makes gravy from her three tablespoons of flour and two cups of milk. She divides the half loaf of bread between seven plates and then pours on the gravy. From nothing, she serves her guests a hot meal. She feeds a multitude, just like Christ broke loaves and fishes and fed his multitude of followers. The woman went from having bare cupboards poverty thinking, to being a miracle working god. She took a small thing and turned it into a big thing.

If your financial cupboards are bare (you are down to your last penny), go inward and ask for an idea to multiply the penny you do have. You have the power to be a miracle worker. You have the power to turn water into wine.

November 22

THOUGHT FOR THE DAY – When we receive unexpected finances from the universe, we must be miracle workers and increase them, not squander them.

MAKING SOMETHING OUT OF NOTHING

The universe has a way of sending you prosperity in unexpected ways. Recently, a deer jumped out in front of my moving vehicle. I absolutely could not miss hitting it. The impact took out the grill, headlights, radiator, hood, etc. of my 1910 Cobalt. My insurance company totaled my car and cut me a check for $6,000.

Before the deer incident, I was getting ready to junk my Cobalt. It was drive-able, but it had a hundred and seven thousand miles on it. The universe had a different idea. Those watching over me turned my worn out auto into a small windfall of cash. Now, it is up to me as to what to do with my financial windfall. I can squander it, or make it grow. My plan for the money is to make it grow and work for me. I will ask my spirit guide for an idea how to accomplish that. Never use yesterday ideas. Ask daily! Our paths on Earth are a daily walk experience that sometimes takes unexpected twists and turns. Talk to your guide daily, so that he can adjust what is happening in your world accordingly.

Spirit Guides will send down daily wealth making ideas that are appropriate for each individual. A mechanic may get the idea to buy tools and go into the car repair business. A seamstress might get the idea to buy a quilting machine and start a home quilting business. I have a brother who loves antiques. He would undoubtedly buy out a small estate and then sell off its contents for a return on his investment. A college student might get the idea of buying a lawn mower and going into the lawn care business during his summer vacation. Spirit guides will send money making ideas down that are in alignment with each human's talents and future destinies. A mechanic will not be given quilting machine ideas. A quilter will not be given lawn mowing ideas.

When we receive unexpected finances from the universe, we must be miracle workers and increase them, not squander them. Spending should be done only out of the profits made on initial windfalls.

Be thankful for all wealth that comes to you in mysterious ways, whether it is a quarter or thousands of dollars. Be thankful enough to make it grow. An unthankful person will spend it on frivolities.

November 23

THOUGHT FOR THE DAY – The use of cursing or blessing words can make a difference in what you get as answers when you request help from your spirit guide.

DAMNING YOUR FINANCIAL OUTCOME

What goes up must come down. Dark words ride requests/prayers upward to your guardian or spirit guide. They then come back down as negative attachments to the answers you need.

A mother prays, "Please help my child in prison!"

She isn't praying for her child to get out of prison, she is praying for her child to remain in prison and get help there.

A demanding, selfish teen might selfishly demand of his

spirit guide, "I want that damned radio!"

What a spirit guide might send him is a broken radio, a damned one.

What do negative and positive words have to do with finances coming to you from the heavens? If you ask for dark ways of making money, dark ideas will come to you with dark attachments such as future jail and prison confinements. Asking for jobs to sell drugs, work as a stripper, bar tending, etc. is dark or bad choices. Those requests with words such as damn will bring back to you dark attachments. A drug dealer may die from taking a bad trip on drugs. A stripper may fall from her pole and break a leg. A bar tender serves and encourages men to become alcoholics. One of his drunks may pull a gun and shoot him in a drunken moment. Dark attachments come with prayers, when curse words are used in the request. Also, those who ask for dark things and jobs are not asking for help from those in the light. Their prayers and requests go to their guides which are demons and devils of hell.

When asking for financial ideas or help from those in the heavens (spirit guides, angels, masters, gods, etc.), ask wisely, respectfully, and in words that are positive and to the point. If you ask amiss, you will receive amiss. If you ask generic, you will get generic. If you ask for heaven, you will have pleasant experiences come to you. If you pray for legal ideas to come to you to use to make money, you will receive light being ideas. Acting on them, you will become a financial wizard on Earth that is known for his integrity.

Totally dark beings do not have light being spirit guides. They have demon guides.

November 24

THOUGHT FOR THE DAY – Hell is poverty and Heaven is prosperity. Between the two experiences is a gate that swings both ways. You can walk the fence line between, or walk thru the prosperity/poverty gate either direction.

PROSPERITY'S GATE

There are laws in the universe and we are subject to them whether we are traveling on earth or other planets. If we apply/use the laws properly, we become perfected ones/gods of great knowledge and resources. As gods in human flesh, we can, at any time we wish, pull from the universe ideas to make our lives prosperous and comfortable as we travel Earth life or other planet life.

I have written before about what wealth is to me. I love coffee. I have decided that wealth to me is being able to go to a café every morning, drink all the coffee I want, have a waitress pour and keep my coffee cup full, and to be able to tip the waitress. To someone else, wealth may be something entirely different.

A friend recently told me that the dividing line between being poor and wealthy to her is being able to have cable TV. She said she would become poor the day her cable was disconnected due to not being able to pay the bill. She loves TV like I love coffee.

What is the dividing line between poverty and prosperity to you?

I know a man who was reared in low income housing by a lifetime welfare sucking mom. He never had a normal life or had proper food and clothing. He speaks of how he was looked down on by school mates for his ratty clothing, etc. As an adult, he has a mental dividing line between poverty and what he feels is prosperity. Name brand, or non-name brands on food and clothing, is his dividing line. He will not purchase anything but name brand foods, name brand clothing, and the most expensive offerings on menus when in cafes. He feels that the day he has to eat generic, buy his clothes in thrift stores, move into low income housing, and fill out a welfare application he will move from wealth to poverty. At the same time, he loves, collects, and will drive old cars or trucks and never give it a second thought. Vehicles are not signs of prosperity or poverty to him.

People pray for wealth, but they don't take the time to think about what it is they feel that wealth is. In order to become wealthy, you must decide what your line between poverty and prosperity is.

November 25

THOUGHT FOR THE DAY – There are times in life when we must choose what is important to us. That choice may be to cease financial investments in order to help out a fellow light being who needs a hand up.

DOLLARS ARE LIKE FLOWER SEEDS

Dollars are like flower seeds. We plant them, just as we do seeds. A seed or dollar investment doesn't look like much till it reaches maturity and produces beautiful flowering plants. Till maturity of our investments come, we are responsible for the watering and caretaking. If we want flowers, investment increase, we must be diligent in our gardening efforts.

My favorite flower to grow is California Mammoth Zinnias. Every year I am known for having beautiful flower beds of the glorious, saucer size blooms. This year, I had a hiccup in my life and caring for my garden of Zinnias was not my top priority. After planting my seeds, my brother became very ill and was at death's door all spring and summer. I had to make a choice whether to be there for him or my flowers. Of course, there was no choice. My brother came first. On the 30th day of July his body gave way and his spirit traveled on to his next appointed round. Afterward, I took a look at my flower beds and saw what a miserable shape they were in. One bed only produced four blooms.

There are times in life when we must choose what is important to us. That choice may be to cease financial investments in order to help out a fellow light being who needs a hand up. There are times when family members have to step in and help pay for funeral or medical expenses for another. Hiccups in your financial investments will happen. However, always remember that you can go within and ask for new ideas to make your seeds and financial investments grow again. Next year, I will plant new seeds in my flower beds, and new dollars in investments.

Life is short. Your friends and loved ones are the flowers in your personal garden. Take care of them.

November 26

THOUGHT FOR THE DAY – Passions determine what wealth is.

OBSERVING THE WEALTH OF OTHERS

Wealthy people walk all about you. You rub shoulders with them every day. If you want to associate with wealthy people, you must learn to recognize wealth and how it is worn or displayed by them. Wealth is not necessarily millions of dollars in a dusty bank vault. Wealth is fulfilled passion.

My Aunt Golden, back in the 1950s, loved antique, carnival glass, flower vases. She displayed her treasures on the surfaces of all her furniture. She was very meticulous and never allowed them to be dusty or dirty. They always shined and glittered when light from her windows hit them. Flower vases are not the average thing that most women collect. However, to Aunt Golden, they were her wealth, her treasures. Being able to purchase an antique carnival glass beauty was to her a sign that she was okay financially. To a man, his sign of wealth might be the finances to buy a fishing rod whenever he wants one. Passions determine what wealth is.

My sister in law goes to the beauty shop religiously every week. To her, being able to have her hair done regularly is a sign that she is doing okay in life. It is her outward sign of being financially okay. My parents thought owning rental property was a sign they were doing okay. A brother of mine sees flashy cars as a sign he is doing okay. A female friend of mine works two jobs. She sees the second job as a sign that she is a go getter, a financially prosperous being on the way up in life. My niece, who is unable to have children of her own, has adopted three little girls. Wealth to her is having children. My deceased Uncle Earl was a fisherman. When he returned home from a day of fishing, he would be all smiles as he displayed his stringer of fish. To him, wealth was not the money he made on his job. Wealth was his catch for the day. My grandson loves to read. His wealth is his library card.

Being wealthy is when you can afford to purchase with cash (not credit cards) items you are passionate about.

November 27

THOUGHT FOR THE DAY – You are the miracle working god in your world. Turn your water (ideas) into wine!

HOME OWNERSHIP OR RENTER HELL

It was during the great depression that my father landed a position as a janitor in a town called Lebanon about 70 miles from Springfield, Missouri where he and my mother lived with my maternal grandparents and three other sibling families who had moved back home to survive the depression. Family members were packed in the house like sardines. 15 people lived in four rooms. Four of the five adult men in my grandparents' house were out of work. Needless to say, my parents were thrilled when my father found work and they were able to get out on their own. My parents moved from Springfield to the small town of Lebanon and rented a tiny house where they chose to live very frugally. They had a dream, an idea for how to own a home without paying mortgage payments or interest.

After about six months, my parents managed to save enough money to purchase with cash a wrong side of the tracks lot back in Springfield near my grandparents. On the lot was a large shed that had been used as a coop for chickens by the previous owner. My parents got the idea to turn the chicken coop into a tiny one room house for themselves. They would turn the chicken coop into what their dollars could afford. Because of the depression, my parents feared my father might lose his job. In their thinking, they would at least have a paid for roof over their head, should it happen, and they would not have to move back in and live with my grandparents and their over load of returned home siblings. Today, moving into a chicken coop seems unfathomable.

On the weekends, my father would purchase a train ticket for my mother and brother to ride in comfort to Springfield, Missouri where their chicken coop/house project was. To save money, my father would hop the back of the train and ride to Springfield with the hobos. Once there, my parents would take what remained of the weekly pay check and purchase a few boards to make improvements to their one room 'shack'. At the end of two years, a few boards at a time, they had their one room remodel completed. Due to the depression, my father did lose his janitor job right after completing the one room house. My parents left Lebanon and moved back to Springfield and into the one room house. I, Jo Hammers the Mystic, was born in that one room house. My father cut wood for a living till the depression ended. My parents embraced and repeated their little house idea. They saved and purchased two more lots on the wrong side of the tracks and built two tiny rental houses one board at a time over the next ten years in spite of hard times. They rented the two tiny houses for 40 years. The rental income took the edge off of their financial hard times. They were wealthy in the depression, because they dared to think mortgage free, home ownership. Ideas are what make a man wealthy.

Go inward and upward to the heavens in meditation,

prayer, etc. Ask for an idea to come to you that you can use to create rent free, interest free, mortgage free housing for yourself. Then, take your idea and turn it into physical form. You are the miracle working god in your world. Turn your water (ideas) into wine (home ownership)!

Home ownership ideas come to man. It is up to man to take them and put them into action. Mortgage free home ownership, no matter how large or small, is a step up out of poverty. Tiny travel trailers are types of one room homes today.

November 28

THOUGHT FOR THE DAY - A baseball thrown into the air comes back down due to the law of gravity. You can catch the ball, or miss it. If you throw a prayer into the heavens, an answer falls back down for you to either catch or miss.

ANSWERS TO PRAYER

When we are children, we think simply and receive simply. For instance: a little boy prays and asks for an idea to make money. He wants a new bicycle. His parents tell him that he must earn the money to purchase the bicycle, because they frankly cannot afford it. So, he closes his eyes, goes within, and asks his deity for ideas of how to make money. He has thrown his baseball like prayer into the air of the heavens. The ball prayer answer falls back down for him to catch. The answer ideas may be to rake leaves, shovel snowy walks, and deliver newspapers. He asked for ideas, he received ideas. The boy runs excitedly out into his world to tackle and become rich form his received ideas, his answer to prayer. Answers to adult prayers come just as easily.

A man we will call Pete has lost his job. He is really confused as to where to go to look for work, or even whether he should look for the same type of position that he has held the last ten years. Going within, Pete asks where and what type of job he is to seek. He throws his baseball like prayer into the heavens. Returning down to him by the law of gravity, his ball answer returns in the form of ideas that just pop into his head. The 'pops' are answers to prayer. He must catch and hold on to the pops.

Pete can miss or not catch his ball answer coming down. Receiving down coming ball ideas and then acting on them is what creates miracle jobs and wealth.

November 29

THOUGHT FOR THE DAY - You are a light being, or a dark being by choice. Taking and not giving back makes you a dark being.

THE LAW OF TAKING AND GIVING

Humans, hitting on hard times, often turn to charities for help. Some do not know that they can use the laws of gravity and attraction to pull what they need to them. So, they get in charity, food bank, and welfare lines. The Christmas season is a peak season for people applying for help. There are two types of people who apply to charities for help. One is those who make a living conning and using charities for lifetimes, and those who ask for a one time hand up. One time uppers are usually aware of the Law of Taking and Giving. They know there are repercussions for taking from charities, when they are able to work. They are just temporarily between jobs.

During the depression, my father had been out of work for six months. During the Christmas season, my mother went to the Salvation Army and signed up for a Christmas Basket. My mother's telling of the story of receiving the basket has become a yearly Christmas tradition in our family. My mother would tell how she went to pick up the basket, thinking it would possibly be a brown paper bag of food because times were bad and charity lines were long. When she got there, she received a cardboard box basket that was so huge that she could not move it. She had to leave it and go get one of her brothers to help her get it home. Every Christmas she told how thankful she was for everything that was in that Christmas basket that year.

The climax to my mother's story is this. Every Christmas season after the huge basket event, she dropped x number of dollars into the Salvation Army's Christmas kettle. She decided that if she gave that amount each Christmas, she would eventually have the value of the Christmas basket paid back, plus some extra to help someone else in need. My mother was in her twenties when she received the basket. At 84 she passed away and her giving back to the kettle ended. She took one basket and then gave back for approximately 60 years. Now, we (her children) put dollars in the kettle every year in memory of our mother.

Light beings, who respect the law of Taking and Giving, do not take repeated charity handouts, or live off of food stamps, welfare, food banks, clothing banks, etc. Light beings only ask for help if they truly need it. Even then, they know that they must respect the Law of Taking and Giving, and eventually return to the same source what they have taken, plus the same amount as universe interest. (Clothing taken from a clothing bank must be paid back to a clothing bank. Food must be returned to a food bank. Scholarship money must be returned to a scholarship fund.) A light being must give back double what he has taken.

Are you a dark being who is constantly raping charities?

There is recompense for not adhering to the Law of Giving and Taking. Making no effort to repay what you have taken in the time of need activates Karma. Future financial doors to wealth will be chained and locked by those in the heavens if you fail to try to repay. Many people live in the gutters of life because they are takers and never givers.

November 30

THOUGHT FOR THE DAY – Every day brings new steps to take or ladder rungs to climb in your financial adventures. The last rung is to decide where your earth wealth is to go at death. Light beings are held accountable for this final choice.

FINAL FINANCIAL DECISIONS

The last major financial decision you will make will be the planning and paying for your funeral. Wealthy people like to be in control, and they do not leave their final financial decisions to be made by others. A rich man who lets a poverty embracing gutter rat relative make his funeral and final financial decisions, may not get the respect due him. Gutter rats don't think like light beings, nor do they show respect.

Example: I have a deceased, lady minister friend who recently died. She left her funeral arrangements up to a dark soul human sister. My minister friend was Pentecostal, and she wore long sleeves, long skirts, long hair, and lived and breathed being moral, holy, and right with her god. Her dark soul human sister is just the opposite. She is a drug addict who lives in the gutters of life and doesn't have a holy bone in her body. After the funeral was over, the dark sister made the decision as to what was to be put on my minister friend's tombstone. My minister friend had already paid for her stone ahead of time. I made a special trip out to the cemetery, after hearing that the stone had been set. I was in total shock. The dark sister had engraved a porn sex goddess on the rock. My minister friend's sister had purposely chosen to disgrace all the holiness and good that my friend stood for.

My Pentecostal holiness friend made a very bad decision leaving her funeral and tombstone decisions to her sister. The sister is a devil in human flesh. An appropriate emblem would have been a cross or a bible. My friend, who was rich in the holiness of her god, was disgraced in death.

Light beings must be careful who they leave their wealth to, as well as whom they leave their final decisions to. Leaving your wealth to be squandered by dark relatives is error. Leaving an organ to a dark being who has destroyed his own with alcohol, drug abuse, and hard living is error. Light beings walk a fine light line in life and death. A light being should choose wisely who his earth fortune and last wishes go to.

When we cross over, we stand in judgment for our deeds and our investments. An organ can be a final investment. If you donate an organ, make sure you know where it is going. You will be held accountable at judgment if you donate an organ to a dark being, enabling him to live longer on earth to do war with the light.

CHAPTER TWELVE
DECEMBER

THE BOOK OF "PASSING IT ON"

December 1

THOUGHT FOR THE DAY - You are a god on earth, and have the power to rescue an arriving soul who has had his silver cord damaged or severed. You have the power to receive communications from the heavens for him.

THE POWER TO SHOW THE WAY

If you have been reading my writings, and have understood them, you have discovered that you are part of a mystical group of Light Being Gods that are on missions and educational assignments on Planet Earth, and that you are just traveling in your human form vehicle. We Light Beings are a brotherhood, just as soldiers are brothers in the military. We light beings are one for all and all for one, with no one left behind.

When we light beings leave Earth life, we leave road maps for those that are lost or coming after us to follow. My writings are my roadmap, my way of 'passing it on'. You must pass on to another arriving or damaged cord light being your map. You are a god on earth, and have the power to rescue a fellow light being! Salvation is not for those of darkness. Salvation and rescue are for those of the light.

On Earth, a group of soldiers will build a military camp in a desolate foreign land. When the builder group of soldiers rotates home, another group will arrive and occupy the camp. The new group will add to, or upgrade the camps buildings, etc. When they leave, another group will arrive and also upgrade. We are soldier type light beings on earth and are responsible for creating a camp of knowledge for those coming after us. My writings are my building blocks on Earth. Those coming after me will add to and build on them, as will future generations of light beings arriving. To pass our military camp of ideas on is the greatest gift we can give to those coming after us.

It is time for you to make your map. It can be simple, a handwritten letter to those of your family coming after you. Your words may awaken some future arriving soul, who has a severed silver cord, to his divinity. Leave letter maps to all your earth family members for future generations. Put one copy of your letter in this book and pass it along to a stranger who loves to read. Let the universe decide where your story of being a light being soldier on Earth should go.

December 2

THOUGHT FOR THE DAY – Man wants his chosen god to have powers. What he does not realize is that he is the god of his world, and it is him that has the power to bless or curse those about him.

GODS WHO SHOW FAVORITISM

Humans believe that their gods have the power to bless or curse them. The Protestant's god is seen as such a being. Sometimes he will bless a particular prophet, and at other times he is angry to the point of killing his prophets and his flock who are not perfect slaves to him. The Protestant's god does not tolerate flaws. Sometimes, the Protestant's angry and vengeful god will play favoritism and heal or bless one or two of his favorites. At the same time he will ignore the cries for help and healing from others. If you are praying to a Christian or other religious persuasion god who is not answering you, you are not on his pet list.

When I was in elementary school, I had a teacher who had serious classroom pets. It was a relief when the school year ended and I got to move on to a new teacher, whom I hoped would be fair. Back in the 1950s, there were not child abuse laws like there are now. The teacher was god and she could spank, verbally abuse, or ignore you with no consequences. Some teachers saw poor children and slow children as not worthy of wasting their time on. In their thinking, it would be the elite and wealthy of the class who went on to higher learning, college, etc. It wasn't unusual back then for poor or slow children to drop out of school in the eighth grade. So, the teachers made pets of the elite and tolerated the poor or slow children. I was a very poor child and was treated by teachers as such.

The snooty teacher above is a type of a god who ignores you. You are not your teacher god's pet or one of his perfect elite slaves. So, you get the unwanted child treatment. No help or answers are sent down to you for your many problems, and god sends no kisses of healing to you for your sick human body ailments. You are treated like a poor or slow child of the 1950s.

The Old Testament Moses Age gave way to the New Testament Jesus Age. That is the same as a child moving from one school year to the next, and having a new teacher. Your god is not answering or paying any attention to you. It is okay to leave the New Testament age and its teacher, and embrace a new school year and teacher in your religious school experience. The New Jerusalem Age or New Age is here. In the New Age classroom you will find new teachers, and discover who god is. You are a God in the New Age if you have embraced enlightenment. You do not need a human created, mythical god who does hot hear you or answer you.

As you travel your path in the New Age, you will be invoked or requested to attend and bless cultural events, just as ancient man invoked his god of harvest to come down and bless his crops. You, a Light Being, New Age God, will occasionally be asked to attend and bless social events on Earth. For instance, you might be asked to attend a wedding. You can choose to bless the wedding couple with a generous gift or one of famine. Today, money is considered to be a gift of blessing. A curse from you (a light being god) might be a recycled, truly awful gift that was once given to you. You may see the wedding invitation as a chance to get rid of the unwanted item. If you curse the wedding couple with your unwanted item, you become a god of darkness, a devil.

You are the god of your new world, and you have the power to bless and curse. Beautiful words of praise and foul language are types of blessings and curses. Words of praise deem you a light being god. Words of disrespect and foul language deem you a devil in human flesh. On Earth there is the power of free will choice. You must choose whether you are a god of light or darkness.

December 3

THOUGHT FOR THE DAY - Brilliant men sleep or languish in mundane jobs and lifestyles. They are the invisible. They are sleeping gods.

GODS OF POWER OR MEDIOCRICY

Since we are the gods of the New Age and our individual worlds, we must choose how to rule and reign. All gods are different in the talents they possess. You may be a hair stylist god, while your brother is healer, and your best friend is a salesman. What we are passionate about in our choice of jobs and lifestyles designates who we are as a god. We can use our talents to be powerful gods, or we cannot use them and be mediocre or sleeping gods. You are only as powerful as you let yourself be.

My sister bakes one of the most scrumptious, butter milk, chocolate cakes ever made. A bite of it is heaven to my taste buds. Baking is her power, a gift that she blesses her world and followers with. Baking a real cake from scratch is what makes her a powerful god. Should she choose to start baking plain old chocolate cakes from mixes, she would then become a mediocre, sleeping god of ovens.

Every light being has unique talents or powers to be used on Earth. Until he starts to use and display his talents, he is a sleeping god in human flesh.

My Uncle Earl was the fisherman god in our family. Back in the late 1940s, before he went to work, he would fish and catch stringers of huge fish. On his way to work, he would stop at our house and place the fish in a galvanized wash tub beneath our outside water faucet. My father would clean them later in the morning. We were a large family. Uncle Earl, our god of fishing, knew we could use the extra meat. Only once, do I remember him bringing a stringer to our house with only one fish on it. On that day, he laughed and explained that he had propped his pole on a rock, and then took a cat nap on the river bank. For that one day, my uncle became a mediocre god of fishing. He chose to let a rock hold his pole instead of his talented fisherman hands. The rock was a cake mix type substitute for the real thing.

What is your special talent or gift? Are you baking divinely from scratch, or taking the easy mix way out? Are you blessing your world with mediocrity or divinity? In these writings, I am trying to give you the best of what I know about Heaven, the Afterlife, the In-between Worlds, and the spiritual paths that will get you to where you want to go. I am baking my cake. It is up to you to eat and enjoy. Some of you, who are narrow-minded and dark of soul, will think I bake fruitcake. Others will enjoy my words knowing they are mouth watering, buttermilk chocolate cake.

December 4

THOUGHT FOR THE DAY- Fences around religious

groups, and their persuasions, are erected by narrow minded devils in human flesh, not gods of light. If a minister, priest, monk, etc. tells you that he and his group are the only way to heaven, automatically know that he is a god of darkness.

THE GIFT TO CALL SOULS TO LIFE

Sounding an alarm, to awaken souls to their divinity, is done by master artists, writers, orators, etc. A soul awakening is like a sleeping human awakening to the sound of his alarm clock. When a human enters an art gallery and views a great painting, he may feel sudden bliss. He feels he somehow sees something more than what is on the canvas. His soul has awakened. The same experience happens when a man reads a good book or listens to the colorful words of a great, master orator. The feeling of bliss that arouses in him is his soul awakening.

Masters, who have the gift to introduce men to their souls, walk the face of the Earth in human flesh. They are sometimes referred to as saviors. They are on missions to all generations, religions, and cultures. No religion or culture owns a master savior rescuer. Masters cannot be fenced in. Fences are built by human, narrow minded religious leaders who want to claim their religious persuasion as the only true path. The door knockers are a good example of a religion believing they are the only path to god.

There is not just one savior or rescuer for the whole world. You are a savior rescuer, if thru your writing, art, music, or words you are causing a soul to awaken to their divinity.

December 5

THOUGHT FOR THE DAY – God spoke to Moses from a burning bush. The bush was his costume in that moment. He did not appear in human form.

GODS IN COSTUMES

Beyond earth life, in the upper heavens, we light beings do not walk about in human forms. We are orbs of light. When we are sent to Earth on missions, we enter and travel in human forms as though they are astronaut space suits. When we leave earth and return to the upper heavens, we discard our human space suits and once more travel our own world as balls of light and energy.

Light beings, or orbs of light, can use more than just human costumes to appear on earth in. God spoke to Moses in the costume of a burning bush. Light beings can also put on costumes of mystical animals or winged angels. Have you ever considered that a master of the heavens can wear the pages of a mystical book as a costume?

If a master light being comes to Earth and takes the form of a book, he will place himself in a position on a shelf or a table where you will be drawn to him and pick him up and hear his words by reading him as words.

December 6

THOUGHT FOR THE DAY – Guardians descend from the heavens to aid light being students who are in need of assistance. Choice of what costume to wear is entirely up to the guardian. Just as humans have different tastes in clothing, so it is with guardians. One may choose an angel costume, while his guardian friend may choose the costume form of a unicorn or leprechaun.

STUDENT'S GUARDIANS

Student light beings come to earth on education assignments. Because they aren't mature beings, they sometimes need guardians to guide and watch over them. Their guardians watch them from the astral shore and will descend to aid them if they are in serious need of assistance. Student light beings are like human college students who have parents living at a short distance.

What does a human college student do when he runs out of money? He rushes to a phone and calls home to mom and dad for financial assistance! When a student light being calls home to the heavens for assistance, it will be his guardian who will answer his phone call and then come down to aid him. Guardians are orbs of light beings. When entering earth life, they will choose a costume to walk about on Earth in. The guardian may choose the costume of a winged angel, fairy, leprechaun, unicorn, etc.

I am Master Barjoraven in the heavens, an orb of light and energy. On Earth, I travel in a human body costume named Jo Hammers. In the heavens, I am a trumpeter of words. On Earth I am a writer and mystic. Who are you in the upper heavens? Who are you on Earth? What costume have you chosen to travel earth life in?

December 7

THOUGHT FOR THE DAY – Men are like buzzing bees, they make noise. At night, when men rest from their noise making, voices of those in the afterlife are easier to hear.

THE GIFT OF BEING A RECEIVER

Did you know that those in the afterlife can speak to you without making a sound that those about you on Earth can hear? If you hear their soundless words, you have the gift of being a supernatural receiver. You are like a radio. You receive and then broadcast. Psychics, seers, mediums, etc. are receivers.

This morning, as I sat in a restaurant drinking coffee and writing, I heard someone at a table behind me speaking my name and talking to someone about me. I also got the strange feeling they were looking over my shoulder and reading what I was writing on my laptop. I immediately turned around. There was no one at the table behind me, nor was there anyone looking over my shoulder. In that moment, I was a receiver of the voices of supernatural beings gracing my presence.

If you hear your name called, and no one is there, beings from other realms are trying to get your attention. They may be asking for an audience with you. Be gracious and ask them to be seated at your table. If you are having coffee, set a cup in front of you and pour them a literal cup of coffee. That is your invitation for them to sit down. Then, let them speak to you.

Graciousness will get you future visits from angels, masters, etc. Some Christians place a plate on their Christmas dining table for Christ. They are aware of the 'Law of Graciousness' and that he will dine with them if they give him an invitation. The setting of the plate is the invitation. Other religious figures such as Buddha or Moses can also be invited to dine by setting plates for them on days of religious observances.

December 8

THOUGHT FOR THE DAY – Senders make requests on the behalf of others. Protestants call them 'prayer warriors'. Intercessor is another term.

THE GIFT OF BEING A SENDER

Just as there are receivers, there are also senders. Being a sender or an intercessor for someone else's need is a gift. My mother, a kind and gentle soul, had that gift. She spent her life praying for people in need that crossed her path. My mother was a prayer warrior in the Pentecostal faith for 84 years. As her child, I wanted to crawl under our bed and hide at times from the constant influx of sick and needy people that knocked on our house door asking for prayer. At the time, I did not understand that my mother had a gift. I saw all the sick and needy people as a nuisance.

Today, I have crawled out from under the bed and now write about some of my experiences watching the miracles performed by my mother and others of the Pentecostal faith. However, as an adult, I am not Pentecostal. I have awakened as a soul and remember who I am. I am not a member of an earth man made religion. I am a light being on earth on a mission. Writing about the spiritual paths and miracles in all religions is part of my mission.

My mother's supernatural gift or expertise was the calling down of a divine one to heal. She channeled a light being nicknamed the 'Holy Ghost'. The Pentecostals called my mother's gift the 'Gift of Healing'. My mother, a light being, prayed for the sick and needy till she vacated earth at the age of 84. Her human body is buried in Hickory Grove Cemetery near Springfield, Missouri. However, she is not dead. She is a light being, an orb of light and energy who has returned to her true home in the heavens. As a light being in the afterlife, she works there as a spirit guide. She has often appeared in dreams to those she once prayed for on Earth.

My mother and I are both light beings. She has returned to the heavens. I am still on my mission on Earth. I am nothing like my mother. My mother was nothing like I am. She was an intercessor calling down healers. I am a map maker, a writer of directions on how to reach the inner heavens.

December 9

Thought for the day – Rescuers or saviors are interested in more than just retrieving souls and escorting them home to the heavens. They can also be healers (astral doctors) or silver cord communication line repairmen (astral telephone linemen).

CALLING ASTRAL DOCTORS DOWN

Being a savior or rescuer of lost light beings on earth is like being a member of an elite group of military forces that rescue downed air plane pilots in enemy territory. They go where no one dares to go to rescue their own kind. Christ was a light being master who entered Earth life to rescue lost light being souls who had severed silver cord communication lines. He did not enter Earth life to rescue devils and dark demons of enemy forces.

(Silver cords are communication lines connecting souls to the heavens. They are invisible to human sight. When severed, cut in two, a soul does not remember that he is a citizen of the heavens or how to make his way home when his human body dies. A severed cord being will need a rescuer.)

Some rescuers are healers, astral doctors. They will descend to earth, wearing a human body costume, to help you with your healing needs. Rescue healers are actually orbs of light and energy. It is man's human brain thinking that expects divine ones to look like him. Divine ones wear costumes to keep from frightening humans.

Example: You find that you are constipated. You make your way to a pharmacy and stand in front of a laxative display trying to pick out a remedy for your minor ailment. In desperation, you mutter, "God help me... which one do I choose?" An ordinary looking stranger may walk up and stand next to you, also seemingly looking at laxatives. When you pick up a box, the stranger might say, "That one is really harsh. You will run to the bathroom for a week after using it." Then he will pick up a different box and display it for you to see, while further adding, "This one works just as well and doesn't have bad side effects." You smile and either take or reject the stranger's advice. You demanded, "God help me!" A divine one came down in costume. You then asked, "Which one do I choose?" A divine one in costume showed you which one.

Astral doctors and other types of divine helpers descend and appear in the costumes of strangers. It is up to you to accept or reject their help. However, the next time you ask for help, divine ones will be reluctant to waste their time on you. They see you as the little boy who cries wolf.

December 10

Thought for the day – The human brain thinker cannot attach enlightened, spiritual meanings to words that he reads and hears. Thus, he takes everything literally. Gifted ones such as psychics, mystics, mediums, and seers go within and awaken their soul to interpret mysterious phrases

THE GIFT OF INTERPRETING WORDS

Two hundred years ago, a Hindu man named Thayumanavar wrote a poem about the powers of Hindu holy men. This is a partial quote . . .

. . . You can control a mad elephant. You can shut the mouth of a bear . . . You can ride a lion. You can play with a cobra . . .)

The Hindu poet was speaking of the supernatural feats that Hindu holy men were performing in his day on Earth. Some people take words literally, while others look for deeper meanings in spoken and written word. Deeper meanings are words of awakening or enlightenment. For instance, the poet spoke of playing with a cobra. The literal thinking Hindu holy man will try to hypnotize a real cobra snake with a flute. The soul thinker holy man will see the cobra as meaning a cobra natured human he is socializing with.

There is a small group of holiness individuals in the United States who take a 'picking up serpents' scripture from their bible literally. A literal thinking holiness leader will charm his copperhead or rattler with the sound vibrations of his congregation's singing and musical instruments. Spiritual interpreters of the 'picking up serpents' would see the serpents as meaning venomous natured humans who would like to do harm to you. Picking up copperheads or rattlers is human brain thinking, and definitely not soul or spiritual thinking.

The human brain thinker cannot attach enlightened, spiritual meanings to words that he reads and hears. Thus, he takes everything literally. Gifted ones such as psychics, mystics, mediums, and seers go within and awaken their soul to interpret mysterious phrases like the Hindu poet's words.

Literal animal brain thinkers will pick up physical snakes, try to ride real lions, attempt to quiet raging African elephants, and put their heads in the mouths of circus bears and lions. A spiritual interpreter will let his soul interpret and assign meaning to what is said by another.

There is great poetry and great writings in all religious traditions around the world. It is up to you to choose whether you want to be a literal interpreter, or a gifted soul interpreter. Literal thinking is lower thought or animal thinking. Spiritual thought is higher thought or soul thinking.

December 11

THOUGHT FOR THE DAY – Adventurous, soul thinking men know what they want out of life; and they do not let fear or obstacles stand in their way of getting it. They do not settle for being normal.

THE GIFT TO JUMP FENCES

A little girl stands in the school yard peering over a tall chain link fence that encloses the recess play ground. The fence is for her safety, but she sees it in a different fashion. She sees it as a hurdle, something she must get over to smell a spring flower on the other side.

Fearless, the little Tomboy girl starts to climb up and over the eight foot fence. She is a fearless 'hurdle crosser'. That is a gift that other little girls on the playground do not possess. She has no fear of heights or what lies beyond fences erected by others. Hurdle crossers know what they want out of life, and they do not let fear or obstacles stand in their way of getting it.

Obstacles on destined paths come in many forms. For example, a chef has made a beautiful casserole and is just about to pop it into the oven. Suddenly, a piece of ceiling tile falls down and into his masterpiece dish ruining it. He quickly grabs out a new casserole dish and makes the dish all over again. He has crossed a hurdle of disaster. He has climbed over a fence.

Hurdle or fence crossers think outside of the box or play ground. They do not settle for the cookie cutter play ground moments that other children or adults are pursuing.

December 12

THOUGHT FOR THE DAY – Being open minded will let you climb to a higher path which will lead to enlightenment or being a master.

THE GIFT OF BEING OPEN MINDED

To understand the supernatural, you must study all the people, cultures, and religions of the world. Being narrow minded (thinking that you and your little religious group are the only ones that have a connection with Divine Source) is ridiculous. God or Divine Source is an open minded supreme being who embraces all peoples, not just one little group of narrow minded religious fruitcakes. Also, God is not the only deity in the heavens. In the Christian's bible, god said, "Let Us make man in our image." Us means that there was more than one creator present at the creation of Planet Earth!

Being open minded is a gift or power. This gift will let you walk thru doors of knowledge around the world and fellowship with all of Divine Source's peoples. The gift will let you understand writings of all holy books,. The gift will enable you to climb higher paths and ladders to enlightenment. The gift lets you become a master of the universe and inner heavens. The gift will let you become one of the 'US'. Being open minded is a power.

Hindu embrace a supernatural power called Mahima. It is the power of becoming mighty and co-extensive with the universe. If we, thru an open mind, become one with all peoples of the Earth and their ideas, we become mighty. Knowledge is power.

December 13

THOUGHT FOR THE DAY – In your tiny part of the world, you might be familiar with or hold in your hand a few supernatural gifts of power. If you study and embrace the supernatural gifts of all peoples and cultures worldwide, you become a treasure chest of divine powers.

SUPERNATURAL GIFTS of the HINDU

1. The power to become the size of an atom, to enter into the smallest of life forms.

2. The power of becoming mighty and co-extensive with the universe.

3. The power to be light, like a balloon, though big in size.

4. The: power or capacity to be heavy though seeming small in size.

5. The power or capacity to enter all worlds. In the west, we call it astral travel.

6. The power to disembody and enter other bodies.

7. Having the creative power of God and control over the sun, the moon and the elements.

8. The power of control over kings and Gods.

To be mighty, you must increase the size of your kingdom. Your kingdom is how much knowledge you have. Study all religions' gifts. To be divine, pass on your knowledge to others.

December 14

THOUGHT FOR THE DAY – The Pentecostals are the only religion that embraces the supernatural side of Christianity. They are the psychics, mystics, channels, mediums, etc. of the Christian faith. However, they are lost in their belief that they are the only ones having god's favor and are the only ones going to heaven. They have fenced themselves in.

THE GIFTS OF PENTECOSTALS

1 The Gift of Knowledge – Supernaturally knowing things about people and other realms.

2 The Gift of Wisdom – Knowing when to speak and when not to.

3 The Gift of healing – The laying on of hands to heal the sick.

4 The Gift of Prophecy – Channeling messages from their god in the heavens.

5 The Gift of Speaking in Tongues – Being a channel for those of foreign languages in the heavens to speak thru them.

6 The Gift of Interpreting Tongues. - The supernatural gift to interpret foreign language messages.

7 The Gift of Helps. They had to have a category to cover all in their ranks that had no particular supernatural gifts. Helps could be cleaning the church bathrooms or handing out church bulletins.

I, Jo Hammers the Mystic, was born into a Pentecostal family and raised in the Pentecostal faith. I see those in the religion of my youth as a group of 'want to be' psychics. They try to walk the walk and talk the talk, but they don't display on a consistent basis that which they believe in. I would say that one in a thousand might actually have mastered a psychic gift.

December 15

THOUGHT FOR THE DAY – You cannot die from any illness or injury unless it is your appointed time to die. If you are a light being, you are on a mission on earth.

THE GIFT OF HEALING

As a child, running barefoot outside, you injured your toe in childhood play. With tears in your eyes, you ran to your mother for comfort. Your mother hugged you, dried your tears, bandaged the cut, and told you that your toe would be just fine in a day or so.

As adults, we are subject to grown up afflictions or skinned toes in our daily walk or play. Masters like Jesus, Buddha, etc. are our adult parents. It is their laps and arms we run to when illness or injury strikes us.

In the Christian's bible, Jesus tells a follower, "Take up your bed and walk!" Healing starts when we run and climb onto our master's lap. It becomes complete, after we take up our bed and walk/run back out to play in our adult worlds.

Our human bodies are designed to heal themselves. We forget that and focus on the pain caused by our illness or injury. In distress we need assurance from a divine parent that we are going to be okay. The Divine parent will hug and kiss us and then remind us of our body's ability to heal its self.

We all have an appointed time for our human bodies to die and us as souls to return to the heavens. When our missions on earth, short or long, are over . . . they are over. Till then, work with your body and let it heal itself. While it is healing, take up your bed and walk!

December 16

THOUGHT FOR THE DAY - Healing and other miracles come from the holy hands of a soul, not human hands laid on human heads.

THE GIFT OF HEALING HANDS

The human body has hands that can be raised in praise when inspired. It is bliss vibrations that cause man to lift his hands, whether in church, possibly a great music concert, or a winning moment in a ball game. Bliss is divine or perfect vibrations.

The soul that travels inside a human body has invisible hands that can be raised in praise. They are not human hands. It is the soul's invisible hands that work miracles. The human soul can reach out of a human form and touch other human bodies and heal them, if it chooses to do so. A soul reaching out to touch another will never be seen by human eyes.

Think of the soul as an auto mechanic. Think of its human body as the car it drives. Not only can the soul repair his own human auto body, he can also repair other human vehicles. A soul has tools, just as an earth auto mechanic does. His tools are holy, invisible hands. An earth auto mechanic heals or fixes cars with wrenches. A soul mechanic heals or fixes human vehicles with holy invisible hands, his wrenches.

Healers heal with invisible hands, not human hands slapped on human heads. If you are in need of healing for your human form, seek out holy hands within, not powerless human hands. The gift of healing is a power of the soul. To find a healer, you must go within to where they are. Souls can reach out and touch each other and transmit healing.

December 17

THOUGHT FOR THE DAY - The purposeful opening of cans of hurtful worms, and releasing the worms in a gossip fashion, is a powerful gift of dark demon beings.

THE GIFT TO OPEN CANS OF WORMS

Opening a can of worms infers sticking ones nose into something or somewhere it doesn't belong, and letting out of the can dirty or illegal secrets that will be impossible to get back into the can. Snoops pry into the lives of others (opening cans) and then tell others about the scandals they have discovered. Once secrets are told, it is almost impossible to stop the spread of gossip.

What does this have to do with power gifts? The purposeful opening of cans of worms is a power gift of dark forces, devils in human flesh. Snoops and gossips are not light beings. The hurtful information they purposely dig up and spread deems them a force of darkness.

Accidentally opening a can of worms is different from purposefully opening one. A teen boy goes to surprise his father, who is working late. He walks in on his dad in a compromising position with his secretary. That is an accidental opening of a can of worms. What the son does with the information comes under the heading of free will choice. He has the choice to tell or not tell his mother. Gossips tell secrets behind people's backs to hurt them. The son going to his mother is not going behind her back.

December 18

THOUGHT FOR THE DAY – With the power of having finances to be charitable, comes the responsibility to give to light causes, not charities supporting darkness.

THE POWER TO BE CHARITABLE

"Charity starts at home!" an old saying states. The reason it starts at home is that Light Beings should only embrace charities or social systems that support light beings. To give to a charity, where you do not know where your money is going, could enable dark devils to live another day on earth to persecute those of the light.

Example . . . you get a flyer in the mail from a charity that is paying for procedures that are restoring sight to the blind. Giving so that a light being receives new sight is a good thing. They will use their restored sight to do good things and complete their missions on earth. A dark being, such as a rapist who has lost his sight, will use his new found sight to look for more victims. Giving to a charity that makes no distinctions as to where the money is going, is blind careless giving.

With the power of having finances to be charitable comes the responsibility to give to the light, not enable or support darkness.

Charity starts at home! That means that those of financial wealth should take care of light beings in need, not welfare dark gutter rats and sociopaths. When we give money, we save someone. Save those worthy of your power. To give blindly will enable rapist and thieving demons and devils to survive another day on earth to rape and plunder those of the light. You will be held accountable for your giving on Earth.

December 19

THOUGHT FOR THE DAY – Holy feet will be found walking to church, mosque, or temple. Unholy feet will be found walking to war, bars, brothels, drug houses, liquor stores, ghettos, gutter living, etc.

THE GIFT OF HOLY FEET

We light beings travel in human bodies. They are vehicle costumes for us. Feet of the human vehicle do the work to move us to where we want to go on earth. They are like the tires on an automobile. When not sleeping in our human forms, we have the power to choose where our human feet take us. When we light beings within human forms sleep, the human brain decides where the human feet go. A soul driven man has holy feet. A human brain driven man has unholy or animal feet.

Holy feet will walk to church, mosque, or temple. Unholy feet, or animal feet, will be directed to walk toward bars, houses of ill repute, or to gutter living by the human brain. Holy feet are god controlled feet. Unholy feet are human brain controlled feet.

Man has free will choice to embrace light or darkness. Day trips to gamble, drink, do drugs, frequent prostitutes, rent porn movies, buy porn magazines, etc. are the journeys of unholy animal nature feet. Holy feet will journey to temples, college classes, art museums, libraries, concert halls, spiritual lectures, etc. Holy feet will walk paths of righteousness and enlightenment. Unholy feet, brain directed, will walk down into the gutters of life.

The Gift of Holy Feet is a wisdom gift. A light being knows where darkness hangs out and he chooses not to walk there. That is wisdom.

December 20

THOUGHT FOR THE DAY – Heaven, is not a welfare state! Those trying to con beings for free finances, food, and housing there are considered gutter rats. When standing before Heaven's judgment for their con tactics, they will be kicked out of the heavens. Heaven is a working state.

THE GIFT TO KNOW WHO IS TRULY POOR

Free will choice is given to each human on earth. You can choose to educate yourself, rise, and become a positive addition to society, or you can choose to be a user of society. Long term welfare recipients are users. They have no intentions of rising for anything other than to get out of their chair and walk to the mailbox to get free monthly money and food stamps. A person, who lives and rapes welfare systems, is not a poor person. He is a user or con artist.

The Afterlife, or Heaven, is not a welfare state! Those trying to con others out of free finances and food on earth are considered to be dark beings or devils there.

A truly poor person is the working man, who has for some reason, fallen on hard times maybe due to losing a job or illness. In spite of hard times, he will seek work, rather than lower himself to become a gutter rat welfare person.

Anyone applying for and staying on welfare for more than 30 days is a rapist of charities. Mothers who have children to get free money and food stamps from systems are gutter rats. To give to or support gutter rats is to embrace or support darkness. The true poor are willing to work for their daily bread. Light beings will not stoop to be gutter rats.

December 21

THOUGHT FOR THE DAY - Spirituality is viewed differently by every human. All spiritual seekers walk paths towards God, but they see and interpret their post card moments along the way according to their particular passions and callings.

THE GIFT TO OPENMINDEDLY LOOK AT ALL POINTS OF VIEW

Three men (a minister, a surfer, and a life guard) stand on a beach looking at the ocean.

The minister blurts out, 'I can just see myself standing out there in those waves baptizing new coverts!"

The surfer returns, "I can see myself out there riding those magnificent waves."

The life guard chimes in, "I see myself quitting my job and letting the sharks swimming out there eat fools like you. "

All three men have different views or ideas concerning the ocean they are looking at. What each chooses to do with the ocean experience is different. The minister could make a baptistery out of the ocean. The surfer could swim out and ride the waves. The lifeguard could choose to ignore his mission to save men from the ocean's perils.

There are many spiritual paths. Personal destinies or missions affect how a man sees things along the way. In the above shared ocean viewing experience, one man saw himself called to baptize believers, one saw himself enjoying a riding high experience, and the third saw himself abandoning his calling.

The Jew, Christian, Buddhist, Hindu, Wiccan, etc. are all walking individual paths to the ocean. They are not look-a- like cookies all cut from the same cookie cutter. They are individuals with religious persuasions and callings that are right for them and their cultures

There are many spiritual highways, roads, and paths leading to the ocean. Those traveling the many paths are seekers of the unknown. If you should encounter a fellow pilgrim along the way, respect his way of seeing your shared view of the ocean.

December 22

THOUGHT FOR THE DAY - You are the Christ miracle worker in your world. Think about it! You turn water into coffee every morning!

THE GIFT TO TURN WATER INTO WINE

The gift to turn water into wine, such as Christ did at a wedding, is a manufacturing gift. People turn one thing into another all the time, in order to feed and clothe multitudes. The cotton farmer harvests cotton. His friend, a mill owner, turns it into cloth. The mill owner has a friend who owns a factory. The factory owner chooses to turn his friend's cloth into wearable items such as trousers and shirts. People join hands on Planet Earth to turn water into wine on a regular basis. Miracle workers walk all about you. Christ was just one. Miracle workers today turn ordinary materials into cell phones, microwaves, computers, big screens, autos, etc.

Animals such as lions and bears (predators) are not blessed with the gift to turn things into something greater. They are survivalists who are always looking for their next meal. Man is an animal and a meat eating survivalist. In extreme hunger situations, he will turn cannibal and eat his own kind. So, what is there about animal man that allows him to walk upright, think, create, and perform miracles?

Man has a light being soul (or a dark being devil soul) that rides in him and drives him as though he is an auto. The driver soul has access to all the knowledge of the heavens and hell. The driver soul is what makes man different from other animals, and enables him to perform miracles. A light being soul tells a man to plant cotton seed, mill cotton into cloth, and make protective clothing from the cloth. It is the spirit being soul driver that makes man a miracle worker.

Are you an animal survivalist or an animal miracle worker? Right now, I have a cup of water heating in the microwave. I plan to add a little of this and that and have a morning cup of instant coffee. Christ's water into wine was instant brew. He put water into wine bags or wine pots. The wine bags or wine pots flavored the water. He did not have years to age instant wine. Perhaps you will make a miracle cup of instant tea this morning.

Take what is available to you and work miracles at home, school, and the office! Turn water into wine, coffee, tea, etc.! You have the gift! You are the miracle worker of your world.

December 23

THOUGHT FOR THE DAY – Masters in the heavens have the privileges to attend the births of divine ones who are entering life forms on different planets. The Wise men from the East were astral travelers that descended from the astral highways of the eastern sky to witness Christ's birth. Christ descended and entered a newborn baby to live a life on earth. Angels descended to herald the event. Wise men did also.

THE WISE MEN WERE ASTRAL TRAVELERS

In the day of the birth of the Light Being Christ into a human body, three wise men followed a star to the place of his human birth. Had you ever considered that the three wise men might have been masters in the heavens who were following astral stars as though they were highway signs? Today, simple minded men picture them as astrologers riding camels. Those of enlightened minds know they were masters light beings from the heavens that were traveling to Earth via light beams highways.

When we leave our human bodies and travel upward to the astral shore or the light, we travel an upward path or astral highway to the light.

On Astral highways, we can travel forward and backwards

in time, as well as travel in the now to other planets, stars, moons, suns, black holes, etc. The wise men were Astral Kings/Masters that descended from the astral highways (took off ramps to earth). The stars they followed were on the astral highway, not desert roads. Today, simple minded humans might call them aliens.

The births and weddings of human kings on earth are celebrated by human leaders of nations who travel thousands of miles around the globe to do so. Masters from the heavens travel light years of miles to witness important events on different planets.

When in a foreign country, it is not unusual for a traveler/vacationer to stop and ask for directions on earth. The Wise Men (masters and kings of the heavens) descended from the eastern sky highways, stopped to ask a human king, (a gas station stop for a roadmap) for simple directions to the place (hospital) where Christ the King was to be born.

(SMILE - Human men get pushed all out of shape at having to stop and ask for simple directions. The wise men were enlightened beings that were smart enough to inquire.)

When you read handed down stories such as the 'THREE WISE MEN', pay attention to the mystical individuals in the tales. If there are characters that have came, went, and were seen no more, they were astral travelers.

December 24

THOUGHT FOR THE DAY - Everyone loves a dinner invitation. The hoopla and enjoyment of companions at dinners is delightful. However, there comes a time when a guest should graciously grab his hat and say good bye. If he doesn't leave graciously at the right time, his host may never invite him again. Knowing when a party is over is a gift.

TO KNOW WHEN A PARTY IS OVER

Have you ever had a guest that didn't know when to leave? Perhaps they were invited for lunch. However, it was way after the evening meal before you could get rid of them? Those thoughtless beings are the human mentally challenged of the social world. They have no common sense or gift of intuition. They just believe every party never ends and that the world is there to entertain them. They have no consideration for the schedules of others.

This is the Christian's holiday season. Their writings say that Mary had a baby, a master. Wise men, shepherds, and angels dropped in unannounced to view her newborn. Some drop in visits from friends and family are acceptable, but not when they stay more than 15 or 20 minutes. Drop-ins hanging out all day are not acceptable.

I am a busy writer and mystic. Personally, I prefer that all guests call first. Drop-ins are not acceptable to me at all! If one shows up, I step outside my front door and visit with them in a standing position. The legs of the uninvited guests will eventually give out and they will go their way.

After giving birth, Mary did not have the conveniences of today. She had personal hygiene to attend to, as well as a baby to breast feed and diaper. Do you think that she wanted strange shepherds and wise men watching or ogling her while she performed those tasks? Of course not! The wise men brought gifts and then went away to never be seen again. The shepherds, I am sure, returned to their sheep. If they were respectable drop in guests at the birth of Jesus, they took a quick look at the baby, presented their gifts, and then excused themselves. They would have known when to grab their shepherd hooks and camels' reigns and go. The wise men and shepherds visited the manager to see a baby, not to interfere with the day's care or hygiene of it or its mother

A host invites you for Christmas brunch. He has not invited you for lunch, afternoon tea, dinner, and then to hang around till after midnight playing cards. The invitation was for brunch, not the meals afterward. There comes a proper time to graciously grab your hat/coat/purse/etc. and say good bye. If you don't show that respect, your host may never invite you again.

There are other types of dinner invitations that pop up in our lives. A man asks a woman to marry him. For awhile, the party is good. However, the invited one should know when the party is over. When a man has given you a black eye, or has thrown you down the steps, that dinner party is over. If you are smart, you will grab your hat and leave. The same goes if it is the man being abused. It is a gift to know when parties of all kinds are over.

December 25

THOUGHT FOR THE DAY – Holidays that are cursed with deaths, illnesses, abuse, and hardships sometimes leaves individuals viewing certain holidays as hells. The returning of the holiday every year is like a recording of a bad song of memories that is played over and over, never ending.

THE GIFT TO DUMP HOLIDAY HELLS

Have you ever broken down in tears after a holiday, because all your effort and good intentions had created a season of hell? Perhaps, your relatives quarreled at the dinner table and one physically attacked another, a loved one died, or your spouse asked you for a divorce minutes before guests arrived. Holiday hells knock in many forms.

When holiday hells knock, you seek consolation in telling yourself that next year you will get the holiday right. The next holiday season arrives. With it come new frustrations/hells equal in disaster to the one before. After years of cursed holidays, you develop a hatred for them. From then on, you just do what you have to do to survive the holidays, and you don't invest your soul in them anymore.

Christmas has become an insane, commercial, holiday in the United States. Riding its coat tails are expectations for it to be perfect. Gifts have to be just right. Children are expected to act perfectly socially like adults. Dinners are expected to be gourmet creations. Grown children are expected to travel hundreds of miles to attend family dinners where they are berated for their lack of success, choices of spouses, lack of children, etc. Christmas lovers will spend their last dollar trying to create a perfect holiday. Their efforts, more often than not, create holiday hells.

The gift to move on and dump holidays that drive you crazy is a choice. You have the power or gift of free will choice. You can choose to continue to embrace that which causes you grief and bad memories, or use your power of choice to dump holidays that no longer work for you. If you choose to remain in holiday hells, it is your choice.

If Christmas insanity was done away with and the holiday

celebrated as it should be, a simple gift would be purchased and presented to a newborn infant as a token of respect on the birthday of the Master Christ. The simple gift would be a bottle of baby oil (myrrh), baby lotion (frankincense), and (gold) a coin. Only the celebrated birthday boy, Jesus, should be given a gift.

December 26

THOUGHT FOR THE DAY – After the midnight of the soul comes morning. Midnights of the soul do not last forever, unless we choose to permanently embrace them in states of depression.

THE GIFT OF MORNING

Dark Nights of the Soul, in earth life are sometimes long and filled with haunting memories, voices, and sounds that are frightening. After trembling in fear in the dark night of the soul, morning is a gift. In the daylight, you do not have to face your demons.

Sitting up at night with someone you love that is dying, seems like a never ending experience. Long recoveries from accidents and illnesses are night experiences, as are long drawn out messy divorces and law suits. Depression and mental illness are night times to the soul. There are many dark, lonely, never ending experiences that man fears will never end.

An abused woman is filled with morning bliss when her divorce papers are finalized and she is rid of her dark night spouse. A stressed mother is relieved when her terminally ill, dying child is no longer writhing in pain and gasping for air. A lonely, sick, depressed older woman (who is contemplating suicide) answers her phone. A relative invites her to come live with them and her dark night of loneliness turns into morning.

There is a 'Gift of Morning'. To receive it, you must be willing to let go of, or turn from what is causing your night experience. Midnights of the soul do not have to be forever. Taking continuous, small steps toward morning will eventually get you there. The sun will come up and you will rise from your night bed of horrors and walk away.

December 27

THOUGHT FOR THE DAY – Amish buggies were the sports cars of the wagon world at the time they were invented. The ancestors of today's Amish drove the latest sports cars of that day! At what point did the Amish become non-progressive in their enjoyment and use of the latest in transportation vehicles? Their ancestors drove them.

THE GIFT TO MOVE FORWARD IN TIME

Some humans are progressive in thought and the way they live. Others are not. Image an elderly lady living down the street from you. In your mind, see her cooking breakfast. You watch as she opens a can of coffee and puts grounds in her shiny metal percolator. The stainless steel coffee pot was given her for a wedding present fifty years prior. You continue to watch as she cooks oatmeal in an aluminum pot that sticks and pancakes in an iron skillet. In a small aluminum sauce pan, she is heating syrup for her pancakes. Prior to cooking, she has set her breakfast table with a china plate and cup, a crystal glass, metal flatware, and a cloth napkin. She is preparing breakfast in the fashion that was in vogue on her wedding day. After breakfast watch as she cleans up. You will see her handwash the dishes and then her cloth napkin in the sink. She does not own a dishwasher or a washing machine. She is stuck in the past with the inventions and ways of doing things of her wedding day.

The Amish are like the elderly lady who has not progressed with the times. They ride in the buggies chosen by their ancestors. They do not stop to consider that their outdated buggies were once the latest in transportation vehicles, sports cars in their day.

I drive a two door, gasoline powered, Chevy Cobalt. I absolutely love the car. Fifty years from now, if I advance with the times, I may drive a solar powered space vehicle that has not been invented yet by Chevy. Refusing to drive anything from this day forward but Cobalt autos is stagnant thinking. That thinking is like the Amish and their refusing to drive anything but buggies.

Today's religions are like outdated Amish buggies and coffee percolators. It is time to move forward in thought and embrace a New Age Dispensation. The Old Testament Age was replaced with the New Testament Age. Now the New Testament Age is passing away. Think of the three ages as buggies, cars, and solar powered vehicles. You can live and drive in past dispensations and their religions, or you can move forward and drive in new thought into the New Age.

December 28

THOUGHT FOR THE DAY - My mother rinsed her laundry in a tub. Today, we have automatic washers with rinse cycles. Perhaps in the future we will wear clothing that never has to be rinsed or washed.

THE GIFT TO INVENT THE UNIMAGINABLE

I am a writer and the electric typewriter was the dream machine of my profession in the sixties. In my high school typing class (about 1962) there were two electric typewriters and the rest were manuals. The electric machines were reserved for those in the class who were advanced, second year typists who planned to be receptionists and secretaries in the business world after high school. The rest of us clunked away on the manuals learning to type. Computers were a fairy tale machine in that time. In 1965, fresh out of high school and working as a telephone operator, I purchased my first new typewriter to start my writing career. I was so proud of that manual machine. Five years later, I managed to come up with the money to purchase an expensive electric one.

Now, it is close to 50 years later and I am writing on a lap top computer. The thought of possibly having to go back to using a manual clunker makes me cringe. With one quick key stroke on my computer, I can back up and correct mistakes. On the clunkers, I had to insert a little white strip and type over errors. Corrections were very time consuming.

I do not know what marvelous machine is coming after the computer that might totally blow my mind. My mother, born in 1914, lived to see the microwave invented, but not the cell phone. Her calls had to be made from a phone that hung on the wall and had a long spiral cord that was always getting tangled up. I have been privileged to witness the inventions of digital cameras, cell phones, and computers. My grandson, who is dyslexic, uses a voice activated computer typing system to write school essays. He will live to see other inventions far beyond our imaginations at the moment.

What does the above have to do with supernatural gifts? We have the power or gift to think out of the box and invent things that are currently unimaginable. We have the gift to be miracle working inventors and progress with the times. Those clinging to the past and its inventions are those who are not opening and using their inventive gifts.

Light beings, traveling in human forms, are the openers of gifts of heaven. They are the creators, inventors, artists, writers, etc. They don't want to type away on an old outdated clunker, when they can use a voice activated computer.

December 29

THOUGHT FOR THE DAY - Life on planet earth is what we make it, or how we create it. How good our lives are is determined by what we embrace. Some of the old is good, but some of the new is better. I have a friend who loves his bicycle. That is a step forward in transportation from riding a horse. He has progressed that far. However, he laughs at the new electric cars that have just hit the market. He is slowly becoming stuck in the past.

SITTING AT THE FEET OF MASTERS

I once looked into the sky thinking that was where god

was. I fantasized about flying like a winged angel to him one day when I died. Now, I have matured in my understanding of god, angels, and modes of supernatural transportation. I do not need bird wings to go within and travel the astral skies to other planets, god's heavens, as well as back and forwards in time. When I want to visit with the Divine, I go inward and upward to the upper inner heavens were god dwells as knowledge, energy, and light. In the higher upper heavens, all beings are orbs of light and they travel in that form.

We must progress in our thinking to become a friend of god, instead of fantasizing about one day meeting him.

I was reared on earth in a family that was of the Pentecostal faith. I once sat on Pentecostal pews and ate my spiritual food from their private Holy Ghost's stew pot. Now, I eat my spiritual food from New Age books, lectures by New Age Thinkers, and private suppers with my Supreme One when I go inward and upward to him.

I no longer travel earth life in the Pentecostals' required long hair, long skirts, long sleeves, etc. I have chosen to walk forward with the times. My preference for clothing is a black hat, red plaid flannel shirt, and jeans. In the future, I might wear something entirely different as my soul progresses in thought. It is okay to walk a certain religious path on Earth, if you are comfortable there. However, it is not okay to live in the past. Light Beings are creators, inventors, trend setters. They always walk forward. Whatever they choose to create, invent, or set as a trend will be light oriented.

Light beings do not create darkness, invent weapons of mass destruction, or set trends that will harm the human body in any fashion. Dark trends include tattoos, tanning beds, etc. Tattooing permanently disfigures the human body and over tanning causes skin cancer and leather like skin when a man is old.

You have the gift to walk forward with the times. It is up to you to open or not open your gift. Heaven doesn't come down to those who have closed their minds to its now possibility.

December 30

THOUGHT FOR THE DAY –Master teachers speak from burning bushes, voices singing in the wind, or the pages of mystical books. The teacher does not have to appear in a human form.

THE GIFT OF A MASTER TEACHER

When a student divine one, traveling and studying in human flesh, is ready, a master teacher will appear on his path. The form the master takes will be in accordance with what the student is comfortable with and understands. Books are the easiest form for a master to use to speak to you. He writes a book, and you walk along your path and read it. If you have discovered a book that speaks to you at soul level, you have had a master appear on your path to guide you. Masters do not have to take human forms. They can take the form of words on pages. Moses spoke to god, who was just a voice in a burning bush. Be open-minded to the forms that divine masters may use to speak to you.

In the upper heavens, we do not walk about in human forms. We are orbs of light. When we come to earth, we travel in human forms as though they are space suits. When we return to the upper heavens, we discard the suits and travel as the balls of light and energy that we are. A master coming to earth can put on a costume form, so as not to frighten man.

If a master teacher takes the form of a book, he will place himself in a position on a shelf or table where you will be drawn to him and pick him up and hear his words by reading him as words. You may discover him as a book in a library, in a box at a garage sale, or on a friend's coffee table. Be open to unusual divine encounters with master teachers that you have been ignoring.

I am Master Barjoraven, a light being. I am this book and its words. I have chosen to take this form so that you may be taught by me. What form will you take to teach others?

DECEMBER 31

THOUGHT FOR THE DAY – What are you leaving behind for those coming after you? Are you leaving a map to darkness or a map of a path to the light?

MY GIFT TO YOU

It is important that we leave behind a record of our spiritual triumphs, and the many twists and turns on our paths that have pointed us to our mastering of educations and missions on Earth. As awakened souls, we are responsible for leaving path/trail/road markers and maps for those coming after us. Without maps and markers, there is nothing but wilderness of mind, the briars and overgrowth of Dark Age thinking on Earth.

I am a writer. So, I am leaving behind what I know about enlightenment and soul life on the written page. Hopefully, a couple hundred years after I am gone from Earth life, someone will read my written words and be inspired to awaken and pursue higher paths. I hope my words will be a stepping stone for someone to take the high road of thought.

Entering Earth life, I was born into a very strict Protestant faith family who felt they were the only church and the only individuals who were going to heaven. In their closed mind, limited thinking, they blindly believed that If you weren't one of them, you were lost and going to hell. They fenced their little religious circle in and anything new out. I, Jo Hammers the Mystic, was a dreamer of dreams, and my dreams didn't always match what Pentecostals taught me as a child. In fear of being branded demon possessed, I never shared any of my wonderful experiences traveling the Astral, nor did I speak of the masters I had met in the heavens that were not Christian or Pentecostal.

Because I feared being ostracized by those of my faith and my parents, my parents never knew me as an awakened one, nor did the Pentecostals I rubbed shoulders with every day. I was my parent's good and quiet child, the one who sat in a corner and never bothered anyone or caused any mischief. The truth is that I was in fear of being beaten by my parents if they discovered that I exited my body at night and spoke with beings that were not Pentecostal. I traveled a path of fear as a child, and as a young adult. Divine ones spoke to me, and I was afraid to tell. I knew nothing about new age thought or soul flight to heavens within. I was about 30 years old before I discovered there was literature about paths to enlightenment, astral travel, time travel, and heavens within.

At a garage sale, I purchased a book by Tom C. Lyle titled 'THE MAGIC POWER OF PRAGMA PSYCHICS' for 50 cents. It was just laying and looking at me on the top of a stack of books that were for sale. The book's words opened me up to the fact that I was a spirit being traveling in a human body, and to the fact that I was capable of drawing to me anything I needed or desired to walk my predestined path. Tom's words resonated with me so deeply, that I threw out my protestant bible. My time had come. I was a student and Tom's words on the written page were the master teacher sent me.

Tom Lyle's book let me discover that there were other new age thinkers out there besides me, that I was not a demon, nor was I alone. His book became my Bible for the next ten years. I read it daily. Tom Lyle, a Master Light Being, left behind a map for me to follow. His map was words he wrote in a book. After years of studying his book, I chucked my protestant faith altogether. That in itself was a gut wrenching decision. It leaves you with no roots, spiritual leader, or family to turn to. My path to enlightenment at the time had only one person on it, me. Eventually, I met others, but it took a few years. There are masters of advanced thought scattered all around the globe. Seek and you will find them.

I am Master Barjoraven in the heavens; Jo Hammers the Mystic on Earth. This book is the road map that I am leaving behind for you. Read it and then . . . Pass it on!

THE END

Jo Hammers

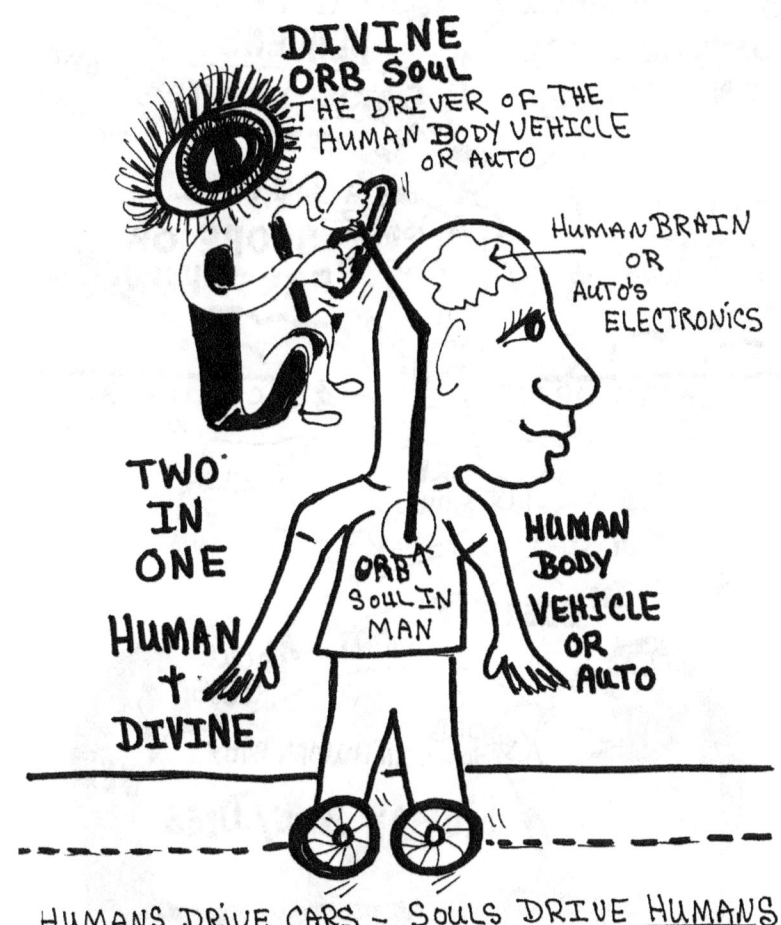

www.ingramcontent.com/pod-product-compliance
Lightning Source LLC
Chambersburg PA
CBHW071956150426
43194CB00008B/895